SACRAMENTO

Gold Rush Legacy
Metropolitian Destiny

Edited by John F. Burns

First Edition

Copyright©1999 by Heritage Media Corporation

All rights reserved. No part of this book may be reproduced in any form or by any means, electronic or mechanical, including photocopying, without permission in writing from the publisher. All inquiries should be addressed to Heritage Media Corp.

ISBN: #1-886483-27-2

Library of Congress Card Catalog Number: 98-073490

Editor: John F. Burns

Photo Editor: Lucinda Woodward

Chapter Writers: Norman L. Wilson, Edward H. Howes,
Walter P. Gray III, James E. Henley, Charles H. Duncan, Melinda A. Peak

Publisher: C.E. Parks

Editor-in-Chief: Lori M. Parks

VP/National Sales Manager: Ray Spagnuolo

VP/Corporate Development: Bart Barica

CFO: Randall Peterson

Managing Editor: Betsy Blondin

Production Manager: Deborah Sherwood

Art Director: Gina Mancini

Graphic Designers: Steve Trainor, Brad Hartman

Production Staff: Jeff Caton, Sean Gates,
Andrea Georgio, Dave Hermstead, Jay Kennedy, John Leyva,
Barry Miller, Susie Passons, Norm Pruitt, Chris Rivera

Sales Coordinator: Teresha Sciortino

Coordinating Editors: Renee Kim, Betsy Lelja, Elizabeth Lex,
Sara Rufner, Adriane Wessels, John Woodward

Profile Writers: Dayna Dunteman, Carella Herberger, Janice Kelly,
Pat Kemper, Stephen M. Kinney, Sarah Mandel, Vicki Mongan, Stephanie Holland, Jackie Thayer

Administration: Juan Diaz, Cory Graham, Letty James, Scott Reid,
Ellen Ruby, Patrick Rucker

Published by

Heritage Media Corp.

6354 Corte del Abeto, Suite B

Carlsbad, California 92009

www.heritagemedia.com

Printed by Heritage Media Corp. in the United States of America

This book is dedicated to Michael Harrison, oldest charter member of the Sacramento County Historical Society and an internationally respected collector of publications on Western history and anthropology. Still active, he celebrated his 101st birthday in 1998 and maintains a detailed cataloging system of his vast collection. This collecting project would never have been put together without the support and assistance of his late wife of 48 years, Margaret B. Harrison, known to her friends as Maggie.

DEDICATION

CONTENTS

ACKNOWLEDGMENTS

Putting this sesquicentennial history of Sacramento together really involved a team effort on the part of many of Sacramento's history practitioners, community supporters, corporate sponsors and the publishers. Initiated and carried forward by Presidents Melinda Peak and Arlean Towne and board members of the Sacramento County Historical Society, and endorsed by the Sacramento Commission on History and Science under the chairmanship of Tedd Freeman, the book features the research and insights of exceptionally knowledgeable authors Norman Wilson, Edward Howes, Walter Gray, James Henley, Melinda Peak and Charles Duncan. James Henley, who has managed Sacramento's historical collections for 30 years, also served as a second reader of the entire manuscript; his judicious comments added substantial quality and depth. Photo Editor Lucinda Woodward labored well beyond the norm to locate exceptional illustrations, many not previously published, that add so much vitality and rich variety to the work. Ruth Ellis, librarian of the Sacramento Room at the Sacramento Public Library reviewed the bibliography and made several helpful suggestions, pointing especially to some of the children's selections. Publishers Chuck and Lori Parks of Heritage Media and their fine staff displayed keen understanding of many of the problems we faced and have presented this compilation in a most attractive design and style that dramatically enhances the way the story is told. The superb efforts of the above individuals, and many other contributors too numerous to name but to whom we are equally grateful, merits long applause and many thanks for the labor of love that was offered.

John F. Burns
Editor

The illustrations feature the collection of the Sacramento Archives and Museum Collection Center (SAMCC). This facility is funded jointly by the City and County of Sacramento and is open to researchers by appointment. Their collection includes objects, manuscripts, ephemera, public records and over 3 million photographs, all related to the people and history of the Sacramento region. SAMCC archivists Patricia Johnson and Anastasia Wolfe made available many hundreds of photographs and other materials for review, provided invaluable advice about appropriate collections to research for particular subject areas, and coordinated the processing of items selected. James Henley, director of SAMCC, provided historical information about nearly all the images under consideration, and assisted in the selection of images for the two chapters he authored. In addition, authors Norman Wilson and Charles Duncan provided similar assistance for the pre-Gold Rush era and the years between World War I and World War II, respectively.

Lucinda Woodward
Photo Editor

Sacramento is a product of its history and is enriched by it. As we celebrate the 150th birthday of the city and county we stand on the doorstep of a new millennium, enlightened by our heritage and challenged by the possibilities that the future holds.

Gold Rush Legacy, Metropolitan Destiny helps provide the perspective we need to meet the challenges of the new century, one in which Sacramento will continue to grow as one of America's significant metropolitan regions. The editor, photo editor, authors and contributors to this work have well described and illustrated the seeds of Sacramento's sustained vitality. From early times through the excitement of the Gold Rush to the economic and cultural diversity that characterizes Sacramento life, this book outlines the contours and highlights of the Sacramento experience.

We are deeply grateful to the Sacramento County Historical Society, Heritage Media Corp. and the many area businesses who have collaborated to produce this new, sesqui-centennial history of the city and county of Sacramento. Through this work the people of Sacramento's past can touch those of the present day, and can contribute to the education of the future generations that will shape the development of next century's Sacramento.

Endorsed by the Sacramento Commission of History and Science as the Sesquicentennial History of Sacramento. The Commission is an official body appointed by:

Sacramento City Council
Joe Serna, Jr., Mayor

Sacramento County Board of Supervisors
Muriel Johnson, Chair

FOREWORD

© Heritage Media Corp.
Photo by Robert A. Eplett

PROLOGUE:
SEARCHING FOR SACRAMENTO

by John F. Burns, Editor & Melinda A. Peak, SCHS President

All of us have certain mental images of places we know or recognize. Prominent features of a city, region or state endure over time and define that place to both residents and outsiders. Los Angeles, for example, has its beaches and world-renowned entertainment industry. San Francisco broadcasts the exotic ambience of the bay, its bridges, Chinatown and Fisherman's Wharf. Seattle promotes its Space Needle and ferries. Such snapshots give people a central picture of these localities. But what characterizes Sacramento? What appears in a person's mind when they hear the name of this particular city and county? What should this book be about?

Ask a Sacramentan that question and be prepared to receive quite a variety of answers, depending on the respondent's orientation and proclivities. Some focus on the celebratory atmosphere that the Camellia, Jazz or numerous ethnic festivals annually evoke. Others see Sacramento as the ultimate halfway point, lauding its fortunate setting midway between the cosmopolitan attractions of the San Francisco Bay area to the west and the glorious natural beauty of the High Sierra and Lake Tahoe to the east, or between Yosemite to the south and Shasta to the north. For those people, Sacramento is a sort of central valley workday parking zone from which one can quickly catapult into a weekend escape.

Another image is that of a "River City," in reference to Sacramento's placement at the junction of two of California's great rivers, the Sacramento and the American. These watercourses are the source of Sacramento's initial fame and much of its current recreational activity, as well as the ruinous floods that have periodically threatened the city's existence and that continue to prompt heated civic debate about appropriate levels of protection. There is no question that dealing with water resources is at the center of the Sacramento and California experience, both historically and today. But the rivers, like the festivals and the central valley location, are only a part of Sacramento's dappled identity.

Probably the most frequent depiction of Sacramento emphasizes its weighty role as California's "Capital City," denoting Sacramento's long service as the Golden State's seat of government. To be sure, Sacramento has something in common with other "second city" capitals, like Springfield, Madison, Salem, Olympia and Santa Fe. More

U.S. state capitals are actually outside the major cities in the states than are found within them. These state capitals often have a "hometown" aura that exists apart from the governance functions, though a majestic capitol building frequently dominates the downtown area, along with surrounding state offices. They are also often situated on bodies of water or rivers, have desirable, well-kept, older neighborhoods that attract residents who want to be close to the political action, have universities close-by, and are connected to the state's primary metropolis via a major freeway arterial. Frequently, families who have lived in these capitals for generations bemoan the loss of a fondly remembered small town environment they feel existed before more muscular government and concurrent business

development sparked a growth surge that continues to worry them.

There is no doubt that Sacramento shares several of these elements with many state capitals; certainly in many ways it is quite unlike its larger California coastal brethren. Visitors from the eastern and midwestern U.S. feel quite at home in Sacramento, seeing the resemblance to familiar settings: the flat terrain, the orderly street grid in the older city, and wonderful large shade trees that provide relief from the extreme summer heat (they note that it is a dry heat though, not that soggy, humid heat that so oppresses most of the rest of the country). This visceral familiarity with Sacramento is not surprising, given the eastern and midwestern origins of the majority of Sacramento's founders. Moreover, visitors find that

Sacramento is not the prototypical California city of the televised media. It is hours from beaches, mountains or redwood forests. It has neither missions nor presidio, Spanish influence originally having been exploratory. It is relatively free from earthquakes and does not resemble the southwestern deserts of popular Western imagination. Few movies are made here and the nightlife is rather more staid than kinky. It is considered a good place to raise a family.

Yet Sacramento is also quite distinct from other state capitals, even those with significant rivers. Sacramento is not just a city; it is also a large county, where two-thirds of the people live outside Sacramento's city limits, and where a different non-capital experience often predominates. Originally the habitat of substantial numbers of California Indians, eight Mexican land grants were eventually established, bordering the principal river drainages in the county. As the area was further settled, agricultural enterprises gradually became dominant, spurred by an astounding proliferation of railroad lines, with some gold dredging activity in the eastern county. Many people were attracted to the area away from the city, and by the onset of World War II a quarter of the population lived in the unincorporated county, mostly on small acreage termed by the census "rural non-farm."

After the war, though, bucolic county life was disrupted, supplanted at an ever accelerating rate by commercial endeavors, shopping malls, suburban housing, defense bases, aerospace industries, miscellaneous businesses and, most recently, extensive computer manufacturing operations. To many county residents, Sacramento seemed to offer entrepreneurial opportunity or lifestyle without much government control, adjacent to but in some ways distant from the capital city; a gulf at times magnified by the disinterest of city leaders in annexing portions of the county even as residential development spread. Though the lines between county and city have blurred as suburbia marches through acre after acre, sections of the county still seek to maintain their own identity, as evidenced by the recent incorporation of Citrus Heights and the proliferation of local area history groups.

But all of the above characteristics of area personality, no matter how interesting or compelling, are sidelights that pale before the one truly monumental event that created Sacramento, a happening that eternally provides a unifying identity for the city and county and that represents its founding soul and spirit. For underneath the seemingly placid, midwestern-like state capital surface is a place that has been at the forefront of the United States' and California's remarkable history. Sacramento has a claim to fame that all other capital cities lack, one that is indelibly etched as one of the extraordinary events of the middle part of the 19th century. Only Sacramento became known throughout the world as the entry gate and commercial nucleus of the great California Gold Rush.

The essence of Sacramento rests within this unique legacy. Many places have rivers, and capitals and pioneer buildings carefully preserved, and attractive, tree-lined avenues, along with growing economies, suburban sprawl, traffic congestion and persistent social problems that come with metropolitan development. But only one city/county has the distinction of being the focal point of California gold seeking, with consequences that set much of the city and county's character to this day and that will continue to affect its future. When people from outside Sacramento are asked what image the place holds, sometimes rivers, music, winter flowers, proximity to other places or its capital status stands out front. But nothing can compete with the legacy of gold that is at Sacramento's heart. That legacy is the source of Sacramento's renown.

Sacramento is initially a product of geographic happenstance. It grew from the point at which river transport could haul prospective miners closest to the goldfields, the earliest mined of which were very conveniently just up the American River from the Sacramento docks. Since Sacramento was the place one could most easily reach in order to be equipped and head for the mines, it was a highly desirable destination. Its rapid growth as the centerpiece of the gold rush led to its becoming the most vibrant city in the state, thus enticing the legislature to fix the capital here. That action, along with the placement of Sacramento as the western intercontinental railroad terminus, ensured that Sacramento would not become just another faded boomtown.

The rivers led to the gold. The quest for gold unleashed explosive population growth that made Sacramento an economic center and legitimized its application as the capital, at the same time prompting a population diversity and transience that remains significant. The trails across the mountains that led to Sacramento and the goldfields became heavily traveled, used by the Pony Express riders, then becoming the transcontinental railroad right-of-way, and eventually the route of highways and freeways, continually cementing Sacramento as the transportation hub of the state.

As the gold diminished, agriculture and food processing escalated in impact, supported by the important transportation infrastructure which itself supplied much work.

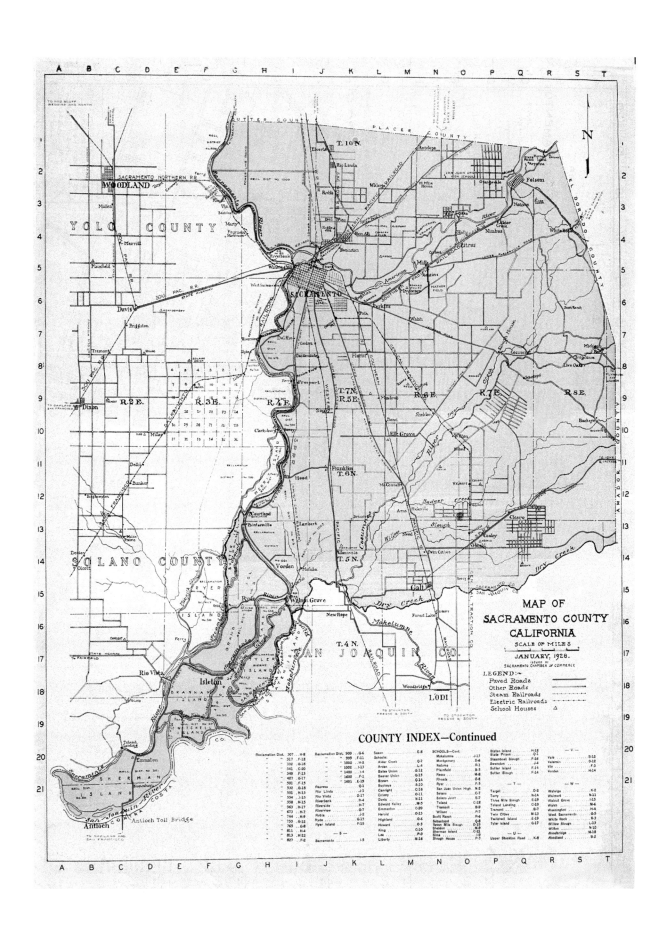

MAP OF
SACRAMENTO COUNTY
CALIFORNIA

SCALE OF MILES

JANUARY, 1928.

ISSUED BY
SACRAMENTO CHAMBER OF COMMERCE

LEGEND:—

Paved Roads	
Other Roads	
Steam Railroads	
Electric Railroads	
School Houses	△

COUNTY INDEX—Continued

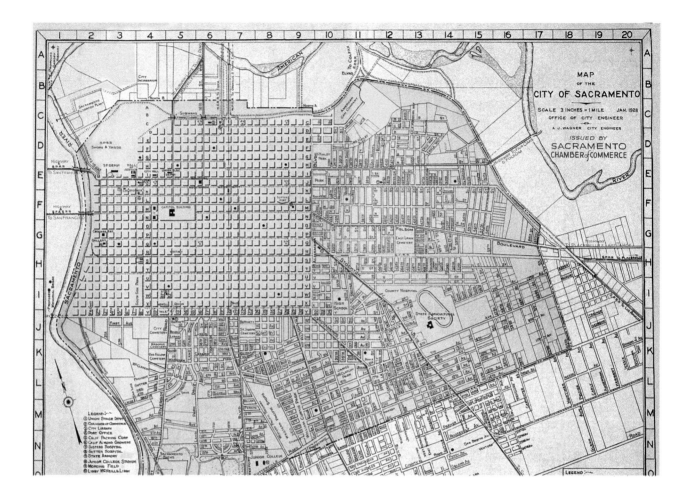

In turn, other services and industries, including defense and aerospace plants, a growing state government, and today's silicon chip manufacturing and financial processing, all became part of Sacramento's evolution. These endeavors were many years removed from the gold rush, but nonetheless, subtly reliant on those earlier efforts by an enterprising Sacramento population that gradually shaped an enduring character for the city and the county.

From the outset, Sacramento's people were of worldwide origin, of all races and beliefs, living and working side by side interdependently. They were energetic, entrepreneurial, distant from the expectations of their home turf and adapting to an unprecedented environment. A traveling physician, commenting on an 1850 Sacramento election, observed a noisy and exciting scene with a "Babel-like jargon of hundreds of voices, in all languages, jabbering, chattering, huzzaing and yelling at the highest key..." These people were not always neighborhood friends or free of intolerance, but they

learned to accept each other to an uncommon degree when compared to the more volatile past of many other localities.

In the restored historic district of Old Sacramento, at Sutter's Fort and in numerous local museums and other sites, the spirit of those initial people is memorialized and renewed. This book will introduce the reader to what makes Sacramento tick, but to most fully savor the rich tapestry of Sacramento history and life there is no substitute for direct contact. Fortunately, in Sacramento, such opportunity is readily available to both those who live here and those passing through. Visitors are often surprised at the range of attractions, since local leadership has not always focused on marketing Sacramento's unique pioneer identity. The ongoing sesquicentennial anniversary of Sacramento and the state has recently sparked greater action to attract tourism through promotion of the gold rush legacy. Hopefully such efforts will be sustained after the birthday parties end.

Trekking through the places that tell the story of Sacramento, one can begin at the beginning, at the State Indian Museum that interprets California's Native American experience. Adjacent to the Indian Museum is Sutter's Fort, the state historic park that is the next stop as the site of the first European settlement. Moving down to the waterfront, the gold rush era ambience of Old Sacramento fronts a host of venues centering around the story of that exciting time and the aftermath, including the distinctive architecture of the old buildings, riverboats at the wharf, the Pony Express Memorial, the California Military Museum, Wells Fargo, the State Railroad Museum and the Sacramento Discovery Museum, with the Towe Auto Museum just down the street.

Nearby are the historic Crocker Art Museum, Stanford House and Old Governor's Mansion, along with myriad other Victorian structures and residences in the downtown area that showcase earlier days. In the center of town the restored State Capitol and Museum, Capitol Park and its many monuments, and the Golden State Museum unveil the development of the state and especially the impact of state government, where eminent political figures like Hiram Johnson, Earl Warren, "Pat" Brown, Jesse Unruh and Ronald Reagan once held forth, and where innovative public policy as well as sometimes loony political theater continues to garner national attention.

Complementary attractions are found further out in the county, where the town of Folsom maintains much of its gold rush flavor in its historic downtown, with the Folsom Dam Powerhouse and Folsom Prison Museums nearby. South of Sacramento's city limits the county's rich agricultural heritage continues to find expression. Orchards and fields lie adjacent to the meandering river as it courses through the Delta, with small towns such as Locke, Courtland and Walnut Grove demonstrating the lasting viability of traditional county life.

Sacramento is also blessed with a large number of publicly accessible libraries and archives, where long-time and new residents, visitors, scholars, students and anyone else can learn more about the topics touched upon in this book and the many other fascinating aspects of the Sacramento experience. The Sacramento Room of the Central Library downtown, the City-County Archives and Museum Collections Center just north of town, the State Library's California Room next to the Capitol, and the nearby State Archives offer broad research opportunities, with materials also available at the Library and Archives at California State University, Sacramento, on the eastern edge of the city. The short bibliography of selected titles that appears at the end of this book can be a useful starting point to gaining further knowledge about Sacramento's many sides and its role in Califonia and U.S. history.

What this book is designed to do is to introduce a number of the pieces that together comprise the mosaic of Sacramento, through a stimulating narrative penned by some of the region's most seasoned and experienced history practitioners joined with a series of photographs and illustrations, some never before in print, selected by a notable local history specialist. Unlike previous treatments of Sacramento, this volume pays conspicuous attention not only to the city but also to the entire county experience, reflecting the book's sponsorship by the Sacramento County Historical Society.

Nonetheless, considerations of space mean that this book is not yet the comprehensive history that an area with the worldwide significance of Sacramento clearly merits. Some notable figures, groups and events could not be included, and the more recent history of the area will be left to a subsequent work. The editor has pushed the limits of page count allocated by the publisher, Heritage Media, and is deeply appreciative for their willingness to expand space in the interest of producing the best history possible in one volume, a book that must remain broadly digestible if it is to meet the needs of its audience. Hopefully some of what appears here will incite others to investigate and record the many layers of the Sacramento story yet unpublished, and will further encourage the political and business leadership of the community to support the Sacramento heritage that is its unique identity.

The historical society board's president who initiated and guided this publication opportunity is a native Sacramentan who has lived here most of her life. The editor is what some consider a typical Sacramentan, a sojourner born and raised in the midwest who settled here as the last and best of many places. Together we are happy to be here and we are extremely grateful to the members of the "Sacramento" team that produced this book. We also appreciate the patience of our children, Alyssa and Katherine, who sacrificed many nights of family time to see this and other work of the historical society completed. We hope that books like these will support their education by giving Sacramento's next generation a vibrant affinity for their heritage. Sacramento's history is a wonderful topic to study. This place is not like other capitals, not like L.A., and not like the Bay area. We think that's just grand, and we hope you enjoy its story as much as we do.

CHAPTER ONE

In The Beginning

by Norman L. Wilson

It was dark and there was water everywhere. Upon this water a raft floated with three figures: Turtle, World Creator and Coyote. Turtle was the builder who dove to the bottom of the sea bringing up dirt on his claws to build the land. World Creator was the religious force who took the dirt from turtle, molded it into the world and put rivers, trees and people on the land. Coyote was the human spirit. These three worked together. Sometimes Coyote would do good and help the native peoples. Other times he would get in trouble and outsmart himself, no different than people have always done. Coyote created droughts and floods, but he also taught the salmon to swim upstream.

Today, as in the Nisenan creation myth, water is a dominant force in California. The first peoples to come into the Sacramento valley followed the rivers and made their villages along the waterways. Spanish explorers followed the streams inland to discover the valley. Later, explorers and trappers took their bounty from the rivers and miners and steamboats would follow the water courses. Farmers would be ruined by droughts or made rich by the alluvial soil on the land. Mining debris would cause great damage in the rivers. Cities would be flooded and massive dams built to control this water. Political boundaries were made and highways and bridges were built, influenced by the rivers and flood basins in the valley. Today we still fear potential flooding of our cities and farms, and we build higher levees. Coyote is helping us as he has always done.

When the Paleo-Indians came into the valley, there were huge rivers rushing from the mountains with melting glaciers and snow fields feeding them. From the north came the great river now known as the Sacramento. It flowed southward joining the San Joaquin River, then west to the ocean which 12,000 years ago was approximately 300 feet lower than today. The valley floor was dotted with lakes and meandering streams, great basins covered with tules that dried up in the summer, and forests that lined the rivers. The valley itself was rapidly filling in with materials left by the floods and, as today, there is either too much water or too little.

The first peoples who arrived over 12,000 years ago found large animals such as mastodons, horses, camels, saber-toothed tigers, huge bears and dire-wolves. Waterfowl by the millions flew in the skies. Giant sturgeon and smaller fish were abundant. There were also large herds of elk, deer and antelope on the valley floor. Grizzly bears were common. Salmon ran up the rivers at least four times a year reaching into the upper drainages. Forests of great oaks lined the streams and were scattered across the plains, which were covered with a luxurious growth of seed-bearing grasses.

These first peoples probably came from the north and east, although some believe that they worked their way down the coast when the ocean was lower. Others think some early inhabitants came from the south. When they arrived in the valley, they found it to be a "Garden of Eden" with grand natural resources. Nomadic hunters initially inhabited the valley; perhaps these people stayed because there was little reason to leave this rich valley, and there was no easy way out over the mountain barriers.

About 8,000 years ago, the people began settling into permanent villages, exploiting the locally accessible resource base. Huge animals of the glacial period were likely hunted to extinction, and the inhabitants turned to other foods, changing their diet by using new plants and using grinding stones to process hard seeds. These early peoples developed fishing technology and learned to hunt waterfowl. Over thousands of years, other groups followed, taking up new areas, and pushing others aside to establish themselves.

These portraits sketched by Swedish artist Emil Lehman during his 1852 visit are among the earliest views of native people in the Sacramento area. *Emil Lehman Sketch Book, Sacramento Archives and Museum Collection Center (SAMCC).*

At European contact, the peoples occupying the valley were Penutian-speaking. Sacramento County had two branches of this language group: The Miwok and the Nisenan. Although the two were related by language and culture, the Miwok probably arrived first. Miwok-speaking peoples occupied the Sierra mountains to the southeast, the valley floor in the Delta, present-day Marin County, and the banks of the Cosumnes River in Sacramento County. The Nisenan were Maidu-speaking and occupied the drainages of the American River and the east side of the Sacramento River. Both Miwok and Nisenan spoke the Penutian language, but the languages were so different they could not understand each other. Nisenan means "of us;" Miwok means "people or man;" Maidu means "man." The group living west of the Sacramento River was the Patwin, who also spoke a different Penutian language.

Around 2,000 years ago, there was a transition to the use of acorns. This meant that the native peoples could harvest and store huge amounts of food to avoid famine when other foods were scarce. The preparation of acorns for food was a complicated procedure. The stored acorns were shelled, ground in mortars, leached with warm water and cooked in baskets using hot stones. The mastery of the use of acorns also helped native peoples to increase their populations.

Use of the bow and arrow probably became common about 1,500 to 1,000 years ago. This made hunting more efficient, especially of small game. It also changed the practice of warfare among the groups living in the area, and later proved to be a serious threat to the Spanish.

When the first Spanish explorers came into the valley, it was one of the most densely populated regions of native North America. These explorers were impressed with the size and number of villages; they reported that some had as many as 500 to 1,000 occupants. They were located along the river's edge on great mounds that became refuges when the flood waters swept over the land. Some villagers would retreat into the foothills to avoid the rising waters. Large villages were located every few miles along the rivers and streams. The village of Pushuni was at the mouth of the American River. Other villages going east along the American were Sek and Kadema. These settlements usually had 20 to 40 houses, a large subterranean dance house which might be 50 to 60 feet in diameter, acorn granaries and brush shade shelters.

By the 16th century, Europeans reached the west coast of North America and started explorations which would eventually range into the Sacramento Valley and the area now known as Sacramento County. Juan Cabrillo (Joao Cabrilho), a Portuguese, was the first maritime explorer to sail along the California coast, in 1542. He landed in San Diego Bay and managed to get as far north as Monterey Bay, claiming this land for Spain.

Cabrillo was followed by Sir Francis Drake, who set foot on the California coast in the vicinity of Marin County in 1579. His party spent a month repairing his ship,

Permanent houses were shallowly excavated and covered with earth. They were often located on mounds above the flood plain. Granaries, constructed of tule mats over poles, stored the year's crop of acorns. *Eleanor McClatchy Collection, SAMCC.*

preparing for a voyage around the world and back to England. His explorations gave England the first knowledge of the width of the continent of North America. When he left, he claimed the land for England. When the Virginia Company on the Atlantic side of the continent was then given its charter, its grant extended all the way to the Pacific Ocean, including the Sacramento Valley, although no one really knew what that meant.

The first explorer to look into the Sacramento Valley and realize its extent was Gaspar De Portola in 1769. He had been sent north by the Spanish to colonize Alta California. By 1808, Lt. Gabriel Moraga ventured into the valley, across Sacramento County and all the way to the Feather River. When he crossed the American River he called it *Las Llagas*. He gave the name Sacramento, for the holy sacrament, to the valley and called the Sacramento River the *Jesus Maria*. The purpose for his exploration was to report on the possibility of inland mission sites, though he found none that were suitable.

Three years later, Padre Abella and Fortuni's party came to the lower Sacramento Valley, also looking for mission sites. Although Abella encouraged the Spanish government to establish missions in the valley, his advice was contrary to Moraga's report and the recommendations were ignored. Padre Narciso Duran and his party came up the Sacramento River by boat commanded by Captain Luis Antonio Arguello in 1817. There were 10 soldiers and 100 native oarsmen with this expedition, which may have gone far enough to pass by the mouth of the American River. Spain's claims to Alta California were appropriated by Mexico when it overcame Spanish rule and established its own government in 1822.

Occasional European forays into the valley continued into the early 1800s without much impact. The Spanish found a Scotsman who had fled his ship and was living with the Indians on Grand Island in 1818. In 1823, the Russian Imperial Navy, led by a German named Otto Von Kotzebue, penetrated the Sacramento River perhaps as far as the American River. Accompanying this expedition were 20 Aleuts and their bidarkas as well as small Russian boats. Their last camp was probably in the vicinity of present day Freeport on the Sacramento River.

One of the first clashes with Native Americans took place on the Cosumnes River in December, 1826. As recorded by Lt. Jose Sanchez, a Mexican officer, and Capt. William Beechey, a British naval officer who was visiting Yerba Buena, this expedition burned Indian villages, killed numerous men on the lower reaches of the Cosumnes River and captured 41 women and children.

The next year, 1827, the famous American explorer, Jedediah Smith, and his trapping party entered the valley from the south. They camped along the American River which they named "The Wild One," near where the campus of California State University, Sacramento, is located today. After exploring the lower reaches of the American River, the party moved south while Smith crossed the Sierra Nevada to attend a mountainman rendezvous at Bear Lake in Utah. Accompanied by more mountain men, he returned to the Sacramento Valley, joined up with his former party and headed north. His reports and maps became invaluable to those who pushed west in later years. After a deadly fight with Indians, he reached Fort Vancouver and told of the large numbers of beaver in the interior valleys of California.

These houses made of tule mats are probably summer houses, occupied during acorn and grasshopper gathering. Women cooked acorn mush by placing hot rocks inside baskets, then vigorously stirring to avoid burning the baskets. This view originally appeared in the April 1859 issue of *Hutchings Illustrated California Magazine*. California State Collection, SAMCC.

The largest structures built by the Nisenan and Miwok were their village dance houses. Excavated to a depth of about four feet, they were topped by a framework of limbs and willow, and covered with earth. These were important places for ceremonies, dances and curing by a shaman. M. Duflot de Mofras prepared this view for an 1844 French publication. *Eleanor McClatchy Collection, SAMCC.*

After Smith's visit to Fort Vancouver, Dr. John McLaughlin, the man in charge of this Hudson's Bay fort, directed Alexander R. McLeod to go south and hunt "The San Buena Ventura." With Arthur Turner, one of the survivors of the Smith party as a guide, the brigade left for a hunt of 12 to 16 months in California. By mid-summer of 1828, McLeod was hunting in the Sacramento area and the Delta. Abel Stearns, who was looking for a land grant, met McLeod and allowed one of his men, an African-American pioneer, George Washington, to join the brigade. McLeod was pleased to have this man since he had been living in California for six years, knew the country and spoke Spanish well. "The Buena Ventura Brigade" trapped the west side of the valley and started north toward Fort Vancouver in October of 1829.

During his stay in the valley, McLeod crossed the trail of a large party of horsemen towing a piece of ordnance. This was Lt. Jose Sanchez and a 42-man punitive expedition from the San Francisco Presidio; he had been in a brutal fight near present-day Galt or Lodi with the Cosumnes Indians, losing two soldiers. He also had 19 wounded members of his Indian auxiliaries with him. The purpose of Sanchez's expeditions and others was retribution for horse stealing in the coastal areas. Escaped Mission Indians, which did not include the Nisenan, began stealing horses in the first years of the 19th century. The stolen horses were driven from the ranchos and missions across the valley to the Sierras, where the Indians felt safe. Captain John Sutter later had similar problems when he first settled along the American River. He mounted several campaigns against the Miwok to retrieve stolen livestock and to punish those he regarded as offenders.

Hudson's Bay Company trappers continued to enter the valley, set up permanent camps and trap along the rivers and streams. Although their primary camp was French Camp near Stockton, their presence was felt along the Sacramento and American rivers. In 1833, a great illness befell the native population living on the valley floor. It is likely that malaria was introduced by the non-native European transients; as many as 70 percent of the Indians in the vicinity of Sacramento died or escaped to the foothills at this time. This was the first of many epidemics to strike and decimate the native peoples.

John B. R. Cooper, an American, came into the valley in 1833 seeking a land grant. He applied to the Mexican government for land embracing the area around today's Folsom, but he never proved up on his grant and he lost his claim. He called the American River the *Rio Ojotska*, a Russian name that means "Hunter's River," alluding to possible exploration into the interior of California by Russians from Fort Ross. By 1837, British boats from the *H M S Sulphur*, commanded by Captain Edward Belcher, traversed about 100 miles up the Sacramento River.

The Mexican government was concerned about these travels by foreign explorers and trappers in California's Central Valley, as they had no control over who was in the area. Juan Bautista Alvarado, governor of Alta California, felt he needed to establish a greater Mexican presence in Central California. Mariano Vallejo, the military commander of Northern California, was too far away in Sonoma to effectively control exploration, settlement and trapping in the Sacramento Valley. But who would provide that presence?

The stage was set for the entrance of John Sutter, a Swiss adventurer, who arrived in California in 1839. He knew about the great Central Valley from information obtained from the British at Fort Vancouver and probably from the Russians at Sitka. He presented himself to Governor Alvarado, and requested an opportunity to establish a rancho. Alvarado wanted a Mexican outpost in the remote Sacramento Valley, and he asked Sutter to explore the central valley rivers, find an area that was suitable for settlement and return in a year for negotiations for the land grant. Sutter obtained a schooner, *Isabella*, and a smaller boat for his expedition up the Sacramento River. While waiting to get his boats outfitted, Sutter visited the Russians at Fort Ross, Mariano Vallejo, and other people who could give him information about the little-known areas beyond the Carquinez Straits. Sutter's group included three German carpenters, two mechanics and eight Kanakas (native Hawaiians) who came with him from Hawaii, courtesy of King Kamehameha.

When the outfitting was complete, the *Isabella* and the other craft worked their way up the Sacramento River. It took several days to find the true mouth of the river in the

Although not drawn until 1849, this view looking toward Sutter's Fort from the north is a good illustration of its pre-Gold Rush appearance. Sutter cleared the ground and used it for crops and grazing. George V. Cooper created this illustration for J. M. Letts' publication, *California Illustrated, Including a Description of the Panama and Nicaragua Routes*, during a trip to the Sacramento area and the gold fields.
J. Brown Maloney Collection, SAMCC.

Delta because of the many islands and false river channels. Sutter encountered the first Indians about 10 miles below the future site of Sacramento City, probably Miwok, perhaps remnants of the village that had been raided by Sanchez. They were armed and hostile but Sutter went ashore, assured them that he wanted a treaty, and that he was going upstream to explore the country. Convincing them, he was allowed to continue on his way.

Sutter explored up to and beyond the mouth of the Feather River, then moved back down to the mouth of the American. On August 12, 1839, traveling upstream a short distance on the American River, his party landed. There they pitched tents and mounted three cannon. Sutter gathered the men and announced that those who were not content could leave aboard the *Isabella*, and he would stay alone with the Kanakas. Three men returned to Yerba Buena and the others remained with Sutter.

After scouting the local area, Sutter selected a gentle, rising knoll well back from both rivers as a place to establish his empire. First came grass huts built by the Hawaiians and soon buildings of adobe were erected. These buildings were joined in a rectangle and eventually resulted in a fort with buildings on the outside perimeter, a central building, walls and gates. When it was finished a few years later, the structure was surrounded by walls 12- to 16-feet high. It was an impressive compound in what was then a wilderness.

Governor Alvarado had indicated to Sutter that if he wanted a land grant he would have to become a Mexican citizen. Sutter made application and on August 29, 1840,

he was awarded his citizenship. He was also appointed judge and representative of the "Government at the Frontiers of the Rio Sacramento." In 1841, he obtained formal transfer of 11 leagues of land or some 44,000 acres which he named New Helvetia. It stretched from the Sutter Buttes in the north to the Sacramento River on the west, margins of the Feather River on the east and down to the American River on the south. Soon, the Mexican government made other land grants in what was to become Sacramento County: Rancho San Juan, Rancho Del Paso, Rancho Cosumnes, Rancho Omochumnes (or the Sheldon Grant), Rancho Cazadores, Rancho Sacayac, Rancho Rio de los Americanos (or the Leidesdorff Grant), Rancho San Jon de los Mokelumnes (or Chabolla Grant) and Rancho Arroyo Seco.

At about the same time, the Russian governor attached to Fort Ross offered Sutter the holdings of the fort for $30,000. Sutter recognized the value and accepted. He dismantled the buildings and the fort walls and moved the boards, mostly of redwood, and other property to New Helvetia where it was needed for additional construction. This sale also gained him a schooner which he renamed *The Sacramento*, and livestock. The herd, which comprised about 2,000 cattle, horses, mules and sheep, was driven overland to the fort by Sutter's men. Aiding in this labor was John Bidwell, a recent arrival and a new employee at the fort. He had come overland in the Bidwell-Bartleston Party in 1841, the first immigrant party to reach California by land from the eastern United States.

William A. Leidesdorff, a native of the West Indies, owned the 35,000-acre Rancho Rio de los Americanos from 1844 until his death in 1848. His father was a Danish planter and his mother was of African-Caribbean ancestry. His land grant was in the vicinity of present-day Folsom. *Eleanor McClatchy Collection, SAMCC.*

Visitors started arriving at Sutter's Fort as early as 1840, with the visit of Peter Lassen and trappers from the Hudson's Bay Company. In 1841, Charles M. Weber, who founded Stockton, and Henry Huber, who became supervisor of farming operations for New Helvetia, arrived. Also in 1841, W. D. Phelps, aboard the American cutter, *Alert,* became the first to carry the flag of the United States into the Sacramento area and Sutter's establishment. In April, 1842, Phelps returned, but finding the road to the fort flooded and impassable, he sent an Indian messenger to Captain Sutter requesting help. By wading and swimming, the Indian reached the fort in about two hours. By 4 p.m., a bidarka, managed by two Hawaiians, arrived with a note from Sutter that Phelps should go in the bidarka to the fort. Phelps reported "This canoe was fifteen to sixteen feet in length, a light frame of sticks and timbers, and covered with seal skins... and extremely ticklish... (I) resigned myself to fate. The waters were madly rushing through the forest and... through it all, we dashed with fearful velocity... the water was so high as to permit the approach to the very walls of the presidio into which I stepped after a half hour's navigation over trees and stumps and was kindly received by Captain Sutter." The bidarka had been obtained with the purchase of Fort Ross, permitting Phelps to reach Sutter and spurring him to pen the early, graphic description of Sacramento flooding in the spring.

In 1840, John Sinclair settled on the Del Paso Land Grant across the American River from Sutter's Fort. Sinclair and his wife, Mary, became one of the first Anglo families to live in the region. They settled the southern part of the grant, raising cattle, hogs and sheep, assisted by Indian labor upon which early settlers relied heavily. When Edwin Bryant visited the Sinclairs on September 1, 1846, Indians were harvesting wheat. Sinclair indicated that the yield would be about 3,000 bushels. Bryant reported that the wheat fields were bordered by ditches five-feet deep and three- to five-feet wide to protect them from the cattle grazing nearby, a technique Sutter also used to protect his fields. Bryant described Sinclair's barn and house as "constructed after the American model" representing "a most comfortable and neat appearance." These ranch buildings were probably in the vicinity of present-day Campus Commons across the American River from California State University, Sacramento. To the east of Sinclair's rancho were the two Mexican land grants known as Rancho San Juan and Rancho Rio de los Americanos.

Other early settlers in Sacramento County and the valley were Jared Dixon Sheldon and William Daylor, who both settled in the Sloughhouse area. Sheldon was a naturalized Mexican citizen who was owed money by the government for carpenter work. He asked for and was given a grant called Omochumnes, or the Sheldon Grant. P.B. Reading, Peter Lassen and William Ide settled in the north end of the valley. John Bidwell, after leaving Sutter's employ, started the town of Chico.

Gradually, more foreign and American visitors and immigrants made their way into the Sacramento Valley and to Sutter's Fort. Some were men who had jumped ship. Some came from Oregon. Others had lived in the coastal area but were attracted to the Sutter establishment. Some settled on ranchos granted to them by the Mexican government, and some simply squatted on the land. The immigrant Bidwell-Bartleston Party had arrived in 1841, and by 1844, the Townsend-Stevens-Murphy Party had brought wagons over what today is called Donner Summit. Two years later the ill-fated Donner Party was trapped by heavy winter snowstorms in the mountains, and several rescue parties were sent from Sutter's Fort to try to save them.

New Helvetia, or "New Switzerland," became a well-known outpost on the frontier. It was a magnet for foreigners who found safety and help. Although Sutter was now a Mexican citizen, he seemed to have welcomed with open arms immigrants, explorers and military expeditions. In a sense, he was caught in the middle between American Manifest Destiny which brought migrations of people to the west from the United States and the Mexican government's attempt to control a distant California province.

In the 1840s, the Mexican governors of California were contesting the governorship and Sutter backed Governor Manuel Micheltorena. Californians Alvarado and Jose Castro led a group which overthrew the Mexican government and, in the process, Sutter was thrown in jail. All of Sutter's holdings were in jeopardy but the new government granted Sutter his freedom and the land that former Mexican Governor Alvarado had granted him in 1841 remained his to rule. Sutter looked at all the land within 40 miles of the fort as his, and evidently thought he was acting within his power when he granted a large portion of land between the Feather and American rivers to Eliab and Hiram Grimes and John Sinclair. Later ratified by the Mexican government, the property extended north of the American River, encompassing much of present-day

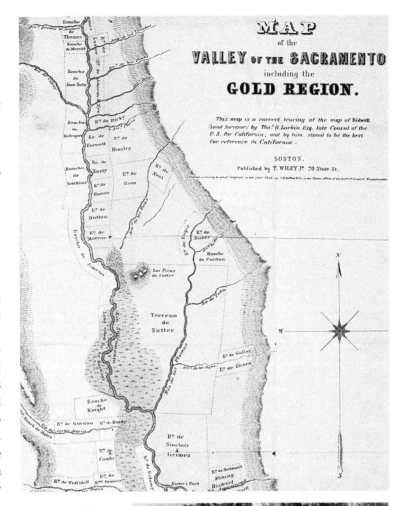

Pioneer Chico settler and land surveyor, John Bidwell, created the base for this map in 1844. It is an important snapshot of the valley's pre-Gold Rush land ownership and land uses. In 1850 it was traced by Thomas O. Larkin, updated to include the mining district along the American River, and given the new title *Map of the Valley of the Sacramento Including the Gold Rush.* *Eleanor McClatchy Collection, SAMCC.*

In 1850, Andrew Jackson Grayson commissioned William S. Jewett to capture a romantic portrait of the Grayson family as they arrived in California. Jewett, a Forty-niner from New York, had the distinction of being California's first professionally trained portrait painter. *Eleanor McClatchy Collection, SAMCC.*

Artist William M'Illvaine, Jr. captured this view of Sutter's Fort in 1849 to illustrate his book, *Sketches of Scenery* and *Notes of Personal Adventure in California and Mexico.* Sutter's vast empire, known as New Helvetia, was based on an European feudal estate model. The fort was a non-military trading post similar in design to Fort Hall, Fort Vancouver and Fort Ross, all places Sutter had visited. *J. Brown Maloney Collection, SAMCC.*

John C. Frémont, a lieutenant in the U. S. Corps of Topographical Engineers, led several exploring, scientific and military expeditions throughout the west. After crossing the Sierra Nevada during the dead of winter in 1844, Frémont followed the south fork of the American River to Sutter's Fort, where Sutter outfitted him for the continuation of his expedition. *Eleanor McClatchy Collection, SAMCC.*

FLAG OF THE FIRST FREMONT EXPEDITION.

North Sacramento, Citrus Heights, Rio Linda and parts of the Fair Oaks-Carmichael area.

More United States government expeditions found their way to Sutter's Fort. In 1841, as part of the Charles Wilkes Expedition, U.S. Navy Lieutenant Ringgold arrived by boat. Lieutenant Emmons and a group of scientists, also a part of the Wilkes Expedition, came south from Oregon and visited Sutter's Fort before going on to meet Captain Wilkes at Yerba Buena. In 1844, Lieutenant John Fremont and a party crossed the Sierra Nevada in the dead of winter and came down the American River to New Helvetia. With them, as a guide, was the famous frontiersman Kit Carson. Sutter generously outfitted these explorers, with mounting concern on the part of the Mexican authorities, although Fremont and his men soon left California.

In 1846, war broke out between Mexico and the United States. The conflict was initially over Texas, but the United States soon expanded its interest to include New Mexico and California. Sutter's Fort had little to do with the war. Many of the Sacramento Valley settlers went to Sonoma, where, led by William Ide, they raised the Bear Flag in a premature effort at California independence. Mariano Vallejo was taken prisoner and brought to Sutter's Fort, which was occupied by the United States forces under the command of Lt. Edward Kern. John Fremont and his military unit, having returned in 1845, traveled through Sacramento on the way to engage the Californios in battle.

Admiral John Sloat, an officer of the United States Navy, declared California annexed to the Union; it became official

with the signing of the Treaty of Guadalupe Hidalgo in 1848. Within a short period of time, Sutter's Fort had been under three flags: the Mexican Flag, the Bear Flag and the American Flag. Under the new American temporary government, John Sinclair, Sutter's neighbor, was elected magistrate or alcalde.

In 1847, after the war was over, Sutter had a difficult time finding skilled workers for his many projects, one of which was a grist mill on the American River near what is today the Howe Avenue Bridge. His work staff was reinforced when some members of the Mormon Battalion arrived at the fort. They had come from the south after marching with the "Army of the West" and, now that the war was over, they were going home. Brigham Young sent a message for these men to stay in California until 1848. Sutter immediately put many to work on the grist mill and on a planned sawmill in the mountains.

Sam Brannan, another Mormon, arrived at the fort from Yerba Buena and was so impressed with the operation in the center of the Sacramento Valley that he decided to build a store just outside the fort. James Wilson Marshall had arrived at the fort from Oregon in 1845. He went to work for Sutter as a craftsman and mechanic, with knowledge of building mills. Sutter was in great need of lumber for his grist mill and other planned projects, including the town of Sutterville. Marshall was sent into the Sierras to locate a lumber mill site. The place he found in the Coloma Valley, on the American River, would soon bring fame and fortune to many, and ruin to John Sutter. In the fall of 1847, Marshall started building the sawmill with the help of the Mormon craftsmen.

Captain John Sutter and John Sinclair had dinner together on New Year's Day, 1848. They probably talked about their successful past year and their plans for the future. Neither would have been able in their wildest dreams to prophesize what changes would come in the new year.

CHAPTER TWO

The World's Gateway to the Gold, 1848-1860s

by Edward H. Howes

Historian Rodman Paul observed that there are sometimes single events that clearly stand out from lesser ones "as sharply as a single tree on a desert plain." The California Gold Rush was one such happening. The accidental discovery of gold at Sutter's sawmill in January 1848 was a small local incident which attracted little excitement or attention beyond the immediate vicinity for nearly four months. There are two reasons for this hiatus of calm between the actual discovery of gold and the explosive period which followed. The first was the effort of John Sutter and James Marshall, his employee who made the discovery on January 24, 1848, to suppress that information while Sutter attempted to protect his proprietary interests in the mill site and his land-grant holdings in the Sacramento Valley. Secondly, because there had been unfounded rumors of gold in California since the Spanish coastal voyages of exploration, the few information leaks that occurred before early May were given little credence.

Once the fact was deliberately revealed in San Francisco, it inspired the first flood of gold-seekers into the American River valley and adjacent areas of the Sierra Nevada foothills in the months between May and December in 1848. These first few thousands, the 48ers, reaped spectacular individual returns compared to the lesser amounts realized by the masses of later arrivals. The news of these early successes were announced to the world by Pres. James Polk's message to the U.S. Congress in December 1848. That message touched off the rush of 1849 and the following years, an unprecedented migration which in a very short time brought dramatic changes in the recently conquered Mexican province of Alta California. The population rush of avid wealth seekers to California measured in the tens of thousands yearly, and the gold produced in California (more than $1 billion by 1900) exerted major influences on the course of United States history, and had a far-reaching impact upon much of the world in the next half-century and beyond. California's gold output multiplied over 70 times between 1848 and 1854, and produced nearly 45 percent of the world's entire gold output in the period from 1851 to 1855. The resulting monetary inflation contributed to an expansion of the world economy, and Sacramento was at the center of this global phenomenon.

The saga of the Gold Rush Era in California and the early development of the Sacramento region begins with the complex person of John Sutter and his ambitions. He was clearly a bold adventurer, an imaginative visionary, and an unabashed self-promoter with an expansive personality and great powers of persuasion. Sutter had an aptitude for recognizing undeveloped opportunities, and began several projects which might well have made him comfortably wealthy in time. Unfortunately, however, he lacked the practical managerial skills necessary to carry his multiple undertakings to successful conclusion. He was also an extravagant spend-thrift and drunken carouser when he had large amounts of cash in his hands. As a consequence, he was constantly in debt, and seemingly, like the White Knight in Lewis Carroll's *Through the Looking Glass*, riding off "in all directions at once."

Sutter himself is partly responsible for airing the secret of the gold discovery. A few days after the event, he went up to Coloma to persuade the workers to stay on until the mill was completed, and he also made an agreement with the local Indians for a lease on the Coloma area. He then dispatched a messenger to the U.S. military governor of California, Col. Richard B. Mason, asking for validation of the leasing agreement. In sending his message to Mason, Sutter revealed the gold discovery and enclosed six ounces of gold as proof. By this means and other information leaks the news was aired,

Emil Lehman, a visiting Swedish artist, captured gold miners at work in this 1852 sketch in the Mother Lode. The men are shown with the standard placer miner equipment of the day, a rocker and a Long Tom. *Emil Lehman Sketchbook, Sacramento Archives and Museum Collection Center (SAMCC).*

Stories about the Gold Rush often emphasize the stereo-typical Forty-niner: a male, who arrived in California from some other state or even from out of the country. What is often overlooked is that some miners, especially during the first year following gold discovery were from California, including Native Americans. This view appeared in *Hutchings Illustrated California Magazine*, April 1859. *California State Library Collection, SAMCC.*

but skepticism prevailed. In March, 1848, the two weekly newspapers in San Francisco briefly informed their readers "it was reported" that quantities of gold had been found at Captain Sutter's sawmill near New Helvetia. That announcement attracted about as much interest as reports of the previous day's weather. One of these journals, the *California Star* actually gave more space to a story, which later proved to be false, about the discovery of a coal mine.

The relative quiet was finally shattered in early May by Sam Brannan, storekeeper at Sutter's Fort, who stormed through the streets of San Francisco waving his arms in the air and shouting out the news that gold had truly been found on the American River. To convince skeptics Brannan displayed a bottle of gold, and that did the trick. Then he hurried back to New Helvetia to be ready at his store for the expected rush to the gold country. As he had anticipated, within a few days the stampede to the mines was on, and life in California would never be the same again.

While the impact of the gold output was of major importance, what was immediately dramatic was the movement of people in the Gold Rush. The first phase in 1848 was primarily movement within California itself, involving mostly Americans who had moved to northern California between 1841 and 1847. By June 1, half of San Francisco's population of 850, almost all single men, had headed for Sutter's New Helvetia en route to the Sierra foothills. It was the same throughout California in a very short time: nearly every town lost a majority of its population. Before he was forced to close down, the San Francisco *Californian's* editor complained: "The whole country, from San Francisco to Los Angeles, from the sea shore to the base of the Sierra Nevadas, resounds with the sordid cry of gold, GOLD, GOLD! while the field is left half-planted, the house half-built, and everything neglected but the manufacture of shovels and pick-axes." In San Jose, the lone official still in town after the alcalde mayor had joined the mass exodus was the jailer, Henry Bee. He was left in the predicament of having custody of 10 Indian prisoners, two of whom were charged with murder. With no higher authority on hand for normal judicial processes, he pondered what to do, finally resolving his dilemma by taking them to the mining area where they worked for him until he had amassed a tidy fortune. He then let them escape to do their own prospecting!

The American military and naval officers at Monterey found themselves in a similarly hopeless situation. In the 18 months after July 1, 1848, the U.S. Army in northern California lost 716 men by desertion from a force of 1,290. Commodore Thomas ap Catesby Jones, commander of the Pacific Squadron, advised the Secretary of the Navy that so many sailors had jumped ship he feared that the government would be unable to maintain a naval establishment in California for years to come. When a soldier on a three-week leave came back from the placers with $1,500 in gold — more than five years' Army pay — servicemen by the hundreds took off for the gold country.

By July, the news had reached Oregon and British Columbia. An estimated half of the male population of Oregon left for the California mines before December. In July and August, boatloads of men left Hawaii, mostly Americans and a few native Kanakas infected by the gold fever. The word also filtered down to Southern California

settlements where Hispanic Californios predominated; they, together with a sprinkling of Spanish-speaking Mexican miners from Sonora, joined in the march of gold-seekers heading to the mines. Almost all of these 48ers passed through New Helvetia on their way to the gold country, except the Californios and Sonorans who trekked north through the San Joaquin Valley to the southern mining camps.

The rapid increase of men pouring into the gold country in the last half of 1848 accelerated disruption of the peaceful, bucolic atmosphere of life in California. This pastoral existence was first disturbed by the arrival of several hundred American soldiers and sailors during the recent war, and by the episode of the Bear Flag Revolt in the north. In May of 1848, the shift of population within the province had brought only a few hundred into the Sierra foothills, but by July those numbers had increased to at least 3,000. In December, with an added influx from outside California, there were perhaps 8,000 to 10,000 miners at work in the gold fields. Significant as they were, those changes were

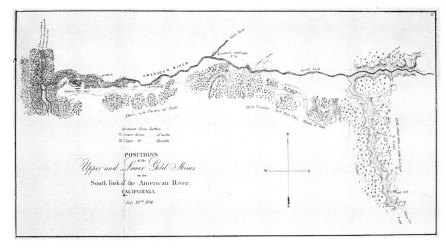

overshadowed by the unprecedented migration of people into California during 1849 and the 1850s.

In July, Colonel Mason decided to see for himself if the stories coming to him at Monterey were true. Mason visited many camps in the foothills north and south of the American River sites first worked by Mormons from the fort and the sawmill. His mid-August report to Washington superiors verified the prior accounts of rich individual finds by the 48ers. He estimated the current production rate of the placers at $30,000 to $50,000 daily. (Later estimates of the total taken by the miners in 1848 set a conservative figure of about $250,000.) To give substance

Wayside Scenes in California provided the cover for a lettersheet that a Forty-niner could use to send a message home. This interesting view illustrates the many cultures represented in the rush for California gold. The view was drawn by Anthony and Baker, and prepared for printing by Charles Nahl. *Eleanor McClatchy Collection, SAMCC.*

The great Gold Rush of '49 began with a flurry of departures by sea routes from eastern United States cities, and from Europe, South America, Australia and China. This seaborne traffic swelled the population of San Francisco to more than 5,000 by midyear of 1849. By 1850, it was a bustling city of 25,000. The huge influx of 49ers also created "instant cities" at Sacramento, Stockton and Marysville. The overland trek from the eastern United States generally followed the Oregon-California trail established in the early 1840s. Some 30,000 came in wagon trains on this route in 1849, twice that number in 1850, plus thousands more through the middle 1850s. Most of these emigrants crossed the Sierra Nevada by the Carson Pass or Donner Summit, with Sutter's Fort as their principal destination.

The flood of Gold Rush emigrants created first an opportunity and finally a disaster for Sutter and his New Helvetia domain. His long-range plans were first disrupted, then altered to meet changing conditions, and finally destroyed by the great number of newcomers who simply squatted on his land between the river landing and Sutter's Fort. Before the gold discovery he envisioned a minor development at the Sacramento riverfront Embarcadero, the growth of a trading center at the fort, a sprinkling of new ranches and farms around the fort, and a townsite south along the Sacramento River and a short

to his report, Mason enclosed a tea caddy packed with 228 ounces of gold.

Between May and September 1848, newspapers in eastern U.S. cities occasionally published brief reports of gold found in California. But these items received little attention until Pres. James K. Polk's December 5th message to Congress indisputably affirmed the large gold strike in California. That announcement fanned the small spark of public interest in California into a feverish reaction.

Mormon Island, shown here about 1850, was located on the south fork of the American River in eastern Sacramento County. On March 2, 1848, two Mormon workmen returning to Sutter's grist mill from Coloma found gold flakes there. It has the distinction of being the first gold camp established after the discovery at Coloma. *Ralph Shaw Collection, SAMCC.*

Sacramento: Chapter Two

distance inland, at Sutterville, near today's Sacramento Zoo.

During the year of 1847, Sutter constructed a tannery and an adobe house near his original landing place on the American River in the vicinity of present-day 28th and B streets. The tannery was operated profitably until the workers left to mine for gold. The Mormon employees left to prospect in the vicinity of Sutter's sawmill. They later established a mining camp at Mormon's Bar and Mormon Island on the American River near Folsom. A thriving settlement on Mormon Island in 1849 included an impressive hotel and a general merchandise store operated by a pioneer merchant from New England, James Lloyd Lafayette Franklin Warren. He also established his famed New England Seed Store on J Street in Sacramento. In 1852, Warren brought a shipment of camellias from New England, introducing the flower which made Sacramento famous in the horticultural world. He was also credited with organizing the annual state fair in Sacramento during the 1850s.

Before the disruption caused by the rush of 49ers, Sutter produced wheat and traded cattle and horses to other settlers in the area and to San Francisco. The frenzied gold-seekers on their way to the gold country in the fall of 1848 trampled his fields, rustled and slaughtered his cattle and took horses from his untended herds. The larger invasion of 1849 continued the depredations on his possessions and men camped uninvited, by the hundreds, in the area between the Embarcadero and the fort. Sutter was floundering with these many problems when his son, John Augustus, Jr., arrived in September 1848, and began efforts to assist his father in the management of his affairs.

In December 1848, John Augustus Jr. commissioned Cpt. William H. Warner and Lt. William Tecumseh Sherman, both Army

engineers, to survey and subdivide a planned new city of Sacramento into building lots. The elder Sutter again was being pressured by debts owed to nearly everyone in the valley, particularly by the Russians for his purchase of the Fort Ross property. To give himself time to pay his creditors, he granted power of attorney to his son and turned over all of his property to him. Sutter Senior then went up to Coloma to prospect for gold while two of his business associates, Sam Brannan and attorney Peter Burnett, stayed with the son to help him raise money.

The three men, young Sutter, Brannan and Burnett, set aside four square miles of the New Helvetia grant lands to

James Lloyd Lafayette Franklin Warren, a Massachusetts merchant and nurseryman, joined the rush to California in 1849. After a brief stint at Mormon Island, he established the New England Seed Store on J Street near Front in Sacramento. He also introduced the camellia to Sacramento and established the Great Agricultural Fair in 1852 that evolved into an annual state fair. *Piera B. Franz Collection, SAMCC.*

California's great Central Valley, including Sacramento County, established its agricultural preeminence early-on. Smith's Pomological and Floral Gardens and Nursery, along the south bank of the American River, provided the specimen fruit for this painting exhibited at the State Agricultural Exhibition in 1855. *Eleanor McClatchy Collection, SAMCC.*

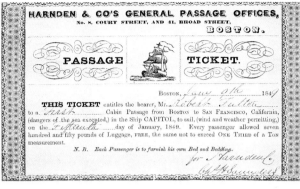

(Above) John Sutter's son, John Augustus, Jr., arrived at New Helvetia in September 1848. In an effort to remove his father from debt, he joined businessman Sam Brannan and attorney Peter Burnett and set aside four square miles, fronting on the Sacramento River at Sutter's embarcadero, to develop the new town they called Sacramento. *Eleanor McClatchy Collection, SAMCC.*

Robert Fulton sailed from Boston to San Francisco aboard the *Capitol* in January 1849. He made his way to Sacramento where he sketched businesses along Second Street near K and L streets. While in California Fulton also drew this *Map of the Gold Region in U. California,* based on an earlier map by C. Richards. His 1905 obituary explained that after engaging in trade for two years, he returned to Bedford, New Hampshire, where he apparently spent the rest of his life. No doubt his two years in California provided him with more adventure than all the rest of his years combined. *Eleanor McClatchy Collection, SAMCC.*

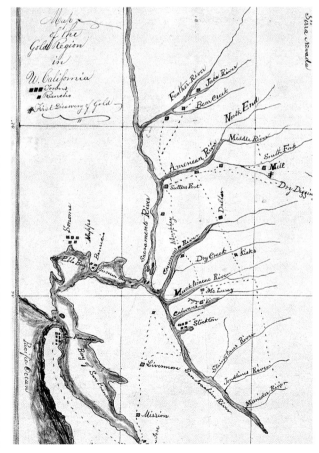

lay out the new town between the fort and the Embarcadero. They named the town Sacramento after the adjacent river. It was soon a busy supply center for the hordes of miners heading for the gold fields. The sale of lots began in January 1849. Brannan, Samuel J. Hensley and Pierson B. Reading moved their businesses from Sutter's Fort to the Embarcadero and erected the first two buildings in the new city at Front and I Street. By April 1849, the city's resident population had grown to about 150. By October, there were 45 wooden buildings and 300 cloth houses in Sacramento and the population had increased to nearly 2,000. Town lots were selling for $1,000.

Besides serving its 2,000 residents, Sacramento businesses supplied goods and entertainment to the thousands of miners passing through the city. Out of a state population estimated at 90,000 in late 1849, there were some 40,000 miners at work in the gold fields. A year later there were an estimated 50,000 mining. In 1852, the year of peak production, $81 million in gold was extracted by a mining population of 100,000, out of a state population of 223,000 persons.

CAPITAL CITY

Even before the 49ers arrived, men in the new settlement of Sacramento recognized the need for an orderly, stable community. Just as Americans throughout California were taking action to establish a state government, activists in the local area moved to create a municipal government, both without mandate or direction from higher authority. In the early spring of 1849, Sam Brannan and Peter Burnett met with a group of interested merchants to draft a code of laws. An election held in July selected a city council of nine which proceeded to name Gen. A.M. Winn as council president. They next created a city charter to submit to voters in September, but the town's gambling interests engineered a defeat of the proposed charter by a vote of 527 to 281 in the September poll. Friends of the council responded by organizing a "Law and Order" party and conducting a vigorous campaign for a revised charter, which was approved by a vote of 808 to 513 in a second election on October 13. In early 1850, the new State Legislature ratified the charter, and the City of Sacramento was officially incorporated on March 18, 1850.

At the same time, Americans throughout California were chafing at the lack of government functions normally found in U.S. states and territories. Congress adjourned in 1848 without providing for civil government in California. The third military governor, Gen. Bennett Riley, was appointed in April 1849, and he recognized the implied threat of political uprising against his authority. With the tacit approval of Pres. Zachary Taylor, he called for a constitutional convention to assemble in Monterey in September. Sacramento voters chose a delegation of eight. These included Jacob R. Snyder and M. M. McCarver from Sacramento City; Lansford W. Hastings, John Sutter and John McDougal from Sutterville; Winfield Sherwood from Mormon Island; Elisha O. Crosby from Vernon; and W. E. Shannon from Coloma, which was then included in the Sacramento district.

In November, California voters approved the State Constitution and elected Sacramentans Peter Burnett as the state's first governor and John McDougal as lieutenant-governor. In its first session the legislature ratified the charter for "Sacramento City," which remained its official name until 1851 when the word "City" was dropped by act of the legislature, though in popular usage the name "Sacramento City" persisted long afterward.

Sacramento County was one of 27 original counties created by the State Legislature in 1850. A year later, the County Court of Sessions divided the county into eight townships: Sacramento, Sutter (the town of Sutterville), San Joaquin, Cosumnes, Brighton, Center, Sonoma and Mississippi (on the American River east of Sacramento). In 1858, the State Legislature chartered a unified City-County government for Sacramento, but experience with that new arrangement apparently caused enough dissatisfaction to produce pressure for restoration of the two separate entities. The State Legislature responded by dissolving the unified government and recreating separate governing bodies for the City and County of Sacramento in 1863.

The first legislature, which met at Monterey in December 1849 and January 1850, was unable to agree on a permanent site for the state capital. For nearly five years the capital was moved each year to a different city. One historian wryly referred to this as the time when California had a "capital on wheels." During this interim, the legislature came to Sacramento and might have stayed had not the great deluge of January 1852 flooded the lawmakers out of the Sacramento Courthouse where they were sitting. They quickly adjourned to Benicia for the rest of the session. That first County Court building in Sacramento burned to the ground in 1854. Work on a new and equally elegant Courthouse began at once with facilities designed especially for the needs of the state government, in anticipation of a return of the capital to this city.

One of the key factors in the selection of the capital was the desire of the northern mining counties for a site removed as far as possible from the influence of San Francisco business interests. The large population of the mining counties

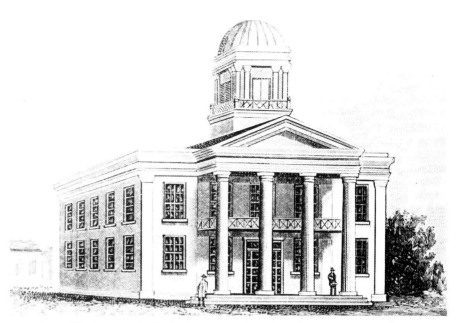

gave them effective clout in the legislature during the early Gold Rush years, so their wishes prevailed in this matter. As might be expected, Sacramento's City and County government officials also played a role in the final decision.

In 1854, Sacramento's State Sen. A.P. Catlin introduced a bill offering the State Legislature free use of the County Courthouse as a temporary capitol until a new permanent building could be completed. The City Council also pledged to give the state a block of land including the Plaza Square for location of the permanent capitol in the heart of the city. The new County Courthouse was completed and ready for occupation by January 1, 1855, three months after the cornerstone was laid. For the next 15 years, except the flood year of 1862, the legislature and state constitutional officers, other than the Supreme Court justices, met in that building. In the final arrangements, state officials returned title for the Plaza area to the city and county, and the county agreed to cede the area where the Capitol Building and the Capitol Park are now located.

BUSINESS

From the first population rush of 1848, Sacramento was a busy center of commerce, providentially located between San Francisco and the mining areas. A variety of businesses provided goods and services for the local community and the gold country. Sam Brannan's stores at Sutter's Fort and Front Street were among the first establishments engaged in this trade. He had bought a sizeable stock of merchandise in early 1848 before the rush to the mines began, and held a near-monopoly on picks, shovels and other hardware items purchased at no more than a few dollars each; he had also

Sacramento's first County Courthouse served as California's capitol from 1852 until it burned to the ground in 1854. It was located at the northwest corner of Seventh and I streets. Eleanor McClatchy Collection, SAMCC.

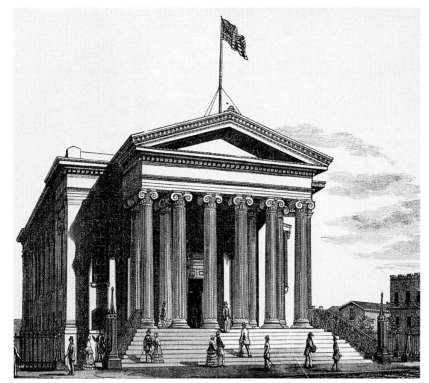

in California. While waiting to get passage on the Pacific side of the Panama Isthmus, he sold his goods to others passing through, and conducted a transport service carrying their baggage to the Pacific port of embarkation. In addition to paying for his transportation, these activities increased his capital to $4,000, enabling him to start his hardware store upon his arrival in Sacramento. He and his partner, Hopkins, gained modest wealth in hardware which they then parlayed into huge fortunes as two of the principal founders of the Central Pacific Railroad in the 1860s.

Among other early enterprises, the Miner's Drug Store, operated by R. H. McDonald between 5th and 6th on J Street, and the Polhemus Drug Store, at 190 J, were the leading dispensers of medicine. A French enterprise, Victor Passenaurd's City of Paris, provided

acquired one merchant's entire supply of kitchen pans at 20 cents apiece. To eager would-be miners he sold the digging tools and other hardware items such as hammers, hatchets and crowbars, for as much as $40 to $50 per item, and the 20-cent pans each went for up to $10 in gold. From sales of these and other commodities he netted $36,000 between May and August 1848, and even more from his store sales and speculation in Sacramento real estate in the boom year of 1849. In this way he built the first of the several fortunes he would make and lose before he died penniless in San Diego, 40 years later in 1889.

Brannan was the first of many merchants who realized that the easiest way to make money in Sacramento was to provide goods and services for miners and local residents, rather than engaging in the hard work and uncertain returns of prospecting for gold. One of the local hardware stores which operated profitably from 1849 through the early 1860s, was run by the partnership of Collis P. Huntington and Mark Hopkins at 54 K Street. Huntington left New England with some cash and $1,000 worth of merchandise which he planned to sell

exotic clothes for women and stylish wear for men. Miners were photographed in tin-types made in Charles King's studio at 130 K Street or in Bell's Daguerreotype Gallery on J near 9th Street. Several establishments engaged in buying gold at a discount from miners returning to the city. Express companies like the Adams and Company and Wells Fargo had offices in Sacramento which received gold shipments from branch offices in almost all the large mining camps and towns, via the network of stagecoach lines converging on the city. Some of that gold remained in Sacramento; most of it was sent by river steamboats to San Francisco, and from there by steamships to Panama and ultimately to New York, Boston and other east coast cities. After the branch U.S. Mint was established in San Francisco in 1857, a larger portion stayed in California in the form of newly minted gold coins.

In 1849, Darius Ogden Mills established the D.O. Mills Bank in Sacramento, the only bank to survive and grow into a major institution. He later established a branch in San Francisco, and became a major partner in William Ralston's Bank of California which played a strong role financing the silver mines of the Nevada Comstock bonanza.

Along with the financial institutions, businesses that were most successful in the early years were the ones which met the immediate needs of the hundreds of transients coming through Sacramento en route to the mining areas. These were hotels, general stores, restaurants, stagecoach lines and express companies. Brannan's Hotel de France opened first with a gala celebration featuring champagne. Despite its spartan sleeping accommodations, the house was full of lodgers from the opening day. The City Hotel was built at an even greater cost, and it, too, seldom had empty space. George Zins opened the first brick hotel in 1850, which, after several name changes, remained in the Pioneer, located at Front and M streets. The Elephant House, on Front Street between J and K, stands out in many of the drawings and paintings of early Sacramento because of its central position on the waterfront and the large figure of an elephant outlined on the hotel's facade. The Orleans, set amid a row of hotels on 2nd Street, was unique in several ways. It had definite Creole associations, being built of prefabricated parts which were shipped around the Horn from New Orleans and assembled in Sacramento. It was one of the buildings destroyed by the great fire of 1852. The ashes barely cooled before a new, attractive brick hotel of three stories came into being as the new Orleans at the same location. It soon was the center of much activity with a reading room, billiard room and saloon, and two upper floors with a parlor, family rooms and furnished bedrooms.

Both mining and the early railroad industry provided work for local iron foundries which primarily produced machinery and tools. The metal-working industries in the city included Stow and Carpenter's California Steam Engine Works on Front Street near the American River, and the Eureka Iron and Brass Foundry opened by Taylor and Woods in 1851, on Front between O and P streets. The Sacramento Iron Works began operations in 1852 between Front and 2nd on I Street. The company was a major employer by 1860, and maintained a work force of 100 in the next decade. Two more plants opened in the 1860s: M.R. Rose's Capital Iron and Brass Works (1862) in the block between 9th and 10th on K Street, and William Gutenberger's Sacramento Foundry at Front and N, in 1867.

TRANSPORTATION AND MAIL

Steamboats appeared on eastern waterways before the 1820s, but the great expansion of steam-powered transportation occurred in the 1850s and 1860s, just in time for the peak years of the Gold Rush. Thousands of people coming

to and through Sacramento from San Francisco in these decades arrived by steamboats which docked at the Sacramento riverfront. By the early 1850s, there were at least 50 ships plying the river route between these two cities. A fleet of shallow-draft vessels operated on the river above Sacramento, carrying traffic to Marysville and as far north as Red Bluff. In the spring and summer months as many as 20 vessels at one time were waiting to dock at Sacramento, with a backup of ships tied to the shore on the Yolo side, and others moored upstream or downstream until they could get access to the landing facilities.

Competition among the steamship companies led to dangerous racing on the river. The result was a series of accidents which took a toll of wrecked vessels, with deaths and injuries to crews and passengers. Public outcry eventually brought a stop to this disregard of safety. In 1854, competition

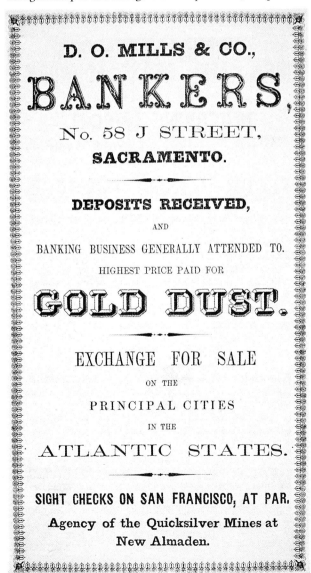

D. O. MILLS & CO.,

BANKERS,

No. 58 J STREET,

SACRAMENTO.

DEPOSITS RECEIVED,

AND

BANKING BUSINESS GENERALLY ATTENDED TO.

HIGHEST PRICE PAID FOR

GOLD DUST.

EXCHANGE FOR SALE

ON THE

PRINCIPAL CITIES

IN THE

ATLANTIC STATES.

SIGHT CHECKS ON SAN FRANCISCO, AT PAR.

Agency of the Quicksilver Mines at New Almaden.

The establishment of banking houses was a natural outgrowth of the Gold Rush. D. O. Mills, who became a nationally renowned financier, started his banking career in Sacramento in 1849. *Coleville's Sacramento Directory for the Year Commencing August 1, 1855, Joel S. Gardner Collection, SAMCC.*

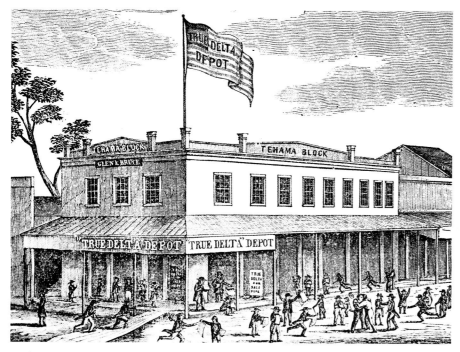

The Tehama Block rose at the corner of Front and J streets in December 1849. This view makes it clear that the *True Delta*, a New Orleans newspaper that provided news from "the States," was available for sale there. The building has been reconstructed as part of Old Sacramento State Historic Park. *Eleanor McClatchy Collection, SAMCC.*

The steamer *New World* was captured by daguerreotype photographer George H. Johnson during the summer of 1850. It is the earliest known photograph of Sacramento City. *Mead Kibbey and Setzer Foundation Collection, SAMCC.*

human history. In Sacramento during the Gold Rush years, the finer breeds of horses pulled the light spring wagons, canopy-covered buggies and more elegant carriages which families used for transportation in town and for short trips. Sacramento boasted seven carriage shops offering as fine a product as any in the United States, as well as providing service and parts replacement for the local carriage trade.

Horses and mules arriving in the overland wagon trains were the first animals used for drayage of small goods and freighting of lightweight commodities. The lowly mules "with neither pride of ancestry nor hope of posterity" made up a majority of the teams pulling the larger freight wagons. In 1858, the *Sacramento Union* reported that 270 individual operators — teamsters who owned their wagons and animals — were then actively engaged as primary haulers of foodstuff and mining machinery over the roads between Sacramento and the mining towns and camps. Local wagonmakers built almost all of the huge wagons used in this trade. These large vehicles normally were pulled by four to eight paired teams of horses and mules, and carried loads of 7,000 to 9,500 pounds. From spring until the late fall one might see 30 to 35 wagons at a time loading at the Embarcadero and making their way east up J Street, heading for the mining towns.

All this animal power required facilities in Sacramento. A busy horse and mule market flourished on 6th Street between J and K streets from 1849 through the 1860s. A harness and saddle shop, a wheelwright and wagonmaker, a hay yard and stable, a carriage maker and blacksmith shop were clustered near the horse market. In addition, the

among independent steamship operators was reduced by consolidation of many companies into one large concern, the California Steam Navigation Company. This giant corporation's near-monopoly control (75 percent of the traffic on San Francisco Bay and the Sacramento River) continued until 1869, when it was taken over by the Central Pacific Railroad.

Until the coming of the automobile in the 20th century, horses and mules were major sources of motive power for transportation. The fact that automobile engines and other machines are still measured in terms of horsepower is testimony to that long tradition of the quadrupeds' role in

Sacramento Union in June 1858 reported the existence of 27 hay yards on the eastern outskirts of the city. Each of these provided shelter and provender for the animals. A blacksmith shop and a wagon factory adjoined nearly every yard.

Stagecoach travel began in California in 1849, with lines operating from Sacramento and San Francisco, and in the south from Los Angeles. James Birch, a 21-year-old New England stage driver, came to California in 1849 with the intention of establishing a stage line in the gold country. With his first partner, Davenport, he began to operate a single "Celerity" stage wagon carrying up to six passengers per load between Sacramento and Mormon Island in the summer of 1849. From the start he had a thriving business on this first local route, charging a fare of two ounces ($32 in gold) each way, until the early winter rains made travel impossible. He returned to New England after that first successful season and arranged for the shipment to California of the first Concord coach seen on the west coast. Its arrival at San Francisco in the early spring of 1850 caused a sensation. As he began his second year of operation in Sacramento, his continuing success inspired others to enter the field, and a keen competition quickly developed.

In 1854, already dominating the field, Birch and his friend Frank Stevens merged several companies into one big organization, the California Stage Company, capitalized at $1 million. After consolidation, Birch's firm operated over 100 coaches, employed 150 persons, and maintained stables of more than 900 horses. The company's stock, originally valued at $1,000 a share, was paying monthly dividends of four to six percent! At the height of its activity during the year of 1856, the California Stage Company controlled almost 80 percent of the stage traffic on 3,000 miles of lines reaching all the major mining camps. The company also had a near-monopoly of contracts for carrying the mail over most of these same routes.

In 1855, Birch's Sacramento-based stage company, abetted by express companies and other business interests, engineered a campaign which secured a legislative resolution calling on Congress to provide an improved overland wagon road and mail route to northern California, and an appropriation for fast mail service on that route, which Birch's company wished to provide. To give more weight to the resolution and to support bills that Sen. John B. Weller and California congressmen introduced for those projects in 1856, the Stage Company gathered 75,000 signatures on a huge petition from northern California. It was the largest petition received by Congress up to that time, and caused quite a stir in the eastern newspapers. Congress reacted by passing a bill for the improvement of four "emigrant wagon

During the 1850s and 1860s, the California Steam Navigation Company controlled 75 percent of the traffic on San Francisco Bay and the Sacramento River. In 1869, it was purchased by the Central Pacific Railroad in an expansion effort. *Coleville's Sacramento Directory 1855. Joel S. Gardner Collection, SAMCC.*

Livery stables, hay yards, harness and saddle makers, horse markets, street cleaners and blacksmith shops were a major component of business communities all across 19th century cities. In Sacramento, the Second Street Livery Stable advertised in *Coleville's Sacramento Directory for the Year Commencing August 1, 1855. Joel S. Gardner Collection, SAMCC.*

roads" (no mention of stagecoaches) to the Pacific Coast, and appropriated $600,000 for a twice-weekly overland mail service from St. Louis to San Francisco.

In 1855, the State Legislature appropriated funds for the improvement of an existing stage and wagon road from Sacramento through Placerville and over the Sierra to the state line. This measure anticipated making a connection with the proposed federal road over the central emigrant route from the Missouri frontier. Telegraph lines already connecting Sacramento and Marysville with San Francisco and other Bay Area cities were being extended along the Placerville road in the late 1850s. By 1861, the wires reached Salt Lake City to meet the transcontinental telegraph line built westward from Omaha. Sacramento and San Francisco finally had their wire connection to all of the eastern United States cities.

For a brief time the later much romanticized pony express offered relatively rapid mail service to the east, but the initial enthusiasm greeting the establishment of the express in 1860 soon waned. Although the young men on their ponies delivered mail from St. Joseph, Missouri, to Sacramento in a record time of 10 days, the small amount that a rider could carry, and the cost of up to $10 per one-ounce letter did not meet local needs and expectations. The company was steadily losing money, and the use of the service was declining even before the pony express was dealt its death blow by completion of the overland telegraph line in October 1861, only 18 months after the ponies began their first run.

DISASTER

Few of California's Gold Rush Era communities escaped the scourge of fire in their first few years. Sacramento suffered its first serious fire in September 1849. Since most of the structures in the city were flimsy tents or frame-and-canvas buildings, they quickly burned, but they were also quickly replaced by similar unsubstantial structures. In April 1850, another fire destroyed eight buildings on Front Street between J and K. Six months later a large fire again wiped out most of the city's canvas and wood structures, which once more were quickly replaced with others of the same kinds. Only a few of the more substantial buildings of brick and stone survived each of these early fires.

The greatest of these fires occurred late in the evening of November 4, 1852. Fire broke out in a millinery shop near 4th and J Street. A strong north wind drove the flames quickly through the downtown section. The blaze raged with such ferocity that observers 100 miles away noted the light in the sky. When the fire subsided only ashes remained in the 55 blocks razed by the conflagration. Relief funds and materials poured into the city from other towns which had experienced previous fires. Reconstruction began almost at once, and the Sacramento Steamer Union announced on December 1 that almost as many buildings then stood as had existed before the fire.

After each of these early fires, the citizens responded by organizing volunteer fire companies; by the late 1850s over a dozen of these groups had been assembled, several with their own firehouse and equipment. A city water works was built atop the new three-story city hall (completed in April 1854) to provide water pressure for fighting fires, but it was not until 1872 that the state authorized the creation of a professional city fire department.

In July 1854, less than two years after the great fire of 1852, the city suffered another destructive blaze. This time the damage was not as great. The volunteer firemen were able to limit the spread of the flames to an area of eight blocks. Unfortunately, one of the buildings lost was the first County Courthouse where the State Legislature had been meeting. Rebuilding soon began, and the new brick building was designed to provide facilities specifically for the use of the state government. By October, the city was comprised of 500 brick buildings and 2,000 wooden frame structures, including hundreds of family homes. Sacramento suffered losses from fires four more times between 1855 and 1870, but none as destructive as the one in 1852.

1850 might well have been called "the Year of Disasters" in Sacramento's early history. The new year was just under way when the city suffered the first of the three serious floods in its initial 12 years. Both the Sacramento and the American River rose swiftly, and on January 9, the American overflowed and left the city under four to 10 feet of muddy water. The flood destroyed most of the flimsy structures in the tent city, including California's first theater, the Eagle, which had just opened on Front Street in October 1849. Merchandise piled on the Embarcadero was ruined, and hundreds of people evacuated the city. Some of the refugees fled to higher ground at Brighton, near where California State University, Sacramento is now located. Merchants set up tents there and carried on trade for a short time. When the flood receded in February, they and the refugee residents returned to the Sacramento river waterfront area and began to rebuild.

The next disaster of 1850 was a "Squatters' Riot." In the heat of summer a long-developing conflict erupted between property owners holding title to lots purchased from Sutter's agents and hundreds of squatters who camped on undeveloped sites in the city. After several confrontations between squatters and property owners, a showdown in August led to violence. A mob of angry settlers led by a man named Maloney and a Doctor Charles Robinson marched toward the Embarcadero, intending to force the release of Richard Moran and James McClatchy, two of their supporters then being held in the city's prison brig on the river. They were met by Mayor Hardin Bigelow at the head of a party of citizens who had responded to his plea for help. The mayor ordered the squatters to disperse peacefully. Instead, a volley

Sacramento's early years as a canvas, shake and clapboard city made it especially vulnerable to fire. On the evening of November 4, 1852, a fire broke out that destroyed 55 city blocks, making it a dramatic subject for this lettersheet. *Eleanor McClatchy Collection, SAMCC.*

SLAVES IN A NON-SLAVE STATE

The gold rush planted the seeds for a significant multi-ethnic population in Sacramento. Large numbers of European nationalities and migrants from the eastern and midwestern United States arrived by 1850, joined with Mexicans, Native Americans (only recently removed from the majority status to a minority population), African Americans, Chinese and other groups from various regions of the world.

Conceived quickly during the gold rush, the original California Constitution in 1849 lacked many elements found in modern law, including those related to civil rights. Although California was admitted to the Union as a free state, the first Constitution merely prohibited slavery; it did not address the details of equality before the law or any of the racial issues that were so volatile at that time. With such matters left to the initial legislature, that body by April, 1850, approved statutes that denied admission into court the testimony of Native or African Americans without a collaborative white witness.

An example of the effects of such law were seen in December, 1850, in the case of *People vs. W. H. Potter.* Sarah Carroll, a "f. w. c." (free woman of color), complained that William H. Potter committed grand larceny against her by taking $700 in gold coins and other articles. Brought before Justice Sackett in Sacramento, the charges were dismissed, with Sackett ruling: "Defendant discharged, he proving himself a white man, and none but colored testimony against him."

In 1852, California passed a fugitive slave law that affirmed the property rights of a citizen from another state while in California. After its passage the law was very controversial, and it was allowed to expire in April, 1855. Nonetheless, the rights of slaves would yet emerge as a major legal issue. In 1857, an enslaved African American, 18-year-old Archy Lee, was brought to California by Charles Stovall, a slaveowner. Stovall hired Lee out, but by 1858 had fears of Lee's loyalty. When Stovall moved to send him back to Mississippi, Lee hid in a Sacramento hotel owned by free African Americans. Stovall had Lee arrested and a long series of legal battles ensued. Top attorneys of prominence such as Edwin B. Crocker and John McKune represented Lee, yet the State Supreme Court, under the influence of a southern-born justice, David Terry, ordered Lee returned to slavery.

Lee was moved to San Francisco but the legal skirmishing continued and Lee's lawyers eventually prevailed in a request to have a final appeal heard before a U. S. Commissioner. Colonel Edward Baker, a Lee attorney, prepared and delivered an extraordinarily vigorous defense of Lee and federal commissioner William Johnson responded that Lee had broken no law, state or federal, and should be set free. Lee was released to freedom on April 14, 1858, four months after he was first arrested.

Like many other communities, Sacramento wrestled with racial and ethnic issues. But unlike certain others, Sacramento from its creation was populated by a significant number of minorities who became part of the economic structure of the community. The presence of these groups did not prevent prejudice, but their numbers and diversity may have prevented Sacramento from ignoring racial and ethnic concerns and may have buffered the region from any substantial rise or enduring effect of radical groups such as the Ku Klux Klan.

of gunfire ensued. Mayor Hardin was seriously wounded (he later died of cholera while recuperating in a San Francisco hospital), and City Assessor J. W. Woodland was killed. On the opposing side, the squatters' leader Maloney suffered a fatal head wound, a man named Jesse Morgan was killed and Dr. Robinson sustained a minor wound.

The next day Sheriff Joseph McKinney led a posse of 20 men to arrest some of the squatters who had taken refuge in a house at Brighton. Gunfire erupted again, leaving the sheriff and three of the squatters dead. That ended the violence, with a toll of eight men dead and six wounded. Two days later, Moran and James McClatchy were released from the prison ship. Dr. Robinson was jailed and charged with murder, but public sentiment was so much in his favor he was never tried on the charge. While he was being held prisoner, his friends nominated him as a candidate for election to the State Legislature. That fall he won a seat in the Assembly.

The third disaster of the year was a cholera epidemic which visited the city in October and November. This dreadful disease was almost always fatal within a day, and no known remedy existed at that time. The plague arrived in Sacramento on October 18 when a steamship passenger, already ill with the disease, was put ashore on the Embarcadero. He died during the night and his body was not discovered until the next day. Two more victims died within 24 hours, and 47 within a week. People fled the city to escape the scourge, sometimes carrying the infection with them to San Francisco or to the mining camps in the foothills. Before the epidemic had run its course in

November, it claimed 600 fatalities in Sacramento. So many unidentified persons died that scores of bodies were buried in an unmarked mass grave.

The city's location at the junction of the American and Sacramento rivers made it a likely target for flooding during the annual winter rainy season. Four times between December 1849 and January 1852 the Sacramento and/or the American River overflowed and covered the city streets with several feet of water. In each successive flood the property losses were huge. Hundreds left the city on each occasion, and were forced to remain away from one to three months until it was safe to return. Each time, the city afterward raised the height of the levees and made some efforts to build up the level of the streets nearest to the Sacramento River.

In December of 1852, both rivers again overflowed and flooded the city. This time the American River also poured into the area outside the eastern city limits, cutting off the roads leading out of the city. Once more entrepreneurs planned a new community on the higher ground to the east. The temporary town of Hoboken was founded one mile east of Brighton in January 1853, and for six weeks 1,000 people

found refuge there. While the flood level remained high the site became a supply depot for the mines. Four steamboats made round trips daily with merchandise from the city Embarcadero, and 70 merchants set up branch stores which took in $80,000 in gold in two weeks. Hoboken even elected a mayor and looked forward to a promising future. But, when the floodwater subsided in mid-February and the roads to Sacramento were open again, the tent city vanished. The flood refugees returned to the city and began to rebuild.

The most devastating floods in Sacramento's history came 10 years later in 1861-62. In March, 1861, the American River swept away the wing dam at Rabel's tannery, again flooding the region outside the city's eastern limits. In the following winter, 26 inches of rain fell in the period between November, 1861, and mid-January 1862. With the city already partially under water from overflow of the Sacramento in December, the American River again breached the levee at Rabel's tannery in January. A huge volume of water broke through the city's eastern levee, drowning Sacramento's streets under five to 10 feet of water in various parts of town. Once again residents and businesses

After both the Sacramento and the American rivers flooded Sacramento City in December 1852, 70 enterprising merchants moved to high ground. Hoboken, a temporary town of frames covered with canvas, appeared east of the city. It was home to about 1,000 people and lasted about six weeks. When the floodwaters subsided, the town lost its reason for being.
Eleanor McClatchy Collection, SAMCC.

had to flee from the city or retreat to the upper floors of buildings which were left standing. Small boats from both rivers moved through the streets as the only local transport. Contemporary observers likened the local scene to familiar pictures of Venetian canals in Italy. For a brief time the projected new town of Mitchville, two miles east of Brighton, flourished as a refuge for evacuees from the flooded city of Sacramento.

Steamboats that normally stayed on the Sacramento were able to navigate up the American River for several miles during the period of high water. One river steamer, the *Gem*, went up the American and sailed through the levee break at Rabel's tannery in an attempt to reach the eastern outskirts of the city. She crashed into the proprietor's home

and destroyed the greenhouse of a commercial nursery and garden at 23rd and B Street before being stranded on a point of high ground. There the *Gem* stayed as an object of curiosity seekers until the Steam Navigation Company pried her loose in April and floated her back down the American River to the Embarcadero.

When the flood of 1862 proved the inadequacy of earlier efforts to raise the height of the levees and street elevations, a more extensive project was begun in the summer of 1863. Streets were elevated for several blocks east from the riverfront, and buildings and homes were jacked up at great expense to the owners. They also had to provide brick bulkheads along the frontage of their properties to contain the dirt fill in the streets, and build elevated sidewalks as well. An important step to lessen the danger of future flooding involved cutting a new channel for the American River to eliminate an S-curve in the river's course just north of the downtown section, near the junction with the Sacramento River. This was done at great cost in 1868, and the dirt from excavation of the new channel was used in the ongoing work of raising the street levels.

PEOPLE AND LIFE

The 1850 census revealed a striking imbalance in the gender ratio of California's population. Out of 115,000 people in the state, about 7,500 (6.5 percent) were women. The social makeup of the two largest cities, San Francisco and Sacramento, reflected that same ratio, while the mining regions had a much smaller percentage of women in communities almost entirely composed of men. The preponderantly single, young male gold-seekers of these early years gave mining towns — and San Francisco and Sacramento — the reckless moral atmosphere of wartime soldiers' towns during payday leaves. The miners' lives took on a recurring pattern: two or three weeks, or, at most a month, of hard, monotonous labor in the diggings, then a trip to Sacramento or Stockton to buy some supplies, get a tub bath, haircut and shave; perhaps get a decent meal (anything but the miners' steady diet of bread, beans and bacon). And then, before returning to the mines — some REAL ENTERTAINMENT AND EXCITEMENT!

The towns of the Gold Rush Era offered many of the pleasures the more conscientious young men had vowed to resist, and which were therefore irresistible. According to historian Donald Dale Jackson, "Sacramento probably offered the most temptation per square yard." In 1849 and 1850 there were more gambling houses and saloons than any other establishments among the hotels along the lettered and numbered streets near the Embarcadero. Even the earliest tent-casinos displayed erotic pictures of buxom, semi-draped females on their canvas walls. One of these "palaces," The Plains, was decorated with huge murals depicting familiar scenes from the overland trails; one, created with skewed perspective, showed a covered wagon drawn by oxen descending a mountain slope in a gravity-defying perpendicular

position which must have staggered the viewer's imagination. Better-built and more richly furnished gambling palaces replaced the first flimsy structures after the 1852 flood and fire.

As a Gold Rush town, a river town and a railroad town, Sacramento had prostitutes operating openly until the years of World War II, despite laws passed in the 1850s and 1870s to ban or limit their activity. In the city's first few decades, many of the prostitutes were quite open about their profession, and so listed themselves to the state census takers in 1852. The federal census of 1860 lists 270 women as prostitutes, almost all of them living in houses or hotels in the streets near the Embarcadero.

Although the 1850 federal census under-counted the state's population, the records for Sacramento City and County are probably more accurate. They report a city population of 6,820 and 9,087 in the county. Applying the male-female ratio in the state to the city, that would mean there were 475 women and 6,345 men in Sacramento at that time. Americans and immigrants of northern European descent, especially English, Irish, Scots, Germans and Swiss, composed the bulk of the population. Only small numbers of Hispanic Californians were found in Sacramento after gold was discovered, as most Spanish and Mexican settlements had been near the coast rather

A careful look at the patrons depicted in *View of the Interior of El Dorado, Sacramento* is evidence of the cultural and ethnic diversity of the Forty-niners. Also, the furnishing of the room is evidence of the elegance that California's gold could provide. *Eleanor McClatchy Collection, SAMCC.*

tions included 62 cooks, 10 barbers, nine eating and boarding houses and 22 men who provided laundry services. The numbers grew to 338 by 1852, and by 1860 had increased to 468, over twice their number in 1850. While they had not grown as fast as San Francisco's African-American resident population, Sacramento's Black community was the first to create stabilizing institutions. By 1851, Rev. Barney Fletcher and his brother, Charles, gathered a small group who began holding regular African Methodist Church services. Elizabeth Thorn, an African-American woman, established a private school in her own home for 14 children in 1854. The next year Rev. Jeremiah Sanderson, a Black abolitionist and educator from Massachusetts, came up from San Francisco and moved the school to facilities offered by the A.M.E. Church.

Along with African-Americans, the Chinese were the most visible and largest of the ethnic groups of non-European origin in Sacramento during the Gold Rush era. Both groups suffered the burden of racial discrimination imposed by the white majority. They were denied the right to vote; their children were excluded from the public schools; and state

than in the Central Valley. Hispanic gold-seekers ventured early in the Gold Rush into the Mother Lode, but many departed in the face of discrimination by the ever-increasing Anglo-European majority. The Native American population, once so numerous in the valley, had virtually disappeared in Sacramento due to disease and depredation. Between 1850 and 1860, the population of Sacramento City and County increased 166 percent to 24,142. As the Gold Rush dissipated, the next decade (1860-70) saw only 11 percent growth, to 26,830.

One extensive study, Rudolph Lapp's *Blacks in Gold Rush California*, describes the African-American community of 200 in Sacramento in the 1850s. They provided services for the transient population passing through Sacramento and miners sojourning from the gold country. The service occupa-

laws banned their testimony in court cases. Chinese who went into the gold-mining areas by the thousands were targeted by the second Foreign Miners' Tax, designed to discourage Chinese miners, until its repeal in 1870. Through the decade of the 1860s, the Sheriff of Sacramento County collected an average of $7,500 a year as his 25 percent commission on taxes collected from the Chinese who were mining in the county.

The few hundred Chinese who settled in Sacramento in 1849 established their Chinatown along I Street. It was almost exclusively a male population until the Chinese Six Companies began to include a small number of women with each shipment of indentured men. By 1860, there were some 1,200 persons in the "I" Street enclave, including only 148 women of whom 110 were prostitutes. The presence of the other 38 women was a significant indication that a small group of married couples had become a part of the community, the beginnings of a stable nucleus in their segregated society. As the number of Chinese miners increased annually, so did the flow of people to Sacramento's Chinatown. By 1870, the Chinese were the largest single ethnic group of miners, including Americans, in the California mines.

Even in the earliest years the city had several "civilizing" factors which in time served to "tame the 49ers," as one historian phrased it. The gradual increase of the number of respectable women through the 1850s and 1860s was reflected in the growing frequency of weddings, the establishment of family homes and the appearance of children in the population, all of which had a stabilizing influence on life in the community.

As early as 1849 there were alternate forms of diversion to the "sinful attractions" in the "old town" section near the Embarcadero. Theaters offered the classic plays of Shakespeare, along with more popular entertainment by famous and notorious stage personalities of the period. Within a few months after the Eagle Theater's demise in the flood of January 1850, five more rose to take its

place. The celebrated Olympic Circus opened in the Olympic Theater in May 1850. Another popular theater entertainment was the appearance of "Dr. Colyer's Living Models," whose scanty attire thrilled the bachelor miners and shocked and titillated the respectable element. All of the Booths except John Wilkes Booth, Lincoln's assassin, appeared in Sacramento theaters during these pioneer years. The Bateman sisters came to Sacramento as well-established child stars after sensational performances in the east. The notorious Lola Montez came to Sacramento preceded by her international reputation. The all-male audience jeered at her bizarre "Spider Dance" and showered her off the stage with eggs and over-ripe vegetables.

Sacramento offered three tracks for race horses. Racing fans also were offered other spectacles at the Brighton track, including a bull fight in July 1850, featuring a Mexican torero and four bulls. The following July a crowd of 2,000 witnessed a bloody fight between a large horned bull and a huge grizzly bear at the same arena. For the less bloodthirsty sportsmen, several amateur baseball clubs played intra-city games from 1859 to 1861 before crowds of fans on diamonds in the city parks. In 1860, a

The Chinese Chapel, located at the corner of 6th and H streets, was dedicated in June 1855. The Reverend Shuck, a Southern Baptist minister and former missionary to China, led the congregation. Barber and Baker's *Sacramento Illustrated,* *J. Brown Maloney Collection, SAMCC.*

team of best players from Sacramento played a series of intercity matches with teams from three other towns. Results: "0 for 3."

The literacy of California's Gold Rush population was quite remarkable. It is attested by the great volume of diaries and letters still preserved in libraries and archives across the country. It was also reflected in efforts to establish a school in Sacramento in 1849 before there was a population of children to sustain it. On February 20, 1854, the city's first public school was opened on the corner of 5th and K. When enrollment increased, a second school was created on I Street near 10th. By July of 1854, more than 500 students were attending public and private schools in the city of Sacramento. The Rhoads School, located on Rhoads family property north of the Cosumnes River, provided education for the children of early settlers (mostly Mormon families) in the Sloughhouse area.

Sacramento was the first community west of the Mississippi River to open high school classes for its teenagers and young adults. In 1855, the school between 8th and 9th on M Street began offering instruction in history, bookkeeping, astronomy and foreign languages. Even after that date, however, much of the education beyond elementary grades was only available in private academies. On October 7, 1857, the Sisters of Mercy, five strong, established a convent behind St. Rose's Church at 7th and K, and three days later opened a school in the church basement with 65 students. In 1860, they bought a block bounded by 9th, 10th, F and G streets, where they built a new school and a home for 65 orphans.

In October 1857, a group of citizens organized the Capital Library Association and raised a capital stock of $25,000 at $25 a share. The money was used to purchase books, fit out library rooms and to purchase a lot for a permanent building. The first library quarters opened in Tukey's Building at 5th and J in November 1857, with 800 volumes acquired by gifts and purchases. The next year, 800 more books were purchased from New York. Reports indicated that 150 books were in circulation from the beginning, and as many as 50 patrons per day came to the library.

In addition to using the library, readers anxiously awaited the arrival of eastern newspapers and magazines. They also patronized the local newspapers, the first two of which were the *Placer Times* and the *Sacramento Transcript.* Some 60 newspapers were started in the city over the next several years but only two, the *Daily Union* and the *Sacramento Bee,* survived into the 20th century.

The early appearance of churches exerted a modifying influence on social behavior in the community. Between 1849 and 1856, 10 Sacramento churches were founded and met regularly in their own buildings. These were: an Episcopal congregation; a Congregational Church; one Baptist and one Presbyterian Church; four Methodist Episcopal Fellowships, including an African-American M.E. Church which hosted the first of three Colored Conventions held in the state; St. Rose of Lima Catholic Church; and a Jewish Community which bought the building of an M.E. Church that was then moving to a new location in the city.

By the middle of the 1860s, Sacramento presented the appearance of a solid, well-established community. It had survived the catastrophes of fires, floods, epidemic and riots. The city had undertaken comprehensive measures against future floods by raising its levees, building up its streets, elevating the foundations of downtown buildings and creating a new channel for the American River near its junction with the Sacramento. Brick buildings and sturdy wood-frame houses had long since replaced the early tents and frame-and-canvas structures. Some of the more affluent residents were occupying handsome new Victorian mansions alongside attractive smaller homes just outside the business district. The

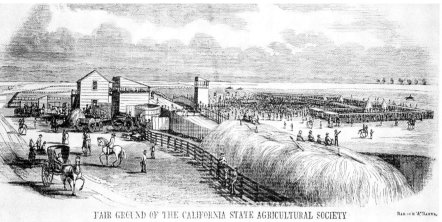

FAIR GROUND OF THE CALIFORNIA STATE AGRICULTURAL SOCIETY
[LOUISIANA RACE COURSE,] NEAR SACRAMENTO, Sept. 26th and 27th, 1855.

The Louisiana Racetrack was located south of Sacramento near the present-day intersection of 12th Avenue and Franklin Boulevard. It was constructed in 1855 and in that September, the State Agricultural Society held the first of several state fair exhibitions there. Eleanor McClatchy Collection, SAMCC.

presence of more women increased the frequency of marriages, followed by the appearance of more children in the population, adding to the stability of the community. A visiting Scotsman, J.D. Borthwick, commented in the late 1850s that the columns of marriage and birth announcements in the California newspapers were becoming as lengthy as they were in the larger cities of the country. The impressive number of churches and schools were institutional symbols of a maturing society. The second largest city in the state, Sacramento, was the county seat, the state capital, and a transportation, communications and commercial center. With the Central Pacific Railroad beginning to build eastward to its junction with the Union Pacific in Utah, Sacramento — "the world's gateway to the gold" — anticipated great benefits from its long-awaited, improved connections with the rest of the nation.

A Methodist-Episcopal congregation built this church on 7th near L Street in Sacramento. In 1858, B'nai Israel purchased the building and used it as their temple from 1859-1861. Barber and Baker's Sacramento Illustrated, J. Brown Maloney Collection, SAMCC.

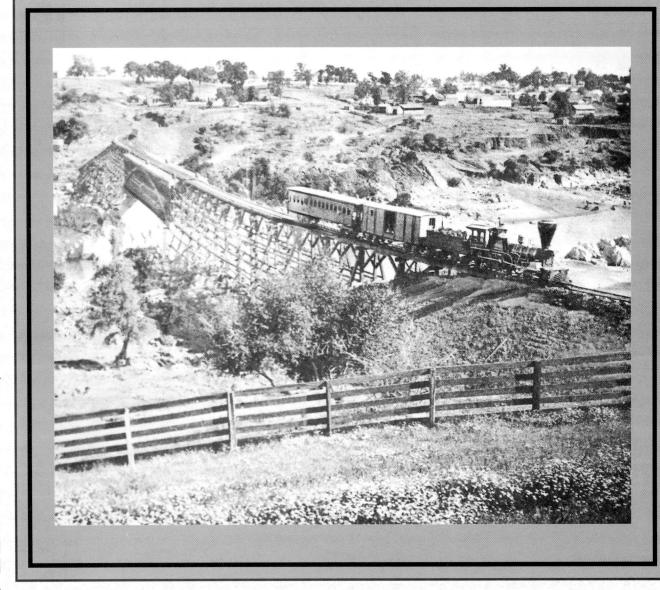

CHAPTER THREE

The Railroad Era in Sacramento, 1860-1880s
by Walter P. Gray III

Sacramento grew and prospered despite fire, flood, disease and a host of other tribulations that threatened to unseat the city from its fragile perch at the river's edge. The wharf at the foot of K Street was the essential bridge between the water and the land, between Sacramento and the rest of the world. As thousands bound for California discovered, Sacramento was a maritime dependency, reliant on ships for most of its connections to the outside world. Sutter's original choice of a site for his settlement was a product of this riverine geography, and the city became a permanent place due in large part to its status as the head of navigation on the Sacramento River. Even though the new residents rapidly created a network of roads radiating away from the Embarcadero, and overland stage connections existed to some degree, Sacramento might well have been an island.

Passengers and freight from the "States" arrived in Sacramento at the end of a 17,000-mile voyage around Cape Horn or via the shorter but more expensive trip across Panama. Both were arduous, hazardous and long: the Cape Horn route was a four-month journey by ship through the world's most treacherous seas, while the "quick" Panama passage still required most of a month and exposed travelers to tropical diseases. After they arrived, people and goods were transferred off the boats to wagons for movement further into the mining areas, but land travel was often no faster or more comfortable. The roads — adequate by horse-drawn standards — were nonetheless slow, dusty and rough in the summer, and could become bottomless wallows during the wet season.

People had long hoped for a better way to reach California. In 1845 — the same year in which the phrase "Manifest Destiny" became popular — a wealthy Boston merchant named Asa Whitney started to promote the idea of a "Pacific Railroad." The Pacific Railroad was to be just that, the railroad connection from the eastern states to the Pacific, the device that Whitney and others believed would conquer the interior of the country and make a continental United States a reality. "You will see," said Whitney, "that it will change the whole world... compelling Europe on one side and Asia and Africa on the other to pass through us." In 1852 and again in 1854, the state legislature had petitioned Congress to support the construction of such a railroad, but without success.

The issue facing Congress was not the concept of the Pacific Railroad itself. Rather, where should such a railroad begin and end? Most Americans thought the idea was a good one, but believed the huge expense of building the railroad would make government involvement a necessity. Government involvement implied government agreement, but action on the matter was paralyzed by the problems of sectionalism and slavery. Northern, typically anti-slavery, interests feared that a railroad that started in a slave state would result in the inevitable extension of slavery into any new states that might be developed along the route. Conversely, slavery's proponents believed that new free states would be engendered by a railroad that began in a free state. Either way, the balance between free and slave states would be upset. Congress' immediate solution to the controversy was to commission a study. A series of surveys were chartered in 1853 to explore the range of possible railroad routes to the west coast. These were published two years later as *The Pacific Railroad Surveys of 1853-55* in 12 wonderfully illustrated volumes. Five feasible railroad routes were identified, but there was no recommendation of the *best* route. That decision would be political, not technical.

Sacramento businessmen knew the economic value of railroads and understood the potential of the Pacific Railroad, even though most thought the idea was too lofty and

The locomotive *L. L. Robinson* was brought to Sacramento by ship where it was put into service as the second locomotive on the Sacramento Valley Railroad. The line ran between Sacramento and Folsom, where this picture was taken. *California State Library Collection, SAMCC.*

costly to become a reality anytime soon. They turned their attention to matters much closer to home, recognizing that a railroad would be the ideal means of capturing the freighting trade that was coming off the ships. Colonel Charles Lincoln Wilson, a Mexican War veteran who had built a plank toll road from lower Market Street to Mission Dolores in San Francisco, saw another way to make a profit by the improvement of transportation. He conceived of a railroad from Sacramento's Embarcadero to the edge of the valley, and in 1853 incorporated the Sacramento Valley Railroad. Although there was a locomotive at work in San Francisco leveling sand dunes, and other proposed lines had been chartered, Wilson's project would be the first actual railroad to operate in the state.

Wilson went east at the end of 1853 to secure a contractor and an engineer. His friend, Gov. Horatio Seymour of New York, suggested the name of a civil engineer that he thought would be competent. Theodore Dehone Judah was bright, energetic, supremely self confident, and by all accounts a difficult man. A native of upstate New York and a specialist in transportation projects, he had worked on a section of the Erie Canal and had been most recently involved in the construction of the Niagara Gorge Railroad.

Judah was only 29 when he arrived in Sacramento with his wife Anna at the end of April or in early May 1854. His first task was to evaluate the business prospects of the proposed railroad. Setting up a survey operation at the city limit near 31st and M streets, (today's Alhambra and Folsom Boulevards,) Judah counted the number of stages and freight wagons heading east on the plank road from Sutter's Embarcadero into the mining districts. His report found strongly in favor of a railroad, concluding "with such a business, it is difficult to conceive of a more profitable enterprise."

Judah laid out a railroad that was planned to run from the river in Sacramento to the Sierra Nevada foothills, with branches north and south along the line of the mountains for a total of 40 route miles. Grading started in February 1855, and the first rail was laid at Front and L streets shortly thereafter. The track ran south along the river five blocks and then turned east onto the R Street levee, destined for the new town of Folsom, 22 rail miles away. An economic crisis later that year forced Colonel Wilson out of the company and slowed the pace of construction, putting the company in debt to lenders in San Francisco. The first locomotive arrived from the east by ship at the end of June.

The new Sacramento Valley Railroad officially opened on February 22, 1856, to moderate success. It had cost much more to build than Judah's estimate, and had mortgaged its future revenues to pay the debt owed to the contractor and the San Francisco financiers. Control passed to the lenders, and the directors who had provided the initial capital — and had aspired to become California's first railroad magnates — lost most of their investment. This cloud of economic uncertainty meant there would be no more capital to build Judah's proposed extensions, and track construction stopped at Folsom. The line's greatest accomplishment was to introduce the railroad to California only five years after statehood, and to inspire the idea that a railroad connection between California and the rest of the Union would not

Railroad, and his wife would later recount that he spoke often of himself as being the man who would make the railroad an accomplished fact. His brother, Henry, had served as an officer in northern California during the Mexican War, and another, Charles, was a lawyer in San Francisco. Talk of California was almost certainly a commonplace around the Judah household even before Theodore ventured west. He read the Pacific Railroad surveys with avid interest, prompting him to explore the passes of the Sierra Nevada on his own. Judah became convinced that it was possible to build a railroad from near sea level in Sacramento over the 7,000-foot summit of the Sierra Nevada only 100 miles away, and then across the Nevada and Utah Territories. These thoughts were pub-

In 1856, Folsom had the distinction of becoming the terminus of the 22-mile-long Sacramento Valley Railroad. This view, from the mid-to-late 1870s, is looking east toward Folsom's railroad yard. The turntable is near the center of the photograph; Sutter Street is to the right. *California State Library Collection, SAMCC.*

have to await the arrival of tracks from the east, but could begin in the west.

While surveying the Sacramento Valley, Judah began to promote the scheme that his new line could be the California-end of a railroad across the continent. But the end of construction at Folsom thwarted the idea that the Sacramento Valley Railroad could continue over the mountains, and besides, the Sierra Nevada was viewed as an insurmountable obstacle which could never be overcome by a railroad, not even one surveyed by as clever an engineer as Theodore Judah.

Judah continued to work for the Sacramento Valley Railroad and undertook other civil engineering jobs, but his thoughts and efforts were increasingly consumed by the challenge of the Pacific Railroad. He had grown up immersed in the ideas of Manifest Destiny and the Pacific

lished in a pamphlet called "A Practical Plan for Building the Pacific Railroad," and he began to lecture on the subject and agitate for public support. In 1856 and again in 1857, he journeyed to Washington D.C. to lobby for congressional support, but the issues of sectionalism and slavery proved to be more daunting and insuperable than those of engineering and track design.

He returned to California more determined than ever to build the railroad, and he was convinced it could only happen with local support. Fruitless meetings with moneyed interests in San Francisco earned him the nickname "Crazy Judah" for the earnest, humorless, single-minded commitment to "his" project. He pursued the matter with disturbing intensity in the face of scorn and derision, and devoted nearly every waking hour planning ways to convince others of the rightness of his cause. Stories circu-

Beginning in 1858, the California Central Railroad was designed to run between Folsom and Marysville, although it was never completed beyond Lincoln. In 1863, the Central Pacific Railroad purchased the company at a sheriff's sale and the line was abandoned between Roseville and Folsom. In this view the California Central rolling stock is leaving Folsom, crossing the American River near the present-day Rainbow Bridge. *Eleanor McClatchy Collection, SAMCC.*

lated of people literally crossing the street to avoid having to speak with him on the subject. Some of Judah's kinder acquaintances merely prohibited the topic of the Pacific Railroad from being discussed in their presence.

Sacramento was not receptive at first, but gradually the attitude began to shift. Tension over slavery and states' rights was straining the very fabric of the nation, coming to a head in the east when Judah made a presentation to a group of Sacramento businessmen in November 1860. The most prominent of these, Leland Stanford, Collis Huntington, Mark Hopkins and Charles Crocker, saw possibilities in Judah's idea. Huntington and Hopkins had found success in their eponymous hardware concern, which later became the largest business of its kind on the Pacific Coast. Crocker, with his brothers, ran a dry goods enterprise. Stanford, after a failed career as a lawyer, also entered the dry goods and liquor business and had been the Republican candidate for governor in 1859. All four were successful Sacramento merchants, prosperous but not wealthy, and had long known one another through their association with the Republican Party. Strangely, they were all raised in the same small area of upstate New York where Judah had originated.

These men were supporters of Abraham Lincoln, who had been elected as the 16th President on November 6, and

they combined patriotism with an equally strong sense of enlightened self-interest. The developing national crisis caused them to take another look at Judah's plan, and they came to share his belief that a railroad along the central route east from California would bind the state to the Union in the event of civil war — and war looked like a certainty. The risks would be offset by the fact that a line into Nevada would capture lucrative traffic destined for the Comstock mines.

Lincoln's election triggered the secession of 11 Southern states. Formal hostilities commenced on April 12, 1861, with the Confederates firing on Union Fort Sumter in the harbor of Charleston, South Carolina. The national tapestry had been torn apart, and back in Sacramento, Judah and his sponsors felt the ideal moment had arrived to launch their enterprise. An organizational meeting for a new company, the Central Pacific Railroad of California, was held on April 30 above the Stanford Brothers' store, and the road was incorporated on June 28. Stanford became president, with Huntington as vice president, Hopkins as treasurer and Judah as chief engineer. Crocker would superintend construction.

The south had withdrawn from Congress, and there would be no more debate about the route of the railroad to the Pacific; the line would clearly be in northern territory. Construction was now a matter of national concern, but the Union, fully engaged in a war for its survival, was in no position to undertake the task. Said Lincoln, "Private enterprise must build the Pacific Railroad. All the government can do is aid, even admitting its construction is a political as well as a military necessity."

Judah spent the summer of 1861 on additional preliminary surveys, and believed he had found the solution to crossing the Sierra. Stanford campaigned for the governorship of the state, winning election in September to a two-year term. Judah was sent east in October "...as the accredited agent of the Central Pacific Company of California, for the purpose of procuring appropriations of land and U.S. Bonds from the government, to aid in the construction of this road." This was his fourth trip east to induce Congress to support a railroad, and he was better prepared than ever with surveys, the support of a company ready to actually build the line and the pressure of a national emergency to lend urgency to the matter. However, Congress and President Lincoln hoped the war would soon be over, obviating the momentous action Judah and his backers urged. A cautious Congress debated a Pacific Railroad bill through the winter and spring of 1862. Finally, the matter was approved by both houses at the end of June, and President Lincoln signed the Pacific Railroad Act on July 1, 1862.

The Central Pacific would build from California toward the east, and the patriotically named Union Pacific Railroad was given the job of constructing west from the Missouri River. The railroads were granted federal lands for rights of way, a construction subsidy in the form of United States bonds that were to be repaid with interest and they were required to finish the job within 12 years. The place of meeting was not specified.

Ground was broken for the Central Pacific at Front and K streets — the most prominent spot in Sacramento — on January 8, 1863. Governor Leland Stanford, still president of the railroad, intoned "We may now look forward with confidence to the day, not far distant, when the Pacific Coast will be bound to the Atlantic Coast by iron bonds that shall consolidate and strengthen the ties of nationality..."

Grading and track construction progressed northeasterly into the foothills. The work was much slower and more costly than anticipated, and a widening rift devel-

oped between Judah and the men who would come to be known as the "Big Four:" Stanford, Huntington, Crocker and Hopkins. Judah disliked the fact that Charles Crocker was given a contract to build one section of line and disagreed with some of his partners' financial practices. Tension escalated as Judah and his small group of supporters on the board were excluded from important decisions. At the end of September the rival camps adopted a compro-

In 1872, Eadweard Muybridge was hired by former California governor and railroad builder Leland Stanford to photograph his family's newly enlarged and remodeled house at 8th and O streets in Sacramento. In this view, Jane Lathrop Stanford and her sister Maria play a game of billiards while four-year-old Leland Stanford, Jr. looks on. Today the house is part of Leland Stanford Mansion State Historic Park. *Eleanor McClatchy Collection, SAMCC.*

Sacramento Company I, 2nd Regiment, California Volunteers proudly display their company cannon, Union Boy, along J Street in 1863. The cannon was purchased by William L. Siddons to be fired in Sacramento to signal Union Army victories. *Eleanor McClatchy Collection, SAMCC, from an original in the California State Library.*

These young women gymnasts from the Sacramento German community's Turn Verein posed for the camera during the 1880s. *Sacramento Ethnic Survey Collection, SAMCC.*

mise: the Big Four agreed to buy out Judah's interest in the railroad for $100,000, and in turn offered to let him buy them out on the same terms if he could raise the funds. This was the opportunity Judah needed to run the railroad; otherwise he could take the money and leave. He boarded ship for New York in the belief he was about to secure financial backing sufficient to buy out his partners and take over the enterprise. Whatever his plan, Theodore Judah did not live to carry it out. While crossing the Isthmus of Panama he contracted yellow fever, and he died in New York City on November 2, 1863. Ironically, the railroad's first locomotive, the *Gov. Stanford*, arrived by schooner from San Francisco on October 6, four days before Judah departed on his final, fatal trip east. The little Norris 4-4-0 was set up at the Goss & Lombard machine shop on I Street, but Judah never saw it run. It is preserved today at the California State Railroad Museum.

Everything the young railroad needed, except timber and the few iron castings that could be made locally, had to be bought in the east and shipped around Cape Horn. The scarcities created by the Civil War drove up prices, and labor was in short supply. Additional locomotives had arrived by 1864, and the road began hauling a few paying passengers

in March. Gangs of surveyors and location engineers ranged out ahead of the end of track, refining Judah's survey and establishing the final location for the line. Graders followed, making cuts and fills and preparing the roadbed.

The railroad was in desperate need of laborers by early 1865. Seven hundred workers, mostly Caucasians, had been hired to build the line, but were "... unsteady men, unreliable. Some would not go to work at all... some would stay until payday, get a little money, get drunk and clear out." Charles Crocker, overcoming an admitted prejudice, persuaded construction superintendent James Strobridge to hire a small number of Chinese in the summer of 1865. Some 20,000 Chinese lived in California and had been systematically driven out of the mines by discriminatory laws. The "experiment" was a great success, and Strobridge eventually employed as many as 10,000 Chinese men at one time. Chinese residents of California were hired at first, but the available supply of workers was soon exhausted and the railroad turned to labor contractors in southern China to furnish workers by the boatload. Between 7,000 and 12,000 Chinese men had come to California specifically for railroad work by 1869.

The line moved slowly east. It took two years to reach Colfax, 54 miles from Sacramento, and it was not until mid-1868 that the tracks entered Nevada. Tunneling was the most arduous and dangerous part of the work. Holes were drilled by hand in the rock face of the bore with drill steels and mauls, and black powder was the explosive most commonly used. Said one engineer later: "When mountain construction was at its height more than 500 kegs of powder a day were used. When the work began, powder cost $2.50 a keg. During the period that the greatest quantity was being used, the price advanced to $15 a keg. Dynamite was invented in 1866, but was never used on the Central Pacific." The grueling work continued through the summer heat and the glacial cold of winter. Everything was accomplished by hand, making the Central Pacific the last, and largest, of the nation's great civil engineering achievements of the pre-mechanized era.

The Union Pacific was moving inexorably toward the west to meet the Central Pacific. Lincoln had decided that the line would begin at Omaha, Nebraska Territory, failing to recognize that the nearest railroad connection was 100 miles away. Ground was broken in December 1863, but it was to be a year and a half before any track was built. The end of the Civil War in 1865 freed men and material for the project, and the speed of construction quickened.

On the western end, the Central Pacific's Chinese track gangs crossed the California stateline in May 1868, and spiked down 305 miles additional of track by the end of the year. The pace accelerated to three miles a day, and the two roads suddenly found themselves in a race to be the first into the rich Salt Lake valley, and quarrelling about where they would connect. A hastily called meeting in New York brought agreement that Promontory Summit, north of the Great Salt Lake, would be the place of final meeting. This was ratified by a joint resolution of Congress as the spot "... at which the rails shall meet and connect and form one continuous line."

Union Pacific Railroad photographer, A. J. Russell, captured Front Street in Sacramento, looking north, in May or June 1869. The open-air building at the center of the photograph is the Sacramento Valley Railroad freight and passenger depot. Going north are the California Steam Navigation Company depot and the Central Pacific Railroad passenger depot. The street dead ends at the multi-story Sacramento City Waterworks. *Sacramento Housing and Redevelopment Agency Collection, SAMCC.*

In the 1880s, Neubourg & Lages, located at 1016-1020 5th Street, was a major supplier of valley hops and grain products to Sacramento breweries. This business reminds us of the close relationship between Sacramento City and the productive farms of the Central Valley. *Eleanor McClatchy Collection, SAMCC.*

The Central Pacific reached Promontory Summit on April 30, 1869, and waited for the Union Pacific to arrive. Plans were made for a ceremony on May 8, a Saturday, and the telegraph wires which followed each railroad carried the news back to the respective coasts. A washout and a labor dispute would keep the Union Pacific away until Monday the 10th. A few minutes before 1 p.m. on May 10, 1869, at a desolate spot north of the Great Salt Lake, the dream of Manifest Destiny was symbolically achieved. Some 1,000 onlookers had gathered to commemorate the completion of the Pacific Railroad. Leland Stanford, who had presided over the railroad's inauguration in Sacramento six years before, brought a tie of polished California laurel wood and the "Last Spike," better known to history as the "Gold Spike," which was to become the icon for the entire undertaking. The telegraph signal "Done" flashed across the nation, now truly "united" states by rail, symbolizing that California was finally connected to the rest of the nation and Judah's goal had been at last, heroically, realized. Sacramento, still the gateway to the goldfields and where

the railroad had begun, was now terminus for the land link with the east.

Anna Judah believed Theodore's contribution had been overlooked by the Big Four on that grand May day, and that the neglect of his memory was intentional. This was a source of resentment to her, living the life of the perfect Victorian widow in Greenfield, Massachusetts, and devoting it to burnishing her late husband's reputation. Upon Judah's death, the task of superintending the grand design fell to Samuel Montague, who became acting chief engineer at the end of November 1863. He did not receive the title of chief engineer in his own right until March 1868, when the Central Pacific was completed as far as Truckee. This delay of more than four years is puzzling, unless one thinks that as long as the Central Pacific was building in the Sierra it was following Judah's route, and that the late engineer was, in essence, still present. The path beyond the Truckee River canyon represented new territory, to be conquered solely by Montague's engineering skills, moving out from under Judah's shadow.

Completion of the Pacific Railroad — it would not be called the Transcontinental Railroad until the early 1870s — made Sacramento the center of a radiating network of new railroads that branched off the Central Pacific and brought railroad connections to every part of the state. This was overlaid on the existing network of rivers and wagon roads already centered on Sacramento, and the pivotal transportation node continued to be the Embarcadero along Front Street. There, ship cargoes and passengers were transferred to the Central Pacific's trains. Expanded freight houses and a covered passenger station appeared on the levee, and the railroad's wharf was extended toward the river. The train station became a focal point of community life, not only the place where passengers boarded trains, but also the indispensable link to the mail, express companies and commercial telegraph. Dependence gradually developed on the railroad network as it grew. What had been a novelty in California only 15 years before became a vital element for travel, business and commerce.

THE CITY TRANSFORMED

The availability of reliable and comparatively rapid rail transportation substantially altered Sacramento's economy. The railroad established its principal shops in the city, and became the major employer. The ability to move agricultural products enabled growers to send their crops out of the local area, and would set the stage for a revolution in California agriculture. Initially, vast wheat ranches in the Sacramento and San Joaquin valleys emerged. The crop was durable and required no refrigeration, making it ideal for shipment in box cars. Development of practical refrigerator cars in the 1880s, cooled by blocks of ice harvested from ice lakes in the Sierra Nevada, prompted further evolution of the agricultural economy. Perishable fruits could now be reliably shipped long distances, propelling California to its modern agricultural diversity. The state's first commercial citrus belt sprung up in the Sierra foothills east of Sacramento, and large-scale commercial cultivation of soft fruits and berries in Sacramento River delta soon followed. R Street,

Carlaw Brothers granite yard at 10th and R streets in Sacramento is evidence of the industry that developed along the R Street railroad tracks. A grocery owned by J. W. Keating at 11th and R streets is at the left. This view, looking east, was taken about 1888. *Eugene Hepting Collection, SAMCC.*

Groundbreaking for California's State Capitol occurred in 1860, but it wasn't deemed completed until 1874. This view of its east elevation was taken about 1868. The semi-circular feature is the apse, destroyed by the post-World War II annex. The light-colored first story is evidence of the granite that was used; brick provided the construction material for the balance of the building. *California State Library Collection, SAMCC.*

the original route of the Sacramento Valley Railroad, became Sacramento's first industrial corridor. Machine shops, foundries, commission merchants, warehouses and breweries developed along the tracks, now owned by the Central Pacific and connected to the transcontinental railroad. The population of Sacramento spurted upward, to 34,390 in 1880, a 28 percent gain in 10 years. The Central Pacific grew in power and capability, and by the end of the century would be rivaled only by the constitutional authority of the state itself. Railroad power was largely responsible for prompting the citizens to rewrite California's Constitution in 1879, creating the document that governs California today, though with many revisions and additions.

State government, however, was not yet a predominant feature of life in Sacramento, being housed temporarily in the county courthouse at 7th and I streets until it was destroyed in the fire of July 13, 1854. One story has Governor Bigler imploring those fighting the conflagration to save the portrait of George Washington from the courthouse: "There is the portrait of the father of your country! Will you permit it to be destroyed?" The painting was rescued, and this same image of George Washington survives today to look out upon the current Senate Chamber from a vantage point high above the dais. A new courthouse, again with "temporary" provisions for the legislature, was completed in January 1855 and lawmakers would remain there for 15 years. Construction of a permanent capitol building was launched at the end of 1856 but was abruptly terminated. Disputes and economic hard times, the same woes that kept the Sacramento Valley Railroad from financial success, put an end to the project.

By 1860, the county, grown weary of sharing the courthouse with the state, arranged to donate property on the four blocks bounded by 10th, L, 12th and N streets as the site for a state capitol building. The Board of Capitol Commissioners in July accepted a design by M. F. Butler. Reuben Clark, designer of the never-built capitol on I Street, was named supervising architect. Clark went insane, and was succeeded by G.P. Cummings and still later by A.A. Bennett. Work on the foundations began September 24, 1860, and had progressed sufficiently to allow the placing of a cornerstone on May 15, 1861, with suitable ceremony and solemnity. But the flood of early 1862, which forced the legislature to relocate to San Francisco, inundated the partially completed building and caused grave concern that the foundations had been weakened. As a result, the walls of the first story were raised six feet, in the hope of preventing the building from ever again being flooded.

Construction on the Capitol continued during almost the same time period as the building of the transcontinental railroad, and the new structure was sufficiently complete for the legislature to take formal possession on December 6, 1869. Six additional square blocks were added to create the present Capitol Park in 1872, bringing it to its present extent of nearly 40 acres. Local marble and building stone from quarries in Rocklin and Folsom had been extensively used in what would become one of Sacramento's principal landmarks. The entire project was finally declared finished in February 1874, at a total cost of $2.6 million.

The 1862 flood had a transforming effect on the growing city. Sacramento had shown great resilience in the face of previous natural disasters, and the rebuildings that had occurred after each previous fire and flood sought to address weaknesses. The fires brought iron-shuttered buildings made of brick and better means of combating conflagration. Floods resulted in the improvement of levees and the employment of an architectural practice in residential structures of elevating the first floor several feet above a so-called "high water" basement. Many of these houses still exist downtown. The flood of 1862 was particularly jarring even to a town rather used to picking up the pieces and starting again.

Sacramento had been a city for 22 years, and the value and consequence of its business and municipal improvements were vastly greater than those that had been repaired after earlier inundations. The city was now the home of substantial enterprises and prosperous merchants with fine residences. Sacramento was now a developing railroad center, and the seat of government with a grand (and expensive) State Capitol building in the works. Clearly, Sacramento had matured to a point where it could no longer afford the loss or even the inconvenience of flood. Dramatic measures were needed in order to keep the rivers, which were the very reason Sacramento itself become a permanent place in the generation before, from threatening the city's future prospects.

Further raising of the levees would help, but risk of a catastrophic levee failure would always remain. There was also a growing awareness that silt from upstream hydraulic mining was slowly filling the Sacramento River. This created the specter of the river bottom eventually becoming higher than the adjacent land, forcing Sacramento to hide behind ever-higher levees from the river, which remained its commercial lifeline. Discussions during the summer of

The State Fair Pavilion occupied the southeast corner of Capitol Park from 1884 until 1905 when the fair relocated to Stockton Boulevard and Broadway in the southern part of the city. The 3-story building to the left of the pavilion was intended to be the governor's mansion, but was used instead as the state printing plant. The small building at center left was a gardener's cottage. Louis Vandercook shot this view, using a glass plate negative, about 1900. *Louis Vandercook Collection, SAMCC.*

1862 brought no solutions, but the city was prodded to action by new flood threats in December. A dramatic solution would "correct" the natural geography on which the town stood by elevating the streets above flood danger.

Sacramento would be raised, literally lifting itself out of the mud. The city trustees directed that the major levees be built up 2 feet above the highest water of 1862, and that the major streets — I, J and K — be filled east to 12th street. A new datum was established at the grade of Plaza Park, and property owners were directed to raise their properties to that level. Some buildings were elevated on jackscrews to the new street level and filled underneath. Other owners decided to fill in around the first story, turning it into a basement, and add new doors to what had been the second floor. Many constructed new second or third stories. Sacramento's sidewalks were impossible to navigate for years. Some sections had been elevated to the new street grade, but other stretches remained at the old. Ladders and ramps connected the various levels, creating a hazard to passersby.

When this prodigious project was completed in 1873, the elevation of the downtown streets had been increased

This view, looking south toward the State Capitol, was taken from atop the Cathedral of the Blessed Sacrament at 11th and K streets. At the end of the 19th century, much of the neighborhood around the Capitol was residential. *California State Library.*

Recurring winter overflow of the American River and subsequent flooding remained a challenge to Sacramentans. They raised the river levees and straightened the curves in the American River. Then, beginning in the mid-1860s, Sacramentans raised themselves out of the floodplain by jacking up their downtown buildings and raising adjacent streets and sidewalks, including the Sacramento County Courthouse at 7th and I streets. *Eleanor McClatchy Collection, SAMCC.*

by 12 feet. At the zenith of the strenuous task of hoisting several dozen buildings a full story above their former street-level frontage, Sacramento was described as "a city on stilts." One historian has referred to this project as "a fantastic feat in engineering and community effort." And it remains one of the city's most remarkable works to the present time.

RAILROAD ECONOMY

The Big Four expanded the Central Pacific by acquiring other railroads and transportation businesses. The Sacramento Valley and other pioneer lines rapidly came into the fold through voluntary purchase or threat, and magnates would soon control the biggest prize of all, the Southern Pacific (SP). The SP became the preferred vehicle for achieving dominance in California transportation, and would eventually be comprised of about 450 subsidiaries and predecessor companies. The SP would own railroads, the riverboats on the Sacramento River, San Francisco Bay ferries, oceanic steamship companies, cable car lines, land and real estate enterprises, timber and oil interests; in fact it influenced virtually every aspect of California society.

In Sacramento, the railroad was the city's largest employer for many years. The Central Pacific's headquarters remained above the Huntington, Hopkins Hardware Store until the late 1870s when headquarters staff and the Big Four left the Valley heat for the more cosmopolitan environs of San Francisco. The railroad employed hundreds of engineers, trainmen, laborers, shop workers and administrative employees. Sacramento was selected as the location for the line's shops, and this enterprise was to become the largest industrial site in the western United States. The Central Pacific used the machine shop and foundry of Goss & Lombard at the beginning of its history. A car shop building was put up near 6th and I streets at the end of 1863 to supplement the Goss & Lombard facilities, and the company was soon bought outright by the railroad to become the nucleus of the largest industrial works in the western United States.

A brick roundhouse and more extensive shop buildings were under construction by mid-1867, on swampland in Lake Sutter (China Slough), which was the remnant of the original mouth of the American River. The shops were

employees, the Central Pacific in 1876 planted 300 eucalyptus trees in the shops, adding 2,700 more in 1877 and encouraging everyone in the city to plant eucalyptus in the interests of community health.

Shops performed every task required for the operation of a great system of railroads, and the railroad's payroll brought Sacramento a stability that helped insulate it to some degree from the periodic economic crises which plagued the state. The men were able to produce almost everything the railroad needed, from pieces of office equipment and brakemen's lanterns to freight cars, passenger cars, cable cars for San Francisco and boilers and engines for bay ferries and river steamers. The city of Sacramento continued to expand and provide its residents and those of the surrounding area with numerous amenities. In 1885, Margaret Crocker donated the family gallery and magnificent art collection to the city; it became the Crocker Art Museum, the oldest museum of its kind in the west.

One of the most remarkable personalities associated with the expansion of the shops was General Master Mechanic Andrew Jackson Stevens. A Vermonter, Stevens became an apprentice machinist for a railroad in New Hampshire at age 17 and rapidly rose through the mechanical department ranks at a number of lines. He became a locomotive engineer for the Chicago, Burlington & Quincy in Illinois and journeyed to California in 1861. He worked for railroads in the San Francisco Bay Area before Leland Stanford appointed him in 1869 to the post of the master mechanic of a Central Pacific subsidiary. Completion of the Pacific railroad triggered the need to increase the Sacramento Shops' capabilities, and Stevens was brought to Sacramento to superintend the Central Pacific's mechanical department as chief master mechanic. Innovation and creativity, particularly in the design, repair and manufacture of steam locomotives, characterized his 18-year tenure. Stevens — he was known as "AJ" — was an inveterate inventor filled with new ideas for improving the efficiency and power of locomotives, and the expanding capabilities of the shops allowed him to exercise his sometimes untraditional ideas. He commenced the manufacture of steam locomotives in Sacramento, and more than 200 would be built under his direction, culminating in 1884 with the world's largest locomotive, *El Gobernador,* named somewhat obliquely after Leland Stanford.

AJ was considered kind, helpful, always concerned about the welfare of his men and a friend to labor. Contemporaries described him as a man who "... held a position far above the average (yet) was never too busy, never too engrossed in his duties, or too occupied in the

planned from the outset to be comprehensive in their capabilities, as the Central Pacific was isolated from the other American industrial centers in New England, the Middle Atlantic and the Ohio Valley. More facilities appeared in the 1870s, and employment grew to 700 men. One of the characteristics of work in the shops was a high incidence of "chills and fever" among the employees. Standing water in the adjacent slough was the source of mosquitoes that carried malaria to the men. At the time, eucalyptus trees were thought to prevent malaria. As a measure to protect its

responsibilities of his high position, but what he had time to listen to and give counsel to the laboring classes." Stevens ensured that all shop employees would work reduced hours during economic hard times rather than instituting layoffs, and kept no "black list" of those fired. His untimely death of kidney failure in early 1888 was a shock.

In a remarkable manifestation of the profound affection with which AJ was viewed, the employees of the Sacramento Shops pooled their modest wages and raised a subscription of $5,292.10 for a bronze statue, with the pedestal bearing the legend "A Friend of Labor." Dedicated by the Governor of California on Thanksgiving Day, 1888, it was installed on the J Street side of Plaza Park, which in the 1990s was renamed in complementary fashion after a more contemporary labor activist, farm worker organizer Cesar Chavez.

The A.J. Stevens monument stands in eloquent testimony to the overwhelming influence of the railroad on Sacramento in the second half of the 19th century. Thousands of people drive down J Street every day under the silent paternal gaze of the tall bearded man whose likeness is rendered in weathered bronze, acknowledging his presence but perhaps not realizing that Sacramento's most prominent public memorial to an individual is not dedicated to a soldier, statesman, merchant or politician, but to a railroader.

Sarah Mildred Jones, center of the back row, was the teacher for Sacramento's segregated and ungraded school #2, located at 9th and O streets. This was her class about 1882. Later, she became the first African-American principal of an integrated Sacramento public school, the Fremont School. *Clarissa Wildy Collection, SAMCC.*

CHAPTER FOUR

The Age of Maturity & Modernization
1880s – 1918

by James E. Henley

THE DECLINE OF MINING

Relatively soon after the Gold Rush began, the easy-to-find gold was gone, and success in mining became a matter of extracting the precious metal from copious amounts of earth. Beginning in 1853, hydraulic mining, or the use of water cannons to knock down and sift through tons of ground, became a predominant mining technique. Almost as quickly, the problems of hydraulic mining were obvious to the Sacramento Valley, as the debris from "hydraulicking" clogged the waterways. The floods of 1875 and 1878 made the struggle one of life and death between the miners and the farmers, river transportation interests, and cities and towns along the Valley's streams. Mining hampered navigation, destroyed river flows, and buried some farm land 20 feet deep in mud along the Feather, Bear and American rivers. Perhaps 1.5 billion cubic yards of debris, in all, flowed down those streams.

After almost a decade of continuous litigation, farmers, valley cities and the railroad teamed up against the miners. By 1880, the state and federal government were involved. In 1884, Judge Alonzo Sawyer, in the landmark case of *Edward Woodruff vs. North Bloomfield Gravel Mining Company, et. al.*, issued a perpetual injunction against dumping debris on another person's land and the state was barred from authorizing the deposit of debris in navigable streams. Farmers would continue to fight the miners for 20 years to protect against the erosion of that hard-won decision, carrying the battle to the state legislature and the halls of congress. Officials of many agencies made frequent trips into dangerous territory to ensure the cessation of illegal mining and to monitor the destruction from prior activity.

Except for the earliest mining activities near Folsom, Sacramento played only a minor roll as a mining county until the technology of gold dredging was refined. The county was not part of those early sites of discovery, except the area above Folsom almost on the county line. Gold extraction below Folsom generally had to wait for the technological evolution of gold dredges. Dredging before 1890 operated in river bottoms and was largely unsuccesful. The major innovation was to set up a continuous bucketline (an endless chainlinked line of buckets) on a huge movable decending ladder which excavated the alluvial deposits over the ancient Pleistocene river channels, further and further away from the modern rivers. In that way, dredging could be profitable by capturing a mere five cents of gold per cubic yard. The new dredges were first employed in the Feather River area near Thermalito. But they were also in production almost immediately on the Yuba and American rivers.

On the American River at Mississippi Bar a dredge was in operation in 1898, with a second dredge in operation at Natoma near Folsom in 1899. By 1910, nine of the 30 dredges operating in California were in the Folsom District, primarily south of the American River. Over $30 million in gold was recovered between 1898 and 1909 by dredging in California. By the 1920s, the Natomas Company was recovering approximately $1 million per month from their dredges.

The environmental destruction by these dredges was immediately apparent and by 1905, the State Assembly was unsuccessfully attempting to force dredge operations to reclaim the land destroyed by dredge activity. Sacramento County was petitioned to restrict dredging and to protect farm land from destruction. A turn of the century anti-dredge convention was held, but adjourned without firm actions or resolutions. Nevertheless, the Natomas Company realized it needed to avoid making the same

In order to determine areas for future dredging, the Natomas Company would test below-surface gravel for gold content. The miners at the left are operating a wench that raised and lowered a bucket for collecting gravel samples from the hole below. The bucket would be emptied into the rocker where it would be worked to determine gold content. The photograph is from the Folsom/Rancho Cordova area c. 1900. *Natomas Company Collection.*

Sacramento County gold dredging commenced at Mississippi Bar on the American River in 1898. By the 1920s, when this photograph was shot in eastern Sacramento County, the Natomas Company was recovering $1 million per month from their dredging operations. *David Joslyn Collection, SAMCC.*

mistakes of earlier mining companies. They thought they could delay anti-dredging action even operating bigger and bigger dredges, if they also experimented with reclaiming the rock piles left behind the dredges. The company claimed it invented the bulldozer to level the rockpiles. But the rock piles were too big and the technology too primitive to turn all the land back into agriculture.

So, it was indeed fortunate that a new, improved building technology emerged which used unimaginable quantities of aggregate, the crushed rock material left behind by dredging. Mixed with an ancient material "cement" and steel reinforcing bars, the aggregate helped to form structural concrete. Natomas, through their dredging operations, had just liberated a huge resource of what was determined to be the highest quality rock.

Before dredging, the Natomas Company had an earlier history in farming near what is now Rancho Cordova. At one point they claimed to have had the largest vineyard in California. That experience, coupled with their early reclamation efforts and combined with a steady stream of wealth from the dredges, prompted them to invest in swamp and overflow land reclamation and real estate subdivision. First they worked their own original 20,000-acre land grant; then they developed the 16,000-acre Reclamation District 1000 and 1001 projects. They purchased in excess of 50 percent of the districts' land, giving themselves voting control. They built a drainage canal, raised the rivers' levees, cleared and subdivided the land and called it Natomas.

The Natomas Company understood dredging and the aggregate business, but selling land in California to mid-westerners was difficult for them. They brought in a partner from Chicago, the Goodwin Land Company, who taught them to market Sacramento's weather during the winter to Chicago and the rest of the American heartland. But, financial success in this endeavor eluded the Natomas Company, and almost destroyed the firm in the face of claims by creditors.

Hydraulic mining interests continued in what was to be a losing effort. Some of the mines continued to operate by keeping their debris behind impound dams. The Caminetti

Engineers proclaimed the debris cleared to Marysville in the 1920s, and by the mid-1950s the tail of the major deposit in the Sacramento River had passed Sacramento. But each year of high water brought new deposits, a situation that persists even today.

Slickins did have a few identifiable benefits. One was to use the mud over the years in construction of the levees in the Sacramento River Delta, where suitable levee materials were scarce because of the peat soil. For decades the river would deliver the slickins where needed. Special clamshell dredgers would take the mud from the bottom of the river and build the levees to protect Delta farmland.

The Natomas Company developed Reclamation Districts 1000 and 1001, the present-day community of Natomas, by building drainage canals, raising levees and subdividing the land. The Natomas Company often featured successful reclamation district farmers, such as Frank L. Azevedo whose home and 174-acre farm are shown here, in their promotional publication, *Natomas News. Eleanor McClatchy, Sacramento Archives and Museum Collection Center (SAMCC)*

Act of 1893 established a federally controlled California Debris Commission. Miners felt that this would give them a chance to resume mining, but the costs of dams to retain the debris were prohibitive.

The essence of hydraulic mining was to use water for almost everything. First, water washed down the gold bearing deposits. Then water carried the processed mud, less its gold, into stream channels to dispose of it. The hydraulic mining mud, known as "slickins," had worked its way slowly down the tributaries of the Sacramento River eventually creeping into San Francisco Bay. The bay's volume was reduced by one fifth or more. The Army Corps of

AGRICULTURAL HUB

From the mid-1860s to the mid-1890s, grains dominated the economy of the Sacramento Valley. By 1892, a million acres were under cultivation. At 16 bushels per acre, 16 million bushels or almost 6.5 million sacks of grain stood along the river banks to be transported to the flour mills of California and the rest of the world. Wheat was a crop that could circumvent the railroads by using river transportation. Steam traction engines were developed to move sacked wheat to the river's edge. The Sacramento Valley would control the world's wheat markets until the markets collapsed with the Depression of 1893. The American midwest and

The Sacramento Valley controlled the world's wheat market until the Depression of 1893. The grain was sacked in the fields, moved to riverbanks by steam traction engines, and loaded onto barges, such as these tied up below the M Street Bridge in Sacramento enroute to California flour mills. *McCurry Company Collection, SAMCC.*

Sacramento County became a center for hop growing, especially along the American and Cosumnes rivers. As a result, Sacramento was able to support several major breweries. In this view, a wagon loaded with beer kegs, perhaps destined for the ship in the background tied up at Front and H streets. The old Southern Pacific Railroad Bridge is at the left. *Eugene Hepting Collection, SAMCC.*

such as the common potato and onion. Even though grain was the biggest agricultural product, vineyards, orchards and row crops were successful and would rise in importance from the 1880s onward. In Sacramento County, special niches for specific products emerged: grapes in the area near Rancho Cordova, pears and asparagus in the Delta, oranges in Citrus Heights and Orangevale, and nuts and olives in Fair Oaks. The editor of the *Sacramento Bee,* C. K. McClatchy, planted two or more of everything he could grow that produced a vegetable, fruit or a nut on his small Fair Oaks retreat. He was representative of many modern Noahs in Sacramento.

With the technique of canning barely 50 years old, the first cannery in Sacramento was operating by 1864. Nationally, the importance and value of canned goods had been demonstrated in the Civil War and in the west with the Comstock rush in Nevada. The first fruit cannery in the Sacramento Valley was established in 1876 by J. Routier near Mather Field. In 1882, the Capitol Packing Company was established and by 1888 it was packing 2.4 million cans per year. In 1929, there were 29 major canneries in the state. Consolidation of the numerous smaller canneries began in 1910. That same year the number of small town canneries diminished. This later reduction was primarily due to the introduction of trucks and improved roads. The remaining, more efficient canneries were centered in large towns like Sacramento where the fruit was "trucked," bypassing the small towns.

central Canada would not dominate those markets until Mennonites immigrating from Russia brought the hearty type of wheat known as "red wheat" to that region.

During the early years of the gold rush, the lure of agriculture attracted many people to provide food for the miners. Great fortunes were made in mundane produce

Sacramento: Chapter Four

The power of the larger consolidated canneries grew until in 1912, when the farmers began to think about organizing. What happened to the canneries is indicative of the progress of the agricultural industry. All facets of agriculture were evolving. The support services of hardware, transportation, processing and financing were reducing competition. The growers and shippers saw this development as a threat and started their own cooperatives, associations or exchanges. The California Peach Growers Association was established in 1917. Other local examples include: California Fresh Fruit Exchange, California Almond Growers Exchange and the California Creamery Operators Association. This economic vibrancy was manifested in modest but steady population expansion, to 40,339 in Sacramento City and County in 1890, 45,915 at the turn of the century, and 67,806 in 1910, nearly doubling the population in 30 years.

THE RISE OF LABOR

The Sacramento Valley before the 1880s saw little labor organization. Labor conflict tended to focus along racial lines. For such a quiet backyard of labor activity, it was quite a shock to the Sacramento region when it became a focus for the unemployed, who banded together as the "industrial armies" of the west coast and organized labor revolts which led to the first national labor boycott. Much of this activity was fueled by the Depression of 1893. By 1894, unemployed laborers organized into "armies," and under the national leadership of "General" Jacob Coxey, started to march toward Washington D.C. demanding jobs. This movement was not unique to the west coast. Coxey hoped to recruit over 100,000 workers from across the country to descend upon Washington, D.C. on May Day, 1894.

The first group from the Bay Area to reach Sacramento were 200 strong, arriving on April 6, 1894, and after a meal they pressed on for Salt Lake City. The main group arrived in mid-April from two separate locations, totaling 1,207 men and three women. They marched up through the Delta from San Francisco and from Stockton. Upon arrival in Sacramento they camped at Snowflake Park at 28th and S streets. The "army" was destitute and would not leave without assistance. The City Council gave them $500 to leave town. Most gave up and marched back to the Bay Area. A small group seized a train and got as far as Rocklin, where the engineer was arrested. Fragmented groups of the armies, also known as the "Industrials," roamed the northern end of the valley above Sacramento causing great fear in the small towns and ranches. Most violence was directed toward Chinese and Japanese.

Attention to these groups waned as the Valley and Bay Area come to grips with the impact of the Pullman Strike of 1894. The strike began on May 1, 1894, in Illinois over reduced wages and benefits at the Pullman factory and

Troops were gathered from San Francisco and valley towns as far away as Fresno. Nearly 1,000 Guardsmen faced off against the strikers at the Sacramento railroad station on July 4th. The Guard was reluctant to advance upon the strikers, as many were friends and acquaintances. When ordered to deploy their bayonets and advance upon the strikers, they refused and were withdrawn. The consequences of the Guard's disregard for orders resulted in the house arrest of an entire Guard unit and the largest Courts-Martial proceedings in the history of the California National Guard. The political fallout would result in the structural reorganization of the Guard statewide.

During the Pullman Strike in 1894, nearly 1,000 National Guardsmen faced Sacramento strikers on the 4th of July. Here, the National Guard is transporting men and equipment south on L Street between 6th and 7th streets. *Sacramento Valley Photographic Survey Collection, SAMCC, from original at California Department of Parks and Recreation.*

On July 10th, President Grover Cleveland ordered all strikers to cease obstructing the railroads by 4 p.m. or be arrested. Shots were exchanged between strikers and guardsmen on July 11. Federal troops arrived and assumed control under the direction of Marshal Baldwin. The depot and railyards were secured by U.S. Marines and Army Cavalry and a train quickly was assembled and dispatched for the bay area. As it entered Yolo County, the train was derailed by a group of strikers, killing one civilian and four soldiers. The derailing of the train and killing of federal troops marked the rapid decline of any significant support the strike had enjoyed. The Marines and Army troops attacked the strikers and seized caches of weapons and ammunition. A number of strikers and perhaps some civilian bystanders were killed.

reached Sacramento on June 25. The local railway union declared a sympathetic secondary boycott and declared that no train would be moved with a Pullman car attached. The Southern Pacific responded by closing their freight operations. The stakes escalated until all traffic stopped and the railroad shut down operations, including the shops.

Almost a third of the region's population worked for the railroad. The economic impact was immediate. Calming forces were ignored and the danger escalated. Federal Marshals were sent to end the boycott. Supervising U.S. Marshal Baldwin, seeing an impasse, asked the governor for National Guard reinforcements.

The shock of the attack on the train, with the resulting loss of life and the federal troop reaction, broke the boycott. The strike was over. Violence had ended by July 13th and trains almost immediately resumed operations. Suspects in the derailment were arrested by the Sacramento Police Department and tried in Yolo County. The organizer of the train's derailment, S.A. Worden, was convicted and sentenced to be executed; later his sentence was commuted to life behind bars. Twenty-seven years after the incident, Worden was pardoned from Folsom Prison.

The last great "army" of unemployed to march into Sacramento during the 19th century was S.A. Leffingwell's group in 1897. Organized in San Francisco during February, the mayor of that city solved his local problems in April by paying steamboat transportation for the relocation of the entire assemblage from San Francisco to Stockton. The leaders of Stockton encouraged the "army" to move to Lodi. In late April, 180 men made it to Sacramento. City officials gave the men food if they would relocate to Yolo County. Once they went to Yolo, Sacramento placed special armed police at both bridges and permitted no one access to the city. The "army" began to fall apart and accepted the railroad's offer of free transportation if the group left in small lots.

Labor strife reemerged in the 20th century. In 1913, the Wheatland farm labor riots occurred, which introduced to the Sacramento Valley the "Industrial Workers of the World" (I.W.W.), nicknamed the "wobblies." Even with the crushing of the riots in Wheatland by private detectives employed by the farmers, the ensuing trial was a focus of wobblie activities. Kelley's "army," assembled from 2,000 Bay Area unemployed workers, arrived in Sacramento in March 1913. They claimed affiliation with the "wobblies." Their goal was to march to Washington D.C. where they would remove

the president from office and abolish Congress. The "army" was hungry, tired and short of funds. The strategy of Sacramento and other communities was to apply pressure, sometimes violent, to relocate the "army." The pressure was coupled with food and some charity, along with forcing the group from place to place until the "army" broke up. World War I would end these violent labor disputes, but the economics of the Great Depression would later bring labor problems dramatically back to the public eye.

BREAKING UP THE LAND GRANTS

The California Gold Rush profoundly changed the course of California. Most Mexican social and political institutional values and traditions were crushed by a quarter of a million determined gold seekers. One result was the dissection of the great land grants. Miners and farmers (many of them squatters) took and used the land without regard for the legal ownership. In a new economic society, dominated by transplanted American values, the established Hispanic families quickly lost title to their ranchos. The Americans theoretically frowned upon large land holdings and absentee ownership, particularly when those lands were owned by people considered foreigners, even though many of those

Kelley's Army, a contingent of some 2,000 unemployed farm workers and unskilled laborers led by "General" Charles T. Kelley, marched on Sacramento in March 1914 to demand legislative support. They camped on the Southern Pacific sandlot at 2nd and H streets before they were driven from the city by a force of deputized citizens. *Eugene Hepting Collection, SAMCC.*

Founded in 1887, Orangevale included about 3,000-acres subdivided into 10 acre parcels. Two years later, when this promotional photograph was taken, plantings far outnumbered residents. *Eleanor McClatchy Collection, SAMCC.*

Fair Oaks developed from an idea for land colonization by V. S. McClatchy, brother of *Sacramento Bee* publisher C. K. McClatchy. In 1895, the Chicago magazine *Farm, Field & Fireside,* in cooperation with McClatchy, purchased 9,000 acres and divided them into 5- to 20-acre parcels. The town center of Fair Oaks included the Fair Oaks Store at the left and San Juan Hall at the right. *City of Sacramento History and Science Collection, SAMCC.*

people had lived in the territory far longer than many of the newly arrived Americans.

Significant new wealth in the hands of new merchants and new companies added more stress on the land grants. The first great wave of immigrants in the form of gold seekers were supplanted by even larger numbers of farmers. The railroads quickly saw that farming reaped greater profits for their companies than would be gained by serving the transportation needs of mining. From the 1870s through the first three quarters of the 20th century, waves of settlers desiring land would arrive by the hundreds of thousands in California. It was inevitable that the land grants would be broken up.

The Central Pacific also had huge landholdings for sale. They mounted a sophisticated marketing plan especially to attract eastern migrants, taking out news and magazine ads and sending traveling exhibits of California produce. The railroads produced numerous pamphlets and even established a flagship magazine titled *Sunset*, but the most aggressive promotions were the excursion trains with cheap fares costing less than $40 for a 12-day trip from coast to coast.

In another maneuver, the railroad and land speculators seized upon the concept of establishing fruit colonies. Colonies were established along the eastern side of the Sacramento Valley from Mt. Shasta to the American River.

The southernmost of these colonies were in Sacramento County. The early crops promoted were oranges, olives, grapes, peaches, plums, nuts and berries.

In Sacramento, an unlikely assortment of groups and individuals would join together to promote Orangevale (Cardwell Colony), Fair Oaks (Sunset Colony) and the Carmichael Colony. Among the most important promoters would be a gold rush water and mining company (the Natomas Company), a real estate speculator (D.W. Carmichael), a newspaper family (Valentine McClatchy and his brother C.K. McClatchy), the Southern Pacific Railroad, and a Chicago magazine *Farm, Field & Fireside.*

Orangevale was established in 1887 and encompassed approximately 3,000 well-planned acres, subdivided into 10-acre parcels. By the mid-1890s, oranges were being planted, but the colony's growth was slow due to the Depression of 1893. The peak growth period for oranges was in the mid-1920s, and the end of significant commercial crops occurred with the freeze of December 1932 which destroyed not only the crops but most of the trees.

In the mid-1890s, V.S. McClatchy, publisher of the *Sacramento Bee*, became convinced that the development of land colonies in the eastern portion of Sacramento County was not only good for the community but also a wonderful personal investment. As his idea coalesced, he gained support from the Board of Trade and many community leaders. With the support of his brother, C.K., he had the full force of the *Sacramento Bee* at his disposal. The *Bee* developed a showpiece soft-bound book, *Where California Fruits Grow*. V.S. then sought support from the Chicago magazine, *Farm, Field & Fireside*. Together they conceived of a new fruit colony which was named "Fair Oaks" after Fair Oaks, Virginia. *Farm, Field & Fireside* bought 9,000 acres in 1895 and lots of five to 20 acres were surveyed and sold at around $100 each. In November 1895, when winter was fast approaching Chicago, an excursion train brought over 100 prospective midwestern buyers. As the train descended into the Sacramento Valley, young girls in crisp white dresses were gathered at strategic locations to throw bouquets of flowers to the awed prospective buyers.

Like Orangevale, growth in Fair Oaks was slow in the economically troubled 1890s, but by 1900, over 2,000 acres were sold and substantial crops of lemons, oranges, almonds and olives were in production. With a bridge to Folsom in place, a substantial rural community center was established. The third colony emerged when D.W. Carmichael put together 3,000 acres from the San Juan and the Del Paso land grants. The Carmichael colony was too late for a citrus colony and developed very slowly until after World War II, when the great Sacramento expansion and post-war boom dominated development.

Changes in transportation would influence the shape and character of these colonies. New paved roads appeared at key locations including the Folsom and Stockton roads. The major boulevards, including Riverside, Auburn and Franklin, were also paved. The Yolo Causeway opened in 1916 and three bridges crossed the American River between Sacramento and Fair Oaks.

THE CALL FOR PROGRESSIVE REFORM AND THE INTRODUCTION OF THE AUTOMOBILE

The Gold Rush created some wealthy individuals, but it was commerce and industry that gave people the most dramatic advances. Hardware, banking, communications and transportation gained phenomenal influence.

But no other force ultimately became more powerful in California than the Central Pacific Railroad, and its contin-

The causeway over the Yolo Basin was completed in 1916. It guaranteed a direct, year-around automobile connection between Davis and other communities to the west with the Capital City.
Maurice Read Collection, SAMCC.

In 1879, the Central Pacific Railroad Company completed a new depot between G and I, Front and 3rd streets. It remained in service until 1925 when it was replaced by the Southern Pacific Depot, still in use by Amtrak. In this 1905 photograph by David Joslyn, the Southern Pacific Hospital is seen at the upper left. *Eleanor McClatchy Collection, SAMCC.*

regulated child labor; a standard number of hours for days and weeks of work; control of gambling and red light abatement; regulation of saloons and consideration of prohibition; and establishing the right to vote for women. Writers known as "muckrakers," such as Sacramento-raised Lincoln Steffens, heightened awareness of the pervasive corruption.

The Progressive movement took hold and eventually bore fruit. Political reformers such as Mayor Clinton White were elected, old line capitalists such as William Land were defeated and Sacramentan Hiram Johnson would become governor. Johnson's election set the stage for an extraordinary personal battle: in an almost biblical sense, progressive son Hiram, the governor, would make war on his father, legal counsel for the Southern Pacific and other large California companies.

Another competitive railroad, the Western Pacific, slowly worked its way into Sacramento. Interurban railroads were connecting Sacramento to the Bay Area and northward to Chico, and river transportation flourished with highly successful boats such as the *Fort Sutter* and *Capitol City.* Sacramento began to issue franchises and attach regulations to everything they happened on, above or below city streets. In spite of railroad resistance, major political reform was slowly occurring. Even public ownership of utilities was being actively debated. All of these forces created a revolution in California, in both politics and in every aspect of community and life. The Southern Pacific's relationship to California and every citizen of the state was redefined by the Progressive reformers.

While all the pressures of reform moved forward, a new force gained the stage. The automobile, which in the 20th century would forever change the role of the railroads and trumpet the death of interurban lines and river transportation, radically altered cityscapes and the nature of land subdivisions. California's love affair with the automobile did not skip by Sacramento. There were 27 registered autos in the county in 1905 and 700 by 1910. By July 1911, in what can only be called an "Auto Frenzy," Sacramentans were buying 75 autos per day.

THE AGE OF ELECTRICITY

As the wonders of electricity were unraveled, a number of inventions led to another series of great changes in Sacramento. The transcontinental telegraph in 1862 first linked the country together in an intimate way with what seemed like instantaneous communication. The Civil War was daily news and the *Sacramento Union's* use of the "wire" gave them an elevated presence throughout the west coast. In 1880, the first telephone exchange was established in the

uation as the Southern Pacific. Little stood in their way: politicians were co-opted, miners felt the consequences of railroad interests siding with the farmers, and newspapers, such as the *Sacramento Union,* discovered the cost of negative editorials when they were bought by railroad interests, with a concomitant change in their editorial positions. The danger for the Southern Pacific, however, was in the public's expanding knowledge of the railroad's power and its willingness to direct and focus that power. By the late 1880s, labor began to effectively organize. Initially, against the Southern Pacific it seemed like an unbalanced fight.

Labor, as it turned out, was not alone in this battle. More and more of the overall population also sought reform. Issues that emerged beyond the emphases of labor included: a demand for municipal services in the form of water, sewers and street improvements; election fraud remedies, governmental reform and an end to political corruption;

The first passenger train on the Western Pacific Railroad arrived in Sacramento on August 22, 1910. Western Pacific, a competitor of Southern Pacific, provided the Sacramento Valley with an alternate transcontinental line. The depot, at the left, still stands on the half block bound by J, K, and 19th streets and the Western Pacific (now Union Pacific) tracks. *Eleanor McClatchy Collection, SAMCC.*

region by the Sacramento Telephonic Exchange. Battery-powered street cars were tried on Sacramento streets in 1888. But the real prize was electric light, and enough reliable power to turn electric motors. Lights were displayed as early as 1879 in Sacramento, powered by steam generators.

In the early 1890s, Horatio Gates Livermore and Albert Gallatin moved to harness the power of falling water to make electricity. A dam and powerhouse had to first be built at Folsom. On July 13, 1895, electric power flowed to Sacramento from the newly completed powerhouse. The *Sacramento Bee* pushed for a grand celebration which on September 9th resulted in the "Carnival of Lights," an electric light parade and display. The *Bee* reported that 30,000 people attended the evening event, a crowd larger than the entire population of the county at that time.

The demand for power was so great that by 1899 a second system was developed on the North Fork of the Yuba River, at the Colgate Powerhouse. This powerhouse transferred power 61 miles to Sacramento. The Sacramento/Folsom enterprise was sold to California Gas and Electric Company and by 1906 was renamed the Pacific Gas and Electric Company. By 1915, the Sacramento urban street scene was an electric one, defined by electric street lights, electric signs and electric streetcars, with only gasoline-powered automobiles breaking the electric panorama.

"THE GATEWAY TO HELL REOPENED" (CLEANING UP THE TOWN)

The closing years of the 19th century were extraordinary for Sacramento. Labor sought a stronger voice, new forms of transportation and communication reshaped the community's life, and political and social reforms moved to the forefront. Child labor was under attack, prohibition gained greater support, the push for public parks and recreation for all classes gained popularity and education faced integration. Women were organizing to demand to vote and wanted full participation in society's business. Coping with reform did not come easy for a wide-open town like Sacramento, which had thrived since the Gold

Children in Sacramento's East Sacramento neighborhood attended the East Sacramento Grammar School, located at the southwest corner of 39th and J streets. Sacred Heart Church now stands at this location. *Eleanor McClatchy Collection, SAMCC.*

Rush in a tradition of liquor, gambling, prostitution and rough politics. The two dominant power monopolies, government and the Southern Pacific Railroad, held sway over the region. Even though one was established by the will of the people and the other was the largest employer in the county, both offered ample opportunity for reform.

Sacramento elected reform mayors around a central theme, corruption. Corruption always seemed to be linked to the police department which always seemed to be tied to saloons, prostitution, gambling, and pool halls. *Sacramento Bee* editor, C.K. McClatchy, was direct in expressing his feelings. His fears for the evils and potential for corruption from saloons and pool halls was encapsulated in the title of one of his editorials: "The Gateway to Hell Reopened." When Sacramento citizen Hiram Johnson was elected governor in 1910, backed by the progressive Republican Lincoln-Roosevelt League, statewide reform moved into high gear, though reform victories were not easily attained and minor diversions frequently distracted the State Legislature and the public. One of these was the unsuccessful attempt to move the state capital to Berkeley or to a number of lesser cities.

In the end, an impressive number of reform actions were approved, including red light abatement, women's suffrage, the direct primary and empowerment of the legislature to set minimum wages. A facet of increasing community maturity in Sacramento was the decision not to demolish the decrepit remains of Sutter's Fort, the city's pioneer symbol, but rather to donate it to the state and see it restored. All Progressive Era actions, however, were not equally enlightened. A major example was the enactment of the Alien Land Law in California, which prevented people ineligible for citizenship from owning land, and which explicitly cemented racial prejudice. Discrimination on the basis of race remained common, primarily directed against those of Asian descent, but any other group in disfavor could also suffer, as German-Americans would find out during WW I.

Men like Hiram Johnson and Mayor White represented a new group bent on societal reform. Trading aggressive pioneer characteristics for larger social values, their efforts were at the center of the California Progressive movement, which thrust California into a leadership role with a few other states to reshape the nation's agenda. This activity forecast the substantial influence that California governing practices, forged in Sacramento, would later have upon the country.

THOSE FASCINATING CROCKER LADIES

The adult lives of two Crocker women, mother Margaret and daughter Aimee, span nearly the first 100 years of Sacramento's existence and pose an extraordinary study in contrasts. Ohio-born in 1822, Margaret Rhodes became Margaret Crocker when she married Edwin B. Crocker in 1852 and moved to Sacramento. Edwin, the brother of railroad "Big Four" partner Charles Crocker, became wealthy as chief counsel to the Central Pacific Railroad. Edwin and Margaret's magnificent home included an art gallery, the core of which was assembled during an extensive tour of Europe in 1869-70. The gallery was at times open to the public by the Crockers, a rare practice in those days. Widowed at age 53, Margaret plunged into civic life by supporting numerous worthy causes. Sixteen years before her death in 1901, she donated the art gallery to Sacramento, and it became an institution now known as the Crocker Art Museum. Aimee, the precocious last of Margaret's five children, was born in 1863, schooled in Europe and wandered down a very different life path. She eloped at age 19 with the first of five husbands, left her child to be raised by grandmother Margaret, and spent most of her life on the east coast. She was a woman who tested the limits of society's conventions in her era. Before she died in 1941, she authored a recap of her venturesome life entitled *And I'd Do It Again.*

WATER AND SANITATION

Since its earliest days and the tragic deaths from the cholera epidemic, Sacramento had feared disease and pestilence. But little was known about sanitation. During the decade of the 1880s, public education through the newspapers stressed the need to eliminate standing water, sewage and garbage. The great slough north of I Street was known by several names, including China Slough and Sutter Lake. Whatever its name, it became a receptacle for filth and garbage of every description and even the dumping ground for railroad scrap including worn-out locomotives and cars. This nuisance would not be filled until 1911.

Prior to 1887, Sacramento had a primitive sewer system of sorts; an open ditch that ran from 31st and Y streets to Riverside Road and exited south of the city back into the river. Some jokingly suggested that Sacramento's weather and the smell of the sewer kept the State Legislature's sessions mercifully short. During the 1880s, the city contemplated pumps to lift sewage over the levies and into the river, but took no action. The city finally constructed many underground brick sewers in the 1890s, some of which are still in operation today.

Drinking water was a special problem. Not only was the Sacramento River laden with mud, its level varied through the seasons and sometimes left the city water intake pipe high and dry. The quality of the water was considered unhealthy. Deep wells were installed in 1893 but failed. Chlorinating was implemented in 1915 but the fight for a water source, be it mountain water, American River water, or filtered Sacramento River water, would continue for more than 30 years with several proposals refused by the voters until a final solution was implemented during the 1920s.

The disposal of the city's garbage for the first two decades was simply resolved. It was dumped in the streets and backyards until it decomposed. For those with river access the solution was even simpler, the waste was tossed over the levee and out of sight and forgotten. A better mechanism was spurred by the excavation of earth to raise the downtown streets in the 1860s. So much fill was taken from the bed of the old American River channel north and east of 28th and B streets that it created a huge hole which evolved into Sacramento's land fill for more than a century. Because of the landfill's proximity to the city, though, the depositing of wet garbage was too odoriferous and called for a neater solution. In 1911, the city built the Incinerator on north B Street, one of the largest municipal incinerators in the western

In 1911, the City of Sacramento built an incinerator to replace its system of depositing raw garbage in the landfill north and east of 28th and B streets. Burning garbage was considered a progressive reform for municipal governments. The structure still stands on North B Street, near 10th. *Sacramento Bee Collection, SAMCC.*

At the July 4, 1916, parade, the Portuguese-American shipbuilders, Nunes Brothers, reminded Sacramentans about the Portuguese troops serving in France. The photograph was taken at 8th and K streets. *Eleanor McClatchy Collection, SAMCC.*

states. With its highly visible, tall, slender stack this great plant was designed to reduce anything that might be collected in public streets, even dead horses.

Prior to the great incinerator, some wet garbage was sold to hog farmers who had multilevel structures to raise hogs, each story of these hog condominiums just high enough for the hogs. But such practices created extreme health hazards and the incinerator ended that practice. The last hog condo, near Grantline Road and Highway 16, finally collapsed and disappeared less than 20 years ago.

Sacramento and the rest of northern California also dreamed of water plans to deal with flood control and irrigation. These were dreams that could not be accomplished locally, not even by the state. It would require massive federal support along with strenuous efforts by the state and local governments to eventually accomodate the desire to control nature.

Sacramento's history is inextricably intertwined with and shaped by the valley's watercourses. The hunger for

gold caused the first serious attempts to contain, divert and manage the water of the Sacramento River and its tributaries. By 1867, almost 4,500 miles of ditches were diverting water for mining. Hydraulic mining had done grievous damage to the rivers and flood plains before Judge Sawyer ended that activity in 1884. It was the farmer's turn next to try to rule water resources to meet their needs, using many of the mining ditches and pressing for both flood control and irrigation on an enormous scale. In 1887, California declared the use of water for irrigation to be a "public use." Fifty water districts were formed, but all except two failed. Into the 20th century, water rights issues dominated the court system and slowed private development, but big plans were envisioned nonetheless.

The first flood plan for the Sacramento valley was developed in 1880 by the state engineer, William Hammond Hall. The plan called for strong man-made levees but Hall conceded that levees could not alone keep the valley from flooding during the giant winter/spring water runoffs. C. E. Grunsky and others added a bypass system with flood basins such as the Yolo, Sutter and Sacramento basins. Full implementation of the plan would take more than 50 years and the combined contributions of both state and federal appropriations. But millions of acres of farmland could and would be irrigated. Regulated water meant a stable source for urban growth, and valley agriculture ensured Sacramento would remain the commercial and agricultural supply hub for the Central Valley.

Wilson even when Bryan resigned over conflicts with the president, as the sinking of the *Lusitania* fueled sentiments against the Germans.

Sacramento was greatly interested in the U.S. military incursion into Mexico. There was conspicuous fear that it would evolve into a second war with Mexico. Tensions were high as U. S. troops crossed the border and Pancho Villa crossed into U. S. territory. The Sacramento unit of the National Guard was called up and occupied Nogales. But,

WAR CLOUDS AND THE "WAR TO END ALL WARS"

Throughout 1915 and 1916, Sacramento, like the rest of the country, was increasingly affected by the growing problems in Europe and the tension between Mexico and the United States. The *Sacramento Bee*, the dominant newspaper with twice the circulation of the *Union*, both reflected and swayed public opinion in the county. The *Bee* was at best lukewarm about President Woodrow Wilson but its favorable disposition to Secretary of State William Jennings Bryan kept the *Bee* in the Wilson camp. The *Bee* backed

by December, U. S. troops were withdrawn from Mexico and attention was focused on European problems.

By the start of February 1917, Sacramento like the rest of the nation, knew war was imminent. German-Americans became the subject of prejudice. In one instance, the Natomas Company promoted small farms that in part could raise cabbage for sauerkraut, but now did not want to use any German words. So, the company printed brochures in which it was suggested that new farmers could support the upcoming war with "Liberty

During World War I, Weinstock Lubin & Company, located at 4th and K streets, offered window space to support the war effort. This display, sponsored by the Jewish Welfare Board, featured a message to civilians: "When we go through this we need all the help and comfort you can give." *Weinstock Lubin Collection, SAMCC.*

Cabbage." In April, Congress declared war against Germany and the Axis Powers.

The war put aside any further meaningful activity on the part of the progressive reformers. Domestic politics were shelved in favor of patriotism. One exception was the bombing of the governor's mansion in December 1917. Credit was claimed by an unknown group, but general consensus blamed the Wobblies.

Sacramento's community focus was on war bonds, war readiness and the draft. Patriotism was defined as "the

across Arizona and New Mexico into Texas where they could be loaded aboard ships for final distribution.

The advent of military aircraft work forecast what would become a vital source of economic sustenance and growth for Sacramento in the years ahead. The military presence also forced the community to look at solutions for saloons, gambling halls and brothels. A Sacramento association of ministers claimed that there were over 100 houses of prostitution in Sacramento and the War Department claimed there was 18 establishments near Mather Field. Yet

below:
In 1911, Oak Park, along with East Sacramento, was part of the first annexation to the City of Sacramento. This view features the Oak Park Grocery and the adjacent Oak Park Pharmacy.
Janet R. Stephens Collection, SAMCC.

opposite page:
This 1914 view features J Street looking west from 5th Street. The Travelers Hotel is at the near left; the California Fruit Exchange building at 4th Street is under construction.
Eugene Hepting Collection, SAMCC.

sinking of the individual into national unity." In October, 1917, Sacramento citizens and businesses bought $1,322,000 worth of war bonds in 28 minutes. Perhaps the greatest effort within the community for the war was the winning of a $3 million contract to build "JN-4" (Jenny) bi-wing military airplanes in North Sacramento at the Globe Iron Works. The contract prompted the company to change their name to the Liberty Iron Works. There was some concern as to where these airplanes would be delivered to the US Government, but that problem was partially solved with the opening of Mather Field in June 1918.

But officials at Mather had to figure out what to do with the assembled planes. The height of the Sierra Nevada stopped planes from flying over the mountains. The solution was for the planes to be flown down the valley while hugging the ground through a pass to Barstow, and then

these vestiges of Sacramento's frontier heritage proved markedly resistant to any substantive control.

In August 1918, a *Sacramento Bee* editorial predicted the war's outcome. "With the ideals of Washington, and the most guns, we cannot lose." Even as the war was drawing to a close, prejudice against German Americans intensified. The State Board of Education recalled books with German music. Experiencing boycotts and violence, German-Americans tried to prove their loyalty. Henry Schaffer, proprietor of the Vienna Bakery, proposed on November 10th in a full-page newspaper ad that he would give $5,000 to the Red Cross if it could be proven he was not a loyal American.

With the close of the war on November 11, 1918, Sacramento moved on past the fulfillment of the dreams of the reformers who had taken control of state and local politics in the early 20th century.

The Age of Maturity & Modernization, 1880s-1918

PEOPLE OF SACRAMENTO:
A LOOK AT THE LINCOLN SCHOOL BLOCKS

by Melinda A. Peak

The history of any locality is largely a product of the activities of mostly lesser-known individuals who go about the business of their daily lives and, in the meantime, shape their communities. Sacramento was settled by, and has continued to attract, men and women from a wide variety of geographic origins, races, religions and lifestyles. Although people often harbored discriminatory views about those who were different, they also managed to set enough of that aside so that various cultures could co-exist while living next door, if not as companions or equals at least with a measure of mutual tolerance and economic interrelatedness.

The Lincoln School blocks between 3rd and 5th and P and Q streets in the downtown area present a fascinating portrait of Sacramento life in a city neighborhood, illustrating how a look in-depth at one section of town reveals a rich tapestry of daily existence that defines some of the overall Sacramento experience. It allows us a glimpse at the routines of Sacramento's past, a slice of the wide-ranging cultural and occupational diversity that developed the city and county character of yesterday and that provides the base for today's and tomorrow's Sacramento. And sometimes what we learn merely tantalizes us, luring us to dig deeper and discover more about these ancestors.

Patterns of settlement and life in the two-block area known for the Lincoln School and now occupied by the PERS building were tied to other events that created the city. Located in a low-lying area near the Sacramento River, the land harbored no Native American habitation but was likely used by Indians for its hunting and gathering opportunities. After European contact, it became a part of John Sutter's original land grant from the Mexican government and was included within the boundaries of Sutter's New Helvetia colony. The land was used as part of the vast grazing grounds on which Sutter ranged his cattle herds. Away from the main lines of travel to and from Sutter's Fort, the area attracted only gradual development attention.

Divided into standard city lots in the first city plans of 1848-49, several of the lots were initially held by investors. The early and middle 1850s were characterized in this part of town by speculative turnover, with lot ownership changing frequently. But by the late 1850s the area became a fairly stable residential neighborhood. Who were some of the people who lived there? Where did they come from? What was their family structure? What did they do to make a living?

William H. Watson owned one half-lot. The proprietor of the Magnolia Saloon, Watson's household in 1860 included his wife, Emeline, two adult sons (one a clerk and the other a printer,) three other sons and a 14-year-old Chinese servant. James McClatchy, patriarch of the McClatchy newspaper family, acquired a half-lot in 1867. McClatchy was born in Ireland in 1824 and came to the United States at age 18. He arrived in Sacramento in late 1849, worked on several early papers, joined the staff of the *Sacramento Bee*, served as sheriff for two years, and purchased the *Bee* in 1866. His wife, Charlotte, was from Charlottestown, Prince Edward Island, Canada.

By 1869, McClatchy had gained ownership of more property, allowing him to expand the residence of his increasingly affluent family. By 1880, the McClatchy household included James and Charlotte, grown sons Valentine and Charles, teen-age daughters Fanny and Emily, and 17-year-old servant Katy Lynch. Next door lived 56-year-old F. S. Hotchkiss, one of the owners of the Sacramento Planing Mills, his 39-year-old wife Eliza and their four children.

Another part of the block was bought by Edwin W. Leach in 1852, splitting it with Thomas Jones in 1854. Leach, a coach maker, sold his property in 1860 to Martin Kilgariff, a native of County Galway, Ireland, who had worked along the levees of the lower Mississippi. In 1858, he brought his family to Sacramento where he worked as a stevedore until his death in 1862. His widow, Ann Kilgariff, then became the owner of the property. In 1870, she had three children at home: Margaret was a seamstress and Henry and John were in school. Mary Scanlon, a dressmaker, and an unrelated teenager also lived in the Kilgariff household. By 1880, Margaret had married, and she and her daughter, Sadie Breen, stayed in the home, along with the two grown sons who were employed as clerks and Julia Smith, a young servant. Thomas Jones, who lived on the other part of the property with his Canadian-born wife, Jane, was a gilder and house painter from England. Their son was a lawyer and their daughter was a school teacher.

A succession of people owned and resided on some parts of the two-block area. A lot was bought by James O'Neil in 1854. A merchant at that time, he later became

Population of Sacramento City & County

(% Growth per decade in parentheses)

YEAR	CITY		COUNTY		CITY & COUNTY		CITY/COUNTY %
1850	6,820		2,267		9,087		75/25
1852					12,589		
1860	13,785	(102%)	10,357	(358%)	24,142	(166%)	57/43
1870	16,283	(18%)	10,547	(2%)	26,830	(11%)	61/39
1880	21,420	(32%)	12,970	(23%)	34,390	(28%)	62/38
1890	26,286	(23%)	14,053	(8%)	40,339	(17%)	65/35
1900	29,282	(11%)	16,633	(18%)	45,915	(14%)	64/36
1910	44,696	(53%)	23,110	(39%)	67,806	(48%)	66/34
1920	65,908	(47%)	25,121	(9%)	91,029	(34%)	72/28
1930	93,750	(42%)	48,249	(92%)	141,999	(56%)	66/34
1940	105,958	(13%)	64,375	(33%)	170,333	(20%)	62/38
1950	137,572	(30%)	139,568	(117%)	277,140	(63%)	50/50
1960	191,667	(39%)	311,111	(123%)	502,778	(81%)	38/62
1970	257,105	(34%)	377,268	(21%)	634,373	(26%)	33/67
1980	275,741	(7%)	507,640	(35%)	783,381	(23%)	35/65
1990	346,586	(26%)	649,414	(28%)	996,9000	(27%)	35/65

a gunsmith and a liquor merchant. His lot was split in 1858 and the south half was sold to Frank Deaver. By 1859, O'Neil had regained ownership of the entire lot with a partner, Alex M. Hayden, a bookkeeper for Wells Fargo, who then became sole owner. In 1870, Fred Berger, 43, and his wife, Lena, 32, owned and occupied the lot, living there with Alice Miller, age 19, all from Hanover, Germany. One dwelling on the Berger property was occupied by the Levy family. Marcus Levy, a native of Prussia, worked as a store clerk and served as a trustee of the Sacramento Hebrew Benevolent Society. His family included his Polish-born wife, Jennete, her three sons, Simon, Nathan and Frank Liebling, and their daughters Rebecca and Rose Levy. Also in the household were two teen-age servants, an Irish girl, Mary Ryan, and a Chinese boy named Jim Ack.

THE LINCOLN SCHOOL ENROLLED MANY STUDENTS FROM DIFFERENT CULTURES, INTRODUCED THEM TO AMERICAN VALUES AND LIFESTYLE, AND AT THE SAME TIME TAUGHT THE NATIVE-BORN PUPILS TO ACCEPT THOSE FROM OTHER CULTURES.

By 1890, Ferguson Burns, a bartender at the Western Hotel, had taken over part of the Berger lot and Thomas Galligan, an engineer at the Capital Gas Works, bought the other part, living there with his daughters, Lizzie and Cassie, and son Frank. Richard E. Goggins, a druggist, purchased a lot in about 1858. In 1860, his household consisted of his wife, Mary, two daughters and a son. But by 1870, Goggins' household structure had changed significantly. His wife and daughters were no longer in the house, and there was another family and an unrelated individual living at the address. The other family was George Maxwell, a 55-year-old deputy sheriff, and Elizabeth and Grace Maxwell, along with 42-year-old Phoebe Anderson.

Ownership and business opportunities were not confined to any single group. William Jones, an African-American tailor from South Carolina, bought a half-lot in the 1850s, then transferred ownership to his Virginia-born wife, Ann. The northern portion was later sold to Jesse Slaughter, an African-American plasterer, whitewasher, laborer and clothes renovator who came to Sacramento in 1849. By 1870, the part of the lot belonging to Jones was again split, with Charles Wolleb taking the eastern portion. He was a music teacher, member of the Philharmonic Society and an officer in the Sacramento Rifle Club. In 1882, Ventura Pimental, a native of Mexico, purchased Wolleb's section, then sold it a few years later to Theophile Demonceau, a railroad machinist. After his death the property went to his widow, Marie, who kept it into the 1920s.

In 1855, Henry Yantis bought a half-lot, with the other half going a year later to Mary Jane Jones, an African-American laundry proprietress. Yantis, born in Kentucky, was an African-American pioneer and leader of Sacramento, arriving in 1852. He was a deacon in the Siloam Baptist Church, helping to establish it in 1856 as the first African-American church in Sacramento, and was also involved with the United Sons of Friendship, an African-American social and benevolent society organized in 1861. Mrs. Yantis was active in the subscription drive which raised the money to buy property for a private school for African-American children. Their household included a son, two daughters and W. H. Stevenson, an African-American physician from Washington, D.C. Mary Jane Jones operated her laundry business and married William Robinson, a teamster from Pennsylvania. Widowed before 1870, her household at that point was comprised of herself, her daughter, Agatha, and a gambler, Charles Foster.

Any given property could host a wide variety of occupations. One lot was broken into quarters, a part acquired by William Orr in 1856. The Pennsylvania-born Orr was a widower with two children who had an ale and liquor store. He sold the operation in 1865 to Peter Miller, a native of Scotland, who listed his occupation as "porter and ale." Another part had the Quong Song laundry in operation, employing 11 Chinese men. In 1884, that lot was sold to N. D. Rideout, president of the California State bank, who six years later sold it to Robert E. Kent, who operated a family bakery on the premises. In 1866, Jesse Hayton, an English shoemaker, purchased a part. In 1870, his household contained his Canadian-born wife, Annie, two sons and a daughter. F. X. Banks, a 34-year-old physician, owned an adjacent part, where he lived with the Parker family: George M., a jeweler from Hamburg, Germany, his wife, Martha, and three children.

It was not unusual for one individual to have several occupations. One lot was purchased in 1854 by George McKee, variously a gardener, farmer, ranchman, stock trader and dairyman. McKee, born in Ireland, brought his family to Sacramento in 1855 from Vermont. By 1870, his household consisted of himself at age 63, his 55-year-old wife, Mary, one teen-age son, an 11-year-old daughter, and an older son, Edwin, with his wife, Emma. Edwin worked as a steamboatman and iron molder until 1877, when he achieved some prominence by being elected City Auditor and ex-officio Clerk of the Board of Trustees of Sacramento. Patrick Birckley, a lawyer, and Edwin's mother-in-law lived with his family.

The Lincoln School gradually became the dominant feature of the two-block property. Classes began in 1857, the initial two-story school building was erected in 1867, and half of one block was purchased from E. B. and Margaret Crocker in the 1870s for school use and expansion. As the 20th century arrived, the lower part of Sacramento, including the Lincoln School neighborhood, began to expand in terms of its ethnic composition and overall population, with more subdivision of lots and the creation of a substantial number of rental properties. The area became an even greater mix of nationalities, with Japanese, Chinese, Mexican, Filipino, Hindu, Portuguese and Italian sections, as well as a scattering of Polish, Yugoslavs and Koreans. Immigrants now made up the majority of the population of this quarter of Sacramento. Nonetheless, some of the older inhabitants remained. As Ernesto Galarza, a Mexican-born immigrant who grew up in the neighborhood, recalled: "The bartenders, the rent collectors, the insurance salesmen, the mates on the river boats, the landladies and, most importantly, the police — these were all gringos. So were the craftsmen, like the barbers and the printers...."

By 1920, Italian and Slavic immigrants were numerous in the area around Lincoln School. One resident was Lorance Yuronich, who bought one of the buildings near 4th and P streets. He put up a one-story frame structure in the back of his lot and included a basement with a bowling alley that served as a neighborhood gathering place for Slavic residents. Galarza observed that once a year when he was a boy the alley behind the lot "was turned into a winery. A large press was brought out of the cellar, and the men, chattering and drinking, pressed the grapes with their bare feet, their pants rolled up above the knees. They offered me nips of wine and lowered me into the press to tramp grapes myself." The Japanese community was also well represented in the vicinity of the school.

The Lincoln School enrolled many students from different cultures, introduced them to American values and lifestyle, and at the same time taught the native-born pupils to accept those from other cultures. Ernesto

SACRAMENTO REMAINS TRUE TO ITS PAST, AS GALARZA SAW IT, "A KALEIDOSCOPE OF COLORS AND LANGUAGES AND CUSTOMS THAT SURPRISED AND ABSORBED ME AT EVERY TURN."

Galarza noted: "My pals in the second grade were Kazushi, whose parents spoke only Japanese; Matti, a skinny Italian boy, and Manuel, a fat Portuguese who would never get into a fight but wrestled you to the ground and just sat on you. Our assortment of nationalities included Koreans, Yugoslavs, Poles, Irish, and home-grown Americans ... The school was not so much a melting pot as a griddle where Miss Hopley and her helpers warmed knowledge into us and roasted racial hatreds out of us. At Lincoln, making us into Americans did not mean scrubbing away what made us originally foreign."

By 1927, the Lincoln School was the largest in the city, despite several disastrous fires and consequent rebuildings. There was a chronic shortage of playground space and a need for more classrooms. The Sacramento Unified School District acquired one whole block in the late 1940s, demolished the existing structures and built a gymnasium. The school then served as both an elementary and junior high school with a student population that numbered as high as 1,200. But by the 1960s, the school-age population had declined and the school was converted to a high school continuation facility. Finally, in the 1970s, the buildings were relegated to strictly administrative uses until the Public Employees Retirement System (PERS) acquired the entire two-block site in 1980, leveled it in 1981 and built the new PERS headquarters.

Today, that office building occupies the land that provided shelter and community for hundreds of Sacramentans over a 130-year period, emblematic of the conversion to government use of many downtown Sacramento areas that once sustained homes and businesses owned by people of both genders, all ages, and a wide variety of ethnic derivations. One can meet their descendants all over the city and county and outlying regions, where they now live adjacent to more recent newcomers. In this way Sacramento remains true to its past, still as Galarza saw it, "a kaleidoscope of colors and languages and customs that surprised and absorbed me at every turn."

CHAPTER FIVE

Best of Times, Worst of Times: Sacramento, 1918–1930s

by Charles Duncan

The postwar period began with elation over the Great War's conclusion and hopes for prosperity and growth spawned by the return of peace. A mere 14 years later, a weary and worried city would look hopefully, and skeptically, to the election of a dynamic new president who promised a "New Deal" to liberate the nation from the consequences of the Great Depression. In between the war and that election, Sacramento experienced the wild ride of a city continuing to shed its "frontier" image amid the excitement of The Roaring Twenties.

Sacramento greeted the armistice that concluded the "War To End All Wars" with tremendous relief. Ninety-nine soldiers from the county had given their lives on the battlefields of France and Belgium. Early in the year following the armistice, the "boys" began coming home to a city eager to show its appreciation for their sacrifice. When the 91st Division of the American Expeditionary Force returned in April, 1919, a huge parade was staged. Ronnie Kemper, a student at Washington School at the time, recalled the big parade as a major milestone in his young life:

"…We got to march in the parade. We were impressed because Col. Philpot had his regiment there, and marching right along side of him was our schoolmate, Little Bob Philpot. He had a duplicate uniform of his daddy. We didn't have to go back to school, either. They gave us passes to a free movie — any movie in town. I went to Moran of the Lady Letty with Rudolf Valentino."

Within a year, veterans had chartered an American Legion Post and temporary headquarters were set up in the city clerk's office.

INFLUENZA

In the midst of the exhilaration over the pending armistice, a global epidemic occurred that was described as "the worst infectious disease outbreak in world history." More than 20 million people died worldwide, with some estimates double that figure. The U.S. counted 675,000 dead. The disease was somewhat late in striking Sacramento, arriving probably in October, 1918 — months after it began devastating other parts of the country. By mid-November, 132 were reported dead, but just one week later, the figure rose to 300.

Gatherings of people were banned. Theaters, saloons and all public buildings except schools were closed, but parents kept children home forcing schools to close on October 22. Church services were to be held outside, unless it rained, and a 30-minute time limit was instituted. For years, *The Bee* had posted election results on a huge outdoor billboard drawing throngs to 7th Street for a gala evening of sharing the returns. That year, the celebration was canceled.

The use of gauze masks became surprisingly controversial. An ordinance was introduced October 17, 1918, to require gauze masks be worn in public. The influenza-preventive measure was debated until January 14, 1919, when it finally was adopted. When it came, it was strictly enforced, however. Violators were arrested and fined. At the end, the *Sacramento Union* placed Sacramento second in the nation on the basis of per capita deaths, at more than 500. And its 5,000 recorded cases put Sacramento 3rd among all California cities.

GOVERNMENT AND POPULATION

After the war, the city government engaged in a self-examination process and a new charter took effect with the election of 1921. Sacramento was one of the original

Sacramentans staged a huge parade in April 1919 to celebrate the return of the 91st Division of the American Expeditionary Force. Lillian Dong Yue led the Chinese contingent. *Ethnic Survey Collection, Sacramento Archives and Museum Collection Center (SAMCC).*

charter cities when the State Constitution first was adopted, and it required state legislative approval of changes. The most recent modification had been in 1911 when a governing body of five commissioners was established. The new charter was crammed with innovations. Sacramento became the largest city in California to adopt the city manager-council system. Clyde L. Seavey was chosen as first city manager.

The influenza epidemic of 1918 reached Sacramento in October. These children, photographed in Capitol Park on November 6, 1918, are wearing the requisite protective gauze masks. *Sacramento Valley Photographers Survey Collection, SAMCC.*

At the same time, Sacramento became the first city in California, and one of the largest in the U.S., to adopt an election system called "proportional representation." It was a complicated scheme for naming a council of nine "at-large" representatives. Voters were asked not just to vote for nine, but to rank their choices with numbers after candidates' names: first, second, etc. It was more a system of elimination, rather than one of election.

Municipal government also spread into the county. Isleton incorporated in 1923. North Sacramento became an incorporated city in 1924, reflecting the successful subdivision of lands in the Haggin Grant. Sacramento County proposed changes as well, a new charter called for a manager system, but controversy arose over a provision to select juries by lot. Widespread bias against the foreign born, especially toward Asians, was commonplace and a not-so-subtle movement opposed the new charter because random selection of juries might impanel Asians. Whether for that reason, or not, the new county charter failed.

By 1920, a total of 91,029 people lived in Sacramento City and County, 34 percent more than in 1910. The relative prosperity of the Sacramento area in the 1920s brought the population to six figures by 1930, at the 141,999 mark, a whopping 56 percent gain in just 10 years, and the greatest 10-year increase since the days of the Gold Rush. Over two-thirds of the people lived in the city proper. However, the doors to Sacramento and the rest of the country were not completely open. The U.S. Congress had enacted increasingly restrictive immigration legislation, culminating in the sweeping 1924 act that served to exclude Japanese. Coupled with earlier exclusion legislation directed against the Chinese, most Asian immigration was halted.

Europeans were placed under formula quotas establishing each nation's maximum immigration at about 3 percent or less of the number from each country already in the U.S. Exempted from these restrictions were immigrants from countries of the Western Hemisphere and the Philippine Islands, which enjoyed special "American" status as a result of the Spanish-American War. After 1924, Philippine natives replaced the Japanese as immigrant workers and, although their numbers were not high, many other groups continued to call Sacramento home. Farmers, the railroads and other industrial employers recruited workers from the Philippines, Mexico and beyond in efforts to secure low-cost labor.

Sacramento had experienced diversity in its population since the Gold Rush. The effect of these new immigration laws was to create what history professor Joseph Pitti called a "migration of races," groups moving from one location within the U.S. to another, as opposed to external migration. Further, those who already had spent some time establishing themselves in this country took advantage of the period of

By the 1920s, Sacramento boasted a professional and up-to-date fire department. Practicing for emergencies took place at the drill tower near the intersection of J Street and Alhambra Boulevard. *Eleanor McClatchy Collection, SAMCC.*

reduced immigration to "settle in" and create more perceptible "turfs," or neighborhoods. In Sacramento, Fourth and I had been unmistakably Chinese since Gold Rush times and remained so. The Irish found Oak Park to their liking as well as the Alkali Flat area, which also housed growing numbers of Mexicans. German Catholics congre-

Funahashi Company was a Sacramento purveyor of fish, poultry and eggs. Sacramento's Japanese community occupied the area roughly bounded by 2nd, 5th, L and O streets. Japantown offered a self-sufficient business district, social organizations and churches. Japanese also settled in Florin and the Pocket area south of Sacramento. *Ethnic Survey Collection, SAMCC.*

When this photograph of the Shiloh Baptist church choir was taken in the 1920s, the church was located at 6th and P streets in Sacramento. Today, the congregation meets at a new location on 9th Avenue in Sacramento's Oak Park neighborhood. *Ethnic Survey Collection, SAMCC.*

gated around St. Francis Catholic Church. Portuguese were tenants and owners in the agricultural Pocket district and also in the recently reclaimed Natomas. The Japanese occupied land near Florin. Jewish residents lived near their Synagogue at 15th and P. Italians centered on the south side up to 17th and X and parts of Oak Park, which also attracted African-American families.

Mexico was a principal target of agricultural and industrial recruitment, resulting in a minor surge of immigration in the twenties. Sacramento's Mexican population grew from just over 1,100 in 1920, to 2,554 in 1930. In mid-decade, 41 percent of all California immigrants were from Mexico, almost three times the number of the English, the next highest group. Whether they were of Asian, Irish, German, Italian, Portuguese, Greek or other origins, they found employment throughout the work force, often in law enforcement, sanitation, street maintenance and agricultural pursuits.

The number of African-Americans in the city and county was less than 1,000 in 1920; a NAACP branch was established by 73 people, white and black, in 1918. By 1930, African-Americans numbered almost 1,500. George Dunlap, who became one of Sacramento's best-known and most successful restaurateurs, began serving food at 612 J in 1917 to an eager and growing integrated clientele. He moved to Oak Park and operated for decades, augmenting his fondly remembered service with a seasonal restaurant at the State Fair, and also as manager of dining cars on the Sacramento Northern Railway.

A blot on racial tolerance was presented by the appearance of the racist Ku Klux Klan in Sacramento. There were no recorded acts by the Klan against the African-American community at that time, and Klan activity overall was sporadic and brief. In one instance, a half dozen Klansmen in full regalia marched to the pulpit of Westminster Presbyterian Church on Palm Sunday, 1922, and presented

During the 1920s, workers from Mexican border towns were recruited by labor contractors for agriculture and industrial work in the United States. The men is this 1927 photograph are repairing a Southern Pacific track near Clay Station in southeastern Sacramento County. *Ethnic Survey Collection, SAMCC.*

the pastor with a donation and a note commending his work. A Klan initiation at Muddox Hall a few days later drew around 300 attendees. Initiations were also held at the Elliot Ranch in Elk Grove and in the rock piles near Folsom, where *Bee* reporters recorded auto license numbers. The next day, 40 public figures and municipal employees were named in the paper as among those at the meeting. City Manager Seavey asked the council to dismiss city workers who joined the Klan, but the council, and later a judge, blocked the action. The visible tenancy of the Klan in Sacramento all but ended in November, 1922, when its Kleigel and local organizer, Edgar Fuller, hastily departed after being discredited by fellow Klansmen for allegedly embezzling funds, among other irregularities.

A FACE "LIFT"

Picture, if you will, what a traveler approaching Sacramento in 1900 might have seen from Upper Stockton Road, or out on Auburn Boulevard, or from the deck of a sternwheeler rounding Portuguese Bend. That overall scene, dominated by the majestic State Capitol, had changed little by the dawn of the Roaring Twenties.

That static face underwent "constructive" surgery in the next decade, and by its end in 1930, 11 buildings exceeded

George Dunlap operated Dunlap's Dining Room out of his 4th Avenue home, a place where many Sacramentans enjoyed Sunday ham or chicken dinners. At the State Fair, located nearby at Broadway and Stockton Boulevard, the Dunlap family managed the cafeteria lunchroom in the base of the grandstand. *Audrey Wilcox Collection, SAMCC.*

100 feet in height. Only two stood that tall before: The Capitol, at 234 feet, and the Cathedral of the Blessed Sacrament at 220 feet. In 1924, the California State Life building stretched itself into 3rd place at 216 feet. Just two years later, the Elks Temple jumped past at 226 feet. Those were the big four and the only buildings over 200 feet for decades to come.

During the decade following World War I, Sacramento developed an identifiable skyline. The California State Life building at the far left (10th and J streets), was built in 1924, and reached 216 feet. Two years later, the Elks Temple at the middle of the picture (11th and J Streets), rose to 226 feet. *Eleanor McClatchy Collection, SAMCC.*

The 1920s saw construction all over the city. Only building permits in Los Angeles exceeded the value of those in Sacramento in 1923. The Capitol Extension, consisting of the Library and Courts Building and State Office Building #1, were built across from the Capitol on 10th Street, using a lot donated to the state by the city to discourage talk of moving several state departments to other cities. A new

State Printing Plant (later converted into the State Archives) was also constructed on 10th Street and O, a block south of the Capitol. Other notables of the twenties were: Sutter and Mercy hospitals (1923 & 1925); the Senator Hotel, 12th and L (1924); the Southern Pacific Depot at 5th and I (1926); The Memorial Auditorium at 16th and J (1927); the Alhambra Theater (1927); and Hughes Stadium (1928).

In 1922, six elementary schools were being built simultaneously. The new high school had been completed, and later the Junior College rose on Freeport Boulevard, followed shortly therafter by its stadium. Residential areas of prestige and beauty were growing south and east of downtown, especially in what came to be known as the Fabulous Forties, between J and Folsom Boulevard, and 42nd to 48th streets. To the north, the city of North Sacramento was attracting families.

THE ECONOMY'S RISE AND FALL

The Chamber of Commerce and other boosters painted a rosy picture of postwar prosperity for Sacramento and the Valley. In 1921, the city topped the state in building gains. The Sacramento River was rated the leading water commerce artery in the nation, based on cargo value per ton. Over 400 manufacturing establishments employing some 8,000 workers were located in the city and county in 1924. These concerns produced over $48 million in goods, 51 percent of which were consumed locally. The Southern Pacific shops still built seven cars a day.

Conditions changed toward the end of the decade, however, as they did everywhere in the country. Seemingly

In 1927, the City of Sacramento completed the Memorial Auditorium, located on the block bounded by 15th, 16th, I and J streets, as a tribute to its war dead. Probably no other building in Sacramento has touched so many area residents. It has been the location of rock concerts, graduations, circuses, boxing matches and flower shows. In May 1942, the Wartime Civilian Control Authority registered Japanese-Americans before removing them to an assembly center at Camp Walerga, near McClellan AFB, en route to permanent camps. *Don Rivett Collection, SAMCC.*

In April 1930, the Pollocks invited friends to a garden party in honor of the American Society of Civil Engineers at their new 45th Street house. More recently, Sacramentans remember this property as the home of Governor and Mrs. Ronald Reagan during his terms as California's governor. *Norwood Silsbee Collection, SAMCC.*

solid companies began to go bankrupt. Among the more shocking failures in 1928 was a Sacramento firm with roots in the Gold Rush, the Natomas Company. It defaulted on bonds and was forced into foreclosure. Automobile sales in Sacramento were over 5,000 in 1930, but fell more than 50 percent to just over 2,000 in 1932. Unemployment and hunger became major social problems. By 1930, the city faced a $50,000 deficit, and near riots were occurring at unemployment offices. Soup kitchens appeared. Theaters put on shows to benefit the unemployed. Salary reductions were common all over town.

Temporary housing along the rivers developed as families threw together shanties of cardboard, tin and whatever else could be found. They came to be known as "Hoovervilles" after ill-fated U.S. Pres. Herbert Hoover who presided over the start of the Depression. Sacramento, an agricultural labor center, once again became a favorite destination of the homeless and unemployed. The Welfare Department served 354 meals per month in 1930; two years later over 1,500 were being served each month. Sacramento joined the rest of the country in 1932, providing Democratic presidential aspirant Franklin Delano Roosevelt with a landslide victory as the hope of the future.

WATER AND POWER

From the days of hydraulic mining, the city's water supply from the Sacramento River had grown increasingly repellent. Drinking water showed discoloration, grit and even unpleasant odors, and it was given the whimsical sobriquet "Sacramento Straight." Compounding the situation, several dry years saw the river all but disappear in the summer months. Years of study showed the choices were wells or filtration. In 1919, voters favored filtration. In 1923, triggered by a telegraphic impulse from Pres. Calvin Coolidge, the Filtration Plant near the Jibboom St. Bridge began operation.

That same year, 87 percent of the voters approved formation of the Sacramento Municipal Utility District, becoming locally known by the peculiar acronym SMUD, to implement the city's claim to water and power rights on Silver Creek in El Dorado County. Negotiations with utility companies to purchase facilities proved fruitless and by 1927, a bond election to construct a dam and power plants at Silver Creek seemed the only solution. Three times (1927 — 60 percent; 1929 — 62 percent; and 1931 — 64 percent), the necessary two-thirds majority for enactment was not achieved, but the obvious public support for the proposal moved PG&E to propose to build on Silver Creek without taxpayer support and pay the district for the privilege. However, an arrangement

By the mid-1920s, the City of Sacramento determined it had a problem with the increasing number of automobiles on its streets. One solution was to provide parallel parking at the curb, plus diagonal parking down the middle of the street, as shown here on 9th Street looking south toward L Street. The Forum Building is at the left. *Eleanor McClatchy Collection, SAMCC.*

satisfactory to both parties could not be reached. Finally, in 1934, a bond issue of $12 million was approved 32,000 to 14,000 (69.5 percent), and SMUD was in business.

PROHIBITION AND LAW ENFORCEMENT

Ed Dickson recalled in a 1970 *Sacramento Bee* article that the Prohibition era was "welcomed" into Sacramento a few days early. On New Years Eve, 1919, raucous final flings were celebrated all over town. Liquor had been banned by Federal law since July, but enforcement under the 18th amendment was to begin January 17, 1920.

Many well-to-do imbibers took advantage of "fire sale prices" and laid in long-term personal supplies as saloons and liquor stores dumped stock before the fateful date arrived. A new, vigorous and illegal "industry" quickly developed to produce and supply the great demand for alcoholic beverages. For the energetic, stills were available in most of the city's hardware stores.

The speakeasy, an establishment where liquor was illegally sold and consumed, emerged in many different forms, some more elegant than others. The Eskimo Club, on J between Front and Second, was one of the better known establishments. The Yosemite was another favorite and the Old Tavern, a building at 28th and Capital, was well patronized. The obvious flaunting of the law drew no sig-

opposite page, inside: North Sacramento was an incorporated city, centered along Del Paso Boulevard, until it was annexed by the City of Sacramento in the 1960s. This view features the North Sacramento Stage, an early form of public transit. *Eugene Van der Cook Collection, SAMCC.*

Rio Linda became a regional center for the poultry business. Antionette Dicks is shown here at her family's poultry farm known as Dixieland. Her husband, Franz, was conductor of the Sacramento Symphony. *Franz Dicks Collection, SAMCC.*

nificant public outcry for compliance. It was observed that many women who never would have entered the swinging doors of a saloon, eagerly sought the excitement and mystery of the speakeasy — escorted, of course.

Not all liquor-serving establishments resembled the stereotype found in the movies. Ronnie Kemper, a Sacramento-born musician, shared his impressions of Sacramento Speakeasies in an oral history:.

"…You'd go quietly and knock on the door. They were mainly homeowners, picking up extra money, in their kitchens. We went to Elma Kurcheler's father. He served in the kitchen. Home brew. Another place was where we got gin with cream soda on top, a gin fizz.

"There was one in Carmichael called the Holland Gardens. There were twins from Holland and that was, I think, the first place Anson Weeks played. (Weeks was a nationally successful Sacramento band leader.)

"We (The Dick Jergens band) played the Shalomar, which had a dance floor. That was a definite Speakeasy, next to Arata Brothers, facing the Plaza, over Blacks, right across from the Blacksmith shop. You go through this narrow side door over the Plaza Theater, or what became the Plaza Theater. You walk up the stairway, and sure enough, there's a double door. Knock, and walk through another, and you got in.

"One time at the Shalomar, a guy said to me, 'I think you've got my seat.' I looked up, and this guy was 25 feet tall, but such a

friendly guy. It was Max Baer, who became World Boxing Champion a little later."

Of course, all the action was not downtown. The tiny Chinese town of Locke in the Delta became important to bootleggers, and county authorities showed little inclination to disturb its enterprises. Riverboat passengers were rumored to stop at Locke for excitement and entertainment.

Bootlegging activity in Sacramento was carried on at a high pitch, but the violence found in connection with it in some parts of the country was largely absent, and there was little public pressure on authorities for strict enforcement. *Bee* reporter Bert Vaughn recalled that, to his knowledge, the Eskimo Club never was raided and it was the most popular and notorious speakeasy in town. Raids were conducted from time to time at other establishments, but even if rare convictions resulted, sentences were light (usually 30 days) and while in the poky, the bootleggers enjoyed many privileges.

Suppliers offered their clients "protection" when liquor was purchased. "Protection" in Sacramento seemed to lack any sinister connotation and meant only that the liquor supplier (of which Sacramento had only two or three) would warn the establishment of any pending raid. Lack of payment, it was said, almost always resulted in a raid. Enforcement was sporadic. The City Council in 1932 revoked 32 business licenses on charges of possession of illegal liquor, but the phenomenon was all but over by that time. Sacramento adjusted without a lot of bother to the fetters of Prohibition and citizens joined the celebration when President Roosevelt's New Dealers allowed stronger beer and led the drive in favor of the 21st Amendment, which repealed the 18th Amendment in 1933.

Possibly due to the pressure wrought by Prohibition, the 1920s brought rapid turnover in the police chief's position, with six different officers occupying the seat: Ira Conran, H. Hugh Sydenham, Bernard McShane, Ted N. Koening, Ed J. Cox and William H. Hallanan. The Police Department opened a Canine unit in 1924. The German Shepherd chosen had been well prepared by a trainer who spoke only German. A departmental history revealed that Patrolman A. L. Gates first had to teach the dog English, before using him on patrol! Other innovations in this decade included a Bureau of Records, a Juvenile Division (one of the first anywhere), and what were believed to be the first Police Science Training classes, offering special instruction in fire arms and self defense. With Sacramento in the forefront of automobile ownership at 14,263 in 1920, a Traffic Division was instituted in 1922. Call boxes were provided and used jointly by both police and firemen. The first police sub-station was opened on 32nd between S and T in 1925.

In contrast to the city police department, the county sheriff's office was remarkably stable in this period. Ellis W. Jones was elected to succeed W. F. Gormley as sheriff in 1918, and he was reelected until he left office in 1932 due to ill health. It was during Jones tenure that the Folsom Prison riot of 1927 occurred. Six convicts began firing homemade weapons during a movie in the prison auditorium. Before it was over, 300 National Guardsmen, police officers and sheriff's deputies representing seven surrounding counties participated in restoring order. Seven died, including one officer. Six convict leaders were tried and five were executed.

AGRICULTURE, RAILS, ROADS AND THE RIVER

The slow but inevitable trend toward urbanization in the county was putting a stress on agriculture, but it remained vitally important in the area. Pastures held livestock throughout remote regions of the county. Poultry production was significant. Florin, Sloughhouse, Galt, the reclaimed acreage of Natomas Company and other rural communities raised diversified crops. Newer "commuter farm" communities like Orangevale, Fair Oaks and Carmichael, had crops growing on small acreages. As an indication of the strong public interest in things agricultural,

the *Bee* reported in 1919 that an enormous week-long Tractor Demonstration was staged on the bare fields at the corner of Watt and Marconi avenues.

The California Crop Reporting Service figures showed 1,392 farms in the county in 1900, 2,975 in 1920 and 3,882 in 1930. Eighty-eight percent of the county's 629,000 acres, or 555,503 acres were in farms in 1920, but it gained only 3 percent by 1930. The number of irrigated farms grew by 50 percent, to 2,613 in the decade. Over 175,000 acres were devoted to livestock in 1930; 105,254 acres were planted in grain; and 75,000 were devoted to dairy pursuits. Fruit occupied just under 80,000 acres and truck crops 46,105, the latter tops among valley counties. A hard freeze of considerable duration in 1932 devastated county crops, and all but permanently eliminated citrus in the area as a cash crop. Citrus production fell from 94,763 boxes in 1930 to only 11,098 boxes in 1934. Peach and pear losses were comparable.

Sacramento's position as an agricultural center, however, was not based on its considerable livestock or crop production, but on its capacity as a processing and shipping center. Sacramento shipped 75 percent of all deciduous crops grown within a 45-mile radius. Del Monte and Libby McNeil & Libby established mammoth canning operations, and the American Can Company built a huge facility to manufacture millions of containers. In the delta region, Bayside Canneries, owned by Chinese, was one of the largest in the world. Southern Pacific's massive fleet of refrigerated freight cars together with an ice plant in Roseville capable of servicing those cars, opened the way for valley fruits to reach the east coast in excellent condition.

Sacramento was a processing and shipping center for Central Valley agriculture. This view by Sacramento photographer David Joslyn features trucks loaded with spinach waiting to be unloaded at the Libby McNeil & Libby cannery at the corner of Alhambra and Stockton boulevards. *David Joslyn Collection, SAMCC.*

The *Delta Queen* and *Delta King* provided elegant overnight travel accommodations between San Francisco and Sacramento beginning in 1927. This view features a party of women enjoying the river from the deck of the *King*. *Eleanor McClatchy Collection, SAMCC.*

The Sacramento River remained vitally important. In 1923, Federal Rivers and Harbors engineers ranked Sacramento cargo tonnage fifth among all ports of America. The increase since 1910 was the greatest in the United States. The river served gold seekers as a highway in 1849, funneling thousands of eager argonauts to the foothills in search of gold, and it continued to be a transport corridor into the 1920s. *The Fort Sutter*, *The Capitol City*, *The Captain Webber* and others carried over 105,000 river passengers in 1925. That same year, heavy barge traffic helped account for tonnage that made the port of Sacramento second in the nation on the basis of cargo value. The opulent *Delta Queen*

and *Delta King* joined the fleet in 1927. The *King* remains moored in Old Sacramento today, serving as a popular local gathering place.

The railroad continued its prominence in the affairs of the city. Southern Pacific remained the dominant employer and shipper, and opened an impressive passenger terminal at 5th and I. In 1931, the depot was adorned by a monument honoring Theodore Judah, designer of the transcontinental railroad. That monument today stands at 2nd and L in Old Sacramento. The Western Pacific, welcomed to the valley a few years earlier, acquired the inter-urban Sacramento Northern Railroad in 1921 and continued service up the valley to Chico. Central California Traction provided service to Stockton and points south, while the San Francisco-Sacramento Railroad served westward travelers. In 1921, an ornate Union Station was constructed near 12th and I to serve all the inter-urbans. Sacramento's streetcar system had expanded to become an extraordinary system, serving all parts of the city and attracting 16 to 20 million riders annually. Buses, or more familiarly "stages", were less significant carriers at that time; more than a half dozen independent lines connected valley and foothill communities to the capital.

EDUCATION

Seventy-nine school districts served the county in 1920 and a few more were added during the decade. Elk Grove Union School District came together in 1921, as did Isleton,

Sacramento Junior College, today's Sacramento City College, established its campus on Freeport Boulevard near Sutterville Road in 1926. This 1931 aerial view, looking east, also shows the Western Pacific Railroad shops and the Curtis Park subdivision just beyond Hughes Stadium. *Sacramento Bee Collection, SAMCC.*

Beaver, and Herald Districts. Folsom High School was formed in 1923, becoming only the second high school serving the northeastern county. Sutterville Heights school was established in 1924.

The Sacramento City Unified School District, the county's education pioneer, entered the field of higher education in 1916, establishing a Junior College at its high school campus at 18th and K. Following closure in 1918 due to the war, the college was reopened in the new high school building at 34th and Y in 1920 and moved to its own campus on Freeport Boulevard in 1926.

AVIATION

World War I provided a great stimulus for aviation, and the region shared in both the excitement and the benefits. President Woodrow Wilson envisioned an aerial highway, coast to coast, with Sacramento a part of it. Before the war ended in 1918, the Army Air Corps selected Mills Station as the site of a military air training school, which became known as Mather Field, leading to a temporary flurry of activity over federal threats to place the school elsewhere unless Sacramento cleansed itself of prostitution. But the war's end led to the closure of Mather as a training school.

Officially abandoned in 1923, Mather continued to serve the community. It was a stop on the 1924 flight around the world. An Air Circus was staged there a year later, thrilling thousands caught up in the hysteria surrounding flight. At about the same time, early attempts at air mail service made Mather a stopping point, and Charles A. Lindbergh landed his *Spirit of St. Louis* there while barnstorming the nation after his epic flight.

Air service began for the Sacramento and San Joaquin valleys in 1928 with Tri State Airlines. Pressure was building on the city to establish a quality air field closer to downtown. A site on Freeport Boulevard was selected for the municipal airport over the one at Del Paso Park. A Boeing aircraft first landed at the new airport in September, 1929, although it was not dedicated until March, 1930.

Mather Field was militarily activated again in 1930 as the central staging area for the United States' first military aviation war game. These "Great Maneuvers," pitted Red and Blue forces against one another, with the Blue Army defending the State Capitol against all attacks. Eighty percent or more of all U.S. Army Air Corps aircraft in the U.S. inventory took part in the exercise, over half of them utilizing Mather. The Blue Army was victorious and the capitol was saved! Among innovations that came from these maneuvers: the use of smoke to obscure targets, such as the Capitol, from the enemy; aerial photography techniques

never before attempted; and the first practical attempts to communicate between airplanes by radio. The Army Air Corps also established a world altitude record while flying in formation.

In October, 1932, the pattern of abandoning Mather Field was resumed, until World War II once more prompted reactivation. But aviation in Sacramento remained healthy. Liberty Iron Works in North Sacramento continued to build the "Jenny" aircraft for the Army after the war, and what is thought to be the first plane manufactured for private use, *The Meteor,* was made in Sacramento.

JOURNALISM, RECREATION AND RELAXATION

The *Sacramento Bee* survived a potentially damaging change in 1923 when a bitter separation of its two owners rocked the community. The McClatchy brothers had vigorously and successfully led The Bee together after the death

Sacramento Municipal Airport, south of downtown Sacramento, was dedicated in March 1930. This 1932 view by Sacramento avocational photographer Eugene Hepting features the United Air Lines terminal, a company offering "Coast to coast air passenger service" for passengers, air mail and express. *Eugene Hepting Collection, SAMCC.*

of their pioneer father, James, in 1883. They had brought The *Bee* to circulation dominance over its one-time close rival, *The Union*, which was the earliest paper in the west. After the breakup, Publisher Valentine McClatchy retired from the scene, and Charles Kenny McClatchy became the sole owner and continued as editor. Two years later, *The Sacramento Star*, a third newspaper in business since 1904, was merged into The *Bee*.

From the time of the clapboard and canvas Eagle Theater in 1849, Sacramento was touted as a place for diversion from the rigors of daily life. Throughout the years, top touring stars and attractions came to the city. By the end of World War I, the reigning vaudeville medium had been forced to share the stage with those blinking black and white herky-jerky images, silent motion pictures, and by

Municipal parks have been a part of Sacramento's cultural landscape since 1850 when the original plat of the city featured public squares. In 1911, former Sacramento mayor and hotel owner, William Land, bequeathed $250,000 to the city for acquisition of parkland. The site of the present-day William Land Park was selected and designed by Frederick N. Evans, a professional park planner. This May 4, 1938, aerial, looks west toward the Sacramento River. Eleventh Avenue separates the park at the upper left from the developing William Land Park neighborhood. *Sacramento Bee Collection, SAMCC.*

From the time John Sutter, Jr., placed "Public Squares" throughout the original plat of Sacramento City in 1850, the city appreciated the importance of public recreation areas. In 1911, the city was faced with implementing a generous bequest of $250,000 from former mayor and hotel owner, William Land. The will specified the money must go for a city park and the leaders spent the next 10 years debating where the park should be.

Some favored improving the rural Del Paso Park, a mostly unimproved area which had been purchased 10 miles out in the northeast country before the turn of the century. The city council, however, voted to purchase property between Riverside and Freeport boulevards, much closer to downtown. That action by the council resulted in a public referendum which favored Del Paso by a two to one margin. The council attempted to rescinded its contract to buy the Riverside acreage, but the court declared the sale valid and the debate finally ended. William Land Park became a showplace, with one of the first public golf courses, and eventually, the city zoo.

1930 all nine theaters in the vicinity were advertising the amazing new "Talkies."

Sacramento, as the "River City", became a favorite of movie makers as well. They found the region's rivers easy to disguise as the Mississippi or other streams and the farm labor pool of Sacramento's West End provided unlimited talent for crowd scenes. William S. Hart shot *Wagon Tracks* in Sacramento in 1919. Charlie Chaplin filmed much of *The Gold Rush* around Truckee, recruiting his "sourdoughs" on Second Street in Sacramento.

Smaller parks were not neglected. Places of leisure were nurtured all over town, starting by maintaining Sutter Jr.'s Public Squares as parks. All told, over 1,200 acres were devoted to parks in the city and county by the end of the twenties. The county, concerned about drownings in the region's rivers, purchased beachfront property at H Street and the American River in 1928. A picnic site and lifeguards were provided, and eventually a towering water slide was built, hurling ecstatic screaming youngsters into the river.

The Days of '49, a mammoth celebration involving the entire

In May 1922, 500,000 people came together in Sacramento over a six-day period to celebrate California's Gold Rush. The Days of '49 was located at the Southern Pacific sandlot, the site later occupied by the SP passenger depot. The event featured an Indian village, mining town, a pageant depicting the founding of the city, fireworks, a rodeo and a parade. This parade entry, driven by Irv Engler of the Engler & Smith advertising agency, paused at the Sacramento Chamber of Commerce office at 917 7th Street. *Arthur McCurdy Collection, SAMCC.*

city, brought an estimated one-half million people to Sacramento over 6 days in May, 1922. It featured a mining town, an Indian village and a towering wooden mountain encircled by a ramp for donkey rides to the top. Days also offered a pageant on the founding of the city, illuminated aerial flights, fireworks, rodeo, parades and much more.

The city opened a family camp in the Sierra at Sayles Flat on the road to Lake Tahoe in 1919. The fee for one week was a very reasonable $20 for transportation, food and lodging. It continues today as Camp Sacramento.

Joyland is a name that brought smiles to several generations of Sacramento's young people. Located in Oak Park, Joyland was a full-service amusement park, with a

The Sacramento Solons represented the capital city in the Pacific Coast Baseball League for several decades. The Moreing brothers of Stockton acquired the Solons in 1920 and ushered in a successful era. They built a new grandstand at the old Buffalo Park at Riverside and Y, and called it Moreing Field. In 1930, lights were added, and in the same year, KFBK broadcast the first baseball game from Sacramento. Future Chicago Cubs star Stan Hack, a Sacramento native, played for the Solons in 1931, before going on to a sterling major league career in which he twice led the National League in hits.

Sacramento interest in the World Series was heightened in 1924 when Orangevale boy Earl McNeeley joined Walter

world class roller coaster. Streetcar lines terminated there while it operated from 1889 to 1927. Much of Joyland burned in 1920 in one of the city's most spectacular blazes and the fun spot never recovered. In 1927, Valentine McClatchy bought the remains and presented the acreage to the city for a park, which was named for his father, newspaperman James McClatchy.

Radio began to envelop the valley in 1922. The government assigned a spot on the dial to this area to be shared by operators at different times and days. Two stations, KVQ and KFBK, began operation the first year. After technical problems were worked out, The *Bee* and Kimball Upson Hardware continued KFBK, which still broadcasts today under a different ownership.

Johnson as a star of the Series. The *Bee* had set up a huge board on the side of their building with lights indicating base-runners and other game data, to the delight of tumultuous crowds. Other sports highlights of the 1920s included: a state basketball championship for Sacramento High School in 1922; the arrival of local legend Coach Hack Applequist at Sacramento High in 1926; an exhibition baseball game featuring Babe Ruth and Lou Gehrig in 1927; and the beginning of the boxing career of Sacramento resident Max Baer who, under the wing of local tavern owner and later county supervisor Ancil Hoffman, won the World Heavyweight Boxing Championship in 1934. So the twenties roared by, a wild ride that gave way to the uncertainty of the thirties.

Sacramento area's older residents still remember the thrill of riding the roller coaster at Joyland. This amusement park operated in Oak Park from 1889 to 1927. In 1927, Valentine McClatchy purchased the fire-damaged property and presented it to the City of Sacramento for development as a city park. *Maurice Read Collection, SAMCC.*

CHAPTER SIX

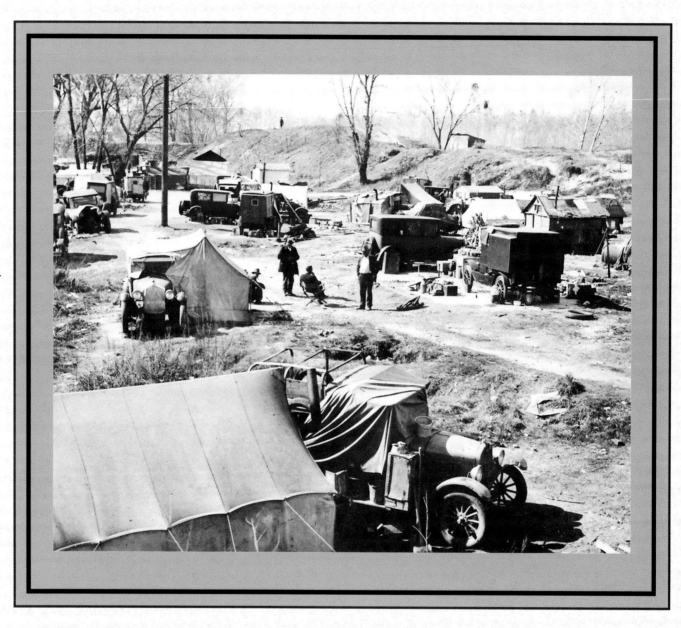

Depression, New Deal, War,
Government and Economic Growth:
The Metropolis Arrives, 1930s–1950s

by James E. Henley

They looked beaten, most of them-having the appearance of a mongrel who does not know why the whip comes down so often on his defenseless back. Therefore they raise pleading eyes when another kick lands them in the gutter, and after a time the gutter seems their only rightful home.

California interested me more than any other state, because everywhere I traveled, everyone to whom I spoke, the word was 'bound for California'. John M. Kennedy 1935.

THE PLUNGE INTO THE GREAT DEPRESSION

From 1929 to 1932, the economy plunged severely. Agricultural crop prices dropped: peaches went from nearly $70 per ton in 1929 to $9 per ton in 1932. Commerce suffered similar declines. Two banks failed in Sacramento and the community was the fourth worst hit by unemployment in the state. More than 25,000 people were without jobs. But in spite of the bad times, the Sacramento region fared better than the country as a whole. The *Sacramento Bee*, with hometown enthusiasm, claimed Sacramento was one of the eight best business spots in the nation.

Franklin Roosevelt campaigned in Sacramento in September 1932 and promised support for many California programs and an end to prohibition. In return for his efforts, Roosevelt received powerful political allies in Hiram Johnson and the McClatchy newspapers. In November 1932, Roosevelt won the presidential election by a landslide. The voters approved of a candidate who looked positively toward solving the economic crisis over Republican Herbert Hoover who suggested little could be done. There was strong Republican sympathy in northern California but Roosevelt, a Democrat, carried every county.

The depression was not an easy problem to fix. Camps of transients had sprung up in many locations around Sacramento, 50 percent of the residents from Sacramento and 75 percent from within the state. Several camps existed in the section that is now identified as the Richards Boulevard area, but in the 1930s it was called the "Jibboom Street Area." These "Hoovervilles" each had 30 to 40 shacks which were constructed of found materials such as paper, tar paper and scrap metal, frequently augmented with brush and tree limbs. Many shacks were actually houseboats moored on the Sacramento River, near the foot of P Street.

The homeless were not confined to the "Hoovervilles." The State Relief Administration (SRA) estimated that there were approximately 165 men between the Southern Pacific depot and 16th Street underpass; sleeping on the ground, mostly along the railroad tracks. Families and small groups were found from one end to another along the Marysville Highway and Highway 99. The SRA reported that along Highway 99, men in small groups and families were usually within eyesight of each other, all the way to Bakersfield.

The most consistently open shelter in the city was run as a joint operation of the City's Recreation Department and the Community Chest. The shelter was at Front and I streets, in the remnants of the City Water Works. Potential clients would line up every day at the Community Chest building at 1428 H Street. Each morning the shelter could only accept usually a half dozen new clients. Five hundred men slept there each day with only 400 beds. A one-day census on February 15, 1934, revealed 1,230 single men in shelters in Sacramento, the third largest number in the state, surpassed only by Los Angeles and Stockton. Sacramento in 1930 had a population of 93,750 within the city limits and 10 percent were unemployed. In 1930, California had 4.7 percent of the nation's population and over 12 percent of its transients.

Sacramento's Recreation Department and the Community Chest jointly operated a Depression-era men's shelter at Front and I streets in what remained of the City Water Works. The men, shown here, are waiting to check in. They had to temporarily surrender their clothing, which were then doused with kerosene and steamed. The wet clothes, shown toward the rear of the photograph, were strung up to dry. This view is looking south down Front Street from the Water Works. *Sacramento City Parks & Recreation Collection, SAMCC.*

Previous Page:
The Great Depression of the 1930s found many Americans unemployed and homeless for the first time in their lives. In Sacramento, several transient camps, thrown together with tar paper and wood scraps, occupied the area known as Jibboom Street, just south of the American River at its confluence with the Sacramento River. They were often referred to as Hoovervilles, a reference to Pres. Herbert Hoover who many felt did not provide enough Depression relief. *Eugene Hepting Collection, Sacramento Archives and Museum Collection Center (SAMCC).*

The proliferation of transients was the result of unemployment, which was the consequence of an unstable economy. Sacramento Valley agriculture saw products drop up to 600 percent from 1929 to 1932. The problems for the farmer would soon migrate to the bankers and other merchants. Then they would reduce the work force, placing more unemployed on the street. Thus a cycle was established.

One City Recreation Department employee recalled that the new men at the shelter had to check all their clothing and were given temporary garb. The clothes they wore into the shelter were steamed in a brick chamber fed by the Old Waterworks boiler after the garments were doused with kerosene. The purpose was to control bed bugs, body lice and other vermin. The wet clothes were scattered around outside until dry. Kerosene was not a particularly pleasant deodorant.

In 1932, the Southern Pacific was evicting as many as 80,000 people per month for non-payment of fares, though the average was 40,000 to 50,000. The record was set in 1933 when 720,000 trespassers were ejected during the course of the year. At times one third of the country's working population was unemployed. Without people earning and saving, banks were failing throughout the northern valley by January 1933. Even so, the problems were worse in other

sections of the country and labor flocked to California and the Central Valley looking for seasonal work. The weather was generally better than the midwest and east, especially for homeless who might be forced to sleep in primitive circumstances. Hopping on a railroad car headed west was a favored mode of free transportation.

REEMERGING LABOR DISPUTES, THE RED SCARE AND RADICAL THINKING

In 1932, a labor strike in Vacaville resulted in a local vigilance committee seizing six strikers who had been arrested and placed in jail. The prisoners were beaten and, after they had their heads painted red, were chased out of town on foot. Labor agitators were commonly called Communists or Socialists. Indeed by 1931 the Communist Party was trying to organize agricultural workers. Strikes subsequently occurred in the Delta, Florin and Gridley in 1933 and 1934. Sacramento cannery workers struck in 1935 and again in 1937. The biggest and most far reaching strike of the period was a general strike of the waterfront in San Francisco in 1934. The strike reached Sacramento and the valley, effectively halting all river transportation.

In Sacramento a great fear of Communism was building. In April 1934, local police stopped a "Communist" demonstration called a "hunger march." By late summer 1934, 24 persons were arrested in a raid of Communist headquarters in Sacramento. Seventeen were charged and 14 were brought to trial on charges of vagrancy and criminal syndicalism. The trial lasted until February 1935. Eight were convicted and sentenced for up to 14 years.

The trial was a political event as much as a legal proceeding. Sacramento District Attorney J.W. Babcock started the trial in the press before it ever got to the courtroom. Amid charges of political motivation, he was soon replaced by California Attorney General U.S. Webb, who hired former Sacramento County District Attorney D.A. McAllister to prosecute the case. The trial continued to be played to the papers. Witnesses included Los Angeles police officers who had no direct evidence or testimony relevant to the defendants but made accusations about Communist actors. Movie industry personalities including James Cagney, Ramon Novarro, Lupe Velez and Dolores Del Rio were branded as Communists. Statewide Communists and Socialists saw the trial also as an opportunity and promoted the defendants as martyrs. Large crowds and demonstrations assembled on I Street in front of the courthouse. Newspaper interest was nationwide.

The fear of Communists in Sacramento was strong even if their numbers were small. Between 1934 and 1940, there were no more than 225 registered in the County. The fear of Communists would be down-played by the allied alliance of WWII only to reemerge in the postwar years.

Communists were but one of a number of groups of radical agitators for political and economic order in California. Muckraking author Upton Sinclair achieved an amazing upset when he secured the Democratic Party nomination for Governor. He had a 12-point program and a slogan for California's economic woes. The slogan was simple: "End Poverty in California," known as "E.P.I.C." His plan would have ended land ownership as it previously existed, completely changed the tax system and assumed control of industry by the state. He also proposed changes to the rights of inheritance and suggested the implementation of a universal pension system. Sinclair was branded as a Communist. The *Sacramento Bee* and the *Sacramento Union* were united in their opposition. Frank Merriam won the gubernatorial race but had there not been candidates of so many factions running for Governor, the outcome might have been in Sinclair's favor.

Two other plans also emerged: "The Townsend Plan" and the "Ham and Eggs" plan. The Townsend Plan was a retirement system endorsed by many in fear of Sinclair. The plan known as "Ham and Eggs" in essence gave every unemployed person in the state $30 each Thursday. Opponents nicknamed the proposal "Ham and Eggs for Everyone." Submitted to public vote statewide in 1938 after a million people had signed a petition to put it on the ballot, the proposal lost by a mere 128,000 votes. The issue was again placed on the ballot in 1939 and lost by two to one. The radical enthusiasm behind these plans was already diminishing. As the radical plans were defeated, a number of other programs were approved. State income taxes were initiated, prohibition had ended, bonds for the Central Valley Project were approved, and veterans received a $1,000 tax exemption.

AN ALPHABET OF PROGRAMS

Franklin Roosevelt's "New Deal" was endorsed and Sacramento and northern California prepared to take advantage of the "alphabet" programs it was delivering. The Roosevelt administration plan was just what the doctor had ordered for the region's turn of the century reformers. Some such as Hiram Johnson and Clyde Seavey were still in powerful positions and able to offer support for the programs.

The CVP (Central Valley Project) was one of the most ambitious water projects in the nation. It consisted of 1) the Shasta Dam, 2) improving Sacramento River drainage, 3) a channel across the Delta, 4) a pumping plant at Tracy, and 5) the Mendota Canal to deliver water to the San Joaquin Valley for agriculture.

Unemployment during the Depression fueled labor agitation and labor disputes. By 1931, the Community Party had moved to organize agricultural workers in the area. This photograph, taken at 5th and J streets in Sacramento, features a 1933 Communist Party parade. The next year, Sacramento police raided party headquarters, which resulted in a trial heavily covered by the media. *Sacramento Bee Collection, SAMCC.*

Hollywood moviemakers often filmed on location at the Sacramento River when they needed a Mississippi River locale or a riverboat scene. In May 1935, Fox Studios began filming *Steamboat 'Round the Bend* in Sacramento. The film starred Will Rogers and featured a steamboat race, shown here. *Sacramento Bee Collection, SAMCC.*

The SERA and FERA were the State and Federal Emergency Relief Administrations, established to oversee emergency food, health, welfare and employment for the unemployed. Next came the CWA (Civil Works Administration) which was to stimulate public projects for employment. The big employer would be the WPA (Works Progress Administration) which between 1935 and 1939 would directly spend $5 million in Sacramento County.

The National Recovery Administration (NRA) was conceived to work with private sector business, but it also established regulations such as a ban on child labor and minimum hours of employment for women. Other programs included the FHA (Federal Housing Administration), and the AAA (Agriculture Adjustment Administration). The FHA, perhaps the most enduring program, is still in operation today.

DIVERSIONS FROM DEPRESSION

1932: When the McClatchy Company purchased the *Fresno Republican,* Sacramento's sphere of influence grew through the entire Central Valley. Sacramentans came off a 13-year dry spell with their first legal beer in April. In May the blimp, *Akron,* visited the Sacramento skies.

1933: Sacramento County adopted a new county charter which gave the County more "home rule" in planning and municipal services, and a professional manager. Charles Deterding become the first County Executive in June. In December, California passed a state water plan. Sacramento County was 8 to 1 in favor.

1934: Eleanor McClatchy attended her first boxing match, a match between Max Baer and Primo Carnera. Her thoughts on the match were published by the *Sacramento Bee.* Eleanor was not a sportswriter but there was no doubt about how she felt about the fighters and the outcome, extolling the handsome and daring Max Baer's victory over the giant brute, Carnera. It was her first and probably last attempt at sportswriting. Mrs. Clunie, who had owned the Clunie Theater and had relocated to Southern California, bequeathed $150,000 to the City of Sacramento for a pool, clubhouse and park improvements in McKinley Park in October.

1935: In March, a new 16th Street bridge crossed the American River. In May, the *Sacramento Bee* won a Pulitzer Prize for journalism for articles about political corruption in Nevada. Filming started in May on the movie

Steamboat Round the Bend in Sacramento. It would be Will Roger's last film. In September at the Fox Senator on K Street, the original Sacramento Mickey Mouse Club was formed. A "Mouser" who was there 63 years ago still sings the club song:

> My name is little Mickey Mouse
> I've got a sweetie down in the chicken house
> She's neither fat or skinny
> She's a horse's whinny
> She's my little Minnie Mouse

In December, the Tower Bridge was opened, replacing the former Sacramento Northern Bridge.

1936: In March, the Hollywood movie, *Sutter's Gold*, premiered in Sacramento at the Alhambra Theater, and the *Bee* soundly trashed it as distorted.

1939: The region celebrated Pioneer Days and the 100th anniversary of John Sutter's arrival, hosting a large community event called "Roaring Camp," a complete mining camp built in Southside Park.

NEW DEAL AND THE WORLD WAR II HOMEFRONT

The New Deal built a huge infrastructure for Sacramento that would handle future growth. The construction of the Silver Creek project with three lakes and powerhouses placed the Sacramento Municipal Utility District in a position to offer high quality, cheap service making it one of the outstanding public utility districts in the nation. Sacramento's water delivery and storage system was upgraded

In 1935, the state of California replaced the Sacramento Northern Bridge, which crossed the Sacramento River at M Street, with the Tower Bridge. This aerial view, looking east, captures the bridge's December 15th dedication, the *Delta Queen* tied up at the River Lines warehouse, and the Sacramento waterfront. *Sacramento Bee Collection, SAMCC.*

to handle future needs. The levees made significantly larger areas available for urban expansion. City Hall was enlarged with an annex to allow government to better serve an expanding population, while the Central Valley Project allowed not only irrigation but also provided flood protection and electric power.

World War II's onset monumentally affected Sacramento's people. Men went off to war. Women often stepped into what were formerly considered men's jobs, launching an unprecedented change in female economic participation that continued to accelerate. Ethnic groups that had traditionally faced discrimination also found greater opportunity, as the country marshaled all of its resources to fight and win a global war. Unemployment virtually ended overnight.

Not everyone, however, was able to participate in the national effort. Ethnic Americans whose country of ancestral origin came to be at war with the United States found they were a special target for discrimination. Perhaps it was most visible with the Japanese-Americans. Anti-Japanese prejudice was significant before the war but

In 1936, Sacramento's Alhambra Theatre provided the venue for the world premier of *Sutter's Gold*. The film, starring Edward Arnold, Lee Tracy, Binnie Barnes and Harry Carey, was a Hollywood version of John Sutter's California years. The *Sacramento Bee* movie critics were not kind. *Photograph by J.C. Milligan, Universal Studio. Don Rivett Collection, SAMCC.*

1939 marked the centennial of John Sutter's arrival in the Sacramento area. Sacramentans acknowledged this historical event by constructing Roaring Camp, a complete mining camp in Southside Park, which was the center of various celebrations. This view of the entrance on X Street, near 7th, was taken in May 1939. *Eugene Hepting Collection, SAMCC.*

Bass player, John Hebert, performed with jazz and big band groups. Here he is performing at the Zanzibar Club, in Sacramento's West End, about 1940. *Sacramento Ethnic Survey Collection, SAMCC.*

WWII brought it to a new level. All people of Japanese ancestry on the west coast (California, Washington and Oregon) were interned in camps such as Tule Lake and Manzanar. They were given seven days notice to arrange for the care or sale of their houses or farms and the storage or disposal of most of their personal possessions. A few Japanese-Americans were able to escape internment by moving to the midwest or east. And, despite the discriminatory treatment, many Japanese-American men from Sacramento and elsewhere joined the 442nd Regimental Combat Team and other units, serving with great distinction and valor.

Upon returning from the camps after the end of the war many had lost everything that they had prior to internment including land, homes, businesses and even personal possessions. Some though, found extraordinary kindness in people who kept their property and possessions safe. The Portuguese community extended protection to many Japanese-Americans in the Florin area and Our Lady of Guadalupe Catholic Church at Southside Park took control of the Parkview Presbyterian Church whose congregation was Japanese-American. Many families stored their personal possessions in the church before leaving for camp. Throughout the war Our Lady of Guadalupe kept the building and its contents secure. On the return of the internees, the Catholic Church returned the Parkview Church to its parishioners and all personal family property was returned.

For civilians in Sacramento the fear of war with Germany and Japan was frequently discussed, but the bombing of Pearl Harbor on December 7, 1941, took everyone in the country by surprise. For most the news came by word of mouth, neighbor to neighbor, originating in a home with a radio. The shock was profound. Charles Duncan was a young boy in Citrus Heights when neighbors brought the news. While adults discussed the meaning and consequences, Charles and another young neighbor took immediate action — they got their air rifles and developed plans to guard a nearby vineyard.

Civic authorities were very quick to react. The City Manager and County Executive began immediate planning and within a day or two police were standing guard at major points such as the Tower Bridge and the City Airport, until the military could be organized to coordinate with civilian authorities. Eventually, many police and sheriff's deputies would be inducted and serve as military police. Uniforms were changing to reflect duties that were not necessarily civilian in nature. The soft caps of city police were exchanged for WWI-style white, military helmets with the word "Police" stenciled on the front. Within a few days the police had developed closer ties with federal agencies and the FBI ordered the police to watch local Japanese leaders and professionals. In response to a federal request, the police also asked Japanese-Americans to surrender all their cameras and radios. The Japanese-American community quickly

Following the bombing of Pearl Harbor, the military coordinated with civilian authorities to protect key properties considered vulnerable to possible attack. Here a soldier stands guard at the Tower Bridge. *Sacramento Bee Collection, SAMCC.*

The bombing of Pearl Harbor by Japan brought prejudice against the Japanese community to a new high. As the result of Presidential Executive Order 9066, more than 93,000 Issei (Japanese immigrants) and Nisei (American-born) in California were moved to internment camps. Sacramento's Japanese community was ordered to relocate in May 1942. This photograph, taken on 4th Street in Japantown, shows families hastily loading up their belongings. *Eugene Hepting Collection, SAMCC.*

Community orangizations rallied support behind the World War II effort. Here, Alice Kwok, Arvella Wong and Norma Wong are providing the musical entertainment at a war bond fundraiser sponsored by the Chinese community. *Margaret Lum Collection, SAMCC.*

obeyed that request. When later asked to surrender all weapons to the police, they lined up at the police station, in some cases turning in the knives from their kitchens and their silver dining services.

As the war progressed, Sacramentans became used to a number of activities, including war bond drives and rationing of food, gasoline and tires. Food was a commodity Sacramento could produce for the war effort both in fact and in symbol. Soldiers at Mather Field volunteered on off-duty time to work in Sacramento's large canneries. Local agriculture maximized its production. The *Sacramento Bee* took leadership in a symbolic and patriotic activity with the Sacramento County Agriculture Commissioner, A.E. Morrison. Together they developed Sacramento's "Victory Gardens." City residents were encouraged to tear up their front and back yards, put in vegetable gardens, feed themselves with the fresh produce they grew and deliver the extra vegetables to the local canneries to be canned under the "V" for victory label. The program was very well received and many front lawns did indeed become vegetable gardens. Once a year, the best produce was taken to Memorial Auditorium for a public celebration. The *Bee* won national recognition for its support and Eleanor Roosevelt thanked Eleanor McClatchy for the company's efforts and the community's spirit.

As the war drew on, residents became accustomed to Civil Defense drills, blackouts, USO dances and mothers'

Since Sacramento was at the center of Central Valley agriculture, Sacramentans provided food for the war effort. In a patriotic, although largely symbolic, effort the *Sacramento Bee* joined with Sacramento County Agriculture Commissioner A. E. Morrison to develop Sacramento's Victory Gardens. Local residents were encouraged to tear up their lawns and to plant vegetables. Extra produce was canned locally under the V (for victory) label. This demonstration Victory Garden, featuring the V logo, was planted at the U. S. Post Office located on I Street between 8th and 9th streets. *Sacramento Agriculture Extension Collection, SAMCC.*

As part of an effort to reduce the visibility of important civic properties, the City's water tower and fire department practice jump tower near Alhambra Boulevard and J Street were painted in a camouflage design. This photograph was shot by Eugene Hepting December 25, 1943. *Eugene Hepting Collection, SAMCC.*

stars in front room windows. The occasional black ribbon on front porches and doors sadly also became a recognized part of community life, as hundreds of Sacramentans did not return from the fighting.

The business community of Sacramento supported the war in many ways. Weinstocks promoted photos at the store of children dressed in soldier's uniforms or caps. Henry Sleeper at Sleeper's Stationary had a very unusual state-of-the-art pantograph milling machine with which he usually engraved dies for tokens and business seals. At certain times he would hear a knock on the door in the middle of the night, get dressed and go down to the store escorted by an Army officer and an armed guard, where he would repair a small part for a secret innovation called the "Norden Bomb Sight," which markedly increased bombing accuracy by U.S. airmen.

THE MILITARY BASES

The Sacramento Valley became a major focus for military air bases to support the Pacific war. The main bases were McClellan in Sacramento, Beale near Marysville, Travis in Fairfield and Mather in Sacramento. Of the Sacramento bases, Mather was the oldest, established in 1918 for World War I and revived in 1935. In 1941, the base was designated a navigational school. By the end of the war, thousands of trainees went through the base. Many then later returned to the Central Valley to continue their military career or to be discharged here. By the end of the 1950s, the base was pumping $45 million per year into the local economy.

McClellan's placement in Sacramento was the product of a political push by the Chamber of Commerce and its manager, Arthur Dudley. McClellan's history was tied to the inadequacy of Rockwell Field in San Diego to serve the Army Air Corps as a supply depot. Rockwell was founded in 1912 but was not large enough to carry out its mission. Sacramento was selected as another supply depot location after Dudley lobbied Congress to appropriate $7 million for a site near Sacramento in 1935. One thousand acres were

Many members of Sacramento's business community actively supported the war effort. Here, members of Sacramento Beverage Industries posed with their delivery trucks in a kick-off for a war salvage drive. The view is looking south toward Broadway and the New Helvetia Housing Project. *Eleanor McClatchy Collection, SAMCC.*

As a result of intense lobbying by the Sacramento Chamber of Commerce, the Army Air Corps selected Sacramento as a supply and repair depot. It was dedicated April 29, 1938, and renamed McClellan Field the next year. By the end of World War II, it had become the area's largest employer. This view, taken two years after the end of the war, shows the repair of P-38 aircraft.

allocated on the old Del Paso land grant. The Depot was dedicated on April 29, 1938 with 50,000 visitors and 623 civilian employees. Completed that year, the main hangar building was proclaimed to be the largest building owned by the U.S. Government. The Depot was officially named McClellan Field on December 1, 1939 after a major who had died in Ohio testing a plane. By the end of WWII the Depot was the largest employer in the Valley.

Camp Kohler, east of McClellan along the railroad tracks, was designed in early 1942. The first block of residential barracks were laid out when the Japanese-American relocation was ordered. The buildings were hastily completed and named Camp Walerga. The first internees to arrive were

volunteers from Sacramento and mostly were professionals. They helped finish the barracks for occupation. Within a few months Walerga's life as an assembly center was over and the buildings joined the rest of the new Camp Kohler. Kohler primarily held troops until they could be forwarded to needed destinations in the Pacific War. The Signal Corps occupied part of the camp until they built the Signal Depot. After the war, administration of Kohler resided with McClellan. Most of the buildings were burned in 1947 and remaining portions were directly combined with McClellan operations.

The Signal Corps did not have their own Army Signal Depot until 1945. The new facility was off Fruitridge Road near Florin-Perkins. It played a significant role supporting

General Douglas McArthur's forces engaged in the occupation of Japan and later in the Korean conflict, the so-called "Forgotten War" in which yet more Sacramentans once again gave their lives.

FLYING FARMERS, POLICE UNIFORMS AND TAPE RECORDERS

The close of World War II introduced the whole country to the benefits of the technology developed during the war. A wealth of surplus military supplies and equipment also became widely available.

The region's farmers had a long history of adapting materials and supplies at hand to perform unique jobs, including surplus property. The Sacramento Valley in the 1910-1930 period had turned rice into a profitable crop. Much of the success came from using surplus WWI airplanes to scare ducks and geese off the fields, thus saving the grain for harvest. The technique was developed by Edmond Moffett in July of 1919. According to local historian Joseph McGowan, the aviator earned the title of the "First Air-borne Duck Herder." It was a great success, but in time the noise was less and less threatening to the ducks. Moffett later tried surplus grenades, but they did more damage than the ducks to the rice fields.

By 1929 aerial seeding was under experiment and, in 1930, a Willows aviator named Nolta planted 9,000 acres at a speed 10 times faster than could be achieved by conventional means. During the same period, aviators were experimenting with "crop dusting" as a means of pest control. By the start of World War II, about 100 planes were involved in agricultural activities. The war stopped any additional significant agricultural progress, but after the war thousands of planes became available. From 1945 through the end of 1946, the number of planes in agricultural use went from 175 to 750.

The City of Sacramento used surplus equipment in street and utility maintenance. Camp Sacramento provided transportation for campers in a surplus troop carrier. The police officers had to purchase their own uniforms and many used military surplus "Great Coats" modified as their uniform coats. *Sacramento Bee* photographers were using military surplus K-10 aerial cameras modified as news cameras. They also used surplus 4-inch roll film recut by hand into 4 x 5-inch sheets because commercially cut 4 x 5-inch film was expensive and hard to purchase into the 1950s.

War technology was as important as war surplus and it was not limited to American technological advances. At the close of the war, the US government established a special task force to quickly recover as much German technology as could be gathered. Military groups with special training scoured German facilities and gathered up German scientists. Lou Heinzman, a sound engineer with KFBK and McClatchy Broadcasting, was a member of one of those teams. He was particularly interested in magnetic tape recording machines which German scientists had been perfecting during the war. In 1945 he sent back to Norman Webster, the chief engineer at KFBK, notes and sketches interpreting what he saw. By the time

Sacramento's recreation program took advantage of war surplus vehicles to enlarge their fleet. This truck is decorated to advertise the Recreation Department's program known as the "Knot Hole Gang." It provided free admission for Sacramento kids at Friday night Solons games. *City of Sacramento Collection, SAMCC.*

A SACRAMENTO FIRST

At a time when women were rarely seen in political office, Sacramento garnered national recognition as the only city of over 30,000 people in the United States to have a woman mayor. Belle Cooledge, an eminent local educator and college administrator, was an elected city councilwoman and became the city's first female chief executive in January, 1948. Cooledge was born and raised in the gold country east of Sacramento and served as dean and vice-president of Sacramento Junior College for over 30 years, with a stint as a U. S. Army nurse in the First World War. She was honored as Sacramento Woman of the Year in 1953, and had a Sacramento Community College scholarship established in her honor. The South Land Park branch of the Sacramento Public Library is named for her.

he arrived back in Sacramento, the notes and drawings had been carefully analyzed. In short order, a "tape recorder" was built out of wood and converted components, placing McClatchy Broadcasting on the front edge of the use of magnetic tape in broadcasting.

POSTWAR GROWTH OF COMMUNITY GROUPS AND ACTIVITIES

In the 19th century a core segment of community social life for both white and blue collar workers were clubs and associations. These could be religious, fraternal or benevolent organizations which brought people of common interest together. The women's organizations came together later but grew steadily throughout the first half of the 20th century. Men's organizations ebbed and flowed with events such as the Depression and wars, but after World War II, most men's fraternal organizations thrived. The largest groups, such as Masons, Odd Fellows and Elks, boasted sizeable memberships, substantial investments in buildings and real estate and booming programs and activities after the war. They frequently helped soldiers who had returned to civilian life reenter society, find a job, associate with old friends and make new acquaintances.

Two strong local women's organizations stand out with their success. Both were formed in the 19th century but blossomed in the 20th century and during both of the postwar booms. They were the Saturday Club, initiated in 1893 and the Tuesday Club, formed in 1896. The Saturday Club was specifically formed to stimulate interest in music. The Tuesday Club was a social group which sponsored lectures and music, and investigated social

issues. Women's clubs frequently paralleled the interests of turn-of-the-century reformers. Their programs included campaigns for schools, the Traveler's Aid Society and rural access to public libraries.

Some groups, on the other hand, declined in the postwar period. The Sacramento Society of California Pioneers was a major influence in the 19th century community, but almost disappeared in the 1940s and 1950s. During the 1880s, the membership was over 400 but during the late 1940s, in spite of a comfortable bank account, clear title to a lot and a two-story hall on Seventh Street, the membership dropped to less than 10 members. It was not until the 1960s that they regained vigor and rebuilt their membership.

These organizations and activities tended to bring people together and establish a sense of community. This identity was especially useful in the 1940s when the large growth in the numbers of new residents sparked a need for a local focus and community identity for the region. These groups and their events helped those of widely different backgrounds and values find a place for interaction.

GOVERNMENT BOOMS

World War II and the three local military bases accelerated patterns of growth. The bases attracted a large civilian workforce in addition to the military population. From 1940 to 1946, the voting population of California more than tripled, which made older California residents a minority. By the end of the war, California state government, centered in Sacramento, was dealing with issues and quantities of service unheard of in its past 95 years. Not only did the size of government grow, revenues were expanding at an enormous rate. By 1946, the growing state surplus was transferred into a special fund called the "Post War Construction Fund." At the same time offshore oil revenues exploded. Those funds were placed in the "Offshore Oil Reserve Fund." Growth of automobile usage meant increased tax collections and fees, including a jump in gasoline sales tax revenues, all of which was placed in the "Highway Fund." When the federal government determined it would invest in a National Defense Highway system, California was ready to participate and had the funds necessary to build an extraordinary network of freeways as part of the system, taking advantage of every available federal dollar.

An unofficial guideline was set up which provided that Southern California development by the state would be handled by the Offshore Oil Revenue Fund and the Post War Construction Fund would handle northern California

projects. Through the Post War Construction Fund, Sacramento would see the construction of many new state buildings to accommodate the growing state government. The state had 18,000 employees in Sacramento by 1958, a dramatic increase over the pre-war period. Under the guidance of Governors Earl Warren, Goodwin Knight and Edmund G. (Pat) Brown, the last to reside in the Old Governor's Mansion which is now a museum on 16th Street, state infrastructure improvements soared with bi-partisan legislative support.

GROWTH OF THE SUBURBS AND DECLINE OF THE CENTRAL CITY

The growth of airfields and industries such as Aerojet, Campbell Soup and Proctor & Gamble brought a significant number of new jobs which required increased services which also brought more jobs. All the new families moving into the area needed new houses. In the 15 years between 1945 and 1960 the Arden area provided housing for 45,000 people and Town and Country 47,000 people. The same kind of development was occurring in other areas of the County. Meanwhile within the city limits existing subdivisions were filling out.

Sacramento's city and county population exploded. Over 100,000 people were added between 1940 and 1950, rising from a count of 170,333 to 277,140. The number of people leaped 81 percent more in the next 10 years, nearly doubling to 502,778, surpassing all other decades but that of the Gold Rush in percentage of growth. Sacramento joined the nationwide baby boom and economic expansion. For the first time ever, more people lived in the county than in the city; over two-thirds were in the unincorporated area by

Freeways are indicators of post-World War II suburban expansion. This c.1950 aerial, looking north, features the new freeway linking Del Paso Boulevard and North Sacramento with downtown Sacramento. Highway 160 leading to a future Highway 40, and later Interstate 80, angles off to the right. *Sacramento Bee Collection, SAMCC.*

1960. Although the new suburbs tended to be largely white, a greater ethnic diversity appeared within the city proper, with expanding concentrations of African-American, Hispanic, east and southeast Asian and other residents.

The first suburban shopping center was Town and Country Village at Fulton and Marconi Avenue, completed right after WWII ended. Almost at the same time, Fruitridge Shopping Center opened at Fruitridge Road and Stockton Boulevard and a short while later Southgate Shopping Center was opened on Florin. In the 1950s, many strip malls opened in addition to larger commercial areas such as Arden Shopping Center, Country Club Center and Florin Mall.

Sacramento State College (now California State University, Sacramento) started in 1947 at City College and moved to its present campus in 1953. In 1947, the Sacramento Yolo Port District was established. Construction began on a port and deep water channel in

1949 with completion occurring 14 years later. By 1954, freeways went east to Roseville and west to Cordelia and by the end of the decade, a new second bridge was completed over the Carquinez Straits; plans were complete to construct a four-lane freeway from Lodi to Sacramento. Freeways were arriving from all points on the compass but the problem of how to get through Sacramento was not resolved until the end of the 1950s. Sacramento was the last major city in California to substantially complete its freeway grid, though a planned crosstown freeway connecting Highway 50 and Interstate 80 near the eastern edge of the county never materialized.

The shopping centers attracted nearby entertainment facilities such as theaters, even as people began to discover economical entertainment in their own home from more extensive radio and television programming. KCCC-TV on channel 40 opened up in a tent on the Garden Highway in 1954. This first channel 40 folded, but KCRA, KOVR, KXTV and KVIE were all in place by the end of the decade.

Suburban development meant there was less need to shop or to be entertained downtown. K Street, the traditional center of shopping and entertainment, was deteriorating along with much of the central city, particularly the west end (the area west of 7th Street). With the growth of suburbs, freeways and televisions in every home, urban deterioration was a national problem and Federal programs were established to address the issues associated with inner city problems. In 1950, Sacramento established its "Redevelopment Agency" to work with the those Federal programs. The first Redevelopment Project area was a 15-block area along Capital Avenue (now Capitol Mall) between the Capital and the Tower Bridge. Later projects would deal with K Street, the balance of the downtown below 7th Street, and Old Sacramento, which eventually was reclaimed from dereliction and became a landmark historic site befitting its role as the portal to the Gold Rush.

Housing was a critical priority throughout the County and the FHA from the New Deal was still around to develop programs. The Sacramento Housing Authority was established in 1939, and Sacramento built its first public housing project along Broadway west of 9th Street in 1942. The Dos Rios project at 12th and North C Streets was opened later the same year.

The suburbs were growing to the north, the east and the south. North Highlands population was only 150 in 1950 but 22,000 by 1959. The Arden area increased 46,000 by 1959. In the south subdivisions filled out the area of Fruitridge and down toward Florin Road. Around the County, subdivisions popped up with names like Orchard Terrace, River Park, Rosemont, Sierra View Terrace, Arden Manor, Arden Oaks, Arden Park and Meister Terrace. Rancho Cordova sprung up as a residential community after Aerojet opened in the Folsom rock piles in 1953. Many of the 15,000 employees would buy houses in the Rancho Cordova area.

As the post-war prosperity boom took hold the tenor of Sacramento life shifted perceptibly from that of its first 100 or so years. A river-oriented gold boomtown that gained world notoriety became as a result the transcontinental rail-road terminus and a transportation crossroads and then a relatively small agricultural processing town that served as a modest state capital. But the 1950s saw the start of what would be a remarkable transformation over the next few decades. Sacramento became a muscular metropolis characterized by rampant suburban growth carrying a diverse seven figure population beyond the county's boundaries, by a significant role as part of the nation's military-industrial-technical complex, by a burgeoning and sometimes innovative state government that gained national and international attention, and most recently by the arrival of electronics manufacturing industries and financial processing centers linked to the global economy. The Sacramento story continues to be shaped, once more on a world stage.

Tony Koester was one of KFBK's most well known announcers. He was most famous for recreating entire baseball games for his radio listeners. The wooden block he is tapping with his left hand would simulate the sound a bat successfully connecting with a ball. Here he is broadcasting from the 1951 State Fair. *Sacramento Bee Collection, SAMCC.*

CHAPTER SEVEN

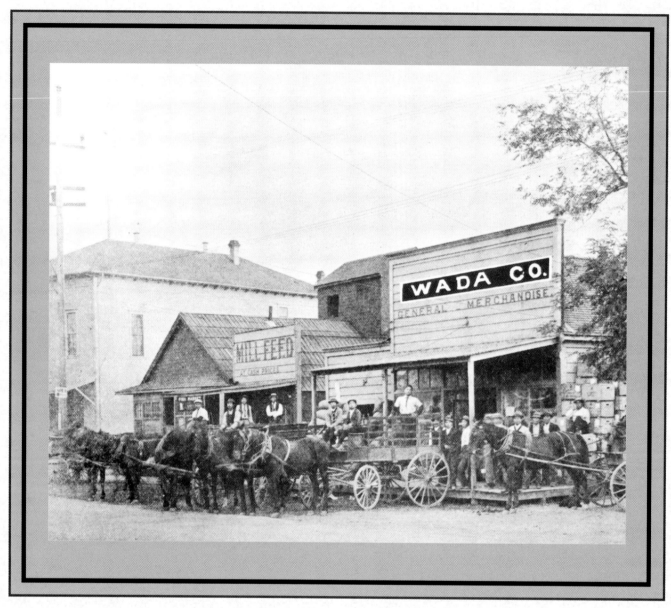

The Communities of
Sacramento County: An Introduction

by Melinda A. Peak

Communities in the County of Sacramento follow one of the following patterns:

- Incorporated City — Sacramento, Isleton, Galt, Folsom Citrus Heights.
- Communities or sites of communities now included within the corporate boundaries of Sacramento or another city — Sylvan/Citrus Heights; Prairie City/Folsom; North Sacramento, Oak Park/Sacramento.
- Communities that still exists with a distinctive history but remain unincorporated — Carmichael, Elk Grove, Fair Oaks, Orangevale, Rio Linda.
- Newer communities that may include earlier small communities — Antelope, Rancho Cordova.
- New planned development communities — Rancho Murieta, Laguna Creek, Gold River.
- Communities that were abandoned and now remain undeveloped — Live Oak, Sebastapol, Hicksville.
- Some locations are not known or uncertain as they were abandoned by the time the first official Sacramento County map was published in 1885 — Viola, Western and Buckner.

In the early years, communities grew up where necessary to provide goods and services to the local region. Many of these communities emerged along transportation corridors. In these years, when the Sacramento River served as the primary means of shipping farm products to urban markets, a number of small communities became shipping points on the river. Other communities formed along the roadways that were heavily travelled by the freight wagons carrying supplies to the miners in the Mother Lode region. The many railroads built over the years also influenced community development. Many of the lines that were created in the Sacramento region are no longer in existence, but at times they supported a number of small communities at the various shipping points.

Some of these communities in the eastern portion of the county were the result of gold discoveries in the region. These communities were short-lived for the most part, dying off when the mineral resource was no longer readily available.

Some of the communities prospered for a short time, and prospects appeared strong enough to establish a post office. A 1955 compendium of post offices includes the names of 85 communities that at some point warranted a formal post office designation. Many communities never had a post office and with a number of other communities developing since that time, the total number of Sacramento County communities might be estimated to total over 100.

Some of the community names are preserved with neighborhood, district or road names. Other names have completely vanished from our collective memories.

Further blurring the distinctions of the communities has been the growth of suburban Sacramento. Lines between communities are somewhat arbitrary, corresponding to zip code boundaries or other lines chosen to distinguish the extent of the "community." Carmichael extends to the boundary of Fair Oaks which runs into Orangevale and Citrus Heights. Within the City of Sacramento and the County, subdivision or neighborhood names are used to identify "place."

Other community distinctions are blurred by post office designations. Many of the unincorporated area citizens may live in communities known as "Foothill Farms" and "Florin," but receive their mail addressed to "Sacramento."

The following text summarizes very briefly the histories of some of the major communities in the County that have had important roles through time as well as some selected smaller communities. For ease of geographical reference they are somewhat arbitrarily divided into five regions: northern, eastern, central, delta and southern.

This essay can only be an introduction. It is not possible to describe the history of every community, nor to give the detail deserved for those profiled.

NORTHERN REGION

Much of the land of the northern portion of the County lay within the boundaries of land grants — Rancho del Paso and Rancho San Juan. Rancho del Paso, consisting of 44,000 acres extending northward from the American River, was held as a tract by James Ben Ali Haggin from 1862 until 1910. The land was first used for grazing, with grain, hay and hops grown on the bottom lands along the American. In the early 1880s, Haggin began using his lands for the breeding and training of thoroughbred horses. Haggin established a nationwide reputation with his horses with a Kentucky Derby winner, Ben Ali, in 1886. Although Haggin quit racing his horses in 1891, he continued to breed them, shipping a number to New York for sale annually until 1905. In 1910, a Minnesota firm purchased the land for $1.5 million and began to subdivide and sell off tracts in the region.

As a result, the northward growth of the City of Sacramento did not begin until this time, and the lands remained primarily rural. The Rancho del Paso lands are crossed by the route of the Central Pacific, and stations were built at Ben Ali, Arcade and Antelope. The area was crossed by a number of roadways leading to other communities to the north and northeast such as Marysville and Auburn.

ANTELOPE

The small community of Antelope started as a shipping point on the Central Pacific for grain from the region to be sent to both Sacramento and the mountains. The first building in the town was a large brick warehouse constructed in 1876, with the townsite surveyed two years later. A post office was established in 1877.

The community remained small, shipping more fruit and almonds as the local agricultural emphasis shifted to those crops. The rail yards adjoining the community was the site of a major 1973 explosion of bombs being shipped to Nevada, resulting in property damage to the remaining portions of the community. The name "Antelope" is now applied to a large tract of residential development west of the site of the original community.

CITRUS HEIGHTS

Citrus Heights is the newest incorporated city in the County of Sacramento. The agricultural lands of this region were sparsely populated. The area was crossed by the Auburn Road, and a number of roadhouses existed along this route to serve travellers. A small community grew up around what is now the junction of Auburn Boulevard and San Juan known as "Sylvan."

In about 1910, several large tracts of lands were laid out in subdivisions of 10-acre plots, each named a Citrus Heights subdivision. On maps as late as 1940, the name Citrus Heights is not used. Eventually, the name became applied to the entire region including Sylvan, with the post office for the community established in 1947. The area was primarily rural until the development of the Sunrise Mall complex in the early 1970s. Growth has occurred at a rapid rate, with virtually every tract of land developed for residential or commercial purposes. The Citrus Heights Historical Society published *A Historical Overview of the Evolution of Citrus Heights* in 1998.

NORTH SACRAMENTO

The North Sacramento Land Company bought a large tract of the Rancho del Paso, and established the City of North Sacramento. The City was incorporated in 1924. North Sacramento has its own post office from 1915 to 1920, with service thereafter from Sacramento. The City of North Sacramento was annexed to the City of Sacramento in 1964.

RIO LINDA

The United States Farm Land Company of St. Paul and Minneapolis began the subdivision and development of the lands of the Rancho del Paso soon after their 1910 purchase. The company advertised nationwide, and described the richness of the area for the production of fruit. The advertisements drew many to the rancho lands, including a group of German Adventists who settled in what is now Rio Linda. Local realtors and developers bought portions of the rancho to subdivide into farms and home sites.

The first rail line to provide service to the area was the Sacramento Northern, an interurban electric railway that was competing with the Western Pacific for service to the

North Sacramento was an incorporated city until it was annexed by the City of Sacramento in 1964. Photographer Eugene Hepting was standing in Del Paso Boulevard looking south, near its intersection with El Camino Avenue, when he shot this photograph November 21, 1940. Del Paso Boulevard remains North Sacramento's main street, and is undergoing a revival as an arts district. *Eugene Hepting Collection, SAMCC.*

Rio Linda developed out of the subdivision of the former Rancho Del Paso. Dixie Land Farm was the name the Dicks family gave to their property, one of the many small farms that characterized the Rio Linda community. *Franz Dicks Collection, SAMCC.*

northern Sacramento Valley. Regular service began in 1906, with a stop "Dry Creek" serving the community of Rio Linda. The post office was established at the site in 1914.

The Sacramento Northern line provided important passenger service between the northern Sacramento Valley and the Bay Area until 1940, when competition with automobile, bus and truck traffic took its toll. Western Pacific converted the Sacramento Northern line to diesel power in the 1940s for continuing freight business. Between 1951 and 1967, the trackage was removed from the railroad berm. The berm now serves as a bicycle trail.

ELVERTA

Just north of the Rancho del Paso, Elverta grew up along the route of the Sacramento Northern as a service center and shipping point for the region. The community was named for Elverta Dike in 1908, whose husband had given a lot for the community church. A post office was established at the town in 1908.

NORTH HIGHLANDS

In 1920, the U.S. Army established an aviation supply and repair depot at Rockwell Field on North Island in San Diego Bay. By 1930, the depot's facilities were becoming obsolete because of the rapidly advancing technology associated with aviation. The leadership within the Army Air Corps could see the need for a larger, more modern facility, in a more central location, further inland to be better protected from possible enemy attack.

Arthur Dudley of the Sacramento Chamber of Commerce worked with the Air Corps to find possible sites in the Sacramento region. Mather Field appears to have been the first choice for the site, but its more distant location from the Southern Pacific trackline and thus from shipping points on the Sacramento River created logistical problems for the transport of large aircraft. Dudley was asked to obtain options on the 1,200-acre site selected on the old Rancho del Paso. Sacramento realtor Carroll Cook drove the muddy roads of the area in November 1935, obtaining purchase options on 17 of the 20 farms in the original site area.

The depot remained a secret undertaking until the $7 million appropriation for the depot was added to another bill in Congress in May 1936. The land title for 1,100 acres, purchased for about $87,000, was finally cleared and transferred to the government in October 1936.

The building of the base brought a need for housing in the area. Dudley encouraged local builders and realtors to build some 400 new houses for the families moving from

Rockwell. The goal was five- to six-room homes, moderately priced and well constructed, that would rent for about $30 a month. By the time the workers arrived in late 1938, many new homes were available. This was the nucleus of the community of North Highlands. The North Highlands post office was established in 1951.

The Sacramento Air Depot was formally dedicated in April, 1939 with the name later changed to McClellan Field to honor Major Hezekiah McClellan, an Army aviation pioneer. In 1948, the name was changed to McClellan Air Force Base, reflecting the 1947 establishment of the United States Air Force as a separate branch of the armed services.

The base served important military needs during World War II, the Korean and the Vietnam conflicts. McClellan acquired additional acreage, and by 1982, comprised 2,790 acres on-base and 928 off-base. For many years, McClellan served as one of the largest employers in the county, but is now slated for base closure.

EASTERN REGION

The eastern lands of the county were recognized early for their valuable gold deposits. The initial communities started along the American and Cosumnes rivers. After the Gold Rush, mining continued to be an important industry in the eastern portion of the county, with many acres dredged for gold between the late 1890s and the early 1940s. Dredging continued after World War II, with the last dredger in the County ceasing operations in 1962. As a result, much of the land had little value. In the early 1950s, the aerospace and defense industries began acquiring tracts of the dredged land, becoming large employers in the region, and stimulating the residential growth of communities in the central and eastern portions of the county.

The agricultural value of the eastern portion of the county was also recognized early in time, with much of the countryside away from the rivers and creeks used for seasonal grazing of sheep and cattle. The need for water for mining led to the development of water conveyance systems that allowed the use of some of the lands east of Folsom for the cultivation of wine grapes and orchards.

MORMON ISLAND

The site of Mormon Island now lies under the waters of Folsom Reservoir. Mormons working for James Marshall at Coloma discovered gold in Sacramento County on the American River just a few weeks after Marshall's first discovery on January 24, 1848. Many members of the disbanded Mormon Battalion gathered to mine in the

area, and reportedly they took out 100 pounds of gold in their first 30 days of mining at the site. In July, 1848, the military governor of the state, General James Mason, accompanied by then 2nd Lt. William T. Chairman, Capt. Joseph Folsom and a military escort, arrived at Mormon Island for an official inspection of the gold regions. The area was occupied by a number of canvas tents and brush arbors, with Sam Brannan's store and several boarding houses present. The site continued to be productive, and a more permanent community grew up at the site. At one point, there were four hotels, three dry goods shops, an express office, a carpenter shop, a butcher shop, a bakery, a livery stable and seven saloons at the site. By 1880, the population had dwindled to about 20. The post office, established in 1851, was moved to Folsom in 1890.

The construction of Folsom Dam and the pending inundation of the town site brought about the need for the final move of the pioneer cemeteries. The Army Corps of Engineers removed 256 interments from Mormon Island, reburying most in a new cemetery located south of the town, on the Sacramento-El Dorado County line.

MICHIGAN BAR

Michigan Bar is the site of an 1849 discovery of gold on the Cosumnes River, near the eastern boundary of the County. The area was intensively mined by placer methods in the early years. A number of ditches were built in the region in the early 1850s to provide a more reliable water supply, with hydraulic mining introduced in 1858. At one time, the population was estimated to total over 2,000.

Important pottery works were established at Michigan Bar for the manufacture of sewer pipe and stoneware in the early years because of the local source for clay. Clay mining continued to be an important industry in this section of the County for many years.

FOLSOM

The City of Folsom has served prominently in the development of Sacramento County. The City was laid out in 1854 on lands of the Rancho Rio de los Americanos, a grant of over 35,000 acres, owned at the time by Joseph Folsom. The rapid growth in California had created a need for improved means of transportation. The first railroad in California was the Sacramento Valley Railroad, completed from Sacramento to Folsom in 1856.

Among the many nationalities who settled in Folsom during the gold rush were a number of Chinese miners. Folsom had a population of over 1,200 Chinese at the height of the gold rush. The Chinese lived on the southwestern edge of town, with their own shops and place of worship. Folsom's "Chinatown" burned several times and was rebuilt over the top of the gutted homes.

The fortunes of Folsom continued to be intimately connected with the American River and the uses people made of it. The Natoma Water and Mining Company was organized in 1851 by A. P. Catlin, to supply water for mining operations. Check dams were built on the South Fork two miles above Salmon Falls, which diverted water into a 16-mile complex of ditches, dams and sluice gates. The company was a phenomenal success, and several affiliated companies branched off from it, which also had great influence on the development of the area. These included the Folsom Water Power Company, the American River Land and Lumber Company and the Sacramento County Water Company.

Horatio Gates Livermore was the driving force behind the Folsom Water Power Company. His dream was a dam at

Folsom, with the power used in an industrial center in the town. By 1862, Livermore and his sons had purchased 9,000 acres of the Rio de los Americanos grant and gained control of Natoma Water and Mining.

In 1868, the State Prison Board was considering Folsom as one of two possible locations for the construction of a new prison. With the hope of minimizing further construction costs, the Livermores succeeded in persuading the board to select Folsom. In a formal contract, the entrepreneurs agreed to turn over 350 acres on the south bank of the river adjacent to the dam for a prison site in exchange for $15,000 worth of convict labor to be utilized in completing the Folsom dam and a power canal.

Unfortunately for the Livermores, however, the state did not complete the prison until 1880, so several years passed before convict labor became available. Convicts first went to work on the dam in July, 1882, one year after the Livermores converted the Natoma Company into the Folsom Water Power Company. The dam and canal were completed in 1892.

By this time, the Livermores had realized that water power as a direct motive force for mills and factories would soon be superseded by electric power. Accordingly they decided to erect a hydroelectric powerhouse below the dam and transmit electricity to Sacramento, in part to power the streetcar system. Work on the powerhouse and an extension of the canal began immediately. The Folsom Powerhouse began transmitting power to Sacramento on July 13, 1895.

Pacific Gas & Electric Company operated the historic powerhouse until November, 1952, when the old Folsom dam was destroyed and a new one erected farther upstream, forming Folsom Reservoir. In 1958, PG&E presented the complex to the California State Park System for preservation and interpretation.

Gold mining remained an active industry in the Folsom area. The Natoma Company introduced dredging in 1899, which enabled the company to reach gold deposits that neither placer mining nor hydraulic mining could easily remove.

ORANGEVALE

The lands of the San Juan grant had been held by a few investors for a number of years. In about 1890, the first major subdivision of the land resulted in the creation of Orangevale. The land was divided into 10-acre tracts that quickly sold. Planted primarily in oranges and other citrus fruit trees, the land was irrigated by water from the North Fork of the American River in Placer County, part of the American River Ditch Company system constructed in the mid-1850s primarily to provide water for mining purposes.

SLOUGHHOUSE

The community of Sloughhouse is located on the lands of Rancho Omochumnes, located on the north side of the Cosumnes. This grant was claimed by William Daylor and Jared Sheldon, both employed by John Sutter. Sheldon and Daylor built a gristmill on their property in 1847. In 1851, Sheldon was killed by miners who were angry about the

This metal bridge preceded the present-day Rainbow Bridge as a vehicular crossing from Folsom to the north side of the American River. The abutments for the former California Central Railroad Bridge are evident just downstream. Sacramento photographer Levi Vandercook about 1910 captured this view of what appears to be a pleasant afternoon outing. *Levi Vandercook Collection, SAMCC.*

The community of Orangevale originated as one of Sacramento County's fruit-producing colonies. The house shown here was both home and office for Harry Beauchamp, physician and surgeon. *Levi Vandercook Collection, SAMCC.*

The community of Sloughhouse is located on the former Rancho Omochumnes on the north side of the Cosumnes River, along Deer Creek. It was named after a public house, known as the Slough House that still operates on the bank of Deer Creek. Nels Westerberg, blacksmith, was one of the early-day residents, and his family remains in the community. *City of Sacramento: History and Science Collection, SAMCC.*

flooding caused by the dam Sheldon built to provide water for running his mill.

Near the site of the gristmill, at the crossing of Deer Creek by the Jackson Road, Sheldon built the Slough House in 1850. The original hotel building burned in 1890, and was rebuilt the same year on the site. This building is still a landmark along the Jackson Highway.

CENTRAL REGION

Most of the land along the American River lies within the boundaries of Mexican land grants — Del Paso and San Juan on the north side, and New Helvetia and Rancho Rio de los Americanos covering most of the south side, from the Sacramento River on the west to east of Folsom. On the south side of the river, four major early transportation corridors brought early settlement — the Coloma Road (roughly the route of Folsom Boulevard), the Jackson Road, White Rock Road and the Sacramento Valley Railroad. Numerous small communities grew up along the roadways to provide lodging and services for travellers and freighters, with many dying out in the 1860s due to the decrease in mining in the Sierran foothills and to the completion of the Central Pacific, the more direct route to the booming mines in Nevada and to

eastern markets. The Sacramento Valley Railroad provided transportation for farm products, and small communities grew up at many of the stations such as Perkins, Mayhews, and Mills.

As with most regions outside the City of Sacramento, agriculture supported the region. The rich bottomlands along the American River proved valuable for the production of a number of crops, including fruit orchards and hops. Wine grapes were another popular crop, and the areas around Carmichael and Fair Oaks were promoted for citrus crops.

BRIGHTON

In early 1849, a group of Sacramento businessmen promoted a townsite east of Sacramento on the Coloma Road. One of the promoters of the site named it "Brighton" after the town of the same name in England. The town promoters built a grand hotel, the Pavilion, in 1849-1850, at a cost of $30,000. The town was divided in lots, with a plat filed with the County Recorder. There was a race track at the site, providing entertainment such as a bull and bear fight in 1851, drawing a crowd of 2,000. The Pavilion Hotel burned down, and the site of the town was abandoned in part due to defective land titles.

In 1861, a new town of Brighton grew up, about a mile south of the original site of the town. This town, located at the junction of the Sacramento Valley Railroad and the Central Pacific line, proved to be considerably more successful. In 1880, the town had a hotel, two blacksmith shops, a distillery and winery, a general merchandise store, harness shop, market and saloon. The town had a post office from 1864 to 1886; it was then moved to Perkins, a small community about a mile east along the Sacramento Valley Railroad line.

CARMICHAEL

Carmichael lies on the lands of the San Juan grant, and is the third major colony laid out on lands of the grant. Clarke and Cox sold the land to D.W. Carmichael, who piped it for irrigation, and sold the land in 10-acre tracts. The land was thought to be especially suitable for olives and oranges. A post office operated from 1921 to 1935. The postwar suburban growth of the region brought the re-establishment of the Carmichael post office in 1950.

FAIR OAKS

The town of Fair Oaks is located on a bench above the American River on lands that were a part of the San Juan grant. In 1849, Frederick Cox, later a state senator, purchased the land grant. He sold about 6,000 acres of it to the Howard

Wilson Publishing Company of Chicago in the early 1890s. The new owners subdivided the acreage into 10-acre tracts, and advertised the Fair Oaks Sunset Colony in eastern newspapers. They offered excursion trains from New York and Chicago for those interested in viewing the land prior to purchase.

The first 150 "colonists" arrived in Fair Oaks in 1895. The promoters helped many of the newcomers to plant orange, olive and almond trees on their lands. By 1897, there were 300 permanent residents in Fair Oaks, primarily engaged in citrus growing. Water was provided to

Perkins was a small community at the intersection of the road to Folsom and the road to Jackson, adjacent to the Sacramento Valley Railroad. The brick portion of this early-day stage stop, store and later service station, still stands. *Eugene Hepting Collection, SAMCC.*

The community of Carmichael, named for developer D. W. Carmichael, grew out of the San Juan land grant. This view, taken in March 1916, shows a fledgling orchard, evidence of the olive and orange groves that were the basis for the colony's founding. *Eugene Hepting Collection, SAMCC.*

Fair Oaks developed on high ground above the north bank of the American River. Like many of the other land colonies in the county, Fair Oaks promoted agriculture, especially orchard and grove crops. The railroad provided the means for growers to ship their crops. This view of the Fair Oaks Depot was taken about 1905. *Levi Vandercook Collection, SAMCC.*

Florin developed along the Central Pacific Railroad's (later Southern Pacific) main line down the valley. It soon became world renown for strawberries and grapes. After 1890, a large Japanese community grew up associated with agriculture. This view of the Wada Co. general merchandise store on Florin Road, was taken about 1910. *Sacramento Ethnic Survey Collection, SAMCC.*

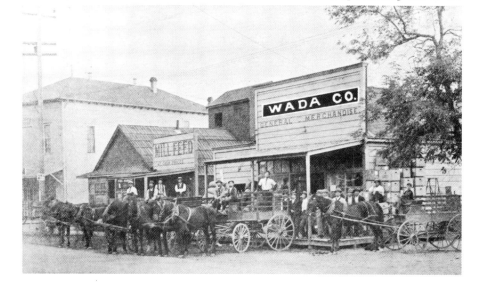

the colonists from the ditch systems of the North Fork Ditch Company. The water supply remained a problem until the establishment of the Fair Oaks Irrigation District in 1917.

The citrus orchards suffered tremendous damage in a freeze in 1932, and less than half of the citrus trees in Fair Oaks survived. The farmers, already suffering due to the lowered prices caused by the Depression, were unable to replant, and many moved from the area.

Almonds and olives did continue to be important products until the 1950s. At that time, the original trees were old and losing productivity. The growth of Aerojet-General and McDonnell-Douglas Aircraft and the suburban expansion of Sacramento brought the subdivision of most of the early agricultural tracts for residential purposes.

FLORIN

The town of Florin grew up as a station on the Southern Pacific line for shipping produce from the surrounding region. A post office was established in 1869, and in the 1870s, a store, hotel and schoolhouse were established. The soil surrounding Florin proved to be excellent for the production of strawberries and table grapes.

The area drew many Japanese immigrants after about 1890. By 1930, the Japanese-American population in Sacramento County totalled over 8,000, second only to Los Angeles County. In 1921, the California legislature amended the school laws to allow the establishment of separate schools for Indian children and children of Asian parentage. Four school districts in the county created separate schools, the only county to do so statewide. The segregation continued until 1942. The only extant building used for a segregated school in the county is the Florin East School in the Florin School District, used until 1939 as the "Oriental School."

RANCHO CORDOVA

Mather Field, later Mather Air Force Base, was initially built during World War I as an Army Air Corps training base. The facility closed in 1932, reopening in 1940. The base remained active after World War II, and the Korean conflict brought further job expansion. The Cold War and Vietnam conflict ensured ongoing employment well into the 1970s. Recent closures of military facilities across the country included this base. The property is now in the hands of the County of Sacramento, with facilities converted to a variety of recreational, industrial and commercial purposes.

Rancho Cordova sprouted on the agricultural lands south of the American River almost entirely as a by-product of the federal defense industry. Mills Station, a shipping point for the produce of the region, was the earliest settlement in the region. The area was one of orchards and vineyards. Starting in the 1950s and 1960s, Rancho Cordova area developers responded to the need for housing for employees of Mather Field and for Aerojet-General with a number of developments on the former vineyards and orchards. Further growth occurred in the 1970s, after the completion of the US 50 freeway, providing a quick connection to the City of Sacramento.

DELTA REGION

The agricultural value of the delta region was soon recognized by disillusioned gold-seekers. Reclamation of the land to prevent annual flooding began early in the 1850s, and continued through the 1930s. Many Chinese settled in the delta region after the completion of the Central Pacific, providing labor for the construction of the levees and for the planting and harvesting of crops. The adjacent Sacramento River provided a means of transporting the agricultural products rapidly to markets in the Bay Area.

ISLETON

Andrus Island was first settled by George Andrus in 1852. The agricultural value of lands in the delta region was recognized quickly, but the annual flooding prevented more than seasonal crop production on some tracts of land. Levees were completed on the island in the 1860s, and the area prospered. By 1874, the population and agricultural production had increased to the point that a market center and river landing for shipping

were warranted. Two major landholders, Josiah Pool and John Brocas, established Isleton in that year. In the next two years, the town grew to include a wharf and a beet sugar factory. By 1880, the community consisted of a Grange Hall, school, hotel, two stores, a post office and a few lesser buildings. The area has remained a prosperous agricultural center. Incorporation of the City of Isleton occurred in 1923.

WALNUT GROVE

The community of Walnut Grove was first settled by John W. Sharp in the fall of 1851. There was an early wharf at the site, and the town served as a shipping point

Walnut Grove is one of the small towns that grew up along the banks of the Sacramento River delta. The town served a largely agricultural population, including sizeable Chinese, Japanese and Filipino communities. The Hotel Kishita, shown here about 1910, provided rooms for Japanese agricultural workers. *Sacramento Ethnic Survey Collection, SAMCC.*

Freeport was established in the 1860s on the east bank of the Sacramento River, below Sacramento, by the Freeport Railroad Company as a "free port." Although by 1930 the property shown here featured a service station, the canopy over the road to protect travelers and their teams from inclement weather was a remnant from the last century. The owner, Joe Souza, poses in front. *Sacramento Valley Photographic Survey Collection, SAMCC, from an original from the Portuguese Historical and Cultural Society.*

Courtland was founded in 1870 by James V. Sims and was named for his son. Both before and after World War II, Delta towns included Filipino communities, drawn to the area by agricultural work. These three young Filipino men are posed in Courtland in 1937. *Sacramento Ethnic Survey Collection, SAMCC.*

for a large area. The post office was established in 1856. By 1880, the town consisted of a schoolhouse, small hall and hotel. The town's population included a number of Chinese and, later, Japanese residents, most of whom came to the region to work in the fields, orchards and packing plants. A disastrous fire in the 1910s in the Chinese section of town led to the establishment of nearby Locke. Little development has occurred in the region, and it remains an agricultural center. Pleasure boating is also popular along the rivers and sloughs in the area and throughout the delta region.

LOCKE

Locke, a unique site, is the only town in America built solely by Chinese. The town is a surprise to most who visit for the first time, with the appearance of a western movie set. The town was built in 1916 after the fire destroyed the Chinese section of nearby Walnut Grove. Locke included a main street with a school, gambling house and many merchants' establishments catering to the Chinese farmworkers and residents. Today, the gambling house and school are museums, and most of the original buildings are still standing. Across the levee, the Southern Pacific wharf and warehouse was built in three stages, beginning in 1906. During harvest season, fruit packers would rent space in the warehouse. The warehouse is now used to store and launch pleasure boats on the river.

FREEPORT

The community of Freeport, on the Sacramento River, was established as an alternative shipping point to Sacramento, as a "free port." The Freeport Railroad Company formed in 1862-1863 for the purpose of building a railroad from the site of Freeport, connecting to the Sacramento Valley Railroad at a point midway between Sacramento and Folsom, thereby diverting the northern trade around the City of Sacramento. Nine miles of the railroad route was built in 1863, and lots were staked off and sold in Freeport. The town grew rapidly, and for about three years, was a significant shipping point. Goods for the mines and other localities were landed here, and produce from the region shipped out. The railroad project proved a failure, and with the completion of the transcontinental railroad, goods could go more directly to the mining regions through Sacramento. In 1880, the town contained a store, blacksmith shop, boardinghouse and shoemaker's shop, and had revived its prospects somewhat as a shipping point for grain harvested in the region.

COURTLAND

Courtland was founded by James V. Sims in 1870. Sims, a native of England, came to California in 1848 as a member of Stevenson's Regiment. He left the army in 1849, mined for a short while, then travelled to the delta region. He became a large property owner and one of the first farmers to grow grapes for commercial purposes in the area. A large wharf was built at the townsite, with steamer service every day in the early years. The place was named for Courtland Sims, the son of the founder of the town. The post office was established here in 1872. As with many of the towns in this region, a large Chinese residential section developed, occupied by the many of the individuals of Asian descent employed in reclamation and agriculture in the delta. The town is the center of a large fruit-growing region, with pears an important crop. An annual "Pear Fair" is held each July.

SOUTHERN REGION

Along the Cosumnes River, the land in the southern region lies within Mexican land grants — Omochumnes on the north side of the river and Sanjon de los Moquelumnes and Cosumnes on the south side. The area is crossed by the major north-south roadways and railroad lines, providing good access to and connections to major shipping points such as Sacramento and Stockton. The southern section of the county has always been agricultural in nature, with non-irrigated crop farming, dairying and stock raising predominating. Until recent years, little development had occurred. The suburban growth of the

county has accelerated southward, particularly along the corridors of Interstate 5 and US 99.

ELK GROVE

The name of Elk Grove was originally applied to a spot about a mile away from the eventual location of the town. James Hall built a hotel there in 1850 and named it after his hometown in Missouri. This hotel burned down in 1857. The eventual site of Elk Grove was on the ranch of Major James Buckner, who also built a hotel on the site in 1850.

Elk Grove began at the intersection of Upper Stockton Road (Highway 99) and Elk Grove Boulevard. After the town relocated about a mile to the east in the 1860s, the intersection became known as Old Elk Grove. In 1930, 19-year-old William Henry Cumpston, who lived just a few doors away, serviced cars at the Old Elk Grove Service Station. *Gail Cumpston Brokaw.*

After the Central Pacific Railroad (later Southern Pacific) was completed down the valley in the 1860s, merchants in the area realized the commercial opportunities for a new town. The name Elk Grove, originally given to a settlement on Upper Stockton Road to the west, was transferred to this railroad-oriented community. The block of buildings shown here about 1930, still stands on the west side of Elk Grove Boulevard, just west of the tracks. *Sacramento Valley Photographic Survey Collection, SAMCC, from an original at Sacramento City/County Library.*

Everson persuaded the citizens to pool their money to form the Elk Grove Building Company in 1876. The profits from the first building, the Chittenden and Everson general merchandise store, fueled further construction which, in turn, brought in merchants from outside the area. Only four years later, the town boasted the original general store and one other, two hotels, a flouring mill, the railroad depot, a hardware store, a meat market, a furniture factory, two drug stores, a harness shop, a grain and hay warehouse, a dressmaking shop, two millinery shops, a boot shop, a wagon factory and a blacksmith. The town continued to grow, first as a commercial center for the farmers in the area and recently as a suburban residential zone for greater Sacramento.

FRANKLIN

The town of Franklin was first settled in 1856 by Andrew George who established the Franklin House. The town was known commonly though as "Georgetown." A post office with the name "Franklin" was initially established in 1856, discontinued between 1858 and 1862, and re-established and maintained until 1943. Buried in the local cemetery is one of the last surviving members of the Lewis and Clark expedition of 1804-1806, Alexander Hamilton Willard, who came to California in 1852, and died in Franklin in 1865.

The hotel was owned successively by Buckner, Phineas Woodward, Mrs. Jared Erwin, and Nicholas Christophel.

The site did not really become a town until after the railroad was constructed. A farmer named Everson saw potential commercial opportunities for a town at this location, but none of the residents, including Everson, had the money available to construct the necessary buildings.

Galt, located near the San Joaquin County line, was established in the 1860s. John McFarland, an early settler, named the town after his birthplace in Canada. This 1895 photograph features Native Americans employed at the McFarland ranch. *Sacramento Ethnic Survey Collection, SAMCC.*

GALT

Although the region near Galt was settled as early as 1849, there was not concentrated settlement until 1869. The first settler in the region was Dr. W.L. McIntyre, who built the first frame house in Dry Creek Township in 1851 at a site near Galt. At first, the area was used almost entirely for stock raising and dairy farming, but crop farming, particularly wheat, soon became a more common use of the land.

The construction of the Western Pacific Railroad through the region led to the establishment of Galt as a thriving agricultural center and railroad junction. The City of Galt incorporated in 1946.

SHELDON

The town of Sheldon provided services to the farmers of the region. Sheldon lies on the edge of the Omochumnes grant, a Mexican land grant awarded to Jared Sheldon in 1844. The town was never large, and the County History of 1880 stated: "This place, as a town, never existed; a blacksmith shop, the inevitable saloon, and two or three house, was the

Sheldon is a small community on Grantline Road at the edge of the Omochumnes land grant. The heart of Sheldon was the store established by the Casey family before the turn of the century. By March 1943, when this photograph was taken, it was owned by Bryan Miles. Although the canopy is gone, the store building remains in use in Sheldon as a restaurant. *Eugene Hepting Collection, SAMCC.*

shipping point for the region's agricultural products. The post office was established in 1869, with the name suggested by an early settler in the region, John McFarland, after his birthplace in Canada. The first two buildings in town were built elsewhere and moved to Galt when the town started. Both were used as hotels serving the railroad, and also the Forest Line Stage Company, which ran from Galt to Mokelumne Hill. This stageline was abandoned in 1876 at the completion of the Amador branch of the Central Pacific Railroad (later the Southern Pacific), who by then had taken over the main railroad through Galt. The Amador branch extended to Ione, where coal deposits had been discovered. Several small towns grew up along this railroad line through the southeastern section of the County including Clay and Conley. Galt became a

extent of it in its most palmy days. It is now deserted." The town had a post office between 1860 and 1874, again briefly in 1887 and 1888, and from 1896 to 1913, when service was moved to Elk Grove for the region. The construction of the Central California Traction Railroad line between Sacramento and Stockton in 1910 through the town of Sheldon provided a means for shipping produce for the local farmers.

WILTON

Wilton is another small town that grew up on on the Central California Traction Railroad Line. The railroad named the station for the owner of the land where it was established — Seth A. Wilton. Wilton was a dairyman and poultry rancher who had been on his land since 1887. The post office was established in 1915.

BIOGRAPHIES OF CONTRIBUTORS

Editor

John F. Burns is History-Social Science Consultant for the California Department of Education's Standards, Curriculum and Assessment Division and directs the History-Social Science Course Models project. He was State Archivist of California from 1981 to 1997, and was responsible for initiating and developing the new State Archives building, Constitution Wall and Golden State Museum in downtown Sacramento. He also established an institute for the training of archivists and created the state oral history program. For over 10 years, he has been an adjunct professor in public history at California State University, Sacramento. Previously he served as a U.S. naval officer, college teacher and grants administrator. He was a county supervisor's appointee to the Sacramento Commission on History and Science and has held many offices in national and state organizations, receiving numerous awards. He is author of *Approaching the Millennium: Prospects and Perils in California's Archival Future,* chief editor of Historical Records of Washington State, and author/guest editor of "World Class Ambitions: History-Social Science Standards for the Golden State," *Social Studies Review,* among other works. Forthcoming publications include co-editing *Taming the Elephant: Politics, Government and Law in Pioneer California,* and a study of the California county courthouse heritage.

Photo Editor

Lucinda Woodward is a historian with the California State Office of Historic Preservation where she supervises the Local Government Unit. She is co-author of *History of the Lower American River*, author of *The Rhoads School: Its History and Recommendations for Use* and *A Documentary History of California's State Capitol,* and the photo editor of *Sacramento: Heart of the Golden State.* Her community activities include appointment to the Sacramento Commission on History and

Science, past president of the Sacramento County Historical Society, former trustee of the Sacramento History Museum Association, past president of the Sacramento History Museum Docent Council, a director of the Sacramento Pioneer Association, member of the American River Parkway Advisory Committee, former member of the Sacramento Public Library Collections Preservation Committee, member of the City of Sacramento Select Committee on Historic Preservation, and a member of the Sacramento Housing and Redevelopment Agency Old Sacramento History Mural Advisory Committee. Her family has lived in California since 1848 and she is a native of Elk Grove.

CHAPTER AUTHORS

Chapter One

Norman L. Wilson was born in Auburn, California. He received his Bachelor of Arts and Masters degrees in Social Science from California State University, Sacramento. He served in the U.S. Navy during the Korean War. His career with the California State Parks system spanned 34 years as a curator, ranger, museum designer, Chief of Interpretation, Assistant to the Director and State Archeologist. He is the co-author of the chapter on the Nisenan Indians for the Smithsonian Institution's *Handbook of North American Indians,* Volume 8, and several other publications and articles pertaining to California history and anthropology. In retirement he continues to write and consult. In 1994, he was awarded the V. Aubrey Neasham Medal for Lifetime Work in Historic Preservation by the California Historical Society.

Chapter Two

Dr. Edward H. Howes is retired as Emeritus Professor of History at California State University, Sacramento, where he taught classes in U.S. History, History of the American West, California History and graduate research seminars for 33 years. His specialty was a class on the history of California during the Gold Rush era (1848 to 1870). He graduated with an A.B. in

History from Knox College in Illinois, where he met and married his wife, Elizabeth, who is also a historian and published mystery novelist. After serving in the Army Air Force in World War II, he earned a M.A. and Ph.D. in History from the University of California at Berkeley. He is co-editor of *Overland to California on the Southwestern Trail, 1849: The Diary of Robert Eccleston.* He is a charter member of the Sacramento County Historical Society, past vice-president, and former editor of the Society's research publication, *Golden Notes.*

Chapter Three

Walter P. Gray III is Chief of the Archives and Museum Division of the California Secretary of State's Office. He had previously been on the staff of the California State Railroad Museum, and served as the Museum's director from 1990 until 1998. A native San Franciscan who grew up in New England, he has a degree in History from California State University, Sacramento, and is a graduate of the University of Virginia's museum management program. He has written or edited numerous books and articles. He is married to Mary Helmich — herself a former staff member of the State Archives — who is the coordinator for Gold Discovery to Statehood Sesquicentennial programs within California State Parks. They live in east Sacramento, and are the parents of a fat brown cat.

Chapter Four and Six

James E. Henley, Manager of the Sacramento Division of History and Science for the City of Sacramento and Sacramento County, has been actively involved in or supervising historic research and project development on Sacramento history for 30 years. This work included the master planning, funding, construction and management of the Sacramento History Museum and the Sacramento Archives and Museum Collection Center. He holds a B.A. from California State University, Sacramento, with a major in California History, supplemented with additional graduate training. He is the city's lead official on matters related to area history, with responsibility for museum and archives buildings and collections, Old Sacramento Historic District research and management

of the Old City Cemetery. Co-author of *The City of the Plain: Sacramento in the Nineteenth Century* and other works, he served as consulting curator for the Oakland Museum exhibit, "Gold Fever," and as graphics editor of a related publication.

Chapter Five

Charles H. Duncan was born in a white house on Pennsylvania Avenue — in Fair Oaks, California. A true native, he has never lived outside Sacramento county, graduating from San Juan High School, Grant Technical College and California State University, Sacramento. He enjoyed a 42-year career in communications with McClatchy Newspapers, in radio, TV (where he portrayed KOVR's Cap'n Delta for five years) and after 1970, as curator of Eleanor McClatchy's collection of printing artifacts on Sacramento and California history and on the development and significance of printing, in general. He lives with his wife of 48 years, Shirley, in the Arcade area and remains active as a volunteer at both the Discovery Museum and the Sacramento Archives and Museum Collections Center.

Chapter Seven and Special Focus

Melinda A. Peak is President of Peak and Associates, an archeological and historical consulting firm that has been in business for over 20 years. A native Sacramentan, she holds a B.A. in Anthropology from the University of California at Berkeley and a M.A. in History from California State University, Sacramento. Author and compiler of hundreds of archeological and historical reports and studies, she is an authority on the prehistory and early history of the Sacramento Valley and adjacent counties. She served as President of the Sacramento County Historical Society from 1997 to 1999 and continues on the Society's governing board, as well as being a member of numerous other professional organizations, including the Western History Association, California Historical Society and Society for Historical Archeology. She lives with her husband, John Burns, and children Alyssa and Katherine on the edge of the gold country.

Partners in Sacramento

Building a Greater Sacramento

Sacramento real estate, construction and visitor service industries shape tomorrow's skyline, while providing working and living space for people.

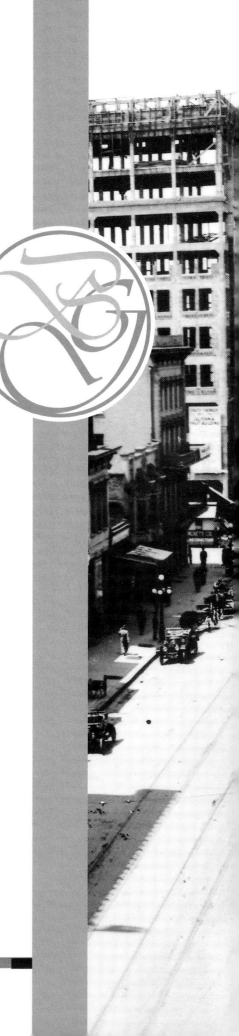

Brown Construction, Inc.

Brown Construction, Inc. is a Sacramento business that's successful from many perspectives. It's a family business founded by a father and son who harmonize their different styles to reach agreement. Together they have built a business team of managers and employees who work respectfully with clients to do a superior job. The high standards that result in solid buildings are applied throughout the entire process of planning and construction. The company's commitment to its clients is reflected in the care it takes with every project.

The AT&T regional headquarters in Sacramento, California

At Brown Construction, Inc., the emphasis is on both excellent workmanship and face-to-face communication. All team members communicate freely with each other and the client, working proactively to plan and carry out the project. Clients are in touch with every step of planning and construction, and their input is an important part of the process. This direct and open style is highly effective and contributes to the company's ability to complete projects in a timely fashion while honoring budget constraints. This capacity has earned Brown Construction, Inc. the respect of both clients and other developers.

Elk Grove Unified School District food-processing facility Sacramento, California

The company focuses on two types of construction — multi-unit housing for families and commercial buildings. Because of this dual focus and its excellent reputation, the firm has a steady flow of work even when demand for construction fluctuates with the economic climate.

The company carries out these residential and commercial contracts in three ways. The first approach is referred to as design/build. This means that Brown Construction, Inc. handles both architectural design and construction. Second is design/assist, in which the company works with an outside architect, functioning primarily as the contractor. The third is the hard-dollar bid, in which the project is planned and completed within a predetermined budget.

Brown Construction, Inc. was established by William T. "Bill" Brown. He began his construction career as a carpenter, and after becoming an independent contractor, he incorporated in 1971 as Brown Construction, Inc. Bill's 30 years of construction experience include work with public and private sector clients, and he has personally overseen the planning and construction of hundreds of homes and commercial buildings. In the process, he's learned a great deal about working with government agencies and developed excellent relationships with agency officials. This expertise ensures that Brown Construction, Inc.'s projects meet governmental guidelines, satisfy community, architectural and ecological concerns and are cost-effective.

For many years, Brown Construction, Inc.'s main focus was on constructing multifamily apartment buildings throughout California. When Bill's son Ronald T. Brown joined the company in 1987, his experience and interest in commercial construction opened further markets. He managed the company's commercial construction projects, concentrating on design/build commercial facilities. He also encouraged use of the latest electronic technology in business management. Within five years Ron was a full partner.

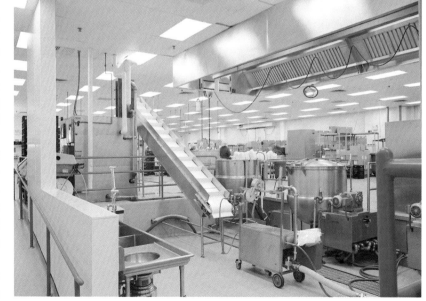

Bill is a generalist, while Ron is a specialist. Bill contributes years of varied experience, and Ron incorporates the latest technical expertise. "We go at things differently," says Bill, "But we wind up agreeing with each other." Together, they have created a solid management team and ensured that every member's intelligence and skills are fully utilized.

The team includes a group of project managers, engineers and architects as well as a superintendent who assumes full-time responsibility for a particular job. This involves conducting an in-depth study of plans and specifications before the project begins, getting the work underway immediately, and keeping the project on schedule. Equally important are the skilled-crafts workers and specialized sub-contractors who do the actual construction and the home office staff that keeps information flowing smoothly. In addition, the team's chief estimator tracks estimated and actual costs and assists with official negotiations.

All team members keep daily track of their work in the computerized, cross-referenced submittal, reference and proposal request logs, which are maintained electronically. These logs provide an ongoing record of planning, spending and construction. This record is open to clients and enables them to check on staffing, materials and expenses. They can see for themselves where savings are realized and how construction is progressing. The logs also help to keep projects on schedule. Brown Construction, Inc. has a history of meeting critical deadlines despite bad weather, completing projects on time and even finishing ahead of schedule.

In the future, Brown Construction, Inc. looks forward to maintaining its current level of quality and integrity, continuing to serve its current markets while expanding in new directions. Ron foresees a paperless office, where projects can be tracked and administered electronically and online. Brown Construction, Inc. is committed to increasing employment opportunities in the Sacramento Valley. Ron Brown says, "Our goal for the region is to construct two million square feet of office space and 500 individual units of multifamily housing per year." To achieve this production goal, Brown Construction, Inc. attracts out-of-state and foreign companies, helping them relocate their operations to Sacramento. One successful example of this process is a Japanese sprout producer now operating locally.

In addition, Brown Construction, Inc. offers its experience and organizational contacts to community groups who wish to undertake their own projects. Together the firm and local leaders work with agencies to negotiate legal requirements and acquire funding. The company derives

Rio Lane Apartments in Sacramento

particular satisfaction from offering its expertise to the leadership of Hispanic communities throughout California. Generous donations to charities such as WEAVE, (Women Escaping A Violent Environment), Summerhouse and other charities that benefit children are further ways that Brown Construction, Inc. serves its community.

Brown Construction, Inc. is recognized as a "developer's contractor" because so much of its work consists of negotiated design/build or assisted design/build contracts. Its 100 percent project completion rate and history of zero litigation are external measures of success. Internally, the firm hires the finest people and exercises dignified and generous employment policies. Employees become long-term, committed team members, skilled in working collaboratively to ensure superior results for clients.

Thus the company achieves success on many levels, creating long-term profitability and a positive, productive work environment that benefits clients, management, employees and the community. Working with integrity and applying the Golden Rule turn out to be excellent business as well as personal policies.

Bill and Ron Brown

Coldwell Banker Real Estate

Coldwell Banker Real Estate rose out of the rubble of the 1906 San Francisco earthquake, pledging to conduct business with courage, integrity, professionalism and neighborly solicitude. More than 90 years later, those values are still the cornerstone of the largest, most widely imitated and one of the most prestigious real estate franchise organizations in the nation.

A more classic embodiment of the California spirit of business would be difficult to find. In 1906, after San Francisco's devastating earthquake and fire, young real

in 1914, and the two remained with the company throughout their lives.

Commercial real estate brokerage was the company's first successful venture. The firm's first residential real estate office opened in San Francisco in 1925, and a full-fledged residential real estate department was established in 1937. Geographic expansion began in the 1950s, with the addition of offices in Southern California. Growth continued in Phoenix during the early 1960s and Seattle in 1969. In the 1970s, Coldwell Banker acquired respected

estate agent Colbert Coldwell was eager to help rebuild the city. But he eschewed the common practice among his peers of acquiring properties, often from uninformed sellers at ridiculously low prices, only to resell them for huge profits. With two partners, he formed the real estate company of Tucker, Lynch and Coldwell, which began a tradition of commitment to customer service that has never wavered. In 1913, Benjamin Arthur Banker joined the firm as a salesman, and he and Coldwell soon discovered they shared similar views and ethics. Banker became a partner

residential real estate firms in Atlanta, Chicago and Washington, D.C.

Coldwell Banker debuted in Sacramento in 1935 under the leadership of Wilbur Brand and two partners by the surnames of Jones and Hullin. In Brand's case, real estate would run in the family: by the late 1990s, his son-in-law, Larry Knapp, had become the first regional vice president in charge of Western operations for Coldwell Banker's parent company, National Realty Trust. Jones & Brand & Hullin was acquired by Coldwell Banker in 1981.

Coldwell Banker's aggressive campaign to expand its holdings originated in the 1980s, a period marked by multiple mergers and acquisitions and subsequent rapid growth. In 1981, Coldwell Banker was acquired by Sears, Roebuck & Co., joining Dean Witter Financial Services Group and Allstate Insurance Group as a member of the Sears Financial Network. Sears provided the resources and framework necessary for reorganization and even more rapid growth in major metropolitan areas across the United States. Also in 1981 came the launch of Coldwell Banker Residential Affiliates, Inc. for the franchising of the highest quality residential brokerage companies. Because of

these two events, Coldwell Banker's share of the residential real estate market grew from 1.3 percent in 1981 to more than 10 percent by the decade's end.

By 1990, Coldwell Banker had offices in all 50 states as well as Canada and Puerto Rico. A new phase of growth began in 1993 when the company was purchased from Sears by The Fremont Group, an investment company formerly known as Bechtel Investments, Inc., and a group of Coldwell Banker senior managers.

Coldwell Banker Capitol Region adheres to a well-worn real estate dogma: location, location, location. The desire to acquire more of this reliable draw was behind the firm's 1998 acquisitions of Coker & Cook Real Estate, Bertrando & Associates, Exceptional Properties and Gerwer & Associates. These acquisitions made Coldwell Banker the largest realty firm in the Sacramento, Placer and El Dorado tri-county area based on market penetration, with its 12 offices and 500-plus agents and brokers.

Currently, Coldwell Banker benefits from the resources and brand affiliation of Cendant Corporation, its parent company. Cendant is the world's largest franchisor of hotels and residential real estate brokerage offices. Under Cendant, Coldwell Banker possesses an organizational structure unique to the industry that enables it to maximize its opportunities nationwide. Coldwell Banker Capitol Region, part of Coldwell Banker of Northern California, is one of 15 real estate organizations nationwide owned by National Realty Trust, a subsidiary of Cendant. As a company-owned organization, it is able to flex its large financial muscle in the quest for greater market penetration. Locally, with Cendant's influence as owner of the largest relocation company in the world, Coldwell Banker Capitol Region has provided relocation services for executives in some of Sacramento's largest companies.

Additional market share is owned by Coldwell Banker franchisees, of which there are five in the Sacramento, Placer and El Dorado tri-county area. These independent operators are part of a network of 2,500 nationwide franchisees, which are governed by the Cendant Corp.'s franchise division.

Coldwell Banker strives to remain a cut above the competition. In 1998, company executives reported that surveys by *Money* magazine and REAL TRENDS listed Coldwell Banker as the No. 1 real estate company in the United States for four out of the last five years. Companies were judged by surveys on customer service, financial well-being, products and services and market share. Based on surveys, Coldwell Banker enjoys a 94 percent customer satisfaction rate — a remarkable feat considering everything that can (and usually does!) happen during the process of buying or selling a home.

Coldwell Banker's repertoire of quality products and services is unmatched in the industry. One such example is the trademarked Coldwell Banker Online, the publicly accessible site on the World Wide Web that gives offices and sales associates the ability to expose their listings 24 hours a day to more than 40 million consumers who browse the Internet. In addition, Coldwell Banker Online offers consumers pertinent tips and financing information that is updated daily.

Coldwell Banker offers the largest preferred-alliance program in the country, allowing its customers to take advantage of discounts through arrangements with businesses complementary to the real estate industry. Coldwell Banker's clients are able to save money on everything from home warranties to lawn mowers to automobiles.

In addition, Coldwell Banker has developed trademarked systems tailored to the needs of special real estate markets. They include the Previews Program for luxury properties and the Resort Property Network for vacation properties.

The future of Coldwell Banker Real Estate can be summed up in two words: bigger and better. But despite the organization's metamorphosis through the years, nothing essential to its beginnings was lost in the transformation. It's a legacy that founders Colbert Coldwell and Benjamin Banker would still recognize as their own.

Jim Ross, senior vice president and regional manager of Coldwell Banker Capitol Region, has been with the firm since 1985.

Coldwell Banker strongly supports the communities in which it resides. Here, a group of Coldwell Banker employees gets set to "Walk for the Cure" in support of the Juvenile Diabetes Foundation.

Eskaton

What began as a group of church members wishing to provide health care and community service has become Eskaton, a multifacility, nonprofit corporation focused on developing innovative solutions to problems faced by senior citizens throughout Northern California.

The corporation, now known as Eskaton, had its beginnings in the 1960s when several members of the Disciples of Christ Church in Oakland formed a charitable organization to provide health care, housing and other services to senior citizens and families. The new corporation's name, Eskaton, was drawn from the Greek language and interpreted to mean "the beginning of a new age."

In 1968, Eskaton took its first step with the acquisition of American River Hospital in Carmichael. Several other Northern California hospitals later became part of Eskaton's family of services.

By the early 1970s, Eskaton had also assumed management of an apartment complex in San Diego that provided housing to low-income families and senior citizens. Although Eskaton no longer offers family housing, the experience provided the "seed" that later grew into the continuum of care for seniors, which now includes housing for retired people and a wide range of other services.

It was in 1974 at Eskaton's first board-level strategic planning retreat that the concept of providing an "umbrella of care" was developed to encompass existing hospital and housing services and expanded to include additional services.

Assisted living was added to Eskaton's "umbrella of care" when the company acquired Annadale Manor in Sacramento. Eskaton no longer operates Annadale Manor, but assisted living has remained a major component of the company's services, and new facilities in Gold River and Cameron Park and an addition at Eskaton Village, Carmichael, opened in 1999. Assisted living is an essential part of Eskaton's multiservice retirement communities. Assisted-living facilities offer seniors the independence of their own room or apartment, with the added help they might need with daily activities, including taking medications, bathing, dressing and grooming. Assisted-living facilities also provide meals, laundry, scheduled transportation and activities.

In 1978, Eskaton added skilled nursing to its portfolio with the opening of Eskaton Manzanita Manor in Carmichael. Although the company had previously managed similar facilities, Manzanita Manor was built to Eskaton's design and included features not commonly found in nursing homes. Eskaton now has four skilled-nursing facilities that provide round-the-clock nursing care and rehabilitative therapy.

Eskaton was able to offer affordable, independent-living housing to seniors with restricted incomes with the opening of President Thomas Jefferson Manor in Sacramento in 1978. Eskaton now offers this service, funded by rent subsidies and construction funds offered through the Department of Housing and Urban Development, at 10 locations in Northern California.

In the early 1980s, Eskaton added home health care and adult day health care, and now provides home-delivered health services through Eskaton Visiting Nurse Managed Care and Eskaton Homecare, and a daytime program for seniors at Carmichael Adult Day Health Center.

The Senior Connection was introduced in 1987, offering workshops for the public on a variety of topics relevant to seniors, from stress to travel to Alzheimer's disease. The Senior Connection's staff of nurses, social workers and care advisors also provides guidance in locating senior resources, including information on health care, housing, social, legal and financial services available in the community. In addition, The Senior Connection provides education and answers for caregivers, including tips on dressing, bathing and lifting a person in their care, as well as tips for taking care of themselves while caring for a loved one or friend.

Eskaton's Centralized Placement Network provides central access to participating skilled-nursing facilities throughout the greater Sacramento area. This service is available to hospital discharge planners, home health agencies and members of the community 24 hours a day, seven days a week. The Assisted Living Registry offers similar access to participating assisted-living facilities.

By the mid-1980s, Eskaton had decided to leave the hospital business in order to focus solely on the development of senior programs and to broaden the range of services targeted to seniors.

THE NEW CORPORATION'S NAME, ESKATON, WAS DRAWN FROM THE GREEK LANGUAGE AND INTERPRETED TO MEAN "THE BEGINNING OF A NEW AGE."

As Eskaton celebrated its 30th year of service in 1998, one of the many noted milestones was the development of Continuing Care Retirement Communities, starting with Eskaton Village in Carmichael. Opened in 1992, Eskaton Village was the first Continuing Care Retirement Community in the Sacramento area, offering cottage and apartment living as well as assisted-living and skilled-nursing services to approximately 500 residents. California has only about 75 such communities, which offer several levels of service in a single setting to a variety of residents, who pay an entry fee and monthly service fees. After the turn of the century, Eskaton will open additional multi-service communities in Grass Valley and Roseville.

Eskaton's TLC program (Talking, Listening, Caring) is one of the ways the company reaches out to the community. Volunteers make daily calls to seniors who live alone and are at risk of becoming isolated. The volunteers check daily on the client's well-being, and, when problems arise, assist the client in obtaining appropriate assistance. There is no charge for this service.

Eskaton Executive Director of Strategic Planning Connie Batterson said there are so many more choices available to seniors today than in earlier years that the challenge is in tailoring services to reflect the changing needs of individuals. "It's not just a 'one-size-fits-all' world anymore," Batterson said.

Despite its many advances in senior living and health care, Eskaton is constantly striving to find more effective and efficient ways of meeting human needs while maintaining high quality and a personal touch. The company's primary mission is still "To enhance the quality of life of seniors through innovative health, housing and social services."

John F. Otto, Inc.

Everywhere in Sacramento, office trailers bearing the name of John F. Otto, Inc. are a common sight. That trailer means there's building underway, and the job is going to be done right. If the building is a new project, it may have been designed as well as built by the company. But new construction is not the only area in which John F. Otto, Inc. excels. When a Sacramento landmark needs a lift, chances are good that John F. Otto, Inc. will retrofit, remodel or restore it. The Crocker Museum addition, the Passenger Railroad Station in Old Sacramento and Frank

The downtown Sacramento office of John F. Otto, Inc.

Fats are all Otto projects, as are additions to Mercy General Hospital, the Sacramento Coca-Cola plant and the Sacramento Zoo.

John F. Otto, Inc. is a homegrown Sacramento company, one whose management and employees are proud to live and work in Sacramento. This dedicated and enthusiastic staff combines respect for tradition with state-

The United States Post Office Bulk Mail Facility at the Sacramento International Airport, built by John F. Otto, Inc.

of-the-art construction skills. At the downtown office, which the company designed as its own headquarters in 1981, a lobby museum of antique tools includes wrenches, levels, drills and bits, and even a giant red-and-gold safe from the old Sacramento Public Market. In an adjoining room, blueprints of upcoming projects are available for subcontractor study, and down the hall, murals of carpenters, masons and painters at work alternate with walls made from classic full-dimension timbers recycled from the railroad warehouse that the headquarters replaced. Retaining the best of the past is a John F. Otto, Inc. tradition. So is a commitment to serving Sacramento.

"When we chose this location," says Carl R. Otto, current president and son of founder John F. Otto, "our first goal was a core Sacramento address."

John F. Otto, Inc. has always been a Sacramento business. John himself began working here after he finished his service in World War II. He tried the public sector, but decided it was not for him. Family legend says that one day in 1947, John simply walked into the house and announced to his wife, "I've quit my job and I am starting my own business." He was already a father, and he brought the principles his family valued into the workplace. There's a heritage of quality and integrity, of a family business built on a secure foundation of hard work, determination and honesty. Respect for the diversity of clients and employees is combined with strict standards of craftsmanship. Just as it did 51 years ago, the company performs all concrete, carpentry and labor tasks with its own work force, guaranteeing that efficiency, cost control and reliable schedules are built into the job.

Carl R. Otto, John's son, heads the business now, and he earned his way in. Carl gained a thorough understanding of the business by steadily advancing in field, office and financial management before his father decided he was worthy of taking the helm. John had too much respect for both his children and his employees to turn the company over to someone who was not prepared to run it properly, and there was no guarantee that his successor would be a family member. Carl is now the head of the company, and it's still a family business. Carl's brother, Johan, is his partner. The company's nonfamily board of directors cooperates in running the firm. The family has controlling interest and could override the board, but they recognize the importance of an outside point of view. The directors' input is invaluable in maintaining an overview of business processes because they can look at issues with fresh eyes.

The company takes pride in meeting high standards. The hospital and medical projects that compose a large portion of its business have special construction criteria, and the firm derives satisfaction from meeting these challenges. Because the company takes this kind of care, clients return the next time they have a project. John F. Otto, Inc. has worked for almost 30 years with Eskaton, a Sacramento-based company that provides residential and continuing care for the elderly. Other current Otto projects are the recreation and office buildings for Del Webb's Sun City of Lincoln Hills, and the seismic upgrades to the state treasurer's office. Making interior improvements to the federal courthouse building is a project with an added incentive. Carl's twin sister will be working in the newly remodeled building, so she's following the process with special interest.

The company's community service commitments are as numerous as its construction credits. John began the tradition of civic involvement, and both employees and family are active in a wide variety of Sacramento organizations. John F. Otto, Inc. is also active in professional organizations, helping to set and maintain high professional standards. In addition, participation in local and state regulatory planning groups ensures that industry guidelines are clear, attainable and well-enforced.

Carl says, "Sacramento is our hometown. It's our community. We all live and work and play here, and our employees do the same. If all the work was right in Sacramento we'd love it. Sometimes we have to travel to do a project, but when it's finished, we come right back. Sacramento's home."

The company culture emphasizes hard work, but that doesn't mean there's never any fun. One of the results of the emphasis on consistent, reliable quality is a company culture that allows for relaxation. When the job is done right the first time, problems are less likely to arise.

John F. Otto, Inc. intends to continue the kind of work the company is doing today. In the future, many of its clients will be ones with whom the company has worked over the years. The same craftsmen and employees will be working side-by-side, meeting the same high standards. John F. Otto, Inc. builds some of the most interesting and best constructed projects in Sacramento. Quality, integrity and workmanship, combined with the finest designs means John F. Otto, Inc. can give superb design a solid form.

Another Otto project, the Sacramento Coca-Cola bottling facility

On the shore of Lake Victoria at the Sacramento Zoo

Eskaton Village Continuing Care Retirement Community

Kimmel Construction, Inc.

There is a construction company in Sacramento that deliberately seeks the most complicated contracts; that prefers to work on the most heavily regulated projects; that draws its greatest pride from the restoration of Sacramento's finest architectural treasures. Kimmel Construction, Inc. has always played in the arena requiring the greatest skill and determination to succeed.

When Albert E. Kimmel founded the firm in 1946, he had already distinguished himself as an Army Air Corps flight instructor in World War II, managed an armored car service, owned a concrete block factory and acquired a glass company. Since his days as a young architecture student in Wichita, Kansas, Albert knew his true calling was in commercial construction. Although he couldn't afford to complete his studies, he turned the craft of building into his life's work.

Kimmel Construction started building residential subdivisions utilizing Albert's concrete block products. The business was doing well, but it was time to join the big leagues.

Armed with a measure of bravado, Albert contacted Pacific Telephone seeking work for his growing business. As luck would have it, the phone company was accepting bids to build a suspended ceiling. Albert jumped at the chance and was awarded the project. The fact that Albert didn't have a clue what a suspended ceiling was didn't stop him from launching his commercial construction career.

With one foot in the door, Albert was on his way to earning one of the best reputations for quality workmanship and unfaltering ethics in the Sacramento market. Kimmel Construction was hired to renovate the Capitol's Senate and State Assembly quarters. By carefully cultivating his government contacts and private-sector clients, Albert grew his business almost exclusively by word-of-mouth.

In 1964, Albert's youngest son Jack got married and found himself in need of a job. He joined his father's business as a laborer, entered the union and became a skilled carpenter. As time went by, Jack managed projects and eventually became an estimator. The elder Kimmel was always on the job, anticipating and preventing complications long before the owner or architect came to sign off on the project. Jack paid close attention to his father's example. When the time approached for Albert's retirement in 1980, Jack was named president of Kimmel Construction, Inc.

Meanwhile, a remarkably parallel story was taking place. Patrick Welch, also a transplant from Wichita, owned a thriving construction company in Menlo Park. In 1968, a young man named Larry Suddjian asked Welch for his daughter's hand in marriage. He agreed, with one condition: "Get a job." So Suddjian went to work at Welch Construction as an estimator. In 1983, following Welch's heart attack, Suddjian was given the yearlong responsibility of winding down his father-in-law's business while moving his family to Auburn.

Jack Kimmel was searching for a highly qualified estimator. In what can only be described as kismet, Larry Suddjian's name came up. On the day after Labor Day in 1984, Suddjian joined Kimmel Construction. Within five years, he was promoted to vice president and went on to become half-owner of the company.

Jack and Larry's formidable partnership catapulted Kimmel Construction into the highest-profile, most prestigious projects in Sacramento and beyond. The bold pursuit of complicated contracts is the true signature of this firm, which tackles projects as delicate as the restoration of beloved historical buildings and as technically demanding as the Vandenburg space shuttle launch-site complex. Among the notable restoration projects completed in the valley are the original River City Bank, the Woodland Courthouse renovation and Yuba City's City Hall. A bridge connected the old Montgomery Ward buildings at 9th and L streets and 8th and K streets. These structures were com-

Albert E. Kimmel, founder

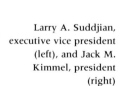

Larry A. Suddjian, executive vice president (left), and Jack M. Kimmel, president (right)

Project: The Landmark
Office Building,
Sacramento

pletely gutted and meticulously rebuilt to house the State Assembly and the Department of Rehabilitation. Kimmel has also been significantly involved in the renewal of old Sacramento's waterfront.

A striking example of Kimmel's progressive achievements is the aptly named Landmark Building, an enormous complex located at Howe Avenue and Arden Way. If Kimmel Construction were to name a specialty, it would be the very demanding and heavily regulated field of health care facilities. The company has built, expanded, renovated or repaired virtually every hospital in the Sacramento Valley. One client hired Kimmel to perform seismic tests on 37 facilities in preparation for the reinforcement and retrofitting necessary to meet government earthquake compliance requirements.

Another distinction of Kimmel's professionalism is the ability to safely complete massive remodeling and expansion jobs while a company is still operating in the location. Roseville Hospital, U.S. Sprint's switching station in Stockton, and KXTV, Channel 10 were all conducting business as usual while Kimmel built around their personnel and patrons. Kimmel's staff works harmoniously with architects to keep the project's atmosphere on a high note from start to completion.

A number of factors have ensured Kimmel Construction's resilience during the economic storms that have depressed the building industry. Jack and Larry sensed the imminent downturn, which started in 1989, and stemmed the tide by restructuring and totally computerizing the entire operation. This efficiency carried the company smoothly through a recession that

ravaged most in the trade, and Kimmel became a high-tech guru in the blue-collar world of construction. Kimmel has always been able to switch between the public and private sectors as conditions warrant. But paramount in Kimmel Construction's enduring success is community involvement.

Kimmel Construction's employees all live and work in the Sacramento area and are proud of their city. The company supports the special interests of employees, strongly encouraging them to participate in a number of causes. Jack is heavily involved with the Salvation Army and serves on the board of trustees of the Mercy Foundation, the University of Southern California's Sacramento Center for the School of Policy, Planning and Development, and is past president of the Rotary Club of East Sacramento. Larry is a charter member of the Point West Rotary Club, has been president and head of the legislative committee for the Golden Gate Chapter of the Associated Builders and Contractors, is a board member of the Private Industry Council and organizes the Western States Trail Foundation's annual Truckee to Auburn 100-mile horse ride.

Jack and Larry credit Sacramento's business diversity for the area's economic stability. Citing the fact that Sacramento is still outwardly expanding and attracting new industries, both are confident that the capital will always adapt well to the coming challenges.

In an industry that has seen little change in the material of its trade since the building of the Great Pyramids, Kimmel Construction has proved that ingenuity, integrity and courage are the best ingredients for success.

Project: the CADA
Office Building, 13th
and O streets

Luppen & Hawley, Inc.

There are few awards given for superb installation of plumbing, heating, air conditioning and electrical systems. A great system is invisible because it causes no problems. But the services these systems provide are crucial. Without sanitation, temperature control, and power and light, businesses, schools and hospitals would be unable to function. In Sacramento, the firm of Luppen & Hawley, Inc. has an award-worthy history of providing these services.

One of the original Luppen & Hawley delivery trucks in front of the Alhambra and J site

The company's current location on 14th Avenue

First-class air conditioning, heating, electrical contracting and plumbing combine with a history of trouble-free installations to give the company name an important place in Sacramento construction history. For almost 80 years Luppen & Hawley, Inc. has been making Sacramento a more comfortable and healthy place to live and work. In addition, it is one of the oldest family businesses in the region.

Luppen & Hawley, Inc. carries the name of its original founders, but the firm belongs to the O'Connor family. The first

Luppen & Hawley completed plumbing and HVAC projects for the California State University Sacramento Student Union Building.

of the family, J. D. O'Connor, joined the company 70 years ago. He worked his way up within the company and helped revive it during the depths of the Depression. In time he bought it and passed it on to his sons. Delbert, the late Kenneth, and now Laurence O'Connor have each succeeded him in continuing the business under its original name.

The roots of the company go back to World War I, when Luppe B. Luppen and John B. Hawley, a pair of Midwesterners, decided to start a business together. They were graduates of the University of Illinois' School of Architecture, and they worked together as engineers for the Division of Architecture of the State of California.

In 1920, the two went into business as mechanical contractors. Mechanical contracting involved setting up systems for plumbing, piping, steam heating, forced-air heating and air conditioning, the same type of construction they had supervised for the state. The firm has the distinction of being one of the oldest Carrier air-conditioning dealers in the country.

Luppen & Hawley, Inc.'s original office was located at 906 7th Street, right across the street from The Sacramento Bee. It was a small commercial office on the ground floor of an apartment building. Five years later, in 1925, they moved to larger quarters near Alhambra Boulevard and J Street, where their business flourished for the next 47 years. They were right next door to the glamorous Alhambra Theater, an air-conditioned mecca for moviegoers. Movie theaters were among the pioneer institutions to provide air conditioning as an essential draw for their customers. An hour or two in the coolness may have inspired many viewers to become Luppen & Hawley, Inc. customers.

After the move to the Alhambra and J Street location, the company also entered the field of electrical contracting. As part of this new aspect of business, the partners hired J. D. O'Connor, the future owner of the company. O'Connor headed the electrical department and in 1933, he became part-owner of the company. After Luppen's retirement, the other partners were A. V. Taylor and J. B. Hawley. Hawley went on to become president of the Master Plumbers of America, and O'Connor served as Western states vice president of the National Electrical Contractors Association.

Through the years, Luppen & Hawley, Inc. continued to perform a variety of services, offering whatever mechanical and electrical services customers needed. One job that stands out is the Campbell's Soup plant. In 1947 the company was selected to install all the plumbing, mechanical and electrical equipment at the new plant, which is still in service on Franklin Boulevard in Sacramento. The work required more than 200 tradespeople, including plumbers, pipe-fitters and electricians. Work was completed in approximately 18 months on the largest industrial plant in the Sacramento Valley at the time.

In 1954, O'Connor became the sole owner of the business but kept the Luppen & Hawley, Inc. name because of its excellent reputation. In 1972, the company moved to its current five-acre site on 14th Avenue. The business employs a combination of old-fashioned skill and advanced technology, using computerized equipment for a range of specialized tasks, from manufacturing sheet metal ducts to pricing and job estimates.

The firm specializes in institutional and hospital projects involving plumbing, mechanical and electrical installations. These facilities require stringent specifications for the installation of piping for medical gases, air conditioning, and complex electrical systems involving emergency power, fire-alarm and nurse-call systems. The company takes pride in meeting the challenge of installing these systems properly.

However, the company doesn't limit itself to medical facilities. It does a variety of mechanical and electrical work on schools, university and state buildings, and sewer and water treatment plants. Current projects include the plumbing and HVAC systems (the trade term for heating, ventilation and air conditioning) for the California State University Sacramento Student Union and the Solano County Education Center. The firm is also carrying out the tenant completion (another trade term for setting up systems to occupant specifications) of the United States Federal Courthouse in Sacramento. Electrical installations include the New Skills and Business Education Center in Sacramento and the Hangtown Creek Waste Water Treatment Plant in Placerville.

Safety in the workplace is always a major concern at Luppen & Hawley, Inc. The company was awarded first place in the 1998 Sheet Metal and Air Conditioning Contractors' National Association Safety Statistics Evaluation Awards Program for having the best safety and health record within its category.

The O'Connors attribute the long-term success of the company to their many loyal office-staff employees and a skilled, union-trained work force. A few years ago, the company celebrated the retirement of four people, each of whom worked for more than 40 years with the company.

The current officers of the corporation are Laurence J. O'Connor, president; John D. O'Connor, vice president; and Richard Padilla, secretary.

If there were a map of Sacramento with a light for every building with a Luppen & Hawley, Inc. installation, it would literally blaze. All over the city, its heating, ventilation and air conditioning, plumbing and electrical services are helping people to be more comfortable and productive. In the years since 1920, Luppen & Hawley, Inc. has grown with Sacramento while nurturing the city's growth as well. A third generation of O'Connors is working

for the company now. The family traditions of quality and service are going strong as the company moves toward its own centennial in 2020.

Another Luppen & Hawley plumbing and HVAC project, the University of California at Davis Medical Center School of Medicine, Building Number Three

The University of California at Davis Medical Center Central Plant, plumbing completed by Luppen & Hawley

Unger Construction Company
Tradition Continues

Unger Construction Co. — originally the Charles F. Unger Construction Co. — has constructed commercial, public and private buildings in the Sacramento area for more than 70 years. The company owes its good reputation to its founder's Midwestern values of honesty, uncompromising quality and reliability, values that permeated his relationships with clients and employees alike.

Charles Frederick Unger was born near Storm Lake, Iowa in 1891, one of four children in a farming family that experienced hard times as he grew up. After working his way through Ames College, where he was also a star football player, he answered the challenge of his generation, World War I, by joining the Army. Following his service as a first lieutenant and field artillery instructor at Fort Sill, Oklahoma, Unger began his career with Parks Construction in Storm Lake. As an architect and contractor he assisted in the construction of several schools, firehouses and city halls.

On a trip to California in 1924, Unger met and married Velma Wyatt of Winters. The couple returned to Iowa, where their first son, Charles Wyatt — known thereafter by his middle name — was born in 1925. The next year Unger moved his little family back to Winters, where he started his own general contracting business, concentrating on carpentry and concrete work. Drawing up the building plans for the Winters National Bank was one of Unger's first projects in his adopted state.

In the 1940s, Unger moved his company office to Sutterville Road on what was then the outskirts of Sacramento, where he had already established a construction yard during the 1930s. The office today is essentially the same building, modestly upgraded over the years to accommodate more personnel. It is located across from Sacramento City College, which did not exist when the office first opened. In years to come, his company would build, remodel or create additions to dozens of projects sited in Sacramento, Yolo and Placer counties, most of them within a 50-mile radius of his office, establishing Unger's reputation as a reliable local building resource.

From its beginning Charles F. Unger Construction Co. was known for high standards and attention to detail. In those years, architects would often rely on their general contractors to add the fine touches to a building; Unger pored over drawings on nights and weekends, adding necessary details to them to ensure that his workers could properly finish their projects. It is not surprising, given their exposure to their father's profession, that Unger's son, Wyatt Unger, became a contractor and his father's partner, and his other son, Dean Unger, an architect. In the 1970s, 80s and 90s, Dean designed Lyon Park Plaza and Lyon Village in East Sacramento, Von Housen Alta Arden Center, Old Spaghetti Factory restaurants in midtown Sacramento, Rancho Cordova and Roseville, and an apartment complex and medical office building in Davis — all built by Unger Construction Co.

Unger, a strong believer in union labor, supported both the local carpenters' apprenticeship program and the Sacramento Builders Exchange (he served as its president in 1963). Many of Sacramento's current general contractors worked for Unger as laborers, apprentice carpenters or cement masons. One such graduate recalls that Unger "ran a very tight ship," often unexpectedly visiting a construction site to check on his workers' progress and craftsmanship, and that he was frugal, legendarily honest, and insistent on meeting clients' expectations. Unger's reputation for trustworthiness meant that he sometimes sealed a contract simply by shaking hands with a client.

Unger projects built during Sacramento's building boom years of the 1950s and 60s and still in use are the midtown Tuesday Clubhouse, the Fremont Presbyterian Church Sanctuary on Carlson Drive (one of the earliest

One of Unger Construction Company's best-known projects — The Tuesday Club, 27th and L streets (1952)

Though Wyatt died in 1992, Nunan and Maxwell uphold the Unger standards. They agree tradition is important and are serious about their roles as trusted caretakers of the Unger reputation.

Through the lean construction times of the early 1990s to today's competitive design/build opportunities, Nunan and Maxwell have kept that reputation intact. They agree that it is gratifying that the company has received industry awards, but they want the company to continue to be known for building quality projects, as Unger would have wished.

However, both men beam with modest pride when they discuss certain Unger Construction Co. projects, such as its at-cost work on St. Hope Academy, its remodels of Sacramento Zoo Fairytale Town attractions, and the ball fields it donated to the Meadowview Community Center, because they directly benefit Sacramento's children. "This is our town," Nunan says simply. Charles Frederick Unger would approve.

local examples of an on-site, precast concrete structure), the Chinese Community Church Sanctuary and Social Hall, Arden Christian Church, four Bank of America offices, Natomas, Northgate and Kenneth Avenue elementary schools, Highlands, Bella Vista and St. Francis high schools, Sacramento City College Little Theatre, and the student health building and corporation yard for California State University, Sacramento.

The self-made businessman liked to continue to make his daily rounds even as he grew older. His distinctive driving style behind the wheel of his 1964 navy blue Chevy pickup became as much a part of his legend as his honesty.

Wyatt, who had joined his father in 1956 as a full partner, ascended to the company's presidency after his father's death in 1973 at age 82. In 1974 the company was renamed Unger Construction Co. and became incorporated. In running the company, Wyatt also exhibited the involvement, reliability and insistence on quality that had characterized his father. "If you got a compliment from him, it stayed with you," says company President John D. Nunan, who started working for Wyatt in 1977. Nunan worked his way up under Wyatt's direction from estimator to project manager to company general manager in 1986.

By that time, Wyatt's health was failing; in 1990 Nunan negotiated the purchase of the company from Wyatt, ending its 60-plus years as a family-owned enterprise. Former journeyman carpenter and local resident Scott W. Maxwell, now vice president of Unger Construction Co., had been with the company since 1986; he started work with Wyatt and Nunan after his graduation from CSUS' construction engineering program. Nunan is now majority owner and Maxwell is minority owner.

The shell of the Fremont Presbyterian Church Sanctuary at 57th Street and Carlson Drive (1963) was an example of Unger Construction Company's use of precast concrete.

Unger Construction Company's restoration of the U. S. Bank Building at 34th and Broadway (1996) makes it an Oak Park landmark.

Wallace–Kuhl & Associates, Inc.

While the Sacramento skyline sometimes appears as if it's floating on a cushion of fog or shimmering heat waves, it stands strongly anchored in the earth — thanks in part to the down-and-dirty work of Wallace-Kuhl & Associates, Inc. Founded in 1984 by Thomas Wallace, Charles Van Alstine and Douglas Kuhl, this award-winning geotechnical and environmental engineering firm has literally been working from the ground up to ensure the integrity not only of many of the landmark buildings downtown, but also of diverse land- and water-development projects within the Sacramento area.

The firm's work is grounded in the sciences, but WKA's emphasis on creative problem-solving elevates that work to an art. Where competitors cite roadblocks, WKA finds a way to help clients achieve their goals in the most efficient, cost-effective manner possible. Short notice and tough jobs inherent in the construction business are all in a day's work for the firm's 50-plus engineers, scientists, technicians and support personnel.

Long before striking out on their own, founding principals Wallace and Van Alstine had been honing their professional skills in Northern California. Engineers at heart, they knew relatively little about starting a business, but that didn't stop them from quitting their jobs and pursuing a $40,000 loan, using their homes as collateral. Soon afterward, Kuhl, an earthwork construction specialist and former engineer for Caltrans, joined the partnership.

Their courage has paid off. Today WKA is a cutting-edge firm worth more than $5 million. It has been honored with two Outstanding Project awards from the California Geotechnical Engineers Association and has been selected as a Fast Track 25 company by Arthur Andersen & Co. and *Comstock's* magazine. WKA has also been listed repeatedly by the *Sacramento Business Journal* as a Top 25 Engineering Firm and in 1995 was recognized as one of the city's fastest growing firms.

Much of WKA's workload involves geotechnical engineering services such as soil and foundation investigations, distressed-building consultation, pavement design and evaluation, feasibility studies and stability analyses. In other words, it is the firm's job to determine through sophisticated testing methods whether a building site is properly prepared, how a structure should be founded, why a structure is having problems and what to do about it. The soft upper soils of downtown Sacramento, for example, necessitate the use of piling to depths of 80 to 100 feet for support of large structures. In other areas, swelling and shrinkage of clay soils are the major problems to overcome.

From the city's Library Plaza to the Community Center expansion, downtown Sacramento has been touched by WKA. One of the firm's most innovative achievements was the foundation of Renaissance Tower, completed in 1988. This was the first building in the greater Sacramento area to be supported upon 170-ton piles, which represented a 31 percent increase over the maximum pile capacity ever used before and resulted in significant cost savings.

But the geotechnical engineering work doesn't end when construction begins. That's where WKA's Earthwork Construction Services department comes in. One notable project under this heading is Serrano El Dorado, a 3,500-acre residential community in the Sierra Nevada foothills. WKA tested and inspected the earth-moving required to provide infrastructure and building lots, as well as golf course and commercial development within the community.

Fans of the Kings and Monarchs, Sacramento's professional men's and women's basketball teams, probably don't think about the details that went into the construction of Arco Arena, but they have WKA to thank for the geotechnical engineering investigation and the construction-materials testing and inspection. WKA also provided similar services for the interim sports arena, now a three-story office building on North Market Boulevard.

Having a bit of old-fashioned fun in this 1984 portrait are, from left, Charles Van Alstine, Douglas Kuhl, administrative assistant Doris Brazil and Tom Wallace, the founding members of Wallace-Kuhl & Associates, Inc.

Since 1990, this building on Industrial Boulevard in West Sacramento has been home to Wallace-Kuhl & Associates, Inc. The building houses the firm's many departments as well as its own construction materials and soils-testing laboratories.

In 1985 came the addition of WKA's construction and inspection testing department as well as the materials laboratory. Certified and cross-trained inspectors in steel, concrete, welding, high-strength bolting, and other materials and processes are assigned to construction jobs throughout Northern California. They have determined plan and specification compliance on some of the most impressive buildings in Sacramento, such as the California Attorneys General building and the Wells Fargo Tower. They also have invented and fabricated specialized equipment for accomplishing difficult tasks more efficiently. This department spent hundreds of hours ultrasonically testing the "skeleton" of Sacramento's Hospital for Crippled Children, completed in the spring of 1997. Supervised by a senior registered civil engineer, WKA's in-house laboratory provides such services as ultrasonic analysis, concrete and asphalt-concrete mix design, testing and research, pavement design analysis, aggregate testing and construction material analysis.

A natural extension of WKA's service was the addition of its geological and environmental services department in 1986. This team of hydrogeologists, biologists and environmental engineers helps clients keep pace with the complex and ever-changing regulations surrounding site contamination and water management. Whether evaluating sources of soil and groundwater contamination or the air in structures for "sick building syndrome," this department plays an important role in the well-being of Northern California's people and wildlife.

WKA's phase I site assessment group, established in 1989, specializes in detecting sources of hazardous materials contamination on industrial, commercial, agricultural and residential properties. With its extensive library of historical aerial photographs, topographical maps and current agency databases, the firm is able to provide a 35-year snapshot of a site's history, often within hours of receiving a request.

Not only does WKA recommend action, it takes action in the form of its site investigation and remediation group. Using state-of-the-art equipment, this group of scientists can characterize the extent of site contamination, produce remediation plans and oversee the cleanup of diesel, solvents, heavy metals and other contaminants. One award-winning project involved the removal of 16 tons of lead from the 40-acre California Hills subdivision, a former gun-club site. The lead was taken to a recycling facility and treated soil was used as road subgrade, paving the way for homes to be built.

Anyone who lives in Northern California is bound to be aware of its geological hazards, including faults and landslides. WKA's group of engineering geologists conducts a wide range of investigations from fault and seismic hazard studies, providing site-specific ground response spectra for structural engineers to evaluate building response during seismic events.

Figuratively speaking, WKA is moving its own mountains. By the late 1990s, ownership of the firm had increased to 10 people. Its main products — the minds of its people — are constantly being upgraded through continuing education, a concept the firm strongly supports. And since the building boom in the Sacramento area shows no signs of abating, the skills of these professionals will be prized for decades to come. Now that's a solid foundation no matter how it is tested.

The staff of Wallace-Kuhl & Associates includes 52 engineers, geologists, scientists, technicians and support personnel.

Allen L. Bender, Inc.

Spans Generations

When Allen L. Bender established his general contracting firm in 1964 he probably didn't know to what extent, more than three decades later, his creations would stand out in the Sacramento landscape. But, as his son Blake Bender remarked, "It's hard to find a place we haven't worked."

Bender is a native Sacramentan. During his early years, he had some exposure to the construction industry through his work in real estate and insurance-related activities. Additionally, his father was a manager for On Your Lot Building, a company that did not stand the test of time.

Downtown Sacramento's Civic Center Parking Garage is an Allen L. Bender, Inc. landmark.
Photo by John Swain

Allen L. Bender, founder and CEO of Allen L. Bender, Inc.
Photo by Larry Lau

Unlike his father, Bender traveled much further down the construction path to become one of the Sacramento area's most prolific contractors. In 1971 his company incorporated and became Allen L. Bender Inc. (ALB). Upon his semi-retirement in 1996, Bender's two sons and two daughters, all of whom have absorbed aspects of the business since they were children, took over the day-to-day operations.

Over a 32-year period, Bender worked at expanding his operation and his clientele with the assistance of his wife, Beverly. His home was his first office, and he opened a modest outside office in the early 1970s. In the early 1980s he built the West Sacramento office the company now occupies.

The company's first experiences included building small, custom and speculative home developments and some custom remodeling work. But as his reputation grew, Bender began taking on small commercial projects in the Sacramento area, building structures like fast-food restaurants and small banks. Eventually, ALB was a full-service general contractor focused on projects involving the extensive use of concrete. ALB currently pursues all types of commercial and public works projects in Sacramento and other Northern California cities.

Some of ALB's notable public projects include a seismic upgrade of the older portion of Folsom State Prison, the $15 million Redding Civic Center, the Rio Cosumnes Correctional Facility in Elk Grove, the Placer County Juvenile Center in Auburn, and various structures at California State University, Sacramento, University of California at Davis and Sacramento City College. ALB strives to create beautiful structures as well as utilitarian ones; the dockside promenade and Plaza of Lights along the Sacramento River are ALB creations, as is the restored historic Shasta Argus Hotel in downtown Sacramento.

When the County of Sacramento decided it was time to upgrade the Sacramento Metropolitan Airport to Sacramento International Airport and expand the facilities, ALB won the contract to create tenant improvements inside the airport's crown jewel, Terminal A, which handles approximately 60 percent of the passenger traffic. ALB's efforts included $13 million in flooring, ceilings, wall finishes, electrical security and duct work.

Over the years, the company also left its mark on the area's military establishment, constructing hangars, commissaries, fire stations, dormitories and runways at Beale, Travis, McClellan and Mather Air Force bases and the Sacramento Army Depot. When most of those installations closed, ALB switched to local flood-control projects like the first phase of the North Natomas levee, which involved

constructing 14 miles of cast-in-place concrete flood walls, as well as building two pumping stations and retrofitting a third.

All of Allen and Beverly's offspring participate in ALB's success: Sons Blake and Brian Bender alternate annually as ALB president and vice president, and their two sisters Kathryn Bender Miller and Jennifer Bender Bittner — office manager and secretary, respectively — are also an integral part of ALB. A third generation of Benders may carry on the tradition: "It's still a little early to tell," Blake Bender said.

Building a Greater Sacramento

Fite Development Company

For four generations, the Fite family has conducted business in both the banking and real estate industries. Known as a strong force in the Sacramento area, the family has maintained a tradition of hard work, honest and well-planned business deals, and exceptional community service.

D. Bruce Fite and his family settled in the Sacramento area in 1968 and started Fite Development Company, a commercial real estate firm. Well-respected for his real estate knowledge, Fite still maintains an influence on the general growth and direction of Fite Development Company. His success in the real estate business brought with it community recognition and the opportunity to participate in other types of business ventures. He is a major stockholder and former member of the Board of Directors of American River Bank, one of Sacramento's most well-respected financial institutions.

Charles D. Fite ("Chet") joined his father Bruce at Fite Development Company full time in 1980. As the company's president, Chet manages day-to-day operations and is involved in virtually every aspect of the company, including development, management, marketing and financing of both existing and on-line projects. Working closely with the construction division, Chet also oversees the design and layout of the company's newest projects. Chet carries on the family's tradition of commitment to quality and honesty in business.

Since its inception, Fite Development Company has helped build, lease and manage more than 5 million square feet of industrial, office and commercial space. Additionally, the firm has developed more than 1,500 residential lots and perfected its own simple formula for success: Buy large tracts of unzoned land on the perimeter of the areas currently being built-out, obtain zoning for mixed uses, then construct speculative buildings or "build-to-suits." Using this method, Fite Development Company has contributed factories, canning plants, mobile home parks, regional malls, strip centers, roller- and ice-skating rinks, movie theaters, auto dealerships, distribution centers, and multi-tenant and Class A office parks to the Sacramento community.

By 1998, Fite Development Company was managing approximately 2 million square feet and owning or controlling more than 1,000 acres of vacant land in the Sacramento and Stockton areas, all of which was in various stages of development.

One of Fite Development Company's most interesting projects is also the closest to home — the Old Mills Winery Office Park houses the firm as well as many other prominent Sacramento businesses. Fite Development Company preserved this historic Sacramento County landmark by converting it into quality office space in a garden setting accented by stately trees, grape arbors and a colorful rose garden. The centerpiece is a dramatic two-story atrium/courtyard. Lush foliage provides a pleasant environment for office tenants and guests.

The original Mills Winery dates back to 1910 when acres of grapes dotted the surrounding countryside and were harvested to produce fine burgundies and port. In all, the park offers more than 61,000 square feet of leasable executive office space. Although Fite Development Company's renovation effort was extensive, most of the structures in the office park are original. Only two of the buildings in the complex are new, and they were designed according to the early California/Spanish influence, which utilized old bricks, wood and red-tile roofs. In addition to the office park's rich history and picturesque setting, its convenient centralized location offers easy access to downtown Sacramento, the Capitol and all local airports.

Other well-known projects from Fite Development Company include the gigantic Chico Mall, the 178-acre mixed-use Beltway Business Park development and Lexington Hills, a 524-acre master planned community with 1,400 residential units, a 31-acre business park and a 7-acre retail center.

Fite Development Company's headquarters, the beautiful and historic Old Mills Winery Office Park

As a major land developer, Fite Development Company continues to be on the leading edge of the Sacramento region's dynamic growth. Operating in one of the fastest-growing commercial real estate markets in the country, the company provides land-users and investors with some of the most desirable and marketable building sites in Northern California. Dedicated to ongoing participation in the market's rapid growth, Fite Development Company has an eye toward the region's bright future.

The Heller Company

Structural engineer Mike Heller had considerable construction experience before coming to Sacramento. Drawn to the area's stable economy, Heller liked the idea of being in the heart of the state's government, which required competitive bidding on public projects. This policy ensured that any qualified contractor had a fair chance to get the job.

With these factors in mind, Heller started his own construction company under the name of Continental Heller Corporation in 1945. The company would soon gain a reputation for technical engineering and construction expertise. Many of the principals of today's top construction

Company President Mike Heller Jr. perpetuates the quality construction techniques passed on by his father, Mike Heller Sr.

firms were trained at Continental Heller. It became one of the largest and most successful contractors on the West Coast. Landmark projects such as Atlanta's subway system, the Anaheim Stadium expansion and the NASA Space Shuttle Complex at Vandenburg Air Force Base in California helped solidify the Heller reputation. Other national clients include Anheuser-Busch, Harrah's, Nestlé and Ralston Purina.

Many of Heller's prominent downtown buildings helped create the dramatic effect of Sacramento's majestic skyline. Locally, Continental Heller has built Weinstocks Department Store, Crocker National Bank, the IBM building, the biological science building at the University of California, Davis, Sutter Memorial Hospital, the Sacramento Municipal Utility District's head office, and 455 and 555 Capitol Mall, to name just a few.

After a competitive bidding process that involved six other national construction firms and was based solely on qualifications, Continental Heller was chosen by the state to restructure and restore its most prized monument. The award-winning renovation of the California Capitol is probably one of the firm's most famous undertakings. The seven-year project, completed in 1982, cost $87 million. Shortly after the project was completed, Mike Heller sold Continental Heller Corporation to an international firm headquartered in France and eased into semi-retirement.

Today, Heller and his son Michael Jr. continue business locally as The Heller Company. While the elder Heller shows few signs of slowing down, his plan to pass his legacy to his son is well-known. Michael Jr., now president of the company, is an MBA graduate of the University of Southern California and holds degrees in both finance and real estate development. Michael Jr. brings 12 years of development experience to the operation. His goal is to blend his own professional philosophy with his father's principles of hard work, strict attention to detail and accountability.

The Heller Company has phased out of heavy construction and now concentrates its efforts on all phases of real estate investment, development, leasing, property management and consulting. During the recession of the early 90s, The Heller Company's primary objective was to purchase quality properties and add value through project renovation, leasing and detailed property management. To date, The Heller Company has purchased six prominent office projects. All are now fully leased, expertly managed and performing better than anticipated. More recently, thanks to a dynamic economy and soaring real estate prices, The Heller Company has resumed new construction by taking on a 90,000-square-foot office development project in Folsom, California.

It is with well-deserved pride that the Hellers, who celebrate their 55th year in business in the year 2000, look forward to another half century of successful business in the capital region.

Sacramento Valley Roofing

The decision to become a builder is often motivated by the desire to leave something behind — a monument to a life's work, a mark on the Earth that shouts, "I was here!" Robert Dixon's greatest works are the crowning glory of such landmarks — the parts that are best appreciated from the air, pinnacles that shape the city's skyline.

When Robert Dixon founded Sacramento Valley Roofing in 1990, he had already spent two decades climbing ladders and reading blueprints for some of the most imposing

roofing projects in Northern California. As a commercial estimator and project supervisor for a major roofing contractor, Dixon worked on massive undertakings like the County Fair Mall in Woodland, the Yuba City Shopping Center, the Folsom Factory Outlets, the United Parcel Service distribution facility in West Sacramento and the monolithic Aetna Life Building in Rancho Cordova.

When he broke away and started his own business, Dixon elected to concentrate on residential, custom residential, commercial and light industrial re-roofing. As the life of his earliest shopping center roofs expired, Dixon was honored to be chosen by many to perform the re-roofing projects. He accepts contracts for construction on new buildings very rarely and only from contractors with whom he has had a strong rapport for 10 years or more.

Now, Dixon does what he likes and likes what he does. He is very happy being able to run his company on a personal level, and Sacramento Valley Roofing has thrived on word-of-mouth referrals. The company's project list includes churches, colleges, banks, law firms, national food chains, apartment complexes, government buildings and hundreds of residences. Dixon is very selective in choosing his projects, contractors, suppliers and associates. Sacramento Valley Roofing is a member of the Western Regional Master Builders Association.

Most of the time, the job at hand requires redoing what has already been done. The surprises don't reveal themselves until the old roof comes off. Discovering that the last contractor was a master of improvisation is usually not good news. Sometimes the roof just won't cooperate. In those rare cases, Sacramento Valley Roofing customers know that Dixon won't rest until the problem is solved. The hands-on, practical knowledge Dixon has accumulated in his career always saves the day.

This is not to say that Dixon never gets to express his creative side. Dixon had the opportunity to participate in the remodeling of a palatial home on 6348 Palm Drive overlooking

the Ancil Hoffman Golf Course in Carmichael, a stunning example of the custom tile roofing design work performed by Sacramento Valley Roofing. A company called the Screenprint Connection bought a historical building on Del Paso Boulevard and contracted Sacramento Valley Roofing to maintain the structure's architectural integrity.

Dixon has successfully demonstrated that roofing is an art that can be appreciated from the curbside. The material selected by the property owner determines the length of the guarantee, and that promise is supported by both Sacramento Valley Roofing and the manufacturer. With the proper choice, a roof that protects life, limb and property can be a thing of beauty and a joy forever — guaranteed.

Aetna Life Building in Rancho Cordova
Photo by John Orfanos

Yuba City Shopping Center *Photo by Robert Dixon & Ron Westen*

Adventist Health Building in Roseville
Photo by Demont Pegram and Robert Dixon

River City Rentals

Now doing business as NationsRent

The clash of big corporate philosophy and Sacramentan common sense gave birth to River City Rentals, which, until its acquisition by Nations Rent in late 1998, was the largest privately held equipment rental company in Northern California.

River City Rentals owner, John Greene, spent 15 years rising through the ranks of U.S. Rentals to become the general manager for the entire Sacramento area operations. In late 1983, the owner of U.S. Rentals handed down an edict which made every branch a separate profit center, effectively forcing Greene's four Sacramento operations to compete with each other for the same customer base. When he voiced his opinion that the change was shortsighted and invited competition, the experts told Greene he didn't know what he was talking about.

River City Rentals had the unique distinction of being the main equipment supplier for both ARCO Arena projects, first in 1985 and the latest shown here in 1988. *Photo by Busselen/Bauer*

Finding himself in the unusual position of fulfilling his own prophesy, John Greene formed a partnership with Del Richbaw, the former vice president of purchasing at U.S. Rentals, and River City Rentals launched into the marketplace. Richbaw's knowledge of acquisitions and Greene's 13 years of operations experience in Sacramento created the perfect marriage.

Most great enterprises have stories of humble beginnings, and River City Rentals was no exception. Neither partner drew a paycheck in the first year. Greene was the only one with a class-one driver's license, so he was the truck driver for the first six months. The yard

didn't have a fence, so the entire inventory had to be pulled into the storage building every night and back out every morning. Those days are remembered fondly because the work ethic developed during those challenging times became the driving force of the company.

River City Rentals' first location on Jackson Road became a sprawling three-acre yard. Three additional Sacramento locations, another in Sparks, Nevada and the latest yard in Roseville have all worked together for the common good of the company. The product offering ranges from party supplies to homeowners' needs to the heaviest industrial and contractor equipment.

Stressing the importance of customer service, Greene earned the enviable reputation of providing well-maintained, reliable equipment with the fastest delivery and response time possible, due to the total cooperation of all his yards. Preferring to be the best rather than the cheapest kept River City Rentals and his clientele mutually loyal and profitable.

River City Rentals was the main equipment supplier for numerous landmark projects including both ARCO Arena complexes, the Foundation Health headquarters, the Silver Legacy Hotel and Casino in Reno, and the Highway 50 landslide repair contract.

When Del Richbaw retired in 1995, Greene became the sole owner of River City Rentals. The definitive hands-on business owner, Greene stunned many of his new employees when they saw him loading trucks and making deliveries to help out, discovering that he'd rather be out in the yard than sitting in his office. There is no chain of command. When an employee wants to speak with Greene, his door is wide open.

An avid outdoorsman, Greene credits Sacramento with being an ideal location for recreation, contributing strongly to the quality of life that continues to keep the organization positive and energetic.

Despite River City Rentals' notable success, John Greene has always given his customers the personal touch of a "fledgling little rental company." That tradition was embraced by NationsRent when Greene brought the industry giant to the West, and his Sacramentan common sense came full circle in the land of big corporations.

SACTO

Job hunters in the Sacramento area have a powerful ally. It probably comes as no surprise that since 1900, the government has been the largest single employer in the state's capital region. Fortunately, a job with the state is not a Sacramentan's only vocational choice — enter SACTO, the Sacramento Area Commerce and Trade Organization. This private, nonprofit economic development corporation was organized to encourage quality businesses to make job-generating investments in the six-county greater Sacramento area.

Jon Kelly of Kelly Broadcasting — a media leader in Sacramento — founded the organization in 1975 in order to broaden the private-sector job base. During that time, almost half of the jobs in the region were with the state. As of 1998, government jobs accounted for only 25 percent of all jobs. SACTO-located companies have invested hundreds of millions of dollars in the area's economy since SACTO's humble beginnings in the late 1970s and early 1980s. Between 1985 and 1997, the number of jobs created by SACTO-assisted companies rose from 2,744 to 32,444. Since 1982, the company estimates it has helped create some 60,000 new jobs through its company recruitment efforts.

According to the company's mission statement, SACTO aggressively pursues new businesses in an increasingly competitive environment by recruiting quality companies in order to create economic opportunity, diversity and stability in the region. First and foremost a marketing organization, SACTO adheres to a systematic marketing program that screens business sectors to determine which types of investments will provide the greatest overall economic return for the area. Once a specific firm has been identified, SACTO demonstrates how they can profit from locating a business in the greater Sacramento area.

SACTO competes with thousands of other economic development organizations throughout the world, nation and state. One of SACTO's major focuses is on attracting and recruiting "major players" — that is, some of the most successful and profitable businesses in the world. The ultimate goal is to ensure that the business growth that takes place in the Sacramento area will be of the highest possible quality. New information-processing, high-tech and food-processing companies are leading the way in Sacramento. Thanks to SACTO's proactive efforts, technology giant Oracle, the world's second-largest software company, built a facility in Rocklin, a small town located just minutes from Sacramento.

When SACTO helps attract other big names, such as internationally known firms like Apple Computer, Hewlett-Packard, Intel, NEC Electronics, JVC Disc America Company and Packard Bell, the result is a win-win, domino-effect for the community — more jobs and an improved local economy are just two benefits. The community can also attract a better-educated, professional class of job seekers and offer better pay as employers compete for high-skilled workers. While a region such as the Bay Area — sometimes referred to as Silicon Valley — has long been infamously overcrowded, Sacramento is still considered uncharted territory by many relocating companies: housing prices are much lower here and freeways are less congested. Another advantage for companies is that the Sacramento area is much more seismically stable than the Bay, where fragile — and expensive — computer equipment can easily be damaged by an earthquake.

While the majority of its energy is directed toward encouraging companies and business-minded individuals to the area, SACTO also enjoys the support of a number of local governments, various community/civic organizations and chambers of commerce. Even though approximately 25 percent of the company's annual $1 million budget comes from local governments and schools, SACTO is careful to point out the difference between itself and the chambers. While the chamber serves as the voice of business in the community by attending to legislative interests, SACTO intentionally avoids involvement in local political issues.

Most of the funding comes from local businesses with an interest in continued growth in the area: established banks, realtors, media and utility companies. In addition to funding SACTO's international recruitment efforts, a considerable portion of that money goes to support the group's research on everything from schools and housing prices to energy costs and income levels.

Well-known SACTO success stories include Kikkoman, AT&T, Blue Diamond Growers, Campbell Soup Company, Shriners Hospitals for Children, S.C. Johnson Wax, Pacific Bell, Bank of America and Mazda Motor of America Inc., to name just a few.

As the century comes to a close, SACTO proudly undertakes a new endeavor referred to as "Project SACTO." This ambitious effort is designed to create some 12,000 new jobs within five years. More than 4,000 of those jobs will be for welfare recipients facing a loss of benefits under the recently passed welfare reform program. Through a combination of research, professional economic development practices and member guidance, SACTO has been instrumental in the recruitment of some of the world's most prestigious companies to the greater Sacramento area.

Exective Director
Alan R. Gianini
© *Sirlin Photographers*

Business and Finance

Investment banking and securities brokerage, insurance and diversified holding companies provide a financial foundation for a host of Sacramento companies.

The Money Store

The Money Store was founded in 1967 to help homeowners take advantage of what for many of us is our greatest financial asset — the equity in our homes. Home equity loans are so popular these days that it's hard to imagine that they were virtually unheard of 32 years ago, when many states prohibited banks from making second mortgages.

The idea that launched The Money Store was simple but revolutionary: A homeowner who builds up equity over years of raising a family should be able to get access to that equity without having to sell the family home. Proceeds from a home equity loan can be used by the homeowner for a variety of purposes.

The Money Store's loans allow homeowners to get back on track financially, ending the stress of too many bills.

One of the country's biggest home equity lenders, The Money Store helps homeowners access the equity in their homes to pay off bills, finance home improvements and pay for college or other major expenses. Interest paid on a home loan from The Money Store is usually tax-deductible, unlike the interest on credit card bills, car loans and most other kinds of debt.

Using loan proceeds, the homeowner can consolidate all debts and pay off car loans, credit-card loans, revolving department-store credit accounts and other miscellaneous bills, by making one monthly payment at a lower interest rate. In addition to debt consolidation, popular reasons for taking home equity loans include financing home improvements, buying a car, paying for a wedding or vacation and paying for college tuition.

Whatever the reason for taking the loan, one major advantage for consumers is that interest paid on a home loan is usually tax-deductible, unlike the interest on credit card bills, car loans and almost any other kind of debt.

The Money Store was among the first companies to use television to promote financial services, and today the company enjoys strong brand recognition in home equity lending as one of the 150 largest consumer advertisers on television.

In addition to being one of the first to capitalize on the use of television, The Money Store pioneered the use of a toll-free consumer response number in its advertising. Busy customers don't have to travel to an office to fill out a loan application — it can be done right over the phone in 10-15 minutes.

Thousands of people call The Money Store's 800 number every day to find out how they can improve their financial situations. Money Store employees at the Sacramento Call Center answer phones 24 hours a day, 365 days a year. The Money Store's substantial investments in technology have allowed the company to reduce the application and processing time for loans in all its business lines. Ongoing technological enhancements are driven by the company's desire to make the loan process faster and easier, providing customers with superior products and service.

In recent years, The Money Store has also been able to serve customers through direct mail and over the Internet.

Fixed- and adjustable-rate home equity loans, refinances, and home improvement loans are The Money Store's main mortgage products. Home equity loans make up about two-thirds of the company's total portfolio. The target customer is someone who — often due to circumstances beyond his or her control, such as a job layoff or medical problems — may have "less than perfect" credit. Every customer's situation is different, so Money Store loan representatives are taught to determine which product works best in each case. One customer may want to refinance high-interest credit-card debt and take additional cash for home improvements; another may need an open-ended line of credit to borrow $40,000 for college tuition, $10,000 at a time over a four-year period.

In addition to selling directly to consumers, The Money Store offers convenient financing, available through home improvement dealers and contractors, for swimming pools, room additions and other home remodeling projects.

Providing innovative responses to consumer needs has paid off for The Money Store, which has shown steady growth over the years. In 1998, the company originated more than $6 billion worth of mortgages. The company has also done extraordinarily well with other business lines. For example, The Money Store has been the country's largest provider of Small Business Administration loans for the past 15 years. And the company's student lending division, Educaid, is one of the nation's biggest originators of government-backed student loans.

In July 1998, The Money Store gained additional prestige and resources when it was purchased by First Union Bank of Charlotte, North Carolina, the country's sixth-largest bank. First Union has $230 billion in assets and serves approximately 16 million customers.

The Money Store has more than 3,000 employees, the majority of them working at corporate headquarters in West Sacramento and other Sacramento locations. Others work in The Money Store's branches throughout the nation. Employees remain dedicated to benefiting customers by successfully providing them with the means to regain their financial health, make home improvements, expand a business or send a child to college.

The company's creative approach to doing business is applied to more areas than the financial bottom line. In 1998, The Money Store was one of only two California companies recognized by the state of California for its recycling efforts, which include purchasing recycled products and encouraging employees to recycle mixed paper. And The Money Store has been actively involved in supporting Sacramento's performing arts organizations and numerous charities serving the area's disadvantaged families. Employees turn out in force for the annual Capital AIDS walk, and they participate in many other local fundraising activities. These donations of time and money help reinforce The Money Store's ongoing message of people helping people realize their financial goals.

Phones are answered by specially trained loan representatives at The Money Store's Sacramento Call Center 24 hours a day, 365 days a year. They have the tools to help homeowners get their finances back on track.

An unusual ziggurat-shaped building, completed in 1998, houses The Money Store's riverfront corporate headquarters in West Sacramento. Architect Ed Kado of Sacramento designed the building, which has become a well-recognized landmark on the city skyline.

Pickett-Rothholz & Murphy

Pickett-Rothholz and Murphy is one of the oldest insurance agencies in Sacramento. Edwin R. Pickett opened the doors to his independent agency in 1919 upon returning to civilian life after military service. The name Pickett was used in business in Sacramento long before it became part of the insurance agency's moniker. Ed Pickett, born in 1893 in Alameda, California, moved to Sacramento in 1911 to work for his father's clothing store, Pickett-Atterbury. World War I called him to the U.S. Army cavalry, and Ed fulfilled this by serving as a border guard with a machine gun company during the Pancho Villa raids in 1916.

Ed Pickett and Jack Murphy walking down J Street in about 1947.

When Ed Pickett started his business, he made the conscious decision to form a brokerage agency rather than work as an agent for a single insurance company. It was risky for him to set up his own office, but he needed the flexibility to shop the industry for the best insurance companies because he was determined to serve the needs of his clients, not the interests of a single insurance company. This fundamental difference in business philosophy attracted tremendous talent to Pickett's new firm. When Morris B. Rothholz, a native

Sacramentan, joined the agency in 1920, the young duo, under the name Pickett-Rothholz Company, began to amass an impressive portfolio of insurance carriers and a prestigious client list that was greatly enhanced by Morris's following by the Sacramento Jewish community. This newly formed team acquired an excellent reputation for community service. Ed was president of Sacramento's Chapter of the American Red Cross and the City/County Chamber of Commerce. Morris also valued community involvement and served as a director of the United Crusade and the Sacramento Chapter of the American Red Cross for over 30 years. He was the first president of the United Jewish Welfare Fund and was also president of B'nai Brith and Sacramento Association of Insurance Agents, and he was a director of Sacramento Savings and Loan Association.

In 1946 Ed was advised to become less active after suffering a major heart attack. Ed and Morris welcomed John J. Murphy and Nathan Forman into their agency as partners. Forman had worked as a broker for Pickett-Rothholz since 1931. Murphy was born in Boston on March 28, 1914, and he graduated from Boston College in 1935. Jack, as Murphy is known, worked as a special agent and underwriter for the Massachusetts Bonding and Insurance Company until he was called to serve during World War II. Jack was stationed in California where he met and married Bettejo Kitt before being sent to Europe in 1943 for the duration of the war. Jack returned to the Sacramento area in October, 1945 and went to work for The Travelers Insurance Company as a reporting agent for its San Francisco branch, while sharing office space with Pickett-Rothholz Company at their office in the Farmers and Mechanics Building located on Eighth Street, between J and K streets. Ed Pickett retired and went on to become known as an authority on bird life of Central California, authoring newspaper articles and a book that was endorsed by the Audobon Society before his death in 1964. The agency flourished in the hands of the new partnership. Arthur Nathan joined the company in 1959 and worked as a partner as well, for more than a decade. Nathan was a native Sacramentan and had attended Stanford University and the Stanford Graduate School of Business. Morris Rothholz retired in 1962 and eventually the leadership was handed over to Jack Murphy in the late 1960s.

Murphy's son, David, joined the agency in 1967. David, who was born on September 26, 1943, when his dad was on his way overseas, was quick to admire the father that he did not meet until he was two years old. Jack had continued the tradition of community involvement and David remembers when, as a young boy walking with his father downtown, he thought that his dad knew everyone in Sacramento. Jack served as commander of Post 61 American Legion, president of Rotary Club of Sacramento, Sacramento Independent Insurance Agents and was often called upon to be the marshal of whatever parade was being held in Sacramento in the 1950s. Much sought after as a master of ceremonies, Jack introduced Adlai Stevenson when he campaigned in Sacramento for the presidency of the United States.

David was prepared to follow in his father's footsteps, not only by his example, but also by participating in a two-year training program with Fireman's Fund Insurance Company after his graduation from Santa Clara University in 1965. When Dave joined the agency in 1967, Ed and Morris had already retired. Appropriately, the agency's name was changed to Pickett-Rothholz and Murphy in 1975, adding Murphy to represent the present and leaving the names of its founders to honor the past. As the agency grew in business holdings and staff, the office moved twice to accommodate this progress, first to Howe Avenue and, in 1985, to its location on Folsom Blvd. Jack retired in 1985, leaving Dave as president of the agency.

Dave has enthusiastically carried the torch of community service throughout his career, volunteering his services to countless worthy causes. He has served as president of Sutter Hospital Foundation, Independent Insurance Agents of Sacramento, Rotary Club of Sacramento, Active 20-30 Club of Sacramento, Camellia Festival Association, Jesuit High School Board of Trustees, St. Francis High School Friars Club and Junior Achievement of Sacramento. He is the 1999 president of the Sacramento Host Committee. He is especially proud of the accomplishments of the Sacramento Regional Foundation, for which he also currently serves as president. This organization is an endowment funded by donors who have a strong passion to contribute to the community. Their investments will ensure a legacy of giving back to the community even beyond their own lifetimes.

Dave is surrounded by a staff of 28 insurance professionals. Jim Coats is executive vice president and other vice presidents are Joe Weber, Candace Holland, Terry Hanson, Larry Evans and Ruth Kindel Johnson. Family members include Dave's sisters, Kathy Tscheu, claims manager, Bettejo Davidson, data processing manager and Dave's daughter, Anna Ryan, customer service manager. Paternal history repeated itself when Dave's son, John Murphy, joined the staff in 1996 and became the newest salesman on board. Vic Cima, who owns P.R.M. Employee Benefits and Life Insurance Services,

Pickett-Rothholz & Murphy offices surrounded by beautiful redwoods.

has complemented the agency since 1980, providing expertise in health and life insurance.

Although the ranks of independent agencies are dwindling nationwide, Dave Murphy feels the Sacramento Valley will continue to demand Pickett-Rothholz and Murphy's style of client advocacy and service. Insurance is its product but detailed personal service, commitment, and unwavering loyalty to the needs of its clients is what sets it apart. This creed was written by Ed Pickett almost 80 years ago and will remain its winning formula into the future.

Standing, left to right: John Murphy, Terry Hansen, Candy Holland and Larry Evans Seated, left to right: Vic Cima, Dave Murphy and Jim Coats.

River City Bank

River City Bank began in 1973 as an idea sketched on the back of a cocktail napkin. It has since grown to become Sacramento's premier locally owned independent bank, with a reputation as one of California's strongest and safest financial institutions.

On a fateful day in 1972, Jon. S. Kelly, owner of Kelly Broadcasting Company and its NBC affiliate, KCRA-TV Channel 3, was sitting with a business associate at the bar at Frank Fat's restaurant, a hot spot for the capital's movers and shakers. The two were discussing their experiences with banks when Kelly came up with the idea for a bank of his own. As he was sketching it out on his cocktail napkin, Wing Kai Fat, part owner of the restaurant, walked by. Fat must have been surprised when Kelly stopped him and asked him not for another bowl of pretzels, but to be on the board of directors for this new bank. The restauranteur agreed and still serves in that position after more than 20 years.

Having garnered support from a select group of Sacramento business people, Kelly applied to the state banking department in September 1972. Approval was granted by mid-1973, and River City Bank began to capitalize itself through the sale of common stock. The initial stock offering on November 9, 1973, was for 280,000 shares at $10 per share, and soon it was fully subscribed. This enabled the bank to open for business on December 14, 1973, at 1010 J Street in Sacramento. Kelly began as president with just 11 employees.

To assist with the bank's marketing and promotional efforts, Kelly established a 17-member advisory board made up of a cross section of successful business people from the Sacramento community. The board's duties were to measure and evaluate community needs and determine how River City Bank could best meet them. The findings of the board launched marketing efforts that embraced three main concepts: no-charge checking accounts, low-interest auto loans and extended hours for customers. This formula was obviously successful, because after the first year of operation the bank had grown to show total assets of more than $12.5 million and had increased its staff to 18 employees.

River City Bank opened an additional branch in temporary facilities at its present-day location on Howe Avenue. Here Sacramento had its first taste of Saturday banking, a breakthrough in customer service. The permanent branch facility was completed in July of 1975, and featured eight drive-up banking lanes, making it the largest facility of its kind in the state. By the late 1990s, the bank had 10 branches.

In the early days, River City Bank made every effort to live up to its name. Female tellers dressed in old-fashioned dresses, and a fully functional — and regularly sounded — boat horn sat atop on the bank's roof. While many of the trappings of the riverboat days faded with the 80s, the bank has retained the old-fashioned habit of doing business on a first-name basis.

By 1980, the bank had six branches and had relocated its head office to the K Street Mall. Three years later, it offered its first automatic teller machine (ATM) and opened two of its branches on Sundays — another first for Sacramento. Throughout the decade, the bank, for the first time under a single holding company called the RCB Corporation, continued to grow and maintain a strong financial position despite the challenges affecting the banking industry during that time. By the end of 1983, its total assets had grown to $150,873,000, taking it out of the "small bank" category. It now has

Broadcasting owner Jon S. Kelly founded River City Bank in 1973.

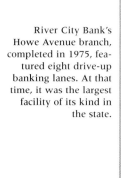

River City Bank's Howe Avenue branch, completed in 1975, featured eight drive-up banking lanes. At that time, it was the largest facility of its kind in the state.

assets in excess of $450 million. In 1988, the bank made its first acquisition with the purchase of First Security Bank of Elk Grove, thus adding two branches to its network.

Two years later, the bank purchased a six-acre parcel of land in the South Natomas area and began construction on a 150,000-square-foot office building. The new landmark headquarters (including one branch) has enhanced the bank's identity in the Sacramento marketplace. On the heels of this move came another milestone with the 1991 opening of the bank's first in-store branch at the Bel Air supermarket on the corner of Cirby and Sunrise in Roseville.

River City Bank is unique in that it knows its customers better than its larger competitors do. That is why it is able to offer them a full range of products and services, from checking accounts for

In 1991, the bank moved its headquarters to a new 150,000-square-foot office building in the southern Natomas area.

senior citizens to tailor-made business accounts to the Moola Moola savings club for kids. Business customers appreciate the bank's willingness to make "office calls" to their workplaces rather than do business behind a desk. This gives loan officers a better feel for each company's unique problems and opportunities.

One thing the bank doesn't do is make foreign loans. Customer deposits are used for loans within a four-county, 50-mile radius of the capital. And because credit is approved and funded locally, the bank is able to act more quickly than larger banks.

River City Bank has always been proactive in the ever-changing scope of technology. Along with 24-hour telephone account access, it offers extensive information on its World Wide Web page and has a convenient on-line banking system, which can eventually be used for loan applications.

As a true community bank, River City Bank takes an active role in improving the quality of life for its neighbors.

Employees come out in full force to support the annual Juvenile Diabetes "Walk to Cure Diabetes." The Make-A-Wish Foundation, the Arthritis Foundation, SACTO, The March of Dimes and "WalkAmerica" are just a few of the organizations the bank helps to sponsor. Individually, all staff members share in the mission to support the communities in which they serve.

The bank's long-term goal is to remain a dominant independent force in the Sacramento area and to retain its niche of commitment to personal service. With the initiative of its people, and the loyalty of those it serves, anything is possible.

Just a few of the awards River City Bank has earned for its community involvement.

Even "Moola Moola" from the Land of Lotta Loot gets involved in community service projects. Special prizes, drawings and parties are given to reward young depositors.

Wells Fargo Bank

The epic stories of the American West and Wells Fargo Bank are so interlaced that they are inseparable. No other modern organization has had a more sweeping economic impact on California's vitality and growth than the "Oldest Bank in the West."

A century and a half ago, the discovery of gold in the Sierra Nevada foothills transformed the harsh and remote Western Territory into the land of opportunity. With hundreds of thousands of fortune seekers swarming into the

Night scene in the big Wells Fargo depot office in Sacramento

Sacramento Valley from every point on the globe, the time was ripe for a professional banking and express company. In the East, Henry Wells and William G. Fargo, founding officers of the American Express Company, failed to convince their partners to head west. Undaunted by this disagreement, they established Wells, Fargo & Co., which was soon buying gold dust, selling drafts, and performing general banking and express services throughout California.

If a prospector actually beat the odds and found gold, he still had a long way to go. Raw nuggets and gold dust were not legal tender. The purity had to be determined before it could be converted into coin, and the hapless miner found himself at the mercy of crooked gold buyers, provided that he was able to get past the confidence men, thieves and scoundrels that lay in wait on his way to market.

Far from simple money changers, Wells Fargo agents were skilled assayers who followed textbook chemistry techniques to reduce raw material of all forms to pure gold. They would then use Gold Standard Balances of

This engraving illustrated Wells Fargo's first location at the Hastings Building in Old Sacramento, the same modern-day location of Wells Fargo's History Museum.

legendary accuracy to weigh the results. When the Wells Fargo agent announced the weight, payment was made in U.S. gold coins, negotiable checks or bank drafts. By eliminating suspicion and relieving the anxieties of miners, Wells Fargo earned the enduring trust of Sacramento's growing community.

That trust extended to the safekeeping and transportation of Sacramento's wealth. Prospectors who made the pilgrimage to the gold country alone utilized Wells Fargo to send money and letters to their loved ones. Strong boxes filled with the most valuable assets of the West were transported in ornate stagecoaches guarded by Wells Fargo's famous shotgun messengers, an elite team of men that included the legendary Wyatt Earp. U.S. Army soldiers stationed in the West to protect settlers received their paychecks from these messengers. Merchants depended on Wells Fargo to transmit payments to their faraway suppliers and to bring back their goods. Over time, Wells Fargo's transportation system would include trains, steamers and river boats. From 1866 forward, Wells Fargo controlled all overland staging west of the Missouri River.

The harsh realities of life in a mining town revealed themselves within a few months of Wells Fargo's arrival in Sacramento. In November of 1852, a devastating fire engulfed the business district, destroying more than 1,600 buildings, including the new Wells Fargo office. Four

weeks after the fire brought the fledgling town to its knees, a levee break on the American River inundated the city. Two weeks later, in a merciless third blow, the Sacramento River rose above its banks and flooded Sacramento again.

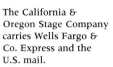

beginning with a modest expansion in 1923 through a merger with the Union Trust Company of San Francisco. Over the course of the next 75 years, Wells Fargo would acquire some of the country's most respected financial institutions and enter the 21st century as the seventh-largest bank holding company in the United States, operating almost 6,000 Wells Fargo stores throughout 21 states.

With the issues of legal tender and assaying well in the past, Wells Fargo Bank's honesty and integrity are now demonstrated by unparalleled service, innovation, convenience and safety.

A lesser company would have packed its bags and left for higher ground, but Wells Fargo showed unprecedented commitment to the region by bringing relief money to the sufferers of these disasters and continuing to provide the banking and express services needed to help rebuild the city.

While some adventurers struck it rich, the vast majority did not. Those who saw their dreams of wealth fade would turn to more realistic trades such as farming. From the very beginning, through the ups and downs, Wells Fargo has supported Northern California's agricultural industry and to this day is the leading lender in this arena. As the impact of the mother lode began to wane, this rural investment proved to be critical in maintaining the viability of the Sacramento Valley.

The image of a Wells Fargo stagecoach heroically running the gauntlet of highway robbers and extreme conditions defines the Old West. The strength of this icon would foretell the courage and fortitude of the company, which withstood the hardships and economic instability of the Civil War, three presidential assassinations, earthquakes, stock market crashes, the Great Depression, two world wars and numerous armed conflicts that dealt deadly blows to the largest banking institutions of the day. Wells Fargo Bank never faltered, never failed to meet its obligations nor even once failed to pay a dividend. The bank maintained its reputation for integrity, strength and full-service capabilities throughout.

In 1918, the federal government nationalized the country's private express companies, and Wells Fargo was forced to turn over nearly 10,000 express offices from coast-to-coast. The proud name of Wells Fargo Bank continued to thrive in San Francisco. Re-establishing its national presence would be a lengthy and arduous task

Always moving forward and changing for the better, Wells Fargo provides commercial and agribusiness banking customers with working capital, term financing and state-of-the-art cash management systems as well as international and investment services. Private banking clients see their savings become secure fortunes through carefully tailored investment brokerage and trust services — managed locally and backed by the strength of a national bank. Commercial real estate developers rely on Wells Fargo's proven expertise and responsive financing programs to fund Sacramento's most important construction projects.

Wells Fargo has shepherded Sacramento through its most trying times. Even in an era of prosperity, there is a need for outreach and renewal. To this end, Wells Fargo continues to support nonprofit, affordable housing development, small business and low-income consumer lending and Community Reinvestment Loan Programs. Wells Fargo is also a strong supporter of the city's cultural and arts programs including sponsorship of the Sacramento Ballet, the State Railroad Museum, the Sacramento Philharmonic Orchestra, the California Historical Society and the Crocker Art Museum.

Wells Fargo Bank boasts its own staff of historians who maintain five museums in California, two of which are in Sacramento. The Wells Fargo Old Sacramento Agency is the restored version of the office opened at that same location in 1854. The other museum is at the Capitol Mall. Visitors to either site are transported to a time when the pioneering spirit reigned supreme and heroism seemed commonplace. They return to the present with the clear understanding that every transaction, every delivery, every building, every business in Sacramento has been touched by Wells Fargo's legacy.

Xebec Management Services

Ted van Leeuwen, Tom Tenge, Stephen Fowler and Jerred Peebles formed Xebec Management Services in 1982 with the desire to provide executive office space and related services to the growing Sacramento marketplace. The founders named their company Xebec after the Mediterranean ship once known for sailing into unknown waters. Xebec was a fitting label for the founders' innovative plans.

During the 1980s, the concept of executive suites was relatively new to the Sacramento region. They were designed to function as branch offices of national and regional companies and as primary locations for entrepreneurial start-up companies and independent professionals. Executive suites offer tenants a range of administrative services, including central reception, copying, faxing, shipping and word processing. The tenant also has the opportunity to lease a small office space for a shorter lease period than is available in a traditional office building. In many cases, executive suites became "incubators" allowing companies to grow without the need for excessive capital and administrative expenses. The building's management staff oversees day-to-day operations, including maintaining the copy machine and managing the phone system and computer networks.

Xebec began by taking over the management of two established HQ executive suite franchises. HQ is an

international organization, formerly known as Headquarters Companies, that manages executive suites. Xebec has operated HQ suites near Cal Expo, at Zinfandel and White Rock, and in downtown Sacramento, Rancho Murrieta, Campus Commons and Roseville. The company ownership and management was reorganized in 1987, leaving Tenge and Fowler to run the business.

In 1988, the founders established a new identity as the "Executive Office Network." Under the new name, Xebec opened or converted existing suites in Campus Commons, Roseville, Greenhaven and Country Club. The company soon became the region's leading company for executive suite services.

Xebec continued to improve its services and embrace the changing needs of the workplace. In 1992, Tom King joined the Xebec team, bringing a passion and talent for the technical aspects of the business. Fowler and King envisioned a larger and even more flexible working environment that offered the same high-tech services available in corporate headquarters — videoconferencing, Internet access and electronic mail — through a centralized source.

In 1996 Fowler, Tenge and King conceived the company's most important innovation: "Business Central, the next generation in business services." Business Central combines existing services with high-tech capabilities and a host of other amenities in a newly constructed and specially designed office building.

long-term lease of three or more years. Within its first year of completion, the building was 95 percent occupied.

Business Central at Gold River offers a professional yet lively and comfortable work environment with services to maximize a business owner's time and resources. In addition to office space, all clients have access to centralized administrative services, a sophisticated phone system, networked computers, videoconferencing, a color copier and a color laser printer. Business Central offers meeting rooms, an inviting and festive oversized break room with shuffle board, television, newspapers and periodicals, and a full kitchen. The break room opens to an outdoor patio with a park-like setting. An in-house espresso bar near the central lobby provides refreshments, breakfast, lunch and catering to tenants and guests.

"The idea is to make employees feel comfortable, relaxed and inspired while they are at work, so they want to come to work here," explains Tenge.

Xebec's tenants include NEC Electronics, CISCO Systems, QWest Communications, Sterling Software, Compaq Software, Peoplesoft, American Woodmark, Accounts, Inc., Employers Health, RWD Technology and a few law firms.

Business Central has many opportunities to expand in the Sacramento region and across the nation. The next step is to connect the worker's home office via phone and computer networking to Business Central. Tenge anticipates that all the administrative and technological services available to the tenants will also be accessible to home-based businesspeople.

As the workplace continues to change, Business Central will continue to redefine and enhance it by providing "next-generation business services" to an array of growing businesses.

In August 1998, the company was sold to InterOffice, a Virginia-based company that shared the vision with Xebec. InterOffice then merged with Alliance Business Centers in January of 1999, and the combined company became Vantas in March of 1999. Tenge, Fowler and King are part of the Vantas management team, which is currently the largest worldwide business center network and intends to expand the company to include more than 500 locations internationally by the year 2005.

Xebec's new concept in centralized, one-stop business services makes it possible for businesses of all sizes to access what they need. The 50,000-square-foot building, located in the affluent, Sacramento suburb of Gold River, is the first of its kind in the nation and allows Xebec to offer more variety and value than other executive suite services. Business Central at Gold River is intended to be a model for offices of the future. Panattoni Catlin Ventures, a prominent Sacramento-based development company, worked in cooperation with Xebec to provide the building and infrastructure.

THE FOUNDERS NAMED THEIR COMPANY XEBEC AFTER THE MEDITERRANEAN SHIP ONCE KNOWN FOR SAILING INTO UNKNOWN WATERS. XEBEC WAS A FITTING LABEL FOR THE FOUNDERS' INNOVATIVE PLANS.

Unlike traditional office buildings, which offer standard-sized suites throughout, Business Central includes various sizes of office space to accommodate different business needs. Business Central continues to offer leases from six months to six years, and clients can upgrade to a larger space in the same building or transfer leases to other projects to meet changing needs. Tenants choose from a variety of office configurations ranging from 140 to 5,000 square feet.

The ground-floor suites offer window offices for a single person and suites large enough for up to 10 employees. Second-floor suites are designed for larger businesses with six to 25 employees, and they require a

Sacramento Commercial Bank

Tradition Continues

When Sacramento Commercial Bank opened for business in 1984, a void in Sacramento's history was finally filled. The cornerstone of a great American city is usually found near the door of its earliest banks. These pioneering banks would grow into Grande Dame financial institutions, fending off outsiders to dominate the business community in perpetuity. Strangely, this didn't happen in the capital city. Although a few of the original financial institutions have persisted, Sacramento has always been dominated by behemoth banks whose home offices are found in San Francisco or Los Angeles or New York.

A core group of respected financiers at First Commercial Bank watched their company swallow California Canadian Bank and become a regional institution. This statewide expansion would clearly erode their standing as a local community bank, and that was the last straw. Daryl Foreman, Robert Muttera and James Sundquist were not interested in living through such an experience.

It was time for a Sacramento bank — one that was born in Sacramento, would stay in Sacramento, and would serve Sacramento exclusively; a bank that would not offend its customers by surrendering to opportunistic mergers; a stable bank with which Sacramento businesses and professionals could forge a personal and permanent bond. Emboldened by their loyal business clients, those idealists opened the doors of Sacramento Commercial Bank and a noble tradition was born.

As business bankers, the founders of this enterprise were immune to the urge to open branches at every street corner and supermarket. Daryl Foreman, president and CEO, Robert Muttera, executive vice president and chief credit officer, and James Sundquist, executive vice president and chief operating officer, all bring the bank to their customers. Every Sacramento Commercial Bank officer makes business "house calls." Depositors who don't have time to come to the bank are serviced by couriers. Thanks to proprietary computer programs developed by subsidiary SCB Financial Software, Inc., some of Sacramento Commercial Bank's biggest customers have never even seen the building. This fundamental commitment to the technology of banking has also brought the institution national recognition for its fiduciary services to bankruptcy attorneys and receivers.

The Sacramento Commercial Bank building is a stunning downtown landmark between 5th and 6th on J Street. Its elegant lobby of rich mahogany carpentry contrasts with the dynamic exterior architecture, a reflection of the company's promise to serve both the traditional banking customer and today's most sophisticated clientele.

With a mission to deliver intelligent financial solutions, Sacramento Commercial Bank's highly skilled team has become the elite of the Small Business Administration loan system. Holding the highest license granted by the SBA, Preferred Lender Program status, Sacramento Commercial Bank has ranked in the country's top 100 SBA lenders. Of the 9,000 banks originating SBA loans, less than 400 are preferred lenders. But most impressive is the fact that Sacramento Commercial Bank is SBA-licensed to lend in San Francisco, Fresno and Reno without having offices in those regions.

The future of Sacramento's economy rests squarely on the shoulders of its small business community, and Sacramento Commercial Bank sees its future in nurturing the ambitions of the Valley's youth. Board members have vigorously supported the Sacramento Entrepreneurship Academy, whose primary goal is to encourage the entrepreneurial aspirations of all university students. Numerous students of the academy have worked for the bank as they prepared to take on their own enterprises, and sponsors believe the program helps to keep young talent in Sacramento.

Destined to be a timeless institution, Sacramento Commercial Bank's goal to dominate the market is well-supported. The bank boasts a senior management team with the longest tenure in the region. Its safety and stability are frequently lauded by financial analysts, buttressed by the fact that approximately 40 percent of the shares of Sacramento Commercial Bank are held by board members. Putting your money where your mouth is speaks volumes in the financial world, and empires are built by such visionaries. Sacramento Commercial Bank's visionaries proudly offer Intelligent Banking® for Sacramento.

Western Sunrise Mortgage

For big businesses and consumers alike, purchasing property is almost always a daunting experience. The amount at stake and the constantly fluctuating real estate market can try the patience of even the most knowledgeable investors. Finding a reliable, professional, organized mortgage firm to underwrite the loan is key and can make the difference between a quick, successful transaction and financial disaster. Since July 1984, Western Sunrise Mortgage Corporation (originally established as the Mortgage Banking Division of Sunrise Bank of California) has been committed to service, efficiency and fostering positive business experiences for its clients.

On August 21, 1992, Western Sunrise Mortgage Corporation was sold to Harbourton Acquisition Corporation, a private investment firm founded in 1990 to acquire, run and operate companies in the financial services sector. Four years later, Western Sunrise Mortgage Corporation became the No. 1 mortgage banker in the four-county Sacramento area (El Dorado, Placer, Yuba and Sacramento). On April 1, 1997, Western Sunrise Mortgage merged with CrossLand Mortgage Corporation of Salt Lake City, Utah.

Western Sunrise Mortgage (WSM) continues to operate as a division of CrossLand Mortgage, with headquarters in Rancho Cordova, California. To say the company has been growing by leaps and bounds is an understatement. The company's CEO, Cynthia Sample, confirmed that the company funded over $7 billion in home loans in 1998 alone. That figure is up from 1997, when it funded $3 billion, and the year before that, when it funded $2 billion.

WSM's client base consists entirely of mortgage brokers, known as "wholesale originators" because the brokers deal directly with the consumers. These mortgage brokers process the loans and submit them to WSM for underwriting and funding. Western Sunrise offers a wide variety of loan products, including first-time home-buyer loans; VA- and FHA-fixed, ARM and 203K loans; 10, 15, 20 and 30-year fixed; and five- and seven-year balloons.

Western Sunrise Mortgage was the first company to partner up with Fannie Mae to do automated underwriting, which, according to Ms. Sample, revolutionized the total-lending environment. State-of-the-art computer systems allow the firm to process loans and get approval within four minutes rather than several days, based on the borrowers' credit profile. Loan processing, which commonly took as long as 60 days, now can be done in as few as 72 hours. Automated underwriting also can bring up instant credit reports and provide automated appraisals within 24 hours. Computer underwriting allowed WSM to increase its volume by as much as 140 percent over 1997, when automated underwriting had not yet been introduced. Advantages of automated underwriting include the elimination of paperwork for borrowers and lenders, and reduced costs that can result in savings passed onto the customer.

Having funded over $20 billion since its inception, WSM now has branches in cities throughout the West, including: Las Vegas, Nevada; Denver, Colorado; Bellevue, Washington; Phoenix, Arizona; Portland, Oregon; Sacramento, Walnut Creek, Santa Rosa, San Jose, Fresno and Irvine, California.

Well-known for its unique equal-opportunity stance, the company was the first recipient of the YWCA's prestigious "Glass Ceiling Award" at the Outstanding Women's Banquet in 1992. The award honors firms for the number of women employed, continuing women's education and promoting

WSM senior management (left to right): Cindy Sample, president; Sharon Bitz, regional vice president; Cyndie "CJ" Johnson, regional vice president; Nora McCaleb, vice president, operations

women throughout the company. Women constitute almost 85 percent of WSM's staff. The company maintains a solid commitment to preserving family life, and employees enjoy flexible work hours as well as encouragement and growth opportunities not traditionally available to women at many companies in the same industry. Ms. Sample, who has been with WSM since 1984, is one of only three female CEOs in California's mortgage banking industry. She firmly believes that happy employees lead to happy customers, which means a happy bottom line. A positive attitude, as well as effort, is always rewarded at the company.

Proud of its excellent reputation for reliability and personalized service, Western Sunrise Mortgage continues to add to its network of more than 2,000 approved mortgage brokers. It is dedicated to supporting the dream of home-ownership in the Sacramento area, which boasts one of the lowest-priced housing markets in the state and one of the most affordable metropolitan areas in the entire country.

Manufacturing and Distributing

In addition to providing and distributing an astounding variety of goods for individuals and industry, area manufacturing and distributing companies also provide employment for Sacramento residents.

Hendrickson Trucking, Inc.

Truck drivers occupy a special place in American legend. Not only are they free-spirited wanderers, rugged descendants of the cowboy, they can also be the kind of grass-roots entrepreneurs who are the foundation of the country's business strength. A smart person with integrity and persistence begins with hope and a single truck. Down the road, his small operation grows into a major business. This is how Sacramento's Hendrickson Trucking Inc. began.

Father and son pose proudly with their first truck.

Bill Hendrickson took out a second mortgage on his family's home to buy his first truck in 1976. He's not sure why he bought that truck. It wasn't for lack of a job. The young father was an executive working full time for the phone company, but the desire to start his own business was strong.

Those first years were challenging, but he never gave up. Family photos capture him and his young son Ward as they spent their weekends tending to the truck.

In 1985 Bill landed his first major contract. Taking an early retirement, he devoted his energy to trucking and soon had a small fleet hauling laminated plastics. As his company grew, Bill concentrated on developing business skills. When the next major contract came along, he needed more trucks and trailers in order to do the job right.

Finding the right lender was difficult, but the search paid off. The Mercedes-Benz Credit Corporation came through with financing to help Bill get the orders on the road in solid, dependable Freightliner trucks. Those new trucks triggered a growth spurt that included moving the company's headquarters to a site that could accommodate continuing expansion, setting up additional office space and bringing in new drivers and office support staff.

The Hendrickson Trucking Inc. fleet keeps expanding. Currently there are 80 trucks on the road, backed by a growing team of drivers, dispatchers, load planners and other business specialists. The business pumps millions of dollars into Sacramento's economy every year.

Bill and Ward, his son and partner, are dedicated to providing their clients with the best possible transportation service. They built their business by saying "yes" when other companies said "no" and by delivering on their promises. As Ward says, "First I'd tell them yes and then when I got off the phone, we'd figure out how we were going to do it." That willingness to satisfy the customer gave Hendrickson Trucking Inc. an edge the company is honing by investing in the best equipment, maintenance, personnel and information technology.

A load from the days when Bill was his own best driver

Two of the principal industries Hendrickson Trucking Inc. serves are food products and building supply. Both industries depend heavily on truck transportation for timely, effective, point-to-point transportation of goods. Hendrickson Trucking Inc.'s dramatic growth reflects the increasing trust it has earned from the manufacturers it serves.

When the company won that first major contract in 1985, Bill Hendrickson committed himself to conducting business with strict honesty, working carefully with regulatory agencies to make sure that he honored every aspect of state and federal law relevant to his business operation. The same steadfast integrity is an important part of Hendrickson Trucking Inc.'s relationship with its clients.

As the company grows, Bill's primary objective is to employ a responsible staff that shares his proactive, earnest attitude about service. Having the right employees is as important as having the right tools, software and equipment. Credible employees who deliver on their promises are crucial to maintaining a consistent level of excellence.

Employees at Hendrickson Trucking Inc. perform a variety of functions. Drivers and road support staff make sure the loads reach their destination safely and on time. Computer systems planning, training and management are also a critical part of keeping the business competitive. Solid sales and financial management staff play key roles in the company's impressive growth.

The drivers are the most visible of Hendrickson Trucking Inc.'s employees since they share the highways with the public. On the road, each driver's behavior represents the company. In order to attract the best-qualified, most responsible individuals, Hendrickson Trucking Inc. offers an excellent benefits package to its drivers, providing them with medical and retirement benefits, vacations and rider programs.

The driver's life is a difficult one; a typical driver travels 3,000 miles a week. But drivers and their families appreciate the independence this way of life affords them.

The home office is run by a staff that offers both drivers and customers accurate information and reliable knowledge. The dispatchers at Hendrickson Trucking Inc. maintain continuous contact with each driver. If the driver has a problem on the road, it's the dispatcher's job to help solve it. Dispatchers help the driver monitor load weights, provide detailed information about pickup and delivery, and supply updates on changing traffic and weather conditions.

While dispatchers work with drivers as they move, load planners serve the clients in assigned geographic

areas, organizing pickup and delivery. Just as the dispatchers talk to the drivers, load planners communicate with clients in their sectors, booking freight, scheduling shipping and providing ongoing information about loads

The third truck — Hendrickson Trucking Inc. begins to grow.

Bill and Ward strategize together.

The Hendricksons pose with their trucks.

A handsome silver
18-wheeler roars up
the hill.

in transit. Load planners also maintain records of loads ordered and delivered.

In addition, the home office staff includes the business specialists so crucial to every firm's success. Human resources, financial management, sales and public contact personnel are all important members of the Hendrickson Trucking Inc. staff, helping to provide superb customer service.

The equipment that hauls the goods is a fleet of Class Eight trucks. They're solid, top-of-the-line beauties, designed for excellent riding and handling, with comfortable sleeper cabs and top-notch load capacity to ensure that both driver and merchandise travel safely. Hendrickson's own staff of mechanics maintains the fleet and keeps them running smoothly at full-performance capacity.

Hendrickson Trucking Inc. recognizes that the trucking industry is rapidly changing and the only way to keep ahead of this change is to take advantage of electronic technology. Staying on the cutting-edge of industry technology requires an inquisitive, analytical approach. The new trucking software programs the company uses to plan its trips and to track trucks and loads along their routes provide the basis for a whole new way of doing business. Just as trucks are faster than horse-drawn wagons, new electronic systems outpace former ways of doing business. These programs require retraining and reorganizing to be fully effective, and Hendrickson Trucking Inc.'s staff is developing new skills and perspectives as they learn to make full use of the new programs. When this technology is combined with an emphasis on service and attention to detail, the business possibilities are boundless.

The firm uses electronic technology in all its departments, training employees to make full use of new technology.

Hendrickson Trucking Inc. employs the database, accounting and word processing systems commonly used by most businesses and also takes advantage of other specialized types of technology. The position of each truck is tracked using the satellite monitors of the GPS, or global positioning system. The driver no longer needs to stop and make tracking calls because information from the GPS is automatically sent to a computer interface. In addition, the GPS provides up-to-the-moment information on traffic and weather conditions, helping drivers meet their schedules. This kind of information tracking allows manufacturers and retailers to plan with confidence since they know when their goods will arrive. Vehicle and load information from the GPS and other sources can also be posted on the company's Web site. Customers can log in and check the progress of their shipment at any time, without going through the Hendrickson Trucking Inc. office.

Another technological application, the electronic data interface, connects the company's system directly to those of its customers. With these interconnected systems, clients transfer information about their shipping needs from their computers directly into the Hendrickson Trucking Inc. system. The Hendrickson system evaluates the load information and accepts or rejects it based on available capacity. The customer is notified of the outcome, and if the load is accepted the information is plugged directly into the database, speeding up load planning and delivery. Because load information passes directly from one database to another, the possibility of error in entering information is lessened.

Despite its rapid growth, Hendrickson Trucking Inc. is still a family operation. Members of the business team respect each other's skills and company headquarters is a friendly place. Both Hendricksons are hands-on managers and keep a close eye on every detail. Together Bill and Ward provide a balance of energy and experience that's the basis for the company's impressive growth.

Bill laid the foundation and used his communications skills to create solid relationships with clients, setting the standards of service. He finds running his own business exciting and enjoys the challenges it offers. He's proud of the company's growth and says nothing gives him more pride than working with his son as they continue to build their business. He's glad to be a part of Sacramento's growth and likes to reminisce about the changes he's seen in the city.

Bill disagrees with those who say California is a difficult place to do business. He insists the keys to success in this aggressive business environment are integrity, service and persistence. The awards Hendrickson Trucking Inc. keeps winning for high-quality service and on-the-road safety come from both its customers and the California Highway Patrol. These commendations demonstrate the company's achievements in safely delivering superior service, year after year.

As Hendrickson Trucking Inc. grows, Ward's role in the company continually increases. He believes in the company's potential, and his willingness to take risks has helped the company expand and move in new directions. Before he worked with the company, he was a flight instructor. Flying taught him to plan carefully, take meticulous care of his equipment and look at the world from a new, broader perspective. His enthusiasm and daring are essential parts of Hendrickson Trucking Inc.'s business philosophy. He's committed to saying "yes" to the customer, and he's eager to see how successful the company can be.

In the trucking industry, good service creates demand. The company has never run advertisements; word-of-mouth reputation is the source of its growth. As new customers ask Hendrickson Trucking Inc. to transport their goods, Bill and Ward are making sure their company has the staff and equipment to serve its expanding clientele. The fleet of silver trucks now travels all over the United States. Bill, Ward and the rest of the team are excited about the direction in which their company is headed. With the best people, technology and equipment working hard to give customers the best possible service, Bill and Ward Hendrickson are turning their business vision into solid, successful reality.

Ninety-nine percent of all items Americans use in their daily lives are delivered by truck. Bill and Ward Hendrickson recognize the importance of the service they offer to American business. That truck they used to wash was the beginning of a fleet, and the Hendricksons have created a business that makes them both proud. Together they're demonstrating the truth of an American legend, delivering the goods by turning hope and ambition into 18-wheeled reality.

A Hendrickson driver photographed his truck framed by the beauty of the Great Salt Lake.

General Produce Company

Cousins Thomas and Daniel Chan know the ins and outs of the produce business and the dynamics of running a successful family enterprise. Tom is chief executive officer and Dan is president of General Produce Co., a wholesale produce business established by their grandfather in 1933.

The only boys born into a close-knit extended Chinese family, Tom and Dan credit a family tradition of honesty and hard work; exceptional customer service; fairness and compassion for employees; a strong

Founded by Chan Tai Oy, who emigrated from Zhongshan in southern China to the United States around the turn of the century, the original General Produce was run by Chan, his three sons, Eddie, Dan and Tom, and his nephew, Davis Sun. Chan initially operated Tong Sung Co. selling produce and fish from 1906 until 1933, when he started General Produce Co.

Grandfather Chan died in 1971 at age 85. Tom Chan Sr., who had worked in the business for his father since he was a teenager, ran the company from the 1950s until

Chan Tai Oy (second from left) in front of Tong Sun Co. in 1910

friendship; and the willingness to accept and embrace change as major reasons for the third-generation firm's ongoing success. The success of the company is truly an accomplishment for a business started in the middle of the Depression.

Site of the 16th Street Market (Sacramento Produce Terminal) which would be General Produce Co.'s home for 51 years.

1991, when he passed the torch to Tom Jr. and Dan Jr. Tom Sr., who passed away in 1998, was well-known as an astute businessman, an intensely hard worker and someone whose word was "as good as gold," according to friends and colleagues.

How people were treated was paramount. One former employee recalled the time Tom Sr. worked side by side with his crew for 28 hours to get a large rush order of bananas to a customer. When the job was through, he treated everyone to a big dinner at a nearby restaurant.

As boys, Tom Jr. and Dan Jr. remember working for their parents during summer breaks. This involved long hours and physically exhausting work. While the two cousins say their family never put any pressure on them to join the family business, Dan, who graduated from the University of California, Berkeley and later became a CPA with Price-Waterhouse, considered the possibility of returning someday. Tom, also a Berkeley graduate, initially vowed he would never come back. While studying in Hong Kong and traveling abroad, he changed his mind.

Manufacturing and Distributing

Tom and Dan both pondered the sweat and toil their family had endured to achieve success, especially during a time when there were many obstacles for minorities. When Tom Jr. asked his father about the most important skill needed to be successful in business, Tom Sr. answered without reservation, "People. Learn about people." Tom Jr. "studied" people as a salesman with Kellogg Sales Company and S.E Rykoff & Co. (now U.S. Foodservice). A sense of tradition, history and family pride drew both Tom and Dan back to Sacramento to join the family business in 1979.

Much has changed since General Produce's early days. Today, General Produce Co. is one of the largest produce wholesalers in Northern California. The once tiny three-

stall produce operation has blossomed into 225 employees. The company's price list, a mere two pages long in 1978, has since grown to 25 pages. Pricing and inventory are tracked by computer. Over 300 tons of fresh fruits and vegetables are physically distributed each day. General Produce's distribution area stretches from Fresno,

California to southern Oregon and east from the coast to Lake Tahoe. The firm serves over 1,200 customers from its main facility in Sacramento and another facility in Mount Shasta, California. Clients include supermarkets, hotels, restaurants, military commissaries, other wholesalers, overseas importers and virtually anyone who buys produce. In addition to produce, the firm stocks some groceries and produce-related items.

Genpro Gifts, the creative products division of General Produce Co., was started in 1996 to address a growing demand by corporate and retail clients for customized gifts for celebrations, thank yous, customer

The founder, his partners and family in 1949 — (Standing left to right) Kitty and Dan Chan, Davis Sun, Eddie and Mae Chan, and their sister Marjorie (Sitting left to right) Lin and Chan Tai Oy, Tom and Mae Chan with daughter Mavis

General Produce Co.'s 77,000-square-foot refrigerated warehouse facility at North B Street in Sacramento

Orders staged and ready to be loaded on trucks

changed since the senior partners ran the business. The company's mission is "We deliver fresh fruits and vegetables and innovative solutions to meet the needs of our customers."

The "secrets to success" passed down from one generation to the next are simple — "Work hard, be dedicated and persevere; surround yourself with good, loyal people; and always leave something on the table for the other person."

As the four senior partners reflected on what kept them together for 65 years, the prevailing concept was "compromise." Work as a family; do not argue; talk things over; and always consider the other person's opinions and feelings. And finally, the lesson they learned from Chan Tai Oy was not only to work hard but to be humble and show consideration for all others. The third generation of Chans, Tom and Dan, are continuing the tradition into the next century.

appreciation, employee recognition, sales incentives and meetings. The family's commitment to quality, service, innovation and value now extends to the art of gift-giving.

Intense competition and an increasingly educated produce-buying public are what makes the business both challenging and rewarding, say the Chans. Keeping quality consistent and prices stable in a commodities-based market is another unique aspect of the business. But Tom and Dan Chan watched and learned. Since it is extremely difficult to distinguish a generic product, General Produce succeeds by providing service that is distinctive and focusing on helping customers be more successful. For General Produce, satisfying customers and nurturing long-term relationships takes priority over short-term profitability. Concern for the customer is a hallmark of General Produce, a fact that has not

Manufacturing and Distributing

Crystal Cream & Butter Company

From humble beginnings as a turn-of-the-century butter-churning plant, Crystal Cream & Butter Company has become a multimillion-dollar operation with cutting-edge technology — and another generation of the Hansen family — firmly in charge.

Few Sacramento companies embody such an amalgamation of old and new. On the one hand, Crystal home-delivery trucks are still a familiar sight in local neighborhoods, evoking memories of simpler, more innocent times. On the other hand, Crystal's state-of-the-art automated fluid-milk processing plant is capable of handling 300,000 gallons of milk a day, untainted by air or human hands.

Crystal began in 1901 as a small butter-making operation, hauling milk from local dairy farms. The company moved in 1913 to a bigger facility at 10th and D streets, where butter and other dairy products continued to be made throughout the 20th century. In 1921 Danish immigrant Carl Hansen, frustrated by his lack of control as plant manager of a dairy cooperative, purchased the company with his wife, Gerda, with dreams of producing a wider variety of products. They did so 10 years later when they introduced bottled milk, a convenience never before available to residents of Sacramento. Cottage cheese, sour cream, ice cream and yogurt soon followed.

The Hansen family grew along with the business, and sons Vernon, Kenneth and Gerald, principals from the 1930s through the 80s and 90s, proved to be instrumental to the longevity of the company. The Hansens also maintained part-ownership of Sacramento radio and television station KCRA from the mid-1940s to 1960, and they sponsored numerous charities.

Today, third- and fourth-generation members of the Hansen family have taken the reins. Under the Crystal umbrella are the historic D Street plant; the automated facility on Belvedere Avenue, which opened in 1996; Vitafreze, a frozen-confections manufacturer; and Crystal Bottling Company, a bottled-water operation which started in 1992.

Crystal products are distributed throughout Northern California supermarket chains, convenience stores, restaurants and schools. Frozen products, including novelties and ice cream mixes, are distributed throughout the West and are exported to several Pacific Rim islands, Taiwan, Russia and China.

But some things never change. Crystal still gets its raw milk from independent dairies in the Sacramento Valley. Because the distance between those 70 farms and the processing plant is so short, the milk stays fresh. Within 24 hours of leaving the farm, it's on the grocer's shelf.

In addition, home delivery has always been Crystal's way of getting up close and personal with customers. At one point during the 1960s, Crystal had the largest fleet of home-delivery trucks in the nation. Now the trucks are owned by independent contractors, many of them retired Crystal employees.

Synonymous with the Crystal name is quality. Thanks to recent technology, the Belvedere plant is able to handle milk in a sterile environment. The shelf life of various Crystal products can be extended dramatically with a new system that pasteurizes at higher temperatures and holds the milk in vacuum-pressurized containers until it is packaged. With this new system, cream with a former shelf life of 18 days will stay fresh for 45 to 60 days.

As marvelous as technology is, nothing can replace good old human initiative and dedication. According to Crystal's executives, the company's 500 employees are its biggest asset of all.

A Crystal home-delivery driver circa 1958

Burnett & Sons Planing Mill
& Lumber Company

The millwork industry involves the manufacture and sale of a large variety of wood products. These products are subject not only to the uncertainty of the general construction market but are also affected by changes in style.

The extent and intricacy of millwork in construction had been in decline for nearly a century, until the mid-1960s. Architects showed a renewed interest in the more

Keeping it in the family From left to right: Fitz Miller, Burnett Miller, Simone Miller and Jim Miller

involved styles typical of earlier buildings. This rebirth brought about increased demand for more elaborate millwork such as radius head doors, arched ceilings, wainscot and heavily shaped moldings. Along with this change came a return to multilevel buildings and, therefore, stair units in many styles. Again fine craftsmen were in demand to create complicated circular staircases, intricate newels and banister work.

This fine-quality millwork and cabinetry had been in the tradition of Burnett & Sons since the late 1850s. As perhaps the oldest millwork company under the same family ownership in the state, it had maintained the expertise necessary to meet the needs of almost any architect or designer.

The Burnett family sailed from Charleston, Massachusetts via the Isthmus of Panama to Sacramento. They arrived in 1849, as many settlers did, seeking their fortune during the gold rush. But the Burnetts had no interest in gold or its accompanying market, which they considered saturated. Although he had been an accomplished carpenter and woodworker specializing in cabinets and staircases, Philitus Watson Burnett was determined to find his niche in a new line of work. After more than 10 years and two failed forays into the sheep-raising and silkworm industries, the Burnetts decided to return to what they had done best in Massachusetts — woodworking.

In 1865, Philitus and his oldest son, Henry A. Burnett, started a small shop in the rear of the family's downtown Sacramento home. Young Henry had just been discharged as first lieutenant from the First California Cavalry and was anxious to have his own business. Soon the pair became known for their fine cabinets and staircases. The rest of the story, as they say, is history — literally. Through several wars, numerous relocations, deaths, changes in partnerships, the Great Depression, even fires, some of the finest architectural millwork in the city of Sacramento can trace its manufacture to the shops of Burnett & Sons.

While fires destroyed many of Burnett's official records, thousands of homes and buildings still display the company's work. One of the most notable examples includes the old state Capitol's famous stairway, which is

The original Burnett's Planing Mill at 23rd and R streets

now used as communion, pulpit and choir loft railings in the beautiful St. Francis Church located at 27th and K streets. This gem of mission architecture showcases exquisite solid black walnut wood, which the Franciscan priests purchased after the staircase in the Capitol was replaced by one of stone and wrought iron. For the 1980 bicentennial, the state restored the Capitol to its original grandeur by calling upon Burnett & Sons to re-create the original stairs as well as many historic pieces of furniture. Due to the impossibility of obtaining black walnut in the quantity and dimensions necessary for the project, they were forced to use Honduras mahogany instead. Many credit the firm for its fine workmanship, which helps the Capitol look as imposing today as it did originally.

Burnett Miller, Philitus's great-great-grandson, who went to work for the company in 1959, currently runs Burnett & Sons. As a former mayor and councilman, he has been an important part of the continuing development of the city, while still remaining a vital part of the family's business. In quality homes and the finest bank buildings, one can find the precision work of the shop. Most of the buildings in the Old Sacramento historic riverfront restoration project exhibit millwork and moldings, windows and doors re-created by Burnett & Sons.

Since its inception, the company has maintained an interest in special craftsmanship and unique construction and production problems. Through the maintenance of an active training and apprenticeship program, Burnett & Sons has been able to continue the traditions of the craft. In an era of mass production, the firm has refused to waiver from the principles of individual and custom production that are becoming more rare.

Miller is proud of his heritage and the successful family business, now in its fifth consecutive generation. Three of his seven adult children work at the mill, which has resided at its downtown location since 1933. Though modernization has taken place — the equipment has been upgraded and computer programs employed — the company's product and reputation remains surprisingly unchanged. Burnett & Sons still creates beautifully crafted custom woodwork for local businesses and homes. Despite the high-tech times, it is interesting to note that the firm, which boasts a booming business, is frequently called upon to re-create the classic work that it did during its first decade.

The Sacramento State Capitol showcases some of Burnett & Sons' most beautiful and well-known work. Shown here is the original famous staircase, which the company was called upon to re-create in honor of the bicentennial.

PRIDE Industries

PRIDE Industries was founded in 1966 in the basement of a church in Auburn, California. The company's founders, a group of parents whose children had developmental disabilities, dreamed of a world where people with disabilities could find employment and be fully integrated into their communities. PRIDE Industries began by providing vocational and life-skills development training,

and in the late 1970s the company moved to Roseville, California to accommodate its continuing growth and success.

Shortly after the company's move to Roseville, and thanks to the vision of two members of PRIDE's board of directors, PRIDE began to transform the company from a

traditional nonprofit organization into a business with a social mission. It was an innovative idea and one that represented an exciting new model for the human service industry. These two men had a vision of self-sufficiency, growth and increased opportunities for people with disabilities.

In 1983, Michael Ziegler was hired as president and chief executive officer. At the time, the company had 15 employees and 50 people with developmental disabilities receiving services. PRIDE's annual budget totaled $250,000, 90 percent of which came from the United Way as well as from federal and state sources. During this transition, PRIDE continued to learn how to operate like a business while advancing its founders' mission to create job opportunities for people with disabilities. PRIDE took an entrepreneurial role in the community, offering services that satisfied the specific needs of its customers, and evolved from a nonprofit organization dependent on state and federal dollars into a self-sufficient company.

Today, PRIDE Industries is self-sufficient and employs more than 3,000 part-time and full-time employees, most of whom have some type of disability. PRIDE is a California-based company with current business in five other states while continuing to expand into more areas every year. PRIDE continues to challenge itself to innovate and improve, and the company recently underwent a strategic planning process that aligned the company's structure and systems to efficiently and effectively support its mission, growth and core lines of business, which include facility support services, light manufacturing, mail services and fulfillment, and government services.

Continuing its focus on providing job opportunities for people with disabilities, PRIDE formed a new division by acquiring YubaShoes, an internationally recognized manufacturer of snowshoes. This acquisition placed PRIDE Industries in the competitive world of the international consumer marketplace and is another example of the company's commitment to showing what people with disabilities can accomplish. PRIDE reached the top of the world - literally! On May 27, 1998, Tom Whittaker became the first person with a disability to reach the 29,000-foot summit of Mt. Everest. Tom's expedition team was outfitted in Sport Snowshoes, a high-tech snowshoe manufactured by PRIDE employees with developmental disabilities in Sacramento.

In 1999, PRIDE Industries ranked as the fourth largest manufacturing employer in the Sacramento region posting revenues in excess of $60 million. The company is consistently included in the region's list of the top 100 fastest growing companies. PRIDE's customers are key to the realization of the company's vision: To be the premier employer of people with disabilities, the vendor of choice in the markets it serves, and the recognized leader in meeting the needs of individuals overcoming barriers to employment. Of PRIDE's customers CEO Ziegler states, "They look to us for quality, responsiveness and value. We are a value-added solution where everyone wins. By working with us our customers become partners in advancing our mission."

PRIDE's clients include Intel Corporation, Boeing, Hewlett-Packard, NEC Electronics, Packard Bell NEC, Wells Fargo Bank, USCS International, The Sacramento Bee, Kaiser Permanente and Pasco Scientific. Offering specialized services like electronic circuit-board assembly and cleanroom maintenance as well as full-service turnkey solutions in fulfillment and manufacturing, PRIDE procures contracts with high-tech and low-tech companies alike. The company also contracts with numerous federal, state and county customers. They manage food services operations at Travis Air Force Base in Fairfield and McClellan Air Force Base in Sacramento, preparing and serving over 100,000 meals monthly.

PRIDE believes that world-class customer service begins with its employees. Everyone knows the corporate mission, and employees are continuously encouraged to make a positive difference in advancing the mission through their own innovation and ingenuity. PRIDE considers this the "Total Quality Entrepreneurship" (TQE) approach to business - the best results come from people who have ownership in their work.

One of PRIDE's most exciting accomplishments occurred in 1997 when the company received ISO 9002 certification. ISO 9002 certification is a comprehensive quality-assurance process that benchmarks processes against a worldwide standard of high-quality business practices. Receiving certification demonstrated to PRIDE's customers

The company's Facility Support Services division provides comprehensive facility maintenance services including cleanroom maintenance.

that the company is committed to quality and continuous improvement. In response to PRIDE's strong partnerships within the community, the company has been honored with numerous awards on a local, state and national level, including the President's Committee Award for Employment of People with Disabilities and Comstock's magazine's Capital Region's Most Admired Company award.

Ziegler describes PRIDE Industries as a unique and powerful partnership between individuals who develop business opportunities, rehabilitation professionals who discover and nurture the capabilities of people with disabilities, and employees who satisfy customers' needs and create new opportunities. "With job creation, the business grows with you and supports the company. Our victories are public victories," says Ziegler.

PRIDE's Mail Services & Fulfillment division offers comprehensive mailing, assembly and packaging with world-class customer service.

American River Packaging

Sacramento was a city in transition when Richard Lamb founded American River Packaging in 1980. The state capital was beginning to shift from a government-driven economy to a more diverse, dynamic economy encompassing government as well as large and small manufacturing and service businesses. This transformation also led to Sacramento's position as a center of high-tech business.

Lamb recognized these trends and seized the opportunity to realize his vision of becoming the leading source for locally manufactured corrugated packaging. He started American River Packaging with a few dedicated employees (some of whom are still working with him) and a minimal amount of equipment. He credits his company with being one of the first in the region to support Sacramento's changing infrastructure. Today, the company is a multiple-facility manufacturer and distributor of sophisticated "total packaging solutions" to Northern and Central California.

The success of the company has been driven by the founder's simple credo: "We don't just sell boxes, we're a service business." Following this guideline, American River has developed a culture that emphasizes unsurpassed customer service. The company has always believed that manufacturing and selling quality packaging is not its sole business. A major component of American River's business philosophy is developing strong, mutually beneficial business relationships that are based on trust. The company believes that a good, communicative relationship is the best path to more cost-effective packaging.

As the years progressed, American River Packaging also grew. Originally a small manufacturing firm focusing on small orders and great service, the company became one of the premier sheet plants serving Northern and Central California, and northern Nevada. The company still processes small orders and provides what many customers believe is the best service available. They have, however, progressed well beyond the original scope of the business.

Today, American River Packaging provides one of the widest arrays of products and services offered in the area — from small to truckload quantities, from sealing tape to stretch film, from contract packaging to "just-in-time" warehousing programs. American River has a blend of products and services that can solve virtually any packaging problem, including protecting package contents against electrostatic discharge. As a matter of fact, the company's specialty is providing "total packaging solutions" — a process that involves engineering the most cost-effective package regardless of the components or processes required.

Typical customers come to the company as they prepare to package their new product or to develop a new and improved package for their existing product. Customers need packaging that is cost-effective; provides maximum protection of the product; is easy to assemble and pack; and is made of recyclable and environmentally safe materials. Ultimately, the packaging must satisfy the customer's customers. Based on a company's needs, American River designs and constructs a prototype box, which is submitted for revisions and improvement, tested on in-house certified package-testing equipment and, upon approval of final graphics, manufactured by American River Packaging. All of these processes are done in-house, which allows American River to reliably and properly balance high-quality, immediate service and cost in supplying the right package.

Other customers that come to the company are experiencing rapid growth and expansion, and often they require highly reliable supply and reduced costs. As prospective customers find that their demand for packaging equals and even surpasses supply, they look to American River Packaging because of its traditional strategy of expanding its manufacturing capacity commensurate with or at a faster rate than the demand of customers. With factories in Madera and Sacramento, California, multiple pieces of equipment at each plant and multiple warehouses, American River Packaging helps customers expand their businesses without experiencing packaging problems.

The core businesses of American River Packaging are the manufacture of corrugated packaging and containers, the distribution of packaging products, and the design and implementation of inventory-control services such as "just-in-time" programs. Other products and services are delivered to customers through "targeted strategic alliances." These agreements are more than just supplier/customer arrangements. They are carefully planned relationships that provide, by intent, a three-way benefit — to American River, to suppliers and, most importantly, to customers.

Rather than trying to be all things to all people, American River concentrates its resources and efforts on its primary business: manufacturing corrugated containers. This is because the product, corrugated containers, is a complete high-performance material, design, manufacturing and delivery system all in one.

The company also focuses on being a low-cost producer. It has achieved that goal by combining new equipment purchases and quality OEM (original equipment manufacturer) restorations. The company has the ability to purchase the appropriate used machinery, often at a substantially reduced cost, strip it to the frame and rebuild it to the original manufacturer's specifications or better.

Additionally, American River Packaging designs and develops "targeted strategic alliances" that give customers specific market advantages as well as a broader spectrum of products and services at the most cost-effective level

possible. As a result of adding its low-cost producer status to the "targeted strategic alliances," the company offers the most complete line of packaging products, multiple-material packages, manufactured products, and inventory control programs to the Northern and Central California markets, as well as northern Nevada, at very competitive prices.

American River Packaging's crowning achievement, however, is not the ability to offer competitive pricing and a vast array of products and services. Lamb places the highest value on customer service that both defines the company and distinguishes it from the competition. "We do what we say we'll do," says Lamb. With such a priority on serving the customer, all employees are empowered to do what it takes to satisfy the needs of customers.

In the future, Lamb sees the company forming additional partnerships with customers and alliances with its suppliers to further push service to a higher level. American River Packaging knows that it must meet its customers' needs better than anyone else. It also knows that the business of service is the company's primary business.

Beutler Heating & Air Conditioning

A young student wiped the sweat from his brow as the schoolhouse baked in the Sacramento Valley sunshine. It was going to be hot. In the 1920s, there was precious little relief from Mother Nature's extremes. But the boy didn't mind; he knew that when the mercury hit 100 degrees, class would be dismissed and he could go have some fun. What Del Beutler didn't know was that one day he would make his living by taming the heat and that he would play a major role in Sacramento's phenomenal growth.

Beutler Heating and Air Conditioning started in the garage of Del Beutler's Carmichael home in 1947. He had honed his skills as a sheet metal specialist during his two years as a Navy foreman at Twentynine Palms, Terminal Island and McClellan Field. He spent a year working for a local sheet metal shop and passed his contractor's license exam with flying colors.

Armed with highly specialized training and practical experience, Del Beutler quickly discovered that his first obstacle to success would be government bureaucracy. While he was away serving his country, Sacramento County imposed zoning restrictions on his property. They declared his new home-based business illegal. The entire neighborhood rose to his defense, and the code enforcers relented until Beutler was able to move his business to a commercial building.

The post-war housing boom promised great prosperity for his fledgling company. In the early days, Beutler concentrated on installing heating and ducting systems for tract-home developments and some commercial building projects. As the demand for cooling systems increased, Beutler became an innovator. His ingenuity was passed down from his father, Lyman Beutler, who invented a safety clamp that prevented the theft of freight-train boxcars. That idea landed Lyman Beutler a job with Southern Pacific Railroad and brought the family to Sacramento from Idaho in 1922.

The first air conditioners on the market were water-cooled, which created constant problems because they required the disposal of massive amounts of water. People would run the spent water into storm drains and streams in ways that would send today's environmentalists into convulsions. Beutler devised systems that repurposed, or recycled, the water, but the contamination problems seemed insurmountable.

Swamp coolers, which used evaporating humidity to lower a room's temperature, were popular in arid regions like Palm Springs but were less effective in Sacramento's climate.

Finally, air-cooled systems were introduced and the entire industry was reborn. The company could then focus on improving the efficiency of fans, ducting, vents and insulation. Never more euphoric than when he was developing something new, Beutler created a think-tank atmosphere for his employees.

A daunting problem with two-story homes has been the dramatic difference in temperature that can occur between the first and second floors. Beutler's design engineers created the Zoned Thermal Equalizer system, which electronically balances the temperature throughout the entire home. Its Smart Vent system was invented to automatically circulate fresh, filtered outdoor air throughout the house while decreasing compressor usage by drawing in the cooler night and early morning air.

When Berkeley lab scientists announced that duct tape was great for everything except sealing ducts, it was no surprise to anyone at Beutler Heating and Air Conditioning. They had long since incorporated a unique sealing technique for sheet metal joints that remains the most efficient in the industry.

Del Beutler, founder of Beutler Heating and Air Conditioning, strikes a dapper pose in this early portrait with his son Gary.

Sacramento Corporate Headquarters

Residential and commercial developers benefit from Beutler's engineering staff, which is thoroughly versed in systems development, government compliance, computer-aided design programs and cost analysis. Beutler's research department has worked closely with the California Energy Commission since 1983 in efforts to improve the efficiency and energy consumption of climate-control systems.

With full-brokerage capability and on-hand inventory worth more than $3 million, Beutler's divisions are responsive and prepared. Since Beutler's roots are in fabrication, the company still has the largest in-house sheet metal plants in the marketplace, allowing for custom or assembly line manufacturing.

In an extraordinary commitment to education, Beutler is the only sheet metal employer in California that offers employees a three-year, state-certified, unilateral apprenticeship program for journeymen.

Five decades and more than 200,000 installations later, Beutler Heating and Air Conditioning has patented numerous inventions and set the standard for excellence in the HVAC trade.

Although he clearly is renowned within his trade for many things, Del Beutler only admits to one claim to fame, which happened while he was in a San Diego boot camp during World War II. Beutler was abruptly ordered to appear before his commanding officer. Fearing that he had done something wrong and expecting a reprimand, he was instead congratulated for being the first recruit in history to score 100 percent on the sheet metal exam, and was told he could name his own reward. He responded that his wife had just given birth, and the CO immediately granted an early release from basic training so he could return home to see his new baby son, Gary.

Gary Beutler, now the chairman of the board of the company his father founded, is credited with creating and maintaining strong customer relations. President Rick Wylie is a brilliant engineer and inventor who has spearheaded the drive for new and better products. Under their guidance, Del Beutler's vision has become the largest heating and air company in Northern California, with more than 700 employees and four locations — Sacramento, Cordelia, Manteca and Livermore.

Beutler Heating and Air Conditioning supports several community causes and projects, including the Shriners Hospital for Children and the Home Aid Foundation, which assists displaced families and

Beutler's full-time, dedicated training staff is unique in the industry.

teenagers. On January 20, 1998, Sacramento Mayor Joe Serna Jr. presented Del and Gary Beutler with a commendation for 50 years of making Sacramentans more comfortable in their homes and, most importantly, for providing quality employment for the community.

Operating out of his garage over half a century ago, Del Beutler faced the business world with little more than his talent and a strong sense of duty. His perseverance then, as well as the legacy his son carries on now, changed the Sacramento Valley forever.

From left to right:
Gary Beutler - Chairman of the Board,
Rick Wylie - President,
Rob Penrod - Vice President/Engineering,
Scott Sahota - Vice President/General Superintendent,
Tom Beutler - Vice President/Controller

Blue Diamond Growers

Sacramento's own Blue Diamond Growers cooperative does everything it possibly can with the almond — it mixes it with breakfast cereal, hickory-smokes it, puts it in soap, grinds it for gourmet crackers, spreads it on toast, even drinks it. But when the company formed back in 1910, it was just plain nuts.

Hardly a domestic market existed for almonds in the late 1890s and early 1900s, when California farmers first experimented with varieties brought from Mexico by

In 1914 Blue Diamond moved its headquarters from San Francisco to 18th and C streets where almonds were transported by rail in burlap bags.

Spanish missionaries. These were shipped, in-shell, to the East Coast, where foreign immigrants bought them to make their traditional holiday marzipan and almond-flavored bakery goods.

In 1929, a five-story processing plant was built to produce ever-increasing Blue Diamond shelled almonds.

In those days, crops were bought by independent dealers whom the growers could never be sure were giving them a fair shake in the marketplace. So in 1910, 230 farmers banded together to form a cooperative called the California Almond Growers Exchange, and they hired professionals to run it. This new arrangement made winners of everyone — in exchange for delivering their almonds to strategically located receiving stations, grower-owners would be assured a home for their product at the best price possible.

The Blue Diamond label made its debut in 1914 on the burlap bags in which the almonds were packed. That same year, the company built a small receiving plant at 18th and C streets in Sacramento. It was around this time that the cooperative began to devise ways to expand the market for its product. Its solution: a new shelling plant that housed the world's first mechanical nutcracker. This was followed four years later by the invention of a revolutionary bleaching system for rain-stained almonds.

In 1929 the co-op built a five-story processing plant, which turned out to be a springboard for the shelled-almond craze of the 1930s and 40s. At that time, the United States was still relying heavily on imported almonds from Spain and Italy, but that changed in 1932, when Blue Diamond shipped 20 carloads of shelled almonds to New York; after that, the Big Apple was hooked on the little nut from California, which was sweeter than its Mediterranean counterparts. Soon folks everywhere learned to "Look for the Blue Diamond," a popular slogan of the period.

Both World War II and the Korean War were a boon to Blue Diamond, which teamed up with candy-bar manufacturers to make chocolate-almond bars for the U.S. armed forces. Growth accelerated during the 1950s, and Blue Diamond erected concrete storage bins, cold-storage facilities and automated equipment. In 1960 it installed electronic sorting machines and expanded its cooking and packing facilities.

Meanwhile, Blue Diamond launched a world-wide campaign, appointing sales agents in Canada, Mexico, South America, Europe, Africa and Asia. Foil packets of trademarked Smokehouse almonds found their way aboard passenger jets, Japanese bullet trains, the Apollo-Soyuz and NASA space shuttles, Air Force One and Amtrak.

Today, because of the marketing successes of Blue Diamond Growers, the almond truly is the ambassador of nuts. The co-op, now owned by about 4,000 growers (about 70 percent of all almond growers in California), produces over one-fourth of the world's annual crop of almonds. The organization markets its crop to all 50 states and more than 90 foreign countries, making almonds California's largest food export and the sixth-largest U.S. food export. Revenues total between $450 and $500 million.

Blue Diamond Growers has always been a solid contributor to the economic health of the city of Sacramento. That's why city officials worked so hard to keep its headquarters there when it considered relocating in the mid-1990s. In exchange for a multimillion-dollar package of incentives and subsidies, the company agreed in 1995 to stay in the capital and spend $30 million to modernize the world's largest almond plant.

Several local charities are glad the company made that decision. Blue Diamond gives generously of its time and money, particularly for the benefit of children right in its own backyard. The downtown YMCA, the Boys and Girls Club, St. Hope Academy, the Salvation Army and the Ronald McDonald House are among the organizations that Blue Diamond supports. The co-op is also involved in an award-winning community project called Shots for Tots, an immunization program for disadvantaged toddlers in the midtown area.

A few blocks away from Blue Diamond headquarters, Washington School and the Washington Children's Center, a subsidized day-care center, are beneficiaries of the co-op's resources. The company underwrites the cost of interns for the school's Head Start program, and employees themselves adopt letters to Santa, making sure each child receives a gift and a visit from Saint Nick, played by a Blue Diamond executive, at Christmastime. Also during the holiday season, the co-op provides tickets to *The Nutcracker* ballet to children who otherwise couldn't afford them.

Named 1998 Business of the Year by the Sacramento Area Commerce and Trade Organization, Blue Diamond Growers is committed to expansion and modernization of its facilities. For example, in 1982 the company purchased the Del Monte Cannery Plant #11 on C Street for $3.5 million. Renamed the Blue Diamond Building, this facility houses a visitors' center, a theater, a factory outlet and offices.

Other facilities include a processing plant in Modesto; several receiving stations located throughout the Sacramento and San Joaquin valleys; and two Blue Diamond Growers stores in Sacramento and Salida. Blue Diamond also has offices in Japan, with a network of brokers throughout major markets of the world. In addition, the co-op markets hazelnuts, macadamia nuts and pistachios, and owns a hazelnut plant in Salem, Oregon.

All this expansion is in preparation for The Big One, which to almond growers is not a giant earthquake, but a colossal crop — one billion pounds of almonds annually by the year 2000. What to do with all those nuts? Blue Diamond has more than a few ideas. Most of them are centered around the concept of the almond as a nutrition-

packed food — not the fatty diet buster it was previously thought to be. According to nutritionists, nuts in general contain high levels of unsaturated, or "good," fat, which may actually help to lower blood cholesterol levels and the risk of heart attack.

That means consumers will see more almonds in what have traditionally been health foods, such as breakfast cereals and milk-substitute drinks. In fact, slivered Blue Diamond almonds are being combined with sardines in Japanese school lunch programs as a way to provide the biggest bang for the nutritional buck. For those Americans whose palates are unaccustomed to such fare, there are new lines of convenience snack products and almond-based gourmet treats.

Of course, the traditional can of Blue Diamond almonds will always be around. Remember the slogan: "A Can a Week, That's All We Ask." But those whose co-workers are constantly stealing almonds from their desks had better make it two.

In the late 1980s, Blue Diamond Growers starred in one of the most memorable U.S. advertising campaigns, "A Can a Week, That's All We Ask." The slogan refers to burgeoning California almond crops that will top one billion pounds in the 21st century. Today they are shipped in 2,000-pound cartons.

Research shows that almonds are a heart-healthy cholesterol-free whole food that protects against major diseases. This is why consumers will see more cereals, confectioneries and almond milk on grocery shelves.

Campbell Soup Company

The red-and-white Campbell's Soup can: It's as much a symbol of Americana as Coca-Cola, Route 66 and Elvis posters. Its contents warmed and nourished legions of baby boomers, who probably still remember that famous Campbell jingle, "M'm! M'm! Good!" In 1962, pop artist Andy Warhol immortalized Campbell's Soup as an important part of the fabric of everyday American life, as a symbol of comfort, fond memories and simpler times.

Begun in 1869 as a small preserve company, the Campbell Soup Company of today reaches far beyond soup and far beyond the borders of this country. Sacramento owns a significant part of the company's rich history as the hometown of the oldest Campbell Soup plant still in production.

The Campbell Soup Company was founded by fruit merchant Joseph Campbell and icebox manufacturer Abram Anderson in Camden, New Jersey, home to the company's first plant and its current international headquarters. The Joseph Campbell Preserve Company marketed its first soup, a ready-to-serve beefsteak tomato soup, in 1895.

Campbell introduced its first condensed soup, tomato, in 1897. Today, Campbell's Tomato Soup ranks as one of the top 10 selling dry grocery items in U.S. supermarkets.

Campbell Soup Company

A revolutionary change in soup-making occurred two years later when 24-year-old John Dorrance, a European-trained chemist who had been hired by his uncle, developed the concept of condensed soup. By removing water from soup, Dorrance was able to reduce the volume of a can of soup from 32 ounces to 10.5 ounces and the price from 34 cents to 10 cents. John Dorrance went on to become president of the Campbell Company in 1914, eight years before Campbell officially adopted "Soup" as its middle name.

Like condensed tomato soup, the famous red-and-white Campbell label was born before the turn of the century. In 1898, company executive Herberton Williams attended a Cornell vs. University of Pennsylvania football game and was so enthralled with the brilliant red-and-white Cornell uniforms, he decided to make a similar statement. Another permanent fixture on the Campbell label was incorporated in 1900 when Campbell's soups won the Gold Medallion for excellence at the Paris Exposition. The medallion has been featured on the label ever since.

Campbell's colorful advertising history also traces its roots to the dawn of the 20th century. The first Campbell's advertisement appeared in 1899 on New York City streetcars. By 1904 those streetcar advertisements featured The Campbell Kids, who touted soup through 1958 and reappeared on television in 1990 to the beat of rap music.

Campbell's first magazine ad appeared in Good Housekeeping in 1905 with the slogan, "21 Kinds of Campbell's Soup — Look For the Red & White Label." Radio spots featuring the famous "M'm! M'm! Good!" jingle debuted in the 1930s when Campbell sponsored such radio programs as the "George Burns and Gracie Allen Show" and "Campbell Playhouse." By 1950, Campbell was on television.

All the while, the Campbell Soup Company was expanding. In 1911 the company began distributing nationally when it entered the California market. Four years later, it acquired the Franco-American Food Company, which manufactures pasta products.

The Sacramento plant, which began operation in September 1947, was the third soup plant built by Campbell and continues to exist today along with Campbell facilities in 22 countries on six continents. In the early days, the local plant helped meet the increased demand for condensed soup, a demand fueled in part by the publication of the first Campbell cookbook in 1916. The cookbook's recipes became the rage of the 50s, and today more than one million cans of soup are used every day in recipes.

Manufacturing and Distributing

Not long after the company went public on the New York Stock Exchange in 1954, Campbell established its international division. From then on, a host of new products debuted on grocery shelves: a line of low-salt soups in 1964, Franco-American SpaghettiOs in 1965 and Campbell's Chunky ready-to-serve soups in 1970. By 1971, Campbell's sales had topped $1 billion.

A decade later, the company's success continued with the advent of products that became instant hits. Prego spaghetti sauces were introduced nationally in 1981, and in 1989, A.C. Neilsen named Prego the No. 1 best-selling new dry grocery product of the decade. A year later, Campbell introduced cream of broccoli soup, which became the most successful new soup in 55 years.

Today, soup is more popular than ever as a convenient, nutritious food ideal for busy families. Keeping up with the demand is the Campbell Soup plant in Sacramento, which employs approximately 1,450 people in a 1.5 million-plus-square-foot facility off Franklin Boulevard. Among the 343 products it manufactures are a wide selection of Campbell's condensed red-and-white soups, Swanson broths, Healthy Request, Franco-American, Pace salsa, Prego spaghetti sauce, V8 vegetable juice and V8 Splash, available in cans, glass and plastic containers.

Each year, more than 37 million pounds of fresh carrots and potatoes and more than 11 million pounds of fresh mushrooms are received at the Sacramento plant. Nearly 30 million pounds of tomato paste, prepared from fresh tomatoes at Campbell's facilities in Dixon and Stockton, are used each year to prepare soups, Prego sauces and Pace salsa.

The Sacramento plant, winner of the 1997 Campbell's World Class Manufacturing Excellence award, produces more than 1.2 billion containers of soups, sauces and salsa annually, a far cry from Campbell's rate of 10 cases per week in 1897.

But the love of soup isn't just an American phenomenon. That's why Campbell can be found all over the world,

tailoring its soups to the tastes of local culture. One of the favorite soups in Australia, for instance, is pumpkin; the soup du jour in China, duck gizzard or fig.

While soup remains the center of the Campbell brand portfolio, the company also owns other big-name brands: Godiva Chocolatier, Pepperidge Farm cookies and crackers, and Arnott's, the leading brand of manufactured baked goods in Australia.

For the future, the company is committed to continuing its Labels for Education program to help fund school materials and to developing innovative ways to connect with consumers. As its vision unfolds, the grandchildren and great-grandchildren of baby boomers may long be singing, "M'm! M'm! Better!"

Campbell has a long, colorful and memorable advertising history.

The Campbell facility in Sacramento occupies more than 1.5 million square feet on 136 acres.

Fong & Fong Printers *and Lithographers*

Fong & Fong Printers and Lithographers, a dynamic family-owned business in Sacramento, attributes its success as one of the West Coast's premier printers to exceptional customer service, a progressive attitude and its dedication to high quality.

The local printing company was founded in 1958 by Sacramento native Paul Fong, who has a printing and graphic arts background, and his wife, Mae, whose college education was in banking, finance and economics. The modest facility at 16th and V streets was quickly outgrown. The next move, to 15th and S streets, saw three major expansions. In 1979, the company made yet another move to a custom-designed building at its present 65th and Broadway location, which houses state-of-the-art equipment.

Today the Fongs, together with a knowledgeable and highly trained staff, produce a high-profile, high-visibility variety of 10-or-more color print products including annual reports, company and product brochures, point-of-purchase materials, direct mailers and posters. Fong & Fong is a printing resource for Fortune 500 corporations, leading advertising agencies and cutting-edge design studios in Northern California, including the Silicon Valley, the San Francisco Bay area and the Sacramento Valley.

"The key to our expansion has been our sales staff and the demand of the public," said son Curtis Fong, executive vice president. "Whenever you accept more work than you can handle, you've got to grow."

Fueling that growth is a zealous quest to acquire the latest in technology. Under one roof, Fong & Fong offers services ranging from complete postscript capability, premium 10-color printing, intricate die-cutting and scoring, precise foil stamping and embossing, to finishing and final delivery.

"We've always been very progressive in adopting new technologies, which sets us apart from the rest," Curtis Fong added. "We're always endeavoring to make our customers' final product better." With its pioneering reputation, Fong & Fong is frequently chosen as a beta (experimental) site by vendors seeking to test new products before releasing them into the marketplace.

"Our greatest achievement," Curtis Fong said, "is the fact that we have become such a highly regarded icon in this industry — and one of the 10 largest minority-owned printers in the nation."

The Fong family attributes this phenomenon in no small part to the cohesiveness of the family unit, which extends throughout the entire work force. Under the leadership of President Paul Fong and Vice President Mae Fong, their college-degreed children have assumed management positions. Besides son Curtis, daughters Karen Cotton and Marsha Fong serve as vice president of finance and vice president of operations, respectively.

"We're like a big family," said Curtis Fong, who started out as a young delivery assistant. "Many of our employees who have been here with the first generation are continuing with the second generation of management. Together we understand the processes because we've all experienced them working side by side. Employees who share our pride will, as a whole, produce a higher quality product."

A natural extension of that pride is a deep regard for the community in which it all began: Sacramento. The Fong family conscientiously works to give back to the city that raised its business from infancy. On that front, Paul Fong, active in Masonic activities, was Potentate of Ben Ali Shrine Temple and takes an active role in hospital, printing, civic activities, and numerous other community affairs. Mae Fong has served on the board of directors of the Sacramento Zoological Society, the Sacramento Area Commerce and Trade Organization (SACTO), the American Red Cross, Junior Achievement and the former First Commercial Bank. Ever proud of their Chinese heritage, the Fongs continue to contribute to and support the activities of the Asian community.

For the future, Fong & Fong is dedicated to continued progress based on the principles that govern its success. "We work hard," said Curtis Fong. "We don't cut corners. And we take a lot of pride in the products we produce. After all, we have an excellent reputation to preserve."

Marsha Fong, vice president of operations; Mae Fong, vice president; and Karen Cotton, vice president of finance

Manufacturing and Distributing

The company's large manufacturing facility on a five-acre site at 65th Street and Broadway is designed for future growth.

Among the first installations in the western United States are the expertly engineered 8- and 10-color Heidelberg presses, which incorporate technical innovations for automation, speed and utmost print quality.

Curtis Fong, executive vice president; and Paul Fong, president

Pacific Coast Building Products

As the city of Sacramento continues to develop from a quiet state government town into a bustling business center, Pacific Coast Building Products provides many of the building materials that help it grow. Through its many divisions, the company supplies lumber products, gypsum wallboard, clay products, concrete products, underground pipe, and roofing products used to build the homes and businesses that shape the active community. The company also distributes other manufacturers' building materials and provides insulation contracting services.

Founder Fred Anderson

Fred Anderson started what was to become Pacific Coast Building Products in 1953, when his father-in-law George Fuller introduced him to the lumber business. A native of Sacramento and engineering graduate of Stanford University, Fred began with a single lumberyard and four employees. Anyone who knew Fred would tell you the phenomenal growth from that single yard to the company's current standing as a Fortune 500 company is no mystery. Fred was the consummate businessman who followed the simple practice of providing quality products and treating his customers so well that he earned their loyalty. Blessed with confidence and good timing, Fred Anderson gradually created or acquired companies that supplied the complementary products necessary to fuel the Sacramento valley's construction boom. Pacific Coast has developed into one of the leading

David J. Lucchetti

suppliers of materials and services to the construction industry. The diverse and growing company is a quiet giant in the region's business community.

In 1970, Fred's son-in-law Dave Lucchetti left his career as a high school teacher and coach to join Anderson Lumber. He gradually moved up to become chief executive officer of Pacific Coast Building Products in 1978, freeing Fred to pursue his many other interests until his death in 1997. Dave continues the company's tradition of providing quality products and solid support to customers that now stretch throughout the United States, and charitable outreach in local areas.

Over the years, Pacific Coast has acquired other companies that have been part of the valley's landscape for more than 100 years. The first was Gladding, McBean in 1976. The Lincoln, California, landmark is one of the country's remaining providers of clay sewer pipe, roof tile, architectural terra cotta and pottery. Gladding, McBean got its start when traveler Charles Gladding first tested the rich clay deposits in 1874 and convinced partners Peter McBean and George Chambers to invest $12,000 to mine and process the clay into vitrified sewer pipe. In the late 1800s, the company expanded its product offerings to include architectural terra cotta and roof tile that soon decorated landmark buildings. Many of the nation's leading architects and historical preservation experts rely on Gladding, McBean to provide ornamental terra cotta for their projects.

In 1980, the company acquired H.C. Muddox, one of Sacramento's first suppliers of pipe and brick products. Originally located at the corner of 30th and L streets, a site purchased from John Sutter's son in 1878, the company moved to Sacramento's southern area in 1965 to make way for the new Interstate 80 freeway. Today, the company is one of Northern California's last remaining brick manufacturers, supplying residential and commercial builders throughout the West.

Located in Utah, the Interstate Brick division also boasts more than 100 years of service since its founding in 1891. The company's proximity to deposits of uniquely colored clay and an advanced manufacturing process that allows for large sizes and custom shapes has made Interstate Brick one of the premier suppliers to customers throughout the country.

Basalite, acquired in 1979, traces its roots to the 1930s and a single manufacturing facility in Napa, California. The company has three plants that mine and manufacture structural concrete block products, interlocking paving stones, segmented retaining walls, wall systems, stucco, sack goods and decorative landscape products. To meet the growing popularity of the company's paving stone products, a state-of-the-art manufacturing facility was built in Tracy, California in 1997. The high-capacity facility creates pavers in a wide palette of colors to meet the needs of the architectural community.

Pabco Gypsum began manufacturing and shipping from its Newark, California facility in 1972. Five years later, Pabco acquired a new gypsum plant and deposit north of Las Vegas, Nevada. These two facilities, combined, supply over 600 million square feet of gypsum board annually. This capacity will increase dramatically with the recent Las Vegas plant expansion. To ensure consistent quality, another division, Pabco Paper, supplies all paper used in Pabco Gypsum products. The company also manufactures laminate and three-tab fiberglass shingles through its Pabco Roofing division.

Although most of its business is in supplying materials to the construction industry, the company does provide insulation contracting to the Sacramento area through its Arcade division. Projects range from single-family residential homes to large-scale commercial construction.

Despite the growth in related products, the company has never strayed far from its roots in the lumber trade. Anderson Lumber, PC Wholesale and Anderson Truss now offer cut-and-packaged lumber, mill-direct lumber and wood trusses, respectively, to builders throughout the region. The company added Northwest Door in 1994 to provide a full spectrum of door and hardware products to the construction trade.

In addition to its reputation for service and product excellence, an important key to the company's success has been its ability to distribute products. Camellia Valley Supply distributes underground water, sewage, and drainage materials to municipalities and private developers. The company's fastest-growing division, Pacific Supply provides roofing, drywall, insulation, stucco, waterproofing, masonry products, and acoustical ceilings and grid from its locations throughout the West. Pacific Supply locations offer retail service for the do-it-yourselfer, though not to the extent of Diamond Pacific, the division that focuses on the retail and independent buildings customer. Diamond Pacific stores include the Pacific Supply line but also sell lumber, windows, hardware, plumbing and electrical products. The large trucking fleet of Material Transport keeps products moving smoothly between the many divisions and

makes it possible to get products quickly into the hands of those who need them.

Pacific Coast Building Products is quite similar to the community that gave it birth: smart and dynamic, yet unpretentious. Though the company has grown far beyond the Sacramento city limits, it has always been an active member of the community it is proud to call home.

Sacramento Bee February 17, 1953

Original Anderson Lumber ad

Tony's Fine Foods

For more than half a century, Tony's Fine Foods has provided top-quality services and products to customers and is widely recognized as a distributor who listens and cares.

Tony's Fine Foods has over 300 employees and a fleet of more than 50 tractor-trailers. It distributes over 6,000 world-class products such as bakery/deli items, prepared salads, pizza ingredients, pastas, condiments, oils, tomato products, finger foods, catering items, specialty beverages, coffee, paper goods, meats, and both domestic and imported cheeses to thousands of customers including major grocery chains, bakeries, restaurants, pizza parlors, delicatessens, hotels and other food service-related businesses across the country. In 1993, the company acquired Cream of the Valley, Northern California's premier distributor of bakery products, and since then has carried more than 2,000 bakery products, including breads, fillings, cakes and pies.

Offering a huge variety of deli and bakery products is just one way Tony's Fine Foods stands above the competition. Tony's marketing materials include pizza and sandwich programs, holiday party tray and gift pack ideas, an extensive point-of-sale library, and educational aids. A fully staffed customer service department is maintained to receive customer orders and answer questions regarding goods

*The early days —
Adele & Tony Ingoglia Sr.
in 1971*

*Tony Ingoglia Sr. and his
prized salami in 1972 —
son Michael Ingoglia is
in the background*

and services. A will-call department is on hand as well to fill immediate, local needs. Embodying the highest standards of service, quality and integrity, Tony's is more than just a supplier; it is a resource for consumer trends, market data, menu analysis and labor-saving systems. The sales staff comprises trained consultants who are food-safety certified and current with market trends. Tony's assists its customers in the handling and presentation of products and encourages the use of in-store demonstrations and sampling to introduce new foods.

While customer demand is instrumental in the surge of its business, Tony's is strongly dedicated to creating partnerships with customers and encourages expansion using new, innovative concepts.

Tony's West Sacramento headquarters, a combination of corporate office suites and a perishable-food distribution

facility, is one of the most modern and efficient in the world. The 120,000-square-foot facility is located on 28 acres. Its fleet of multitemperature trucks and trailers are carefully designed for hot Valley temperatures. Twenty sealed loading bays allow perishables to be kept in a constant 35-degree fahrenheit climate whether in storage, on the dock or in a truck. The Tony's plant accurately keeps track of every single product and ensures freshness by using state-of-the-art software for tasks such as radio frequency computers, "real-time" inventory, automatic product rotation, multiple-order picking and bar-code scanning of each item shipped.

While incorporating progressive technology, Tony's remains old-fashioned in many respects — specifically the treatment of the customer. Like the company's employees, customers are considered more like family than business associates — consistent with the Ingoglia's proud Italian heritage. Many similar businesses conduct their ordering procedures via telephone, fax and other contemporary timesaving devices. Tony's has always believed in sending its sales staff to call on each customer personally. Representatives are trained to answer questions, help customers identify needs and establish accurate re-order levels.

Since the beginning, the company's goal was to dependably deliver the freshest food of the finest quality. It is this commitment to customer service and reliability that keeps Tony's Fine Foods on a steady growth track. The company prides itself on delivering quality products at competitive prices along with an unmatched level of customer service.

Born in Cantania, Italy, Anthony "Tony" Ingoglia Sr. immigrated to the United States in 1912 when he was less than a year old. He arrived at Ellis Island with his older brother Joe and his parents, Adolfo and Anna. The family first lived in Boston, where Adolfo became a salesman with Mussolino-LaConte, an importer of Italian specialty foods.

By the age of 12, an industrious Tony was helping out around the plant, oiling cheeses to prevent them from drying out and filling out freight bills. After a toboggan accident severely injured his left leg, he was in and out of hospitals for the next three years. By the seventh grade, he quit school to help support the family.

By 1934, young Tony Sr. had landed a job with California Salami Co. in Oakland. As a salesman covering territory in Sacramento, Sonoma, Napa, Petaluma and Santa Rosa, Mr. Ingoglia convinced the firm to let him sell cheese and other Italian meats. That same year, he married 19-year-old Adele, whom he had met three years earlier. They were married for 60 years until she passed away in 1994.

The young couple moved to Sacramento in 1934 and started Tony's Salami Co. It was just Tony and Adele in those days. She took orders over the phone and over the next few years, he would make literally hundreds of trips

Adele & Tony Ingoglia Sr. and their four children in 1979. Pictured left to right: Joanie Berger, Michael Ingoglia, Anthony Ingoglia Jr., Adele, Tony Sr. and Donald Ingoglia.

between Sacramento and San Francisco. He would leave the house at 3 a.m. and return after 10 p.m. His tiny refrigerated company truck doubled as a warehouse, and he tracked pricing and inventory levels in his head. Embodying the values he had learned from his parents, he worked demanding hours, conducted an honest business and always put the customer first. Within a few years, his reputation for trustworthiness and dedication had spread, and Tony's Fine Foods became an industry name.

Tony's is legendary for its commitment to the customer. Several rival companies have been quoted in news articles praising the firm's reputation for delivering exceptional service and quality products. Though Tony Ingoglia Sr. retired long ago, he remains active in the business by observing, advising and supporting. Tony's Fine Foods prides itself on partnering with the customer and delivering success from the service line to the bottom line — a fantastic goal for the next generation.

The tradition continues — four generations of Ingoglias planning the future of Tony's Fine Foods

Milgard Windows

Northern Californians have high expectations of their windows. Not only must windows imbue a home with grace and character, but they must be tough enough to withstand summer's searing heat and winter's driving rains. Just as importantly, they must be built to satisfy the ideals and pocketbooks of an energy conservation-minded public. Consumers here also expect much from their window company — value, superb customer service and promises it can keep.

For more than 40 years, Milgard Windows has consistently met and surpassed the expectations of its West Coast customers. Established in 1958 by Maurice Milgard Jr. and

his son Gary, Milgard Windows began as a small glass company in Tacoma, Washington. In 1962, Gary Milgard left the glass company to start an aluminum window fabrication company called Milgard Manufacturing.

Milgard has since grown to include window manufacturing plants in Sacramento, Hollister, Simi Valley and Temecula, California. Other window manufacturing operations are located in Washington, Oregon, Nevada and Colorado. Milgard Manufacturing also operates two tempering plants in Tacoma and Dixon, California, a state-of-the-art vinyl extrusion and injection molding plant in Tacoma and sales offices throughout the West and Midwest.

Milgard's Sacramento-area operation, located in Rancho Cordova, employs about 350 people. It began in 1981 as a sales distribution center and has quickly grown to become a full-service manufacturing facility. Aluminum, vinyl, wood or fiberglass — whatever the type of window, Milgard can suit virtually any architectural possibility, residential or commercial, new construction or replacement. With a dealer base made up of local glass shops, Milgard has a strong presence in the greater Sacramento area. Broadstone, a master-planned community in Folsom, fea-

tures Milgard windows, as does the Serrano El Dorado community in the Sierra Nevada foothills.

The Milgard name has always been associated with quality. Each Milgard window is designed for maintenance-free durability and smooth operation. The structural performance and quality of the company's products exceed every industry standard.

Milgard windows are also designed for supreme comfort and energy efficiency. The company's trademarked SunCoat product is the most energy-efficient glass option on the market. When the California Energy Commission and the National Fenestration Rating Council met to revise the energy code in 1991, Milgard was there, doing its part to help standardize testing for energy efficiency and educate the public. Milgard also works with the Sacramento Area Utilities District and Pacific Gas & Electric in providing rebate programs for homeowners who take steps to make their homes more energy-efficient.

Customer service is the cornerstone of Milgard's business. Customers who select Milgard windows are promised on-time, in-full delivery, servicing for all items sold and the Milgard Lifetime Guarantee, which states that any properly installed Milgard window, skylight or door with a materials or workmanship defect will be fixed free of charge for as long as the customer owns the home.

As a solid contributor to the Sacramento economy, Milgard Windows is proud to be a neighbor and benefactor. Through the Milgard Gift-Community Action Team (MG CAT), the company donates to such nonprofit organizations as Habitat for Humanity, the Ronald McDonald House, the

"Christmas in April" home rehabilitation program and the Loaves and Fishes homeless shelter.

Serving its neighbors will continue to be a priority as Milgard Windows expands its facilities and workforce in the Sacramento area. Care, service and quality — put it all together and Milgard is the clear choice for windows.

Governor's Mansion

Marketplace

Sacramento retail establishments, service industries and leisure/convention facilities offer an impressive variety of choices for Sacramento residents and visitors alike.

California Surveying
and Drafting Supply, Inc.

As the old tools of a trade become scarce, the desire to continue a tradition creates a niche market. As the new tools of a trade are changed by science and technology, the desire for the absolute state-of-the-art creates a niche market. The desire to bridge the old with the new created California Surveying and Drafting Supply, Inc.

There is no older art than that of the builder. The ingenuity to invent and then re-create a structure or device of efficiency requires the skill to measure and document; design templates, plans or diagrams; and then reproduce faithfully from those instructions. For thousands of years little changed about the instruments ancient guilds used to build King Solomon's temple — a time when the square and compass were the tools of a secret craft. The earliest navigational instruments used the same plotting and triangulation theories to explore the oceans and, once on solid ground, to map new territories. As the Industrial Age gave way to the Computer Age, the ancient building arts were torn between traditional and high-tech design. Since both disciplines had to coexist in the practical world, there was a great need for mediation.

With a solid foundation of experience in their trade and a focused fascination with new technology, Bruce Gandelman and Tom Kubo founded California Surveying and Drafting Supply in 1986. They were well on their way

A technician troubleshoots a Total Station.

A classic surveying transit theodolite — fine art and function

to becoming industry authorities on everything from the most obscure drafting tool to the most advanced satellite surveying systems.

Bruce Gandelman has lived in Sacramento his entire life. His father was a cartographer with the United States Geological Survey in the 1950s and later a draftsman with Aerojet. Strongly influenced by his father's lifelong engineering career, Gandelman earned his degree in landscape design and worked as a field foreman before accepting a position in a surveying supply firm. There he met Tom Kubo, who had joined the company after seven years in the military. Together, they rose through the ranks of management and eventually decided to start their own business when their employer scaled back operations in Sacramento.

Gandelman and Kubo ambitiously sought to redefine the role of a surveying supply house. The very name, California Surveying and Drafting Supply, is a major departure in itself. As curious as it may seem, surveyors and draftsmen had traditionally been supplied by separate vendors, even though their professions work in tandem. The broad appeal of an extensive variety of maps has attracted a large market of hikers and sports enthusiasts to the business, and California Surveying has become a major supplier of stakes and striping paint to contractors and government agencies. Any one of these facets could stand on its own, but incorporating all in one organization has made California Surveying unique and highly successful.

Paramount in this success has been a relentless effort to accommodate every request possible.

Dozens of highly informed and enthusiastic tenured employees field questions from all over the

GPS's pinpoint accuracy allows a surveyor to move quickly in the field.

country, going to extraordinary lengths to validate the company's reputation for being the best at what it does. The staff sources products and inventories special items for clients to provide on-hand availability. If a requested item simply does not exist, California Surveying is willing and able to create it from scratch. Special projects have been particularly important to the firm's development.

California Surveying took the initiative to research and compile the first master map of Sacramento County's postal zip codes, influencing Thomas Brothers to include such maps in its annually updated guides. The California Department of Waterways commissioned the company to develop special templates used by investigators to diagram boating accidents. Boating enforcement agencies throughout the United States have since been requesting these templates. The California Department of Transportation engaged California Surveying for the arduous task of converting its engineering templates and measuring instruments to the metric system.

The surveying trade was evolving at a rapid pace when California Surveying and Drafting Supply entered the market, becoming more efficient as instruments were integrated, automated and computerized. But Gandelman and Kubo knew that the satellite technology the military was developing to map the Earth would inevitably transform the business as surely as the calculator caused the extinction of the slide rule.

The advent of global positioning system (GPS) surveying was regularly delayed by the space shuttle program and military priorities, and the earliest systems were admittedly cumbersome. A handful of satellites transmitted radio signals to ground stations, and to take measurements users had to compute the optimal time to survey based on when all the satellites would be overhead. Finally, the constellation system of 24 satellites was fully deployed and GPS could deliver around-the-clock, pinpoint accuracy. California Surveying has become the area's authority on GPS systems through its long-standing alliance with industry giant Trimble Navigation.

Not all surveyors have been anxious to adopt the new technology. Many established firms consider the change to GPS economically unfeasible because of the enormous investment already committed to conventional equipment. California Surveying has found that GPS has helped to level the playing field for young surveying firms that may only need one or two units to conduct all their field operations.

While the drafting table is rapidly being replaced by computer-aided drawing systems, many still prefer to take mechanical pencil and T square in hand. The encroaching obsolescence of drafting equipment is a major challenge for California Surveying because decreasing demand has prompted manufacturers to discontinue many products. The company constantly searches for reliable sources and strives to maintain large inventories and selections in both its Sacramento and Santa Clara locations.

The service and repair department supports every product sold by California Surveying and Drafting Supply, but as historians of the trade, the technicians are also experts on products that have long since come off the market. One repairman on staff is among two or three in the nation qualified to repair Hewlett-Packard's original Total Station, a surveying device that revolutionized the industry in its day. Another technician worked in England for the manufacturer of instruments used by the California Department of Transportation; a skilled machinist, he now remanufactures replacement parts that have not been available for over two decades. Yet another specialist performs restorations of beautifully crafted antique instruments, objects of art as much as devices of the trade. There are likely few surveying or drafting instruments used throughout time that are unknown to the staff of California Surveying — a claim all-comers are welcome to challenge.

California Surveying mentors aspiring architects and designers through generous contributions of equipment and material to high school drafting competitions, which are ultimately judged at the California State Fair. The firm works closely with American River College, where drafting instructors continue to teach the fundamentals of the art while struggling with the impulse to teach only computer applications. It is easy to make the argument for computer-aided design systems when one realizes how many expensive tools are eliminated, but there will always be the nagging concern that the skills and wisdom of the ancient arts will become only dim memories.

California Surveying and Drafting Supply has assumed the role of shepherd for the new technologies — turning the page toward the future while bookmarking the past for guidance.

Emigh Hardware

A couple of classic tales come to mind when one steps into the Emigh Hardware store near the corner of Watt and El Camino: David vs. Goliath. Or *The Little Engine That Could*. But then, Sacramento's largest family-owned hardware store is a story in itself, holding its own against the giants of home improvement.

While Emigh Hardware doesn't look old-fashioned (it stopped selling horse buggies and combine harvesters long ago), it feels old-fashioned. Small by today's huge chain warehouse-style standards, Emigh Hardware nevertheless sells just about everything a homeowner or professional

James Emigh, co-founder of Emigh Hardware

Colby Emigh succeeded his father, James, in the family business.

needs. The atmosphere is comfortable — the kind of store Ward Cleaver would shop in. People, not computers, answer the phone here, and an always-packed parking lot attests to the blessing of many happy return visits.

The reason customers keep returning to Emigh Hardware — some from miles away — is the same reason they've been returning for more than 90 years: service that starts with a smile and doesn't end until customers find what they want and know how to use it.

The first Emigh Hardware store was opened in 1908 by brothers James and Clay Emigh, who set up shop at 1208 J Street after moving from Suisun City. Four years later, the company merged with Winchell and Cline and moved to a larger location at 310 J Street. Another move in 1918 took the business to Seventh and J Street, where it remained for 14 years under the leadership of the brothers.

With the retirement of the senior Emigh brothers in the early 1930s, the next generation took the helm. James' sons Albert, James Jr. and Colby moved the business farther

uptown to 13th and J Street, the current location of the Sacramento Community Convention Center. During these years of the Depression and World War II, even steel garbage cans were scarce and dear. Brandishing his credo of customer care, Colby Emigh, always alert to promotional opportunities, put his garbage cans on sale — much to the consternation of competitors who wanted to keep prices high.

By 1952, Colby was ready for another move. Attracted by the postwar building boom in the suburbs, he took a risk and relocated the business to "the country," the newly developed Country Club Centre at El Camino and Watt whose only neighbor was a goat farm.

The newer, more mobile population here had trouble pronouncing the name Emigh, so in the 1960s the company introduced a cartoon character depicting a pigtailed girl in overalls saying, "Call me Amy." Little Amy, a composite of Colby and Jesma Emigh's daughters Carol and Mary, is still a familiar feature in Emigh Hardware advertisements. During the 1960s, Emigh became an affiliate of Ace Hardware and increased its purchasing power as a result.

Colby Emigh's son-in-law, Rich Lawrence, took over as general manager in 1971 and in 1973 moved the business across the street to the present 35,000-square-foot location on El Camino Avenue. Lawrence's son Brian is the fourth generation to contribute to the family legacy.

During Rich Lawrence's tenure at Emigh Hardware, much has changed. When he started, mail orders to Chicago took six weeks for delivery; now they take one or two days. Other things have stayed exactly the same — especially the commitment to personal service that has been a part of the Emigh tradition since the beginning.

At Emigh Hardware, customers are treated to extras they just can't get elsewhere. The store's 100 knowledgeable employees, some of whom have been with the company for more than 20 years, ensure more customer assistance per square foot than any other hardware store. At no cost, customers can have their faucet parts cleaned. Power equipment is set up, serviced and ready to go. Whatever is purchased can be delivered free of charge within the Sacramento area. The little things add up, too: Cashiers do not interrupt sales to take phone calls — all calls are handled in the back office by an operator.

"Our customers take ownership of the store," Rich Lawrence says. "They feel it's their store."

While Emigh Hardware prides itself on selection in all areas, it also has a few specialty departments, including an extensive lawn and garden section; a large patio equipment selection featuring brand-name furniture and barbecue grills; and high-level paint and plumbing departments.

To check out what's new, customers no longer need to set foot in the store. Through the Emigh Hardware Web site, they can learn all about the latest shipments, plus receive advice on common problems from its handy "Ask Amy" how-to guide. The Web site also gives store hours and location and offers an online mailing list.

Emigh Hardware, ever conscious of its position as a Sacramento institution, has always done its part to improve the quality of life in the city it has called home for so long. A longtime champion of youths, the company donates to several area schools and cosponsors the "Friends for Kids" golf tournament to benefit five different youth charities in the Sacramento community.

As Emigh Hardware looks forward to its 100th birthday, the store will continue to maintain the quality of service and selection of products customers have come to expect. Emigh Hardware: "Where service has been a tradition since 1908."

The Emigh, Winchell, Cline Company at 310 J Street, circa 1912

Emigh Hardware moved to Seventh and J Street in 1918.

Folsom Lake Ford
and Folsom Lake Toyota

Serene, sophisticated surroundings; calm, sensitive, considerate personnel; computer work stations, a beautifully appointed lounge and a celebrated theme restaurant for those who wish to make good use of their downtime — attributes usually reserved for the elite world of luxury shopping. Actually, this is a description of two of California's biggest and most beautiful automobile outlets — Folsom Lake Ford and Folsom Lake Toyota.

Founder and CEO of Folsom Lake Ford and Folsom Lake Toyota, Chuck Peterson

The man in the driver's seat of this multidealership automotive empire is a soft-spoken gentleman who is proud of his old-school upbringing and the strong work ethic instilled by his parents. Chuck Peterson, founder and CEO of Folsom Lake Ford, Folsom Lake Toyota and Folsom Lake Used Car Outlet, was raised in a small southeastern Idaho community, where his parents both worked for a major retail organization. While growing up in Preston, Idaho, Peterson worked from sunrise to sunset on a farm during the summer breaks of his early teenage years and later pulled 12-hour shifts, seven days a week, canning beans and sauerkraut for Del Monte.

By the time he was ready to attend the University of Michigan, Peterson was thoroughly accustomed to an honest day's work. As he toiled to earn his master's degree in business administration, he took on part-time jobs and even interrupted his studies for a while to run a stereo store. He developed an instinct for merchandising and customer relations, which would pave the way to his future career.

Armed with his graduate degree in 1972, Peterson was hired as an internal auditor at Ford Motor Company's world headquarters, where he had a chance to observe virtually all facets of the business. The allure of sales seemed to beckon him, and he was granted a transfer to Ford's fleet division, rising to management ranks in unprecedented time. As good as that job was, Peterson preferred sunny California over chilly Michigan and was given the position of truck merchandising manager for Ford's San Francisco operations. Shortly after that move, he left Ford to become the vice president of a Bay area holding company overseeing nearly two-dozen automotive-related businesses. Peterson found himself wearing too many hats in a frenetic organization, and he decided instead to buy a 20-percent interest in the Swanson Ford dealership in Los Gatos. He honed his marketing skills for 10 years as Swanson's general manager.

1988 was the year Peterson decided to strike out on his own, acquiring the former Bennett Ford dealership at Greenback Lane and Madison Avenue in Folsom. He renamed the franchise Folsom Lake Ford and struggled to get the business on its feet. A year and a half later, Folsom Lake Ford became the top-volume Ford dealership in the area.

In early 1990, Peterson seized the opportunity to buy a Toyota dealership, located on Zinfandel Drive near Sunrise Boulevard, from the legendary car mogul Cal Worthington. Peterson had always felt that Ford and Toyota would make a winning combination, but both Folsom Lake Ford and his new Folsom Lake Toyota operations were in poor locations. He decided that he would move both dealerships to a single site.

A man with a vision shared by very few at the time, Peterson decided that a 21-acre parcel of land along the Interstate 50 corridor would be his businesses' new home.

His existing Ford dealership was in the city of Folsom. His Toyota dealership was in Sacramento County. Literally considered "the sticks" at the time, the land for the new site was in an unincorporated area outside of the Folsom city limits. In a skillful political move, Peterson orchestrated the annexation of the land to make it part of Folsom, and he offered to continue compensating Sacramento County for the revenue it would lose as a result of the Toyota dealership's relocation. The tax-sharing agreement made everyone happy.

California was in the throes of a miserable economy, and the city of Folsom had suffered some financial losses in the past when it made concessions for an auto mall that failed, so Peterson had to develop his auto outlet without any of the city incentives usually afforded a major auto-mall development.

Undaunted by the many obstacles and doubting voices, Peterson designed his new location to be like no other. His dream became a reality heralded by a massive gala affair on January 18, 1995, when an estimated 7,000 guests (including Edsel Ford II) celebrated the grand opening of Folsom Lake Ford and Folsom Lake Toyota to the live sounds of the Beach Boys. Visitors to the new outlet marveled at the manicured grounds, the progressive architecture, the creature comforts, the children's playroom, the impressive saltwater aquarium and even the full-service, automotive-themed restaurant, Chuck's Grill.

Peterson's auto business soon became Folsom's top tax-revenue producer and one of the city's Top 10 employers, with annual sales exceeding a quarter of a billion dollars. The site became a magnet for new businesses in the area, and the gigantic American flag that marks the Folsom Auto Mall's location can be seen clearly from the freeway.

Folsom Lake Ford and Folsom Lake Toyota support numerous community causes and charities — most notably, the annual Sacramento Kings Celebrity Golf Tournament.

The world of automobile manufacturing and distribution has become a contraction of strange bedfellows, and Peterson sees the ranks of producers shrinking to six international conglomerates in the future. A similar trend is also taking shape at the dealership end of the industry as more and more franchises are acquired by enormous public corporations. Peterson cites the mind-boggling prices being offered

to independent dealers and wonders how this phenomenon will affect the buying public. He does credit this environment for the stabilization of new-car prices — a clear benefit to the consumer. He has major expansion goals as well, but the signature style that has brought him to such heights is always at the forefront of his plans.

Hungry customers can fuel up at Chuck's Grill

Absent in Peterson's repertoire are the mind-numbing commercials with screaming announcers and jungle-beat jingles that led to the invention of the remote control. Equally absent are the predatory salespeople who swoop down upon potential buyers before they have even come to a complete stop in their trade-ins. Peterson is very serious about making the car-buying experience at Folsom Lake Ford and Folsom Lake Toyota a memorably pleasant, dignified, professional and exciting event for his customers.

Raley's
A Family Store

In the depths of the Great Depression, an ambitious young man with a positive outlook came to California searching for gold — and he found it. Thomas P. Raley opened Raley's Drive-In Market in 1935. His store in Placerville was to be the first of more than 100 stores in Northern California and Nevada owned by Tom Raley and his family.

Tom Raley leveled an empty lot next door to his Placerville market and boldly advertised his store as "the

Raley's Drive-in Market, Thomas P. Raley's first store in Placerville, California, was located in the heart of the Gold Country.

nation's first drive-in market." Until then it was unheard of for a market to offer its own parking lot for customers. Raley's entrepreneurial spirit led to many innovations. Customer convenience, quality and service were the impetus for any change or improvement — a theme continuing today in all Raley's markets.

While Raley's success is the result of skilled and innovative leadership, a look back in time reveals several events to be the most significant in its history. Raley's was

A new Raley's store opens on the Mount Rose Highway south of Reno, serving the growing population of Northern Nevada.

one of the first markets to install a self-service meat counter. Cellophane had just been introduced into the marketplace, and Raley capitalized on the new trend by selling individually packaged meats.

Another milestone in Raley's history was the opening of a drugstore alongside the market in 1958. The stores were located side by side with a common wall between them, and they operated as separate businesses. Operating a drugstore was a completely new venture for Raley, but he was certain his grocery-store customers would enjoy the convenience. He learned the drugstore business from recognized leaders in the industry who willingly shared their expertise and encouraged him to move forward with the idea.

In 1973, Raley's acquired the Eagle/Thrifty chain in Nevada. It was a grocery and drugstore that operated as one business. It took quite a bit of convincing for Raley to finally decide to "tear down the wall" between his grocery and drugstore on Freeport Boulevard in Sacramento to create a "superstore." After he created his first supermarket/drug center, sales volume doubled. Raley decided that most of his stores would become "superstores" and remodeled more than 20 stores during the 70s. Raley's pioneered the "superstore" concept, distinguishing itself from other grocery chains at that time.

Another Raley's innovation was the addition of the "NutriClean" label to its fruits and vegetables. The store works directly with growers and an independent testing laboratory to test for pesticide-free produce. To maintain high quality produce once it reaches the store, Raley's employees are extensively trained in safe food handling and storage.

Joyce Raley Teel created a new chapter in company history in 1985 when she re-joined the organization. As Tom Raley's only child, she couldn't remember a time when her father's stores weren't in her life. Her vision added a new dimension to the company — community involvement. As a longtime community volunteer and patron of the arts, Teel extended Raley's dedication to customer service even further. In 1986, she and Chuck Collings (then president of the company) developed Raley's own nonprofit organization,

Food for Families, to aid in feeding the hungry. Food for Families collects donations of cash and food through in-store collection canisters. By 1998, cash donations surpassed $6 million. Raley's covers all administrative costs, so 100 percent of every dollar collected goes directly to feeding hungry families. For this, the organization has received national acclaim.

Through Joyce Raley Teel's commitment to serving her community, Raley's has also supported local arts groups, youth programs and education, and she established the Thomas P. Raley Foundation. The foundation has donated funds to build the Boys and Girls Club of Sacramento, created an endowment fund for the Sacramento Crisis Nursery and supported other community organizations.

Raley's is the title sponsor for the Senior Gold Rush Classic golf tournament to help raise money for local non-profit organizations. The tournament is one of many nationwide sites for the Senior PGA Tour. Also influenced by Joyce Raley Teel's passion for supporting the community, Raley's, in partnership with AT&T, launched the Sacramento inaugural Race for the Cure fund-raising event in 1997 to help fight breast cancer.

By 1998, the Raley's chain included 117 stores throughout Northern California, extending south to Yosemite and east to Elko, Nevada. Raley's Superstores, Bel Air Markets, Nob Hill Foods and Food Source are part of the Raley's family of stores. The company employs about 14,000 people and earns revenues of approximately $2.4 billion.

The company attributes its success directly to excellent customer service, valuing its employees, partnerships with suppliers, high-quality merchandise and innovation. As a family-owned company, Raley's makes decisions based on the impact on customers and employees as much as on the financial bottom line. Raley's also looks at the bigger picture by considering the impact on the community at large.

Employees are given the opportunity to participate in the decision-making process, which has created a family of employees who realize the difference they make every day in the success of the company. "How can I help you?" is a way of doing business that Raley's is especially proud of. Customers are considered guests and every employee works to satisfy the customers' needs.

Suppliers are treated as partners. Raley's is proud of its relationships with suppliers. As a result of Raley's reputation as a leader in innovation, companies often approach the chain to test-market new products. Manufacturers are assured their products will be prominently displayed and promoted.

Since the death of the company's founder in 1991, Joyce Raley Teel has been the company's sole owner. Her son, Michael Teel, became Raley's president and CEO in 1998. While other grocery chains merge, Raley's stands solidly based in West Sacramento, preferring to expand its own store base. Raley's plan for the future is to build on the foundation that Thomas Raley laid in 1935 — understand customers and continue to meet their changing needs through innovation and excellent service.

Fully prepared meals and indoor banking centers are important features in Raley's Superstores.

Hot rotisserie chicken is a popular item at Raley's Old Fashioned Deli, where it is served by deli clerks Amber Perales and Erica Garcia.

Tower Records

The Long and Winding Road: The Beatles sang it, but Russ Solomon, founder/chairman of Tower Records, has traveled it — mostly without a map, but with the instincts of a born opportunist and lover of culture. His serendipitous journey from owner of a small Sacramento record store to king of a $1 billion global empire has been nothing if not a testament to luck and good timing. Today, Solomon's company, MTS, Inc., oversees more than 227 record, book and video stores, outlets and galleries in 18 countries.

Born in 1925, Solomon learned about retailing from his father, who owned a business called Tower Cut Rate Drugs at 16th and Broadway in Sacramento. The original neon sign still glows above what is now the Tower Cafe. After serving in the U.S. Army during World War II, Solomon started a "rack jobbing" business, in which he invento-

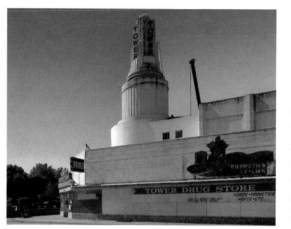

Tower Drug Store, on 16th and Broadway in Sacramento, as it looked in 1960, is where Solomon first began selling records.

The Tower Theater, from which Tower Records takes its name, still anchors the corner of 16th and Broadway in Sacramento.

ried and serviced small record sections in variety and department stores.

Going broke after eight years, he borrowed $5,000 from his father to start his own store, which he determined should sell nothing but records — all available titles, and lots of them. He opened for business in 1960 in what is now the back room of the Tower Cafe on Broadway, and he named his company Tower Records after the theater that anchored the shopping complex.

Solomon's unprecedented concept of offering a huge selection and quantity caught on instantly in Sacramento, but nobody in the music merchandising industry was paying attention to such a small town. From the beginning, Solomon's store operated on the premise that his customers were serious about their music, and he wanted them to know that Tower was, too. The same philosophy was applied to the bookstore he opened three years later. While the stores were big by the standards of the day, the atmosphere was comfortable, allowing customers to browse or just hang out until midnight every day without being pressured by salespeople.

Then in 1967 Solomon took a trip to San Francisco for a weekend of carousing, but what happened on that trip became pivotal to the Tower storyline. The morning following a late night out, Solomon was sitting at a drive-in along Fisherman's Wharf when he happened to spot a "For Lease" sign on a 5,000-square-foot storefront at the corner of Columbus and Bay. There he saw the kind of potential he'd been dreaming of for a decade.

Within a week, Solomon signed a five-year lease and thus began the West Coast's first large, supermarket-style record store. And San Francisco, by then a fountainhead of music in that era of peace, love and rock 'n' roll, was ready for it. Fillmore Auditorium, just a few blocks away from the store, was packing thousands of people in every weekend with the likes of Duke Ellington and the Grateful Dead. Fifty miles away, the Monterey Pop Festival was making its legendary imprint on the landscape of entertainment. And people were snapping up records by the Beatles and the Rolling Stones as fast as Tower could stock them.

The company's success in San Francisco enabled it, two years later, to launch a store on Sunset Boulevard in Los Angeles. During the 1970s, the Tower network expanded throughout California to Seattle, Washington, and Phoenix, Arizona. In 1980, a store was added in Honolulu, Hawaii.

At about the same time, Solomon discovered that a store in Japan, no doubt impressed by Tower's showy success on the U.S. West Coast, was using the trade-marked Tower name. He saw this not as a violation, but as an opportunity to sell it some records. Eventually he bought out the company and established a base of operations in Tokyo, Japan.

Even though Tower had reached across the Pacific, it had yet to infiltrate the East Coast. That changed in 1983 when Tower opened its flagship store in New York City. The store, located on Broadway in Greenwich Village, currently stocks more than half a million records in a 55,000-square-foot facility. The resulting culture clash as East met West has become something of a joke over the years. Solomon, every inch the casual Californian, habitually steals what he calls "stuffy" neckties from visiting East Coast business associates and displays them in Plexiglas cases around his office.

Tower's next landmark location was to be No. 1 Piccadilly Circus in London, England, arguably the most beautiful and best known of the stores. The early 90s saw more international expansion, with stores in Osaka, Japan; Taipei, Taiwan; Mexico City, Mexico; Dublin, Ireland; Tel Aviv, Israel; Singapore; and Hong Kong.

The largest Tower store in the world, possibly the largest ever, opened in 1995 in Tokyo, Japan. The store fills nearly 83,000 square feet on eight floors and includes a cafe in the basement. The record/video/book store shattered sales records from the opening day.

Key to Tower's success is the authority given to each store's management team to customize its stock and merchandising techniques to suit local tastes and the overall local marketplace. To further enhance the Tower experience for its clientele, the company has its own publications division, under which the award-winning music-scene magazine *Pulse!* is produced.

Tower, always capitalizing on the fast-changing wave of technology, partnered with The Good Guys! in 1995 to open the first multimedia superstore, WOW!, in Las Vegas, Nevada. The proliferation of Internet and commercial online services has also provided the company with the opportunity to develop a niche in digital shopping.

However, Solomon is convinced that the large-store concept is here to stay, because people who buy books and music want instant gratification.

The largest Tower store in the world is located in the Shibuya district of Tokyo, Japan.

They like the experience of physically being at the store — the sights, the sounds, the feel of a new book or compact disc in their hands. His outlook for the future is dedicated to further expansion.

Thanks to the "wisdom of Solomon," the beat goes on.

Tower opened the landmark No. 1 Piccadilly Circus store in London, England, in 1985.
Photo by Andrew Putler

Scofield's
Home Furnishings

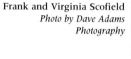

The outside of a residence is much like the clothing one wears in public. The inside of the home is where one's true personality can be found, but creating that intimacy doesn't come easily. That's when Scofield's enters the room.

The creative wisdom accumulated over two-thirds of a century goes into the selection of every item in Scofield's breathtaking showroom at Sacramento's prestigious Town and Country Village. Those who seek inspiration in blending function and decor are guided by Scofield's recognized dynasty of interior design consultants — an unsurpassed team of highly

Frank and Virginia Scofield
Photo by Dave Adams
Photography

qualified, long-term employees. Scofield's enduring and well-deserved reputation for excellence in a highly competitive industry was arduously earned.

A young family man in the early 1930s, Miles Scofield toiled as a machinist in Torrance, California, while dreaming of going into business for himself. A shoe store seemed intriguing, but his other choice beckoned more strongly. He decided to work gratis for a furniture store on Crenshaw Boulevard in Los Angeles to learn the business and then opened a store in Covina. Being 25 miles outside of the city taught him the three most important rules of operating a successful retail business: location, location, location. Miles knew he had to be in a hub city and was torn between Phoenix and Sacramento.

When he opened Scofield's Furniture at the corner of 14th and K streets in February 1936, he soon learned that Sacramento was the tougher of the two markets. He was facing several well-established, dominating competitors who were firmly rooted in the community. But Miles had a secret weapon — an irresistible personality. He was able to garner exclusive lines with the most respected furniture manufacturers in America.

A decade later, Miles' 23-year-old son Frank began running the family enterprise. Growing up in the business gave Frank a unique insight into the world of fine furnishings. Frank successfully cultivated his father's industry relationships and built a clientele that now extends well beyond the Sacramento Valley.

When the time to expand the business arrived in 1979, Scofield's moved to Exposition Boulevard. The move to Town and Country Village took place during Scofield's 60th anniversary in 1996. It was during these moves that the Scofield family realized just how much Sacramento had bonded with their company. The commotion caused by the relocation seemed to demonstrate the community's feelings of ownership; the old neighborhood expressed a sense of loss while the new locality welcomed Scofield's with open arms.

Scofield's has numerous exclusive lines in its collection. Beautifully crafted imports are joined with such eminent American names as Stickley and Baker Furniture and many others in an offering of style and elegance unequaled in the Sacramento area.

Scofield's has always promoted finer furnishings as the most prudent purchase because of the durability of quality products. This philosophy has carried through generations of loyal customers. A Scofield's delivery truck in front of a customer's home is a great status symbol in Sacramento — a fact Frank discovered from a vociferously disappointed client when a delivery had to be made in a rented van without Scofield's name on it.

Frank Scofield's wife Virginia holds a bachelor of science degree in interior design and has spent her entire adult life in the profession. Recognizing the public's growing interest in interior decorating, Virginia regularly conducts design seminars. Her consultation activities carry her all over California and the neighboring states.

Frank Scofield is highly regarded in the country's elite group of high-end retailers and has won the respect and admiration of his peers. Frank's impeccable taste, instincts and knowledge of furniture construction are legendary. He enjoys sharing his wisdom and has counseled many people in the industry. This level of success is extraordinary in any trade, but the fact that Frank has achieved his dreams despite his lifelong struggle with dyslexia is a true story of triumph over adversity.

While it could be assumed the company's client list would read like a Who's Who in the Sacramento Valley, that is confidential and all lips are sealed at Scofield's. With expertise and gracious actions, Scofield's brings a touch of class to Sacramento.

Shari's Berries™

Shari's Berries has satisfied Sacramento's love for chocolate-dipped strawberries since 1989, when Shari Fitzpatrick left her position as a stockbroker to turn her passion into a successful business. Fitzpatrick often prepared chocolate-dipped strawberries for clients to enjoy at special occasions and as gifts. After catering many events with attractive and delicious chocolate-dipped strawberries, Fitzpatrick realized her special talent.

She built her business through aggressive networking in the community, radio promotions and giving out product samples at every function she attended. Knowing that the telephone was the lifeblood of her business, Fitzpatrick forwarded all her calls to a pager with a message stating that all calls would be returned within ten minutes. With a basket full of quarters, Fitzpatrick responded to calls immediately by driving to the nearest phone booth.

By 1991, Shari's Berries opened its first storefront in Sacramento. The company later opened in the prestigious Wells Fargo Center on Capitol Mall in 1994 and opened a third Sacramento store in 1998. The stores are adorned with shiny displays of silver gift baskets, platters, gift boxes and an assortment of photographs featuring elegant chocolate-dipped strawberry gifts.

Fitzpatrick formed a second corporation under the name of Strawberry Enterprises in 1997 that oversees the growth of the company on a national level, and she patented the company's signature long-stemmed,

chocolate-dipped strawberry rose bouquet in 1993. As a result of her company's continued success, Shari's Berries provides jobs to more than 25 people. (And well over 100 during Valentine's Day!)

The company considers itself a delicious alternative to the traditional florist. Strawberries are dipped within hours of delivery to ensure the product is

Shari's Berries special chocolate-dipped strawberry

as fresh as possible. It is common to dip 80,000 strawberries the night before Valentine's Day.

Customers will find edible gifts appropriate for any occasion and recipient. Strawberries, dipped in either dark, milk or white chocolate and topped with chocolate chips, almonds or coconut, or maybe decorated to simulate a tuxedo, are delivered with a chocolate-dipped champagne bottle or chocolate-dipped goblets for weddings, anniversaries, birthdays, a special romantic evening or any other occasion. Strawberries are also combined with balloons, teddy bears, treasure chests and mirrored heart boxes. Shari's Berries also makes a simulated wedding cake covered in 100 strawberries and features a line of silver-plated collectibles, glassware and other items to accompany the berries.

Fitzpatrick donates many of her chocolate strawberries to charity auctions and other fund-raisers every month.

The chocolate-dipped strawberry gifts of "Sacramento's edible florist" continue to expand in response to customer requests. In fact, many new product ideas come directly from repeat customers. Customer satisfaction is a key element in the company's loyal following. Shari's Berries has a call center for nationwide mail orders and its own Web page, and its next goal is expanding nationally through its proprietary Digital Franchise™ system as well as more traditional franchise opportunities. Even as new opportunities for Shari's Berries come along, Fitzpatrick still builds her business one berry and one season at a time.

Shari's Berries chocolate-dipped strawberry silver ice bucket with a chocolate-dipped champagne bottle is perfect for weddings, anniversaries or other special occasions.

Networks

Sacramento transportation, communications and energy companies keep people, information and power circulating throughout the region.

SMUD
The Sacramento Municipal Utility District

When electricity first came to Sacramento in 1879, it was a wonder. In town, a crowd of 5,000 gathered one September afternoon to see two arc lamps in front of the Mechanics Store on K Street. When the lamps flared on at dusk, the crowd applauded.

For the next few years, Americans flocked to circuses and state fairs across the country to be dazzled by electric lights and electricity-driven engines. In less than 100 years, this circus-tent marvel would completely transform the economy, the landscape, and the shape of everyday life in Sacramento and throughout the nation.

In September 1895, Sacramento celebrated the advent of the electric age with a nighttime display of lights that could be seen 50 miles away. Across the brightly-lit Capitol, the names of the leaders of electricity development were emblazoned in electric lamps. Lighted bulbs illuminated the trees in Capitol Park. Downtown was lit by a parade of electrically lighted floats drawn by electric railway cars.
Photo courtesy of David Joslyn Collection, City of Sacramento, History and Science Division, Sacramento Archive and Museum Collection Center

The history of electricity in the Sacramento Valley is the story of the development of what most people regard as modern life. And the story of the Sacramento Municipal Utility District (SMUD) is inseparable from it. From the start, the people who live and work in these communities have shaped the District's business, because they created and own the utility.

By 1890, electricity was fast replacing steam as the workhorse of manufacturing and industry, and most cities were at least partially illuminated by electric light. In Sacramento, J and K streets were lit by suspended electric lights, and summer concerts at 9th and J streets played to the accompaniment of a powerful arc lamp. Four manufacturers in town powered their operations with steam-generated electricity.

For Sacramento, though, steam-generated electricity was proving to be too costly for common use because the price of coal was five times higher here than in the East. In the high price of coal, local businessmen saw a shining opportunity. In 1895, they teamed up with the General Electric Company to bring affordable electricity to Sacramento. They built the Folsom Dam and Powerhouse on the American River — California's first successful hydropower plant.

The Folsom Powerhouse generated 11,000 volts at half the cost of steam electricity. Overnight, it looked possible for Sacramento's ordinary working people to afford the light and comfort that electricity could bring. Sacramentans celebrated by raising $20,000 to fund the Grand Electric Carnival, a parade and display of lights so brilliant it could be seen 50 miles away.

For the next 20 years, two private electric companies served Sacramento businesses and homes. These competing systems had incompatible voltages and their prices fluctuated dramatically, but businesses and most town dwellers were able to enjoy at least some electricity. Sacramento farmers, however, had none because the private power companies could not see a profit in building power lines for relatively few customers.

By the 1920s, increasingly dissatisfied with the unreliable electric service and fluctuating rates, Sacramento citizens started studying the drive for nonprofit, community-owned power companies in other towns and cities across the United States. In these communities, citizens saw electric power as a natural extension of services provided by local governments, such as schools, parks and public safety. They were pushing for referenda and elections to buy out private electric companies or to set up a competing system. Community-owned systems were bringing dramatically lower electric rates and improved electric systems.

In 1921, Sacramento city officials took up the idea of community ownership of the electric system. In 1923, they placed the issue on the ballot. According to *The Sacramento Bee*, private power interests waged a turbulent and bitter campaign against the measure. Nevertheless, on July 2, 1923, the voters of Sacramento approved the creation of their own electric utility — the Sacramento Municipal Utility District.

By 1910, electric streetcars were becoming common. Here, the electric trolley picks up passengers at 6th and K Streets in downtown Sacramento.
Photo courtesy of Eleanor McClatchy Collection, City of Sacramento, History and Science Division, Sacramento Archive and Museum Collection Center

They also elected a five-member Board of Directors. With the additional services of a city lawyer, an engineer, a secretary and an accountant, the Sacramento Municipal Utility District was launched.

As tough as it had been, the fight was just beginning. The following years were a tangle of engineering studies, political battles, elections and court filings and counter filings. The longest battle was for the electric distribution system – the poles and lines carrying electricity from its source to the consumer. Finally, in March 1946, the owner of the distribution system was ordered by the court to sell it to the utility that Sacramento's citizens had created 23 years before.

For the Sacramento Municipal Utility District, the real work was just beginning. The distribution system the District had fought for was antiquated, some of it dating back to 1895. It had not been well maintained since 1923 and had suffered particular neglect during the years of war shortages, 1941-1945. Furthermore, it was a remarkable jumble of competing systems.

"It had bits of almost every conceivable distribution voltage," said the District's chief engineer in 1946, Paul Shaad.

In addition, requests for hook-ups had been piling up during the war years. Some 3,000 customers were waiting for electric service, and more joined the waiting list every day. Demand for electricity was climbing, too, as the postwar economic boom began and Sacramento residents discovered they could afford luxuries like electric washing machines and window air conditioners.

"Everything was overloaded," said Eugene Clark, the District's chief dispatcher (retired), "to the point that it could all go down in a heap, and we knew that."

In addition to repairing the electric system and hiring and training a work force to take over its operation, the District had to acquire 4,000 items necessary to the inventory of a going electric utility, all in a time of severe postwar shortages.

To this day, District employees and retirees recall those days with pride.

Working closely together with an optimistic attitude, the District's 400 new employees got the fledgling utility up and running in six months. During the blistering summer and fall of 1946, they worked long hours in rented rooms and sweltering tin Quonset huts setting up metering, billing, communications and office systems. On poles and underground, they struggled against tall odds to put into order the outdated, patchwork electric distribution system.

And it paid off. On December 31, 1946 at 6 p.m., with no fanfare and no dimming of the lights, the Sacramento Municipal Utility District started supplying the power for Sacramento, just as Sacramento voters had requested so many years before.

Sacramento practically exploded with prosperity during the postwar economic boom of the late 1940s and 1950s. In the next 15 years, the number of District customers went from 65,000 to 170,000 and electricity use more than tripled.

While the economy rocketed upward, Sacramento homes went through a transformation, too. In 1946, many homes in Sacramento and almost all farm homes were lit by kerosene or gas lamps and kept warm by wood stoves. But by 1960, the average Sacramento home was a veritable electricity consumption showroom. Not only were there electric

At noon on December 31, 1946, in Superior Court, the final order was signed authorizing the Sacramento Municipal Utility District to take over the electric distribution system. Left to right are William L. Oliver, PG&E attorney; Malcolm Tuft, American Trust Company attorney; Judge Warren Steel; Stephen W. Downey, the District's consulting attorney; Donald E. Wachhorst, District Vice President; Martin McDonough, the District's attorney; and James E. McCaffrey, the District's General Manager and Chief Engineer. *Photo courtesy of Sacramento Bee Photo Morgue, City of Sacramento History and Science Division, Sacramento Archive and Museum Collection Center*

Growth was explosive in Sacramento in the postwar years. Electricity use skyrocketed as Sacramentans discovered electric heating and air conditioning and scores of electric appliances. The top photo shows Arden and Watt in 1946; the bottom photo is the same location in 1956. *Photo courtesy of Photo Archive, Sacramento Municipal Utility District*

lights, but Sacramentans had snapped up electric ranges, central heating, electric washers and dryers, dishwashers, and a remarkable range of small appliances from waffle irons and griddles to electric blankets and bathroom space heaters. Most of all, Sacramentans discovered air conditioning. In 1959, sales of room air conditioners jumped 92 percent from the year before, and for the first time electricity use in Sacramento peaked in the summer rather than at Christmastime. It has peaked in the summer ever since.

Community ownership of the electric system brought benefits beyond the city and its suburbs. The District began connecting farms to the distribution system. Farmers and ranchers installed seasonal irrigation pumping and sprinkler systems, freeing themselves from the drought cycles typical to the Sacramento Valley. They discovered electrified dairy barns, infrared brooding, refrigeration and other electrical

consumers enjoyed one of the best reliability records in the country.

By 1975, the District's electricity distribution system was 95 percent new or rebuilt. "The system is now so flexible and modern," the general manager wrote, "that with a minimum adjustment it can serve any customer of any size anywhere in the area with practically any amount of load." The completed powerhouses on the American River were able to meet almost all Sacramento's energy needs with low-cost power.

At this same time, Sacramento confronted two challenges that would change the way its residents used electricity. The Arab oil embargo triggered an energy crisis in the United States. And in Northern California, a drought began that by 1976 would leave some reservoirs dry and cut the District's hydroelectric power output almost in half.

The District has built a variety of recreational facilities around the beautiful mountain reservoirs on the upper American River as a condition of operating powerhouses within national forest lands. Visitors can enjoy camping, fishing, boating, horseback riding and biking. *Photo by George Turner, Sacramento*

farm helpers. In short, they grew more prosperous, and farming changed from a family affair to a multibillion-dollar industry.

During its first 15 years, from 1946 to 1961, District employees steadily engineered and built a flexible, well-integrated system. "We put in a good system, properly done," recalls pioneer lineman George Moore. "We spent a little more on a quality system rather than an inexpensive one like the other utilities did, because if you spent less, you would have costly failures."

The District improved the power supply, as well. Low-cost contracts were negotiated for federal hydroelectric power, and in 1958, the District began construction on its own system of hydroelectric power plants on the upper American River.

All this planning paid off. By 1961, the District had lowered its rates three times, and Sacramento electricity

Sacramento's utility responded by expanding power generation sources and dedicating resources to teach customers how to use energy wisely, offering free energy efficiency inspections and low-interest financing for insulation and energy conservation equipment. A new program was tested, using radio-controlled cycling of air conditioners in exchange for a rebate on one's bill.

Consumers caught the spirit. In 1979, for the first time ever, electricity usage dropped at peak summer times in Sacramento.

Also in the mid-1970s, the District's promising new nuclear power plant began operating. Initially, excitement ran high that when the plant, known as Rancho Seco, was operating fully, energy would again be abundant in Sacramento. However, by 1979, operating problems showed that nuclear energy was not living up to its original promise. And in the aftermath of the Three Mile Island

In August 1984 and 1986, the District opened two photovoltaic power plants near Rancho Seco. They are only part of a diverse array of generation resources that includes wind, cogeneration, rooftop photovoltaics, hydroelectricity, geothermal and fuel cells. *Photo by George Turner, Sacramento*

government and industry to recruit new businesses to Sacramento and encourage businesses to stay here and expand. District cogeneration energy projects with local businesses help to provide more permanent jobs and tax revenue to the community as well.

The electric utility industry is undergoing dramatic changes. After 100 years of monopoly, utilities in California and across the United States are opening their service areas to competition, much the way long distance telephone service was deregulated. In July 1997, the Sacramento Municipal Utility District led the way by becoming the first utility in California to offer customers a choice of energy suppliers. California's investor-owned utilities have permitted competition since March 1998.

nuclear accident in Pennsylvania, the Nuclear Regulatory Commission mandated higher safeguarding standards on all nuclear power plants. Rancho Seco, which only a few years before had produced more energy than any of the more than 200 operating nuclear plants in the world, would require years of upgrades. In 1989, Sacramentans voted to close Rancho Seco for good.

In the 1980s, anticipating a slowdown in nuclear power, the District had turned to its customer-owners for direction. Using extensive customer input, the Board of Directors determined to move away from the concept of a large centralized power plant and move toward a diverse array of power sources.

Throughout that decade, the District took part in construction of a third electrical transmission intertie to the Pacific Northwest to allow the purchase of inexpensive, surplus electricity and built an impressive solar energy plant at the Rancho Seco site. These new sources of energy plus aggressive power buying and a customer base eager to conserve energy kept plenty of power flowing to Sacramento homes and businesses throughout the 1980s.

The 1990s were a powerful decade for Sacramento's electric utility. Cogeneration plants, low-cost purchased power from the Pacific Northwest and Canada, and development of renewable resources and advanced technologies are the foundation of a solid resource plan that kept customer rates constant beginning in 1990. The District is regarded internationally as a leader in energy efficiency and advanced and renewable technologies research and development. By keeping power costs low and promoting air quality improvement and job growth, the District helps the Sacramento community cultivate a thriving economy. The utility works with

Sacramento's utility is well positioned for the challenges of competition. In 1946, the District was a small, struggling utility with 65,000 customers, an antique distribution system, and no power generation whatsoever. Today, the District serves more than 500,000 customers and generates over 360 million kilowatt-hours of electricity from remarkably diverse resources. Thanks to the transmission lines built in the 1970s and 1980s, the District is able to buy power from many different sources at good market prices.

Reliable electric power at stable and reasonable rates — that was the original promise of municipal power when Sacramento's voters created their own utility in 1923 and that is what their electrical utility delivered. With the continuing guidance of its customer-owners, the Sacramento Municipal Utility District will keep that promise for as long as the people of Sacramento need electrical power.

SMUD's new Customer Service Center opened in 1994. Here, customers can start and stop service, pay bills and handle other business related to their accounts, sign up for energy efficiency programs, and visit the building's Energy & Technology Center, a major resource for energy information. The building is an impressive model for energy efficiency. *Photo by Glen Korengold, Sacramento*

The Jones Companies

Sacramento, as the focal point of the 1849 California Gold Rush, drew prospectors and entrepreneurs from around the world in search of the earth's riches. Nearly 100 years later, a young Stanford geologist named Vern Jones also arrived in Sacramento in search of the earth's resources. His was a quest for oil and gas. Today, decades later, Vern Jones and his family have quietly established a local and worldwide presence in the energy industry.

Collectively called The Jones Companies, the firm is run by Vern Jones, his wife, Gloria, and son and daughter, Derek and Sandra. The company currently specializes in energy management services (as Energy Operations Management Inc.), oil and gas exploration (as Vern Jones Oil and Gas Corp.), natural gas marketing (as California Energy Exchange Corp.), a number of proprietary natural gas pipeline companies (Sacramento Valley Pipeline, Delta Gas Gathering, California Gas Gathering and Yolo

Vern, Gloria, Sandra & Derek Jones

Vern Jones Oil & Gas is pictured drilling for natural gas south of Sacramento.

Pipeline), and geological and engineering services (as International Logging Inc.).

In 1952, Vern Jones, a Stanford graduate with a degree in geology, and a partner started their first company, Exploration Logging (EXLOG). The business provided geological formation services for companies drilling for natural gas in the Sacramento Valley. For those not familiar with the industry term, "logging" describes the recording of all aspects of a well-drilling operation, such as the drilling parameters of the well, formation evaluation and hydrocarbon monitoring. Fully contained laboratories, or "units," were constructed and equipped complete with monitoring equipment and a laboratory designed to work around the clock.

After a time, EXLOG's founders decided to branch out into the international market, and in 1962 the company received its first international job in Bolivia, South America. They would provide logging services for Standard Oil of California (better known as Chevron).

During the mid-60s, to meet the needs of oil companies exploring around the world, EXLOG expanded internationally, opening offices around the world. In 1972,

EXLOG kept its name but merged with Baker Hughes (formerly known as Baker Oil Tool), a large oil-service company, as a means of providing additional capital to fund EXLOG's aggressive growth plans. Vern stayed on as president and chief executive officer until he retired after 28 years in 1980. He continued as a director of Baker until 1985. Between 1952 and 1980, the company operated more than 200 units, employed more than 800 professional geologists and provided services in 26 countries worldwide.

From 1972 through 1980, EXLOG was the largest company in the world providing formation evaluation services to the energy industry.

By 1980, Derek and Sandra had finished school and decided to join Vern and Gloria in pursuing new opportunities, which included the formation of Vern Jones Oil and Gas. Though most of their endeavors included oil and natural gas exploration, the Jones family also owned a vineyard/winery operation known as Valfleur Winery. By the mid-80s, these diverse ventures began consuming considerable resources, time and effort. The family members concluded that the energy business was its future so they sold the vineyard and winery operation in order to dedicate all their resources to the energy field.

Vern Jones Oil and Gas discovered a new gas field in Northern California in the early 80s and then expanded into other areas such as Texas, Louisiana, Colorado, Kansas and Oklahoma until the early 90s. Today the company's primary focus is natural gas exploration in Northern California.

A roughneck is lighting a flarestack for Vern Jones Oil & Gas on a new gas-well test in the Clarksburg area.

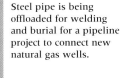

Steel pipe is being offloaded for welding and burial for a pipeline project to connect new natural gas wells.

In 1989, the Jones family started another business, California Energy Exchange Corporation (CEE), as a marketer of California-produced natural gas. Prior to this time, the California utility companies controlled gas pipelines and thus controlled gas bought and sold in Northern California. The advent of deregulation of natural gas in the California natural gas market provided the opportunity for transporting private sector gas on the utility system. Since its inception, CEE has continued to expand its services to assist major and independent gas producers and end-use markets in achieving their energy goals by structuring and coordinating both long- and short-term gas and sales arrangements.

With the combination of the utilities' effort to refocus on the gas transmission and distribution pipelines and de-emphasize gas-well hookups, the Jones family has formed a group of pipeline companies that interconnect local gas wells and their traditionally nitrogen-rich gas to specific end-users. In addition, as a resource management company, Energy Operations Management (EOM) helps

fill the void left behind by the utilities by providing expertise in all aspects required for pipeline project development such as: biological and environmental compliance, permit and right-of-way acquisition, and all forms of design, engineering, and operations.

From EOM's gas control center, located in the Sacramento headquarters, operators employ a high-tech SCADA (Supervisory Control and Data Acquisition) system to oversee and control the flow of natural gas through a pipeline grid that can extend from the wellhead to the customer's burnertip. Sophisticated monitoring and alarming features help ensure the safe, reliable passage and measurement of gas through the various pipeline systems on a "real-time" basis. The SCADA system utilizes conventional and Internet telecommunications to acquire and disseminate data from often remote locations in the field. This information allows EOM and its clients to effectively manage these valuable resources in this new era of energy competition.

In 1990, Vern Jones and a group of local investors created a new formation evaluation company, International Logging Incorporated (ILI), similar to EXLOG. The company has grown steadily, averaging 40 percent growth each year since 1995. The new company currently provides formation evaluation services only in the international market. The main regional office for Southeast Asia is located in Singapore, where there is a manufacturing facility where all new logging units are constructed and the bulk of the area operations are run. Additional offices are located in Jakarta, Indonesia; Kuala Lumpur, Malaysia; Beijing, China; Sonkla, Thailand; and Perth, Australia. Maracaibo, Venezuela

Sixty percent of International Logging's geological and engineering services are provided to offshore drilling operations.

right and bottom photo: International Logging's formation evaluation "units" are laboratories that house geologists, engineers and the necessary computers and instruments to monitor all aspects of a well-drilling operation.

is the regional office for Latin America with an additional office in Rio de Janeiro, Brazil.

Much like EXLOG, ILI was formed to provide the international energy sector with specialized formation evaluation and engineering services. The management and staff have been directly involved in the development and implementation of new technology and practices used in the well-logging industry.

ILI constructs environmentally controlled steel units that are designed to protect personnel and sensitive computer equipment from harsh climatic conditions ranging from the sub-freezing temperatures of the arctic to the jungle heat of the equator. Utilizing state-of-the-art software, hardware, and hydrocarbon sensing equipment, ILI's geologists and engineers are able to monitor all aspects of the drilling operations from often-remote parts of the world. This information is communicated by satellite to oil companies' home offices for analysis and review.

ILI has approximately 140 geologists employed worldwide with nationalities including Filipino, Indonesian, Malaysian, Bangladeshi, Indian, Pakistani, British, Chinese, Singaporean, Russian, American, Peruvian, Colombian, Venezuelan and Brazilian. This diverse employee base allows the operational flexibility required to provide these international services.

In 1998, ILI and the other Jones Companies relocated to a newly completed facility in a business park in the Sacramento suburb of Rancho Cordova, which will serve as corporate headquarters for the various energy-related businesses.

A long history in the Sacramento area and an established presence in the community have lead the Jones family to support both charitable organizations and industry associations over the years. Family members have held a variety of executive positions throughout the years, and their involvement has been widespread, reaching such organizations as the Crocker Art Museum, Sacramento Children's Home, Sacramento Opera, Sacramento Philharmonic Orchestra, Sacramento Symphony, International Host Committee, Stanford University, American Association of Petroleum Geologists, Independent Petroleum Association of America, and California Independent Petroleum Association.

Despite advances in alternative energy sources, oil and natural gas will continue to meet the majority of the world's energy needs for decades to come. Natural gas, with its clean-burning characteristics, is the environmental fuel of choice for meeting the growing energy demands of California. The Jones Companies plan to meet the energy challenges of the future by continuing to expand their role in the domestic and international marketplace.

KCRA-TV

A fortunate accident of nature gave the gift of gold to Sacramento's earliest pioneers. A century later, the same ancient seabed that produced the mother lode provided the ideal geography for another kind of pioneer to discover gold — over the airwaves. When KCRA-TV, Channel 3 transmitted its first television programming on September 3, 1955, the station's unobstructed signal could reach viewers as far north as Yuba County, south beyond Stockton and approaching Oakland to the west. Over the decades that followed, that range nearly doubled while KCRA-TV dominated one of the country's most coveted broadcasting markets — a blueprint for success in the television industry.

Ewing C. "Gene" Kelly, founder of KCRA-TV

Post-World War II America was vibrating with optimism and opportunity. The country was building at an incredible pace; material and personnel that had been dedicated to the war effort were now free to make dreams come true. The population was exploding with the "baby boom" and a prosperity previously unequaled in American history seemed unstoppable. Manufacturers were flooding showrooms and stores with new products, all clamoring to reach a very receptive consuming public.

It was in these exciting days that commercial television was introduced to the world. An audience that had previously been reached only by radio or the printed word was mesmerized by the flickering images on a tiny picture tube. Nevertheless, many prominent captains of industry saw the television as nothing more than a gadget or a toy with an expensive price tag.

KCRA-TV at the 1955 California State Fair, attended by Governor Goodwin Knight (left in light colored suit)

The old dairy truck barn that would become KCRA-TV

Ewing C. "Gene" Kelly, a 10-year broadcasting veteran who founded radio station KCRA-AM in 1945, had been encouraged by network executives at NBC for several years to consider getting into television. Ewing became convinced that television was well worth a gamble. He joined forces with partners C. Vernon, Gerald and Kenneth Hansen, the brothers who owned Crystal Cream and Butter Company. The Hansens provided the dairy truck barn at 10th and D streets that was converted into the original KCRA-TV studios and later became the permanent location of the station.

Brand-new KCRA-TV took the case for a television in every home directly to the people, making its broadcasting debut from the grounds of the 1955 California State Fair. Attendees, including California Governor Goodwin Knight, were shown how television worked and saw themselves on TV sets exhibited at the KCRA booth. With programming that featured the legendary Groucho Marx and local news briefs, it didn't take long for the public or the advertisers in Sacramento to fall in love with Channel 3. KCRA-TV was turning a profit after only three months on the air — well on its way to the top of the ratings.

Ewing C. Kelly's sons Robert and Jon assumed the roles of president and executive vice president of the parent company KCRA Inc. after their father passed away in 1960, sharing half ownership with the Hansens. The station became the Kelly Broadcasting Company in 1962 when Robert, Jon and their mother Nina purchased the Hansen half of the corporate shares.

The station has been an NBC affiliate since its inception, as was KCRA-AM, and although the network's standings have fluctuated wildly over the decades, KCRA-TV has consistently been a nationally dominant station. News programming has been the driving force of the station, proving to be the key ingredient in KCRA's irrefutable market conquest. "Where the

"News Comes First" has been the station's slogan since 1957. With the philosophy that the greatest service to the community is the responsible delivery of accurate information, KCRA devotes as much as one-third of its broadcasting day to news. Many of KCRA's news broadcasts are consistently ranked among the highest in the country.

Such innovations as live talk shows, the "news magazine" format, programming about medical breakthroughs and a chronicle of the West fueled a successful syndication enterprise that became Kelly News and Entertainment. KCRA's bold advocacy project "Call Three" assists viewers who are deadlocked in consumer disputes. The station is also highly regarded for its community awareness programming about the diverse ethnic communities of Northern California.

The demands of efficient news-gathering have kept the field crew on the cutting edge of technology, being the first Sacramento station to use color film, the first to use videotape, the first to use remote cameras and the first to use a helicopter. Adding another dimension, KCRA has a long history of directly covering world news affecting Northern Californians.

KCRA-TV's frequent excursions into the international news scene began with Stan Atkinson's groundbreaking coverage of the earliest stages of America's involvement in the Vietnam conflict. After accompanying Vice President Lyndon B. Johnson on a fact-finding tour of Indochina in 1961, Atkinson convinced joint-owner Bob Kelly that there was an important story to tell in Southeast Asia. The young reporter traveled to Binh Hung to record the tiny village's fight against the Viet Cong. An hour-long documentary titled "The Village That Refuses To Die" was syndicated nationwide and later used as a training film for military personnel preparing for duty in South Vietnam.

The closing days of the 1990s brought challenging issues to the television industry, which weighed heavily on the Kellys. The Federal Communications Commission (FCC) mandated that all broadcasters must completely convert to the digital high definition television (HDTV) format by 2006, with the first HDTV transmission in the top 30 markets required by November of 1999 — a demand that would cost the station tens of millions of dollars to retain its license.

The Kelly family, which had fought the good fight and won for over 40 years, had to come to terms with a brave new world; it was time to find a buyer who was in a position to bear the financial cost of maintaining KCRA-TV's dominance. The Kellys agonized over the decision until a deal was struck with Hearst-Argyle Television, Inc., the industry's fourth-largest independent TV station group at the time. The Kelly family left millions of dollars on the table with other suitors when they closed the deal with Hearst-Argyle because they needed to know that the new owners would embrace the KCRA legacy of journalistic excellence and community service.

Hearst-Argyle's roots in broadcasting reach back to 1928, and the corporation's commitment to television news is indelible. With the financial clout to meet the new FCC compliances and a hard-earned reputation as a builder and innovator, Hearst-Argyle was prepared to continue KCRA-TV's pre-eminence in the Sacramento market. The Kellys turned over the keys to the station on January 5, 1999, ending one era of excellence in broadcasting while ushering in the new.

California Independent
System Operator

The California Independent System Operator, or Cal-ISO for short, is key to enabling Californians to shop for power and creating open competition in the electric industry. It was created by the state in 1996 to act as the electricity traffic control center for California's "electron highway," which covers 124,000 square miles and three-fourths of the state. The mission of the Cal-ISO is to ensure the power grid is safe and reliable and that there is a competitive market for electricity in California. Increased competition should ultimately lower the cost of purchasing electricity.

The California ISO is the high-tech electricity traffic controller for the state's open market power grid where reliability of the system is driven by competitive energy markets. Hour-Ahead Resource Coordinator Kimberly Brown monitors the markets in the hour before electricity is consumed. *Photo by Charr Crail*

The California ISO is a one-stop energy emporium for electricity traders in the final hours before energy is consumed. Information technology is the heart of the operation, which requires leading-edge computer systems and highly trained professionals such as (from left to right) Systems Administrator Danny Bennett, Consultant Amit Sharma and Market Operations Senior Engineer Mark Rothleder. *Photo by Charr Crail*

The Cal-ISO is located in Folsom, a small Sacramento suburb. It is not far from the site of the historical Folsom Powerhouse on the American River, where in 1895 the country's first long-distance transmission of power took place. On March 31, 1998, this impartial, not-for-profit corporation assumed computerized command of the long-distance, high-voltage power lines that deliver electricity throughout California and between neighboring states and Mexico. The power grid, a transmission system made up of high-voltage power lines supported by 100- to 150-foot towers, delivers 164 billion kilowatt hours of electricity every year. That's enough power to serve the annual energy needs of 27 million

current customers of California's investor-owned utilities: Pacific Gas & Electric, Southern California Gas Company, Southern California Edison and San Diego Gas & Electric. In addition, the grid will transport significant amounts of power for others in the region.

California is the first state in the nation to offer access to an open market power grid where reliability is driven by energy markets. In other words, the buying and selling of electricity by market participants is the force behind the delicate balance of supply and demand that keeps the transmission system stable. Hundreds of power plants supplying up to 45,000 megawatts during peak demand are connected to the Cal-ISO, making its control area the second largest in the United States (the Pennsylvania-New Jersey-Maryland interconnection is the largest) and the fifth largest in the world.

The first participants in the Cal-ISO are the state's three investor-owned utilities. These utilities are mandated by landmark state legislation (AB 1890 as of September 1996) to release control but not ownership of their long-distance transmission lines to the Cal-ISO. The legislation guarantees that all power marketers (nonutility companies generating or brokering electricity) who wish to do business in California will have the opportunity to generate and/or deliver power over the state's electricity grid. These companies use scheduling coordinators to schedule deliveries of electricity over the Cal-ISO controlled power grid.

The scheduling coordinators are the intermediaries between the Cal-ISO, retailers and customers. Via computers, they call in the route on the transmission grid they plan to use to transport electricity, showing how they will match their customers' demand with supply. The Cal-ISO then takes these schedules and runs them through a large computer program to determine the chances of "congestion" on the power grid. If no congestion is found, the Cal-ISO gives scheduling coordinators the green light to proceed. If congestion is discovered, the Cal-ISO gives them the opportunity to either sell or buy more power, with the Cal-ISO eventually choosing the least costly option.

The nerve center for Cal-ISO operations is a 15,000-square-foot control room. The control room contains computer consoles and a 160- by 12-foot mapboard that provides a window into California's electrical backbone. This giant mosaic mapboard gives an instant overview of where electrons are flowing throughout the state. Dynamic indicators show which circuits are closed or open and the status of key power plants and substations. This enables the Cal-ISO to monitor the security and transmission reliability of California's high-voltage lines, as well as those extending into Nevada, Oregon, Arizona, New Mexico, Idaho, Washington and British Columbia, Canada. As one of four Western Systems Coordinating Council (WSCC) Security Coordinators, the Cal-ISO monitors transmission security for a portion of 16 Western states.

Since transmission reliability is a 24-hour job 365 days a year, operators need to assess the status of the transmission system at all times. The mapboard provides a picture of critical information that is updated every four seconds. The high degree of visibility allows operators to clearly view the board and check real-time system security from any one of 12 computer consoles. In the event of a natural disaster or other emergency, there is another control room in Alhambra that serves as a backup for the Folsom control room. Four redundant computer systems provide enhanced reliability.

Along with operating the power grid, the Cal-ISO is a one-stop energy emporium for electricity traders in the final hours before energy is consumed. Cal-ISO is like a bank, acting as a clearinghouse for energy transactions but never buying or selling power itself. The markets allow the ISO to make adjustments in power deliveries in response to changes in energy consumption. Cal-ISO has three open markets that help lower the cost of providing electrical services such as regulation and voltage support. Two of the markets are conducted the day before and the hour before electricity is used. The Ancillary Services Market helps fine-tune the flow of electricity when the unexpected happens, such as a power plant failure or a sharp rise in demand for power. The energy that is bought and sold can be dispatched within seconds, minutes or hours.

The Congestion Management Market allocates space on the transmission lines. When there is not enough room for all the electrons on a line, congestion zones are established and scheduling coordinators operating in these zones can play the congestion management market, curtailing their power deliveries or generating more as needed. In the Real-Time Imbalance Market (also called the "Spot Market") supplemental energy is quickly bought or sold every 10 minutes to accommodate energy needs just moments before it used. Scheduling coordinators receive payment for the extra electricity they supply or are billed for extra energy they need to meet the demand of their customers.

The electricity market in California is worth more than $23 billion. But the economics of this market encompass a much broader spectrum. Affordable, reliable, competitive electricity helps keep the entire economy in California

California's emerging energy markets are spawning new growth in renewable energy sources such as wind power. *Photo by Tom Myers*

healthy — one of the primary goals of the state's ambitious restructuring efforts.

As California continues to find new uses for electricity, yesterday's technology isn't lost; rather, it is recaptured and revitalized. The winds of change are bringing new opportunities to California, a state clearly regarded as a leader in the energy industry. The Cal-ISO's responsibilities will grow as transmission and generation needs expand and neighboring states follow California's lead in opening the doors to competition.

To find out more about the California ISO, people can call or visit them on the World Wide Web.

California's "electron highway" spans 124,000 miles or three-quarters of the Golden State. Investor-owned utilities have been mandated to turn over their transmission systems to the Cal-ISO, but the utilities still own and maintain the towers and lines. Photo *by Mark Cohen*

Pacific Access

Think for a moment about the size, scope and complexity of the ever-changing global communications industry. In this deregulated environment, the rivalry is fierce and the challenges enormous. Working as partners with some of the major players in the communications market, Pacific Access found its strength as a strategic network services and solutions provider to some of the largest communications companies in the world.

Pacific Access was founded in 1985 by Dennis and Julie Pulos, who seized the opportunity to create a high-tech niche following the divestiture of AT&T. Seeing tremendous potential in customizing solutions for the seven newly created Regional Bell Operating Companies, Pacific Access quickly became a strategic partner rich in technological and telecommunications expertise.

More than a decade later, Pacific Access has grown to become a premier, multidisciplined provider of quality technology services and solutions. The $100 million privately held company, headquartered in Rancho Cordova, includes

PACIFIC ACCESS IS A CORPORATE SPONSOR OF SEVERAL NONPROFIT GROUPS, AND ROUTINELY DONATES EQUIPMENT TO LOCAL SCHOOLS AND SENIOR CENTERS.

a nationwide network of branch offices with over 100 employees. Customers, including AT&T, Lucent Technologies, SBC/Pacific Bell, Bell South, US West, Bell Atlantic, MCI and AirTouch, trust Pacific Access to address their business challenges and design a network infrastructure that optimizes business efficiency and allows those customers to become more competitive in their marketplace. The company delivers network audits, network design and capacity planning, project management of network and systems implementation, network growth and transition plans — these are just some of the strengths that Pacific Access brings to the table.

The company's proven track record in mission-critical applications has earned it some impressive awards from clients and partners, such as SBC/Pacific Bell Quality Partner, Hewlett-Packard Best in Class, Bell South Master Services Provider, Pacific Bell IVEN Certification, AT&T MWBE Partner Award and more.

Pacific Access has also been recognized by several business publications, honored as one of *Inc.* magazine's Fastest Growing Companies and one of the top Nationwide High Tech Companies by *Hispanic Business*. Other honors, from the *Sacramento Business Journal*, include No. 1 Certified Woman-Owned Business, No. 3 Certified Minority-Owned Company and the No. 12 Software Development Company in the area.

While the vision and drive of its founders has provided the basic building blocks of Pacific Access,

Dennis and Julie Pulos, cofounders of Pacific Access

the company has evolved into a unique business model consisting of six divisions, which were created for maximum focus, entrepreneurial spirit and growth. Pacific Access strives to attract staff who can understand the communications market and thrive in a changing environment.

Pacific Access (PAC) is the recognized worldwide network and systems integration division that provides services, internally developed hardware and software products, and "best-of-breed" third-party products from companies such as Lucent Technologies, Hewlett-Packard, Sun Microsystems, Cisco Systems, IBM, Newbridge and others.

Strategic Global Services (SGS) is an industry leader in consulting and deployment services for data network environments. SGS has conducted numerous network audits worldwide to help Fortune 500 companies obtain maximum efficiency of assets and network utilization. It is also a leader in central office deployments of the latest in technologies, in conjunction with legacy equipment removal.

PAC Labs is the hardware and software development division of the company. PAC Labs develops products that are globally accepted by customers in the communications industry, including products that are used for communications transport and network systems management.

Pacific Access Capital is the finance division of Pacific Access, which offers a variety of leasing and financing services to all of the company's divisions and customers.

WORKING AS PARTNERS WITH SOME OF THE MAJOR PLAYERS IN THE COMMUNICATIONS MARKET, PACIFIC ACCESS FOUND ITS STRENGTH AS A STRATEGIC NETWORK SERVICES AND SOLUTIONS PROVIDER TO SOME OF THE LARGEST COMMUNICATIONS COMPANIES IN THE WORLD.

REPAC focuses on inventory management of legacy (older) network and computer systems to help communications companies maximize the use of their assets. It transitions older technology out and partners with PAC to replace those products with the latest technology solutions.

The company's Intelligent Power Systems division (IPS) provides innovative power resource management systems for automated power, environmental and facilities management. IPS's products and services help reduce costs and improve efficiencies for companies with large infrastructure management needs that rely heavily on electrical power.

THE COMPANY'S PROVEN TRACK RECORD IN MISSION-CRITICAL APPLICATIONS HAS EARNED IT SOME IMPRESSIVE AWARDS FROM CLIENTS AND PARTNERS, SUCH AS SBC/PACIFIC BELL QUALITY PARTNER, HEWLETT-PACKARD BEST IN CLASS, BELL SOUTH MASTER SERVICES PROVIDER, PACIFIC BELL IVEN CERTIFICATION, AT&T MWBE PARTNER AWARD AND MORE.

With corporate success comes community responsibility — a role Pacific Access takes seriously. To that end, Julie Pulos serves on the board of directors for the California Chamber of Commerce, and she also serves on various subcommittees of the chamber, such as the Technology Task Force. Julie also has participated on the Sacramento Area Commerce and Trade Organization's (SACTO) high-tech advisory panel, which works to attract high-tech businesses to the area, and serves as a member of SACTO's board of directors. The Puloses are long-standing members of the Sacramento Metropolitan Chamber of Commerce, the Rancho Cordova Chamber of Commerce and the Sacramento Hispanic Chamber of Commerce.

Pacific Access is a corporate sponsor of several non-profit groups and routinely donates equipment to local schools and senior centers.

These are just a few examples of how partnerships with Pacific Access serve to improve the quality of life for its customers, employees and the community. The company's expertise spans the globe, and it is no wonder that the world's leading communications companies take advantage of the innovative and intelligent network services and solutions offered by their partner, Pacific Access.

Pacific Gas and Electric Company

The basic ingredients of civilization — housing, running water, heat, light, food distribution — were nonexistent in the West when masses of settlers flocked to Sacramento's gold fields. Those ingredients had been left behind but not forgotten.

Fortunately, many pioneers failed miserably as gold prospectors and were forced to turn their ingenuity to meeting the demands of a burgeoning population. As they planned their courses, these trailblazers replaced the flickering candle with the gas light and then the electric bulb.

One such disgruntled miner, Peter Donahue, and his brother James moved to San Francisco and built a successful iron foundry. Creatively, the Donahues embarked on another business venture that launched the race for energy supply in California. Operating from a small waterfront plant that produced gas from coal, the San Francisco Gas Company began lighting the city streets with lamps in 1854. Meanwhile, gas suppliers started appearing in the inland towns of Central and Northern California. The Sacramento Gas Company, founded by banker Darius Ogden Mills, first offered service to the Valley in 1855.

A young San Francisco moneylender named George H. Roe became the unlikely founder of PG&E's origins as an electricity supplier after repossessing a primitive electric generator from one of his debtors. He became so obsessed with the potential of electricity that he formed the California Electric Light Company — the first central-station provider in the United States to deliver electricity to the public.

The frenzy of competition that followed would be fierce and sustained, with motivations ranging from adventure to avarice and arrogance. One attribute shared by all was vision. The steady flow of intruding gas and electricity suppliers would be met with resistance and then cooperation. When the massive Edison General Electric Company expanded to the West Coast, George Roe merged his company into the Edison Light and Power Company. By 1894, this entity was combined with the Donahues' to form the San Francisco Gas and Electric Company.

On the other side of the Bay, the Oakland Gas Light and Heat Company was expanding under the command of John A. Britton, the man who would become the first president of Pacific Gas and Electric Company. Further inland, partners Eugene J. de Sabla and John Martin were wrestling with the dynamics of long-distance, high-voltage transmission of electricity. The most breathtaking of their ventures was the unprecedented 4,427-foot aerial crossing of the Carquinez Straits near Vallejo that they completed in April 1901.

De Sabla and Martin acquired Britton's Oakland concern in 1903, and after careful courtship, the San Francisco Gas and Electric Company was added to form the Pacific Gas and Electric Company on October 10, 1905. Three months later, John A. Britton was installed as president.

The ensuing century staged PG&E's growth to stand as the largest investor-owned utility in the United States, providing service to 48 of California's 58 counties. PG&E has been a leader in the development of every source of energy used in California, including natural gas, hydroelectric, geothermal, nuclear, solar and wind generation.

Through strength, perseverance and cooperation, PG&E has become California's lifeline, braided from over 500 individual strands of enterprising companies.

A familiar Sacramento Valley landmark, the Folsom Powerhouse was acquired by PG&E in 1903 and remained in service until 1952. It has since been deeded to the state and preserved as a museum.

Sacramento Regional County Sanitation District

Sacramento-area leaders, realizing the tremendous potential for the area's growth, joined forces in 1973 to form the Sacramento Regional County Sanitation District (SRCSD), which conveys and treats wastewater for the Sacramento region. Back then, the organization of the District was unique because many treatment plants were, and still are, owned and operated by municipalities. The District represents one of the few examples within the state of a regionalized effort to serve an entire urbanized area within a county.

As a result of the postwar growth in California, the small rural treatment plants of the 1950s and early 1960s quickly became enveloped by neighborhoods and urban population centers. As people moved into the area, Sacramento County clearly needed a more comprehensive wastewater management plan. Sound planning and vision helped the District stay ahead of the rapid changes fueled by the county's expanding customer base.

The Sacramento area's inevitable growth was factored into plans for a new regional wastewater treatment plant serving the needs for most of the county's residential, business and industrial customers. Today, the District-operated Sacramento Regional Wastewater Treatment Plant in Elk Grove serves more than a million people. Several innovations to accommodate both its expansion and the growth of communities around the plant have contributed to the uniqueness of the facility. Among the innovations is a 2,500-acre buffer between the plant and surrounding neighborhoods. Today the buffer provides natural odor control and serves the community as a nature preserve.

Most people create about 50 to 100 gallons of wastewater every day as they shower, wash their hands, do laundry and dishes, and flush the toilet. Businesses and industries also produce millions of gallons of wastewater each day. Before the wastewater can be treated, it must travel to the treatment plant. The District operates a large pipeline conveyance system, which connects to a web of smaller pipes that intricately cover the county — and ultimately reach every home or business in its service area. Wastewater travels up to 30 miles from the far corners of the county before it arrives at the treatment plant.

Every day, 165 million gallons of wastewater reach the treatment plant, which is operated around-the-clock. Cleaned wastewater returns to the Sacramento River, where it can be used again for fish habitat, recreation and other uses. Biosolids, the organic solids removed from the wastewater, can be reused as a fertilizer or soil amendment. Methane gas, a byproduct of the treatment process, can be recycled into an energy source. An on-site cogeneration facility converts some of this energy into electricity for the Elk Grove community.

The District is governed by a board of directors. The eight-member board includes the five supervisors from Sacramento County and council members from the cities of Folsom, Sacramento and Citrus Heights. As Sacramento continues to grow, the board faces new challenges to ensure safe and cost-effective wastewater services. For Sacramento, the region where flowing rivers are its signature, well-managed wastewater remains at the heart of its growth and continued prosperity.

A view of natural wetlands on the grounds of the Sacramento Regional Wastewater Treatment Plant in Elk Grove

Workers perform regular maintenance at the Sacramento Regional Wastewater Treatment Plant.

Professions

*Artists, photographers, electricians, engineers,
newspaper and realty organizations provide
essential services to Sacramento.*

Lionakis Beaumont Design Group, Inc.

"Designing the future...building on experience"

Good architects design good buildings. Great architects design brilliant futures. Lionakis Beaumont Design Group, Inc., Sacramento's oldest and largest architectural firm, has banked on decades of experience, longstanding community relationships and the progressive minds of its people to make that leap into greatness.

While the firm boasts a loyal client base and a sterling reputation dating back to 1909, its approach is as undeniably fresh and energetic as that of an emerging firm determined to prove its mettle. Lionakis Beaumont's 21st-century vision of Sacramento is dynamic, cosmopolitan, globally connected and socially and environmentally enriched. The firm expects no less of its buildings.

A Commitment to Service

The hallmark of Lionakis Beaumont Design Group has always been service — not just the timely production of construction documents and computer models, but the

ability to perceive what the client wants and to create an experience that exceeds client expectations from start to finish. It's a tradition in excellence that began in 1909, when George Sellon, a Chicago-educated architect, founded the firm after a two-year term as California's first state architect. Sellon quickly became known

as a pioneer, designing Sacramento's first steel-reinforced building and its first high-rise office structure. The landmark 926 J Street building is one of Sellon's most impressive works. His firm, known as George C. Sellon & Liemmings Architects until 1923, also designed many of the capital city's churches, schools and places of business.

Sellon's retirement in 1950 ushered in a new era for the firm. For the next 30 years, Whitson Cox, J.R. Liske,

George Lionakis and engineer Klyne Beaumont distinguished themselves as some of Sacramento's premier architects, designing buildings for such clients as *The Sacramento Bee*; Sacramento County; Pacific Bell; California State University, Chico; the Los Rios Community College District; Kaiser Permanente; and the Rio Linda Union School District. The relationships the firm cemented then still hold today as a testament to its commitment to service and pursuit of quality.

As Sacramento established itself as a major metropolitan area, daring new ideas began to take shape within the firm. During the mid-1980s, new partners came on board who significantly changed the way Lionakis Beaumont Design Group thought about architecture. Counting on its unparalleled reputation in the community, partners Bruce Starkweather and Joshua Reyneveld knew the firm had what it took to become one of the leading architectural firms in Northern California. They believed that as a firm that grew along with the city it served, Lionakis Beaumont Design Group had a vested interest in the future of that city. Therefore, its buildings should be designed to enhance the quality of life not only in the present, but for decades to come. Thus began the concept of designing futures rather than buildings.

The new generation of principals, including Starkweather, Timothy Fry, Etienne Louw, Nicholas Docous, Don Mariano and Dave Younger, are committed to positioning the firm for this mission. A major move was the addition of expanded services. Now under one roof, the firm houses the disciplines of architecture, planning, facilities management, interior design, and structural engineering. This multidisciplined approach is a key differentiation that sets Lionakis Beaumont Design Group apart from its peers.

Unlike other firms that contract out for many of these services, Lionakis Beaumont pools its talent for each project, providing the client with a "single point of contact" environment. From a project's inception, the key staff involved will remain the same through its completion. This team approach not only facilitates communication, but ensures harmony in regard to overall goals and philosophies.

As "steward of the process," the firm offers clients a broader view, inviting them to think 20 years ahead while providing a framework within which to make decisions. Nowadays, as buildings are constructed less expensively and more quickly than ever before, the firm contends it is even more important to make the right decisions early on to avoid spending a lot of money on a building that doesn't meet all the client's needs.

Part of exceptional service is the ability to perceive what the client wants. Lionakis Beaumont Design Group is in tune with today's trends. The firm recognizes that one of the ways employers seek to increase employee output is through increased employee satisfaction. It obliges by designing workplaces with pleasant and comfortable surroundings, with ample natural light, places for greenery, ergonomically correct equipment and amenities.

"We design buildings for real people and serve real needs," Starkweather says.

The Pursuit of Excellence

The most valuable commodity Lionakis Beaumont Design Group has to offer is the critical thinking skills of its staff.

"The magic for us," says Starkweather, "is who we are, not what we do."

As a result, the firm consistently approaches new projects with innovative ideas, achieving a level of appropriate risk. Problem-solving skills are utilized to achieve success whether or not the firm has experience with a given building type. Whatever the job, the attitude is "We can do it."

Lionakis Beaumont Design Group, Inc.'s midtown studios

For Lionakis Beaumont Design Group, the highest compliment is not, "What a beautiful building!" but "You have exceeded our expectations." Staff members maintain that going to one of the firm's newly completed schools and seeing the pride and joy on the faces of students and teachers is tantamount to receiving the highest honor possible.

A testament to the firm's many talents is the Kaiser Permanente Point West medical office building on Cal Expo across from the California State Fairgrounds, completed in May 1997. At 230,000 square feet, this complex is designed for easy access and minimal confusion. Its three separate buildings, connected by atriums, each have different color schemes that help visitors navigate the vast office space.

On a smaller scale, Lionakis Beaumont Design Group received a merit award from the Coalition for Adequate School Housing for its design of the Foothill Oaks Elementary School in the Rio Linda Union School District. This is the latest of 21 schools the firm has designed for the district in a relationship that has endured nearly half a century. Designed with bright colors and to reflect the existing neighborhood context, the school was developed

The principals of Lionakis Beaumont Design Group, Inc., are, from left, Etienne Louw, Bruce Starkweather, Don Mariano, Dave Younger, Timothy Fry and Nicholas Docous.

around a historical oak tree dating back to George Washington's birth. The firm took special care to incorporate educational features in its designs, such as a plaque commemorating the age of the tree and a wall measuring the tree's "drip line" circumference of about three-quarters of an acre.

Current noteworthy projects include Franchise Tax Board Phase 3 expansion; new Education Classroom Faculty Office Building and renovation and expansion to Bell Memorial Union at California State University, Chico; projects at *The Sacramento Bee*; new corporate headquarters for Radiological Associates of Sacramento; administrative support building for UC Davis Medical Center; new adoption center for Sacramento SPCA; seismic upgrade and renovation of DMV Headquarters; and the competition-winning design for the Sacramento River water intake structure.

Smart use of technology is crucial to capitalizing on new opportunities and meeting the demands of the future. Lionakis Beaumont Design Group strongly believes that technology is a way to bring people together, not a tool of isolation. The emphasis is on technology with a human touch — after all, what is architecture but a marriage of art and science, emotion and pragmatism. Increasingly, building design is being done by computer, and blueprints are being replaced by large-scale photocopies, which are recyclable. Whatever the method, the

professionals at Lionakis Beaumont insist on blending sound design principles with aesthetically pleasing environments. Technology helps them do that.

Lionakis Beaumont Design Group's extensive client list has resulted in a broad range of project-type expertise. Its work in both the public and private sectors enables the firm to bring the strengths of each to the other. For example, its state building projects often borrow cutting-edge concepts from private industry projects.

A Legacy of Added Value

As Sacramento comes into its own as a major destination on the West Coast, Lionakis Beaumont Design Group wants to be relevant to the capital city's progress, just as it has always been. Because its staff members live and work in the community — Starkweather himself is a fourth-generation Californian — the firm is committed to improving the quality of life for all residents. It diligently works at cultivating what it calls the legacy of added value — putting more into the community than it takes out.

Its own mid-town studio is a shining source of inspiration. When a stint of rapid growth in the late 1980s and early 90s forced the firm to find a bigger studio, it chose not to add to urban sprawl, but to do its part toward downtown revitalization by buying a building in the heart of the city.

The firm renovated a 1940s brick warehouse, the former home of an industrial glass company, and paid special attention to energy efficiency and the environment. The building itself is located near light-rail public transit lines, making it easy for employees to leave their cars at home. In addition, there is a recycling room with bins set up for pickup by a

nonprofit organization and a storage area for three special commuter bicycles, which were purchased in Holland and are used by the staff for lunch or errands. One of the most important design features of this studio is the widespread use of natural light. Attractive, multipaned windows are placed throughout the building, making it as functional as it is beautiful. Input from the entire staff of architects, engineers and interior designers was combined to make Lionakis Beaumont Design Group's studio a unique and stylish place to work.

Lionakis Beaumont Design Group is a proud sponsor of several charitable organizations, including public tele-

vision station KVIE-TV Channel 6. The firm also supports the Leukemia Society, the American Cancer Society, The Ronald McDonald House and Families First.

These relationships, along with those the firm has maintained with clients old and new, are proof that Lionakis Beaumont Design Group, Inc. is and always has been about people, not structures. With a philosophy like that, the future of Sacramento looks promising indeed.

Foothill Oaks Elementary School — the 21st school in the Rio Linda Union School District to be designed by Lionakis Beaumont Design Group, Inc.

Sacramento River Water Intake Structure — The competition-winning design by Lionakis Beaumont Design Group, Inc. Anticipated completion, fall 2001.

The staff at Lionakis Beaumont Design Group, Inc.

Buehler & Buehler Associates

Buehler & Buehler Associates Structural Engineers, Inc. is a Sacramento-based structural engineering firm. Since 1946, Buehler & Buehler Associates and its predecessor firms have maintained many long-term relationships with architects, designers, developers and various public sector clients in California and throughout the western United States. Walter A. Buehler began a career in structural engi-

neering in 1946 and then formed Buehler & Buehler in 1953 with his son Walter D. Buehler. Together, they built the firm's successful reputation by providing quality structural engineering for projects such as the IBM building and the Pacific Telephone and Telegraph building in Sacramento. In 1982, when the firm grew larger, they formed Buehler & Buehler Associates. Although neither of the Buehlers are still with the firm, the current principals, Patrick Vujovich, David Hutchinson, Ronald Migliori, Todd Thorp, Lawrence Jones, William Rader, Scott Hooker and Larry Summerfield, continue to provide ongoing leadership and the same level of quality service that has been synonymous with the Buehler & Buehler name for over 50 years.

The firm has over 30 employees, the largest structural engineering staff in Sacramento. More than half of the staff are licensed professional engineers experienced in working with all forms of construction materials and procedures. As structural engineers, their responsibility is to create construction plans that ensure that a building's foundations,

framing and floor systems will withstand the force of an earthquake. Throughout its history, the firm has designed thousands of projects including low- and high-rise office buildings, federal and county buildings, data centers, telephone and utility facilities, warehouses, military facilities, medical office buildings, hospitals and more than 400 educational facilities.

Specializing in new design, seismic retrofit, tenant improvement, rehabilitation, renovation and preservation of historic sites, Buehler & Buehler Associates has engineered buildings that can be found throughout much of the Sacramento region's landscape. The firm's designs include the widely recognized five-story Lincoln Plaza, the 26-story U.S. Bank Plaza, the 24-story Capital Square, the Sacramento Convention Center renovation and the Sacramento International Airport's Terminal A. The firm has also contributed to the seismic renovation and analysis of many historical buildings such as the Sacramento Main Library, the Sacramento Municipal Utility District headquarters and the GSA Cottage Way. As a result of Buehler & Buehler Associates' analyses, innovative procedures for strengthening these types of buildings have been used to satisfy current building code requirements. The firm attributes its success to responsiveness, service, reliability and dependability. Clients can depend on the firm's engineers to maintain active roles in all phases of every project, from the formation of a preliminary concept through the

completion of construction. Buehler & Buehler Associates strives to provide optimal designs for every project, regardless of size and scope, while providing the most economical and efficient solutions possible.

The firm's design approach is founded on both innovative and practical engineering concepts. To maintain the highest level of service, Buehler & Buehler Associates' engineers are committed to staying current on recent developments within the structural engineering design industry. They are active members of building code committees, attend professional seminars and enroll in continuing education courses.

state of California. Dispatched by the Office of Emergency Services, Buehler & Buehler Associates prepares safety assessments immediately after disasters let by principal Ron Migliori. The firm's engineering teams visited the 1989 Loma Prieta and 1994 Northridge earthquake sites to assess and note deficiencies that would influence building code changes and the requirements for designing and renovating buildings. The findings were immediately integrated into the firm's design philosophy.

While structural engineering design continues to change, so does the technology used to create and evaluate drawings.

Sacramento International Airport Terminal A — Completed in 1998, the 275,000-square-foot Terminal A at Sacramento International Airport doubled passenger capacity and accommodated international travel.

Members of the firm are frequently invited to share their expertise as guest speakers for the Structural Engineering Association of California and to instruct engineering classes at California State University Sacramento (CSUS). Dr. Ajit Virdee, one of the firm's principals until his death in 1997, made significant contributions to the community and CSUS for nearly 40 years. Virdee, a former chairman of the civil engineering department at CSUS, dedicated his career to structural engineering research and education, writing textbooks and influencing code developments.

Buehler & Buehler Associates' staff are members of various building code and regulation committees that influence structural design code development. Vujovich, the firm's president, serves on the State Building Seismic Program Peer Review Board, which operates as an oversight body for the State of California-Seismic Retrofit Program of State Buildings. As members of the Structural Engineers Association of Central California (SEAOCC), several of the firm's principals serve on the Board of Directors, the Seismology and Code Committee, the Ad Hoc Committee for Masonry Design and the Committee to Evaluate Response to Seismic Design. The firm's executive vice president, Hutchinson, co-authored the 1997 Uniform Building Code (UBC) Seismic Design Manual for the Structural Engineers Association of California (SEAOC), which assists practicing structural engineers in interpreting the 1997 UBC requirements for structural design.

The firm also shares and broadens its experience by registering as disaster service workers with the

Buehler & Buehler Associates uses computer workstations equipped with the latest structural analysis and computer-aided drafting (CAD) software and hardware.

Throughout its history, Buehler & Buehler Associates has supported community fund-raising events and nonprofit organizations, including the CSUS Association of Students in Civil Engineering (ASCE) Concrete Canoe Event, local high school events, Special Olympics, YMCA and the American Heart Association.

The firm's contribution to Sacramento's landmarks will continue to impact area residents and visitors for many years to come — as a source of entertainment, shopping, education and commerce. As the Western landscape changes, Buehler & Buehler Associates' expertise continues to expand. With an eye on the future, the firm will continue to pursue opportunities to do what it does best — design buildings that combine artistry with stability, providing the most effective solution to the challenges faced by its clients.

Sacramento Convention Center — This 200,000-square-foot addition and renovation, completed in 1994, tripled the size of the 20-year-old convention center in downtown Sacramento. For its structural design, B&B received the 1996 Best Public/Municipal Building Design Award by the Prestressed Concrete Institute (PCI).
Photo by Erich Ansel

Dokken Engineering

Richard A. Dokken established Dokken Engineering in 1986. Before the inception of Dokken Engineering, Mr. Dokken was a founding partner at Engineering Computer Corporation, which was formed in 1976 after he left his position of associate engineer at the California Department of Transportation. Mr. Dokken brings more than 30 years of experience designing bridges and highways to the firm.

As a multidisciplinary civil engineering consulting firm, Dokken Engineering is proud of its creative and cost-effective solutions to the transportation dilemmas faced by communities and surrounding regions. Dokken Engineering plans and develops highway interchanges, overpass bridges, channel crossings, seismic retrofits, transit guideways and light-rail elevated structures. Most of the projects are located in California, although Dokken Engineering has been involved in construction projects in China and other parts of the United States.

Clients include community builders, transportation authorities such as Regional Transit (RT) in Sacramento and the Metropolitan Transit Authority (MTA) in Los Angeles, cities, counties and state transportation agencies.

With offices in Sacramento County (Rancho Cordova), San Diego, Tustin and Salinas, as well as more than 60 employees, Dokken Engineering offers personalized and hands-on services to the communities where projects are located. Dokken Engineering's staff works in partnership with clients from concept to completion. Dokken Engineering goes out of its way to provide exceptional client service. During the course of a given project, Dokken Engineering is accountable to many different "bosses." The firm's biggest challenge is to simultaneously meet the demands of individuals, government agencies and private industry. Dokken Engineering staff must be keenly aware of local traffic patterns and community development issues long before they reach an agreed-upon solution for the clients.

"It's a lot more than math," says Richard Dokken.

Dokken Engineering projects are often valued at as much as $2 million. Developing final plans, specifications and estimates can take several months, depending on the parties involved, the environmental impact and the number of design changes made during the process. Site visits before and during construction are critical to learning the lay of the land. The firm identifies soil conditions, environmental concerns and any animal habitat that may be disturbed as a result of the new construction. The firm works in cooperation with private devel-

Sacramento's "R" Street elevated light-rail platform

Professions

opers and the community to satisfy the interests of all concerned.

Although Dokken Engineering becomes a valuable source of knowledge and advice for its public- and private-sector clients, it is often a silent partner of the communities it serves. In the booming Laguna Creek community south of downtown Sacramento, Dokken Engineering designed the Laguna Boulevard-Bond Road/SR 99 interchange to be a close and convenient entry and exit point for commuters.

Another project is the Truxel Road/Interstate 80 interchange. This interchange created easier access to Arco Arena, a major center for Sacramento sporting events and entertainment. The interchange is also an excellent example of using alternative funding sources instead of traditional financing from state or federal agencies. Local development bonds paid for the Truxel Road interchange. In recent years, dramatic changes in state and federal funding have made it necessary for local agencies to seek other means to finance their ongoing construction needs. Truxel Road is one of several projects receiving construction financing from nontraditional sources.

Another Dokken Engineering project using an alternate funding source is Crossroads Parkway in the city of Industry (Los Angeles County). The parkway was designed to accommodate the needs of private industry companies located alongside Interstate 605. It represented the first privately funded highway project and was used as a prototype for future development.

Dokken Engineering also has extensive experience with light-rail facilities and elevated structures. The firm developed the "R" Street elevated structure for Sacramento Light Rail. In Southern California, Dokken Engineering designed five major aerial light-rail transit structures and two elevated station platforms for the Metro Blue Line, which runs from downtown Los Angeles to Long Beach. The challenges in designing the Metro Blue Line involved the integration of artwork and sculpture into the design of each rail station along the entire length of the route.

For every project, regardless of scope or size, Dokken Engineering is equipped with state-of-the-art computer-assisted design programs and engineering software that precisely calculates measurements. Gone are the days of using hand-lettered drawings and manual calculations to measure dimensions and stress loads. Computer software gives Dokken Engineering the ability to complete project plans and revisions much more quickly and precisely.

"Now that we have computers, we have even more changes on a job site than we did before. If we want a ditch to be a little wider or deeper, we change the measurements

The Truxel Road/Interstate 80 Interchange offers easier access to Sacramento's ARCO Arena.

on the computer and it redraws the sketch for us in an instant," said Richard Dokken.

Computer models also show three-dimensional drawings of projects at various stages of completion. Dokken Engineering's computer technology also uses video conferencing via computer. Desktop computers also provide a link to extranets facilitating regular communication with clients, the intranet to talk between offices and the Internet for its own Web page.

Dokken Engineering's technology and experience continue to grow as it keeps pace with the changing

The Olympic Boulevard bridge in Los Angeles was retrofitted to better withstand the force of an earthquake.

needs of communities. Even with computers as the tool of choice for communications and design, Dokken Engineering accepts no substitute for the hands-on collaboration and community-driven solutions it continues to deliver.

LPA Sacramento, Inc.

The gold rush first drew the world's attention to Sacramento, and the city's unique setting still attracts people from around the globe. Located in one of the world's most fertile farming regions, Sacramento has a climate and agricultural heritage that has profoundly shaped the built environment over the past century. Gradually, however, architecture became less locally oriented and distinctive. Then, 25 years ago Lynn Pomeroy formed LPA Sacramento to approach architecture in a new way that reflected an acute awareness of the physical environment.

This multidisciplinary approach combines architecture, urban planning, landscape architecture, and interior design to create memorable places that add to the quality of people's lives, enrich the physical location and add economic value to the surrounding area. This design philosophy, which Pomeroy refers to as "place-making," guides every LPA project, large or small. The firm's projects, from Sacramento to Taipei, demonstrate in compelling visual terms how a sensitivity to place produces unique designs that are well suited to the environment and purpose and are inviting places where people can live, learn, work or relax.

In each new situation, place-making begins with what LPA principal and design director Curtis Owyang describes as getting a "sense of place." Although it is based on a thorough understanding of the purpose of the structure, the existing built environment, the local climate and knowledge of building codes and regulations, acquiring a sense of place goes further, delving into the history and culture of each location. Each building LPA designs truly fits into the fabric of its community and neighborhood.

"By looking closely and listening carefully, ideas emerge naturally," Owyang notes. "Projects seem to design themselves, as existing relationships present themselves and solutions take form."

LPA's Natomas Marketplace, a retail complex located at Interstate 80 and Truxel Boulevard, demonstrates the application of the approach. Owyang and principal Ron Metzker drew on the Central Valley's agricultural heritage to design this project, making use of building shapes and materials such as shed roofs and corrugated metal, which recall traditional agricultural buildings. While these forms in the complex evoke farm structures, new materials and colors energize this vibrant retail setting. At Natomas Marketplace, principal Alan Porter, who directs landscape architecture and planning services at LPA, designed groups of trees and plants in parking areas to resemble orchards. Porter plays an active role in the planning of each project. By integrating landscape elements into the larger design, he ensures that the spaces between buildings are accorded as much care and attention as the buildings themselves.

Throughout the area, LPA's projects reflect the distinctive qualities of the Sacramento region by responding to the character of the older structures and the materials from which they were built. At the same time, the local climate, vegetation and intended use also influence the outcome of the design process. Sacramento is as well known for its delta breezes as for its sweltering summers and mild winters. For much of the year, people want to be outdoors. Careful planning of outdoor space can create places that people find both useful and enjoyable all year long.

That's the idea behind the landmark Pavilions Shopping Center on Fair Oaks Boulevard, an outdoor, pedestrian-oriented shopping and dining environment uniquely suited to Sacramento. Meandering walkways and cool corridors connect a network of specialty shops and restaurants. Visitors relax comfortably in inviting alcoves. Landscaped outdoor spaces feature art, fountains and other water elements that form interesting spaces for music events and receptions visitors can enjoy year round.

Place-making, with its emphasis on space, use, history and culture, leads to building designs that are aesthetically superior. At the same time, these projects also perform well in

This interior corridor of the Coca-Cola headquarters in Sacramento features a curved ceiling that resembles the swirl logo found on all Coke products.

The headquarters of the California Farm Bureau Federation is located in a park setting along the Garden Highway in Sacramento.

the marketplace, demonstrating LPA's strategy to develop "value-added design." Value-added designs are cost-effective to build, operate more efficiently after completion and lease more successfully. Mark Posnick, an LPA principal, works closely with clients to analyze building systems and components right from the start, to decrease initial design costs and to reduce operating costs over the life of the structure.

LPA has applied value-added design to a wide range of buildings including commercial, residential, retail, governmental, cultural, educational, industrial and seniors' communities here in the Sacramento region and abroad. Recent projects include headquarters for Coca-Cola, Vision Service Plan and the Sacramento Department of Utilities, as well as the Mather General Aviation Terminal and the California Senate Rules Committee hearing room in the State Capitol. Whenever possible, LPA will design the interiors of the buildings they build using the principles of value-added design and place-making exemplified in the California Farm Bureau Federation Headquarters. Robi Kaseman, who directs LPA's interior design services, developed these interiors using natural materials and finishes which recall the colors, patterns and textures of the California landscape.

The Pavilions shopping center in Fair Oaks has become a Sacramento destination for fine dining and shopping.

The firm designed Folsom Lake College, a new campus for the Los Rios Community College District, which is scheduled for completion in 1999. Principal Rod Round points out that this is the first new community college built in California in 20 years. This campus will serve a population of 15,000 students by taking advantage of technologically advanced learning systems.

Several unusual projects have been designed in Taiwan. One involves a master plan and headquarters complex developed for the 200-square-mile East Coast Scenic Area near Taitung. LPA also developed the master plan and design guidelines for Tan Hai Newtown, a new city for 300,000 people near Taipei, which will include residential, governmental, educational, commercial, cultural and recreational facilities.

From designing distinctive interiors to planning and developing whole new cities, each project receives the same level of attention and design quality at LPA. This commitment to excellence has long been recognized within the architectural profession with national and international honors and acclaim. In 1990, the California Council of the American Institute of Architects presented LPA with the prestigious Firm Award for its outstanding achievements.

While many people understand architecture as simply the design of buildings, LPA's multidisciplinary approach is quite different. The firm's four-fold emphasis on architecture, urban planning, landscape architecture and interior design combines with its philosophy of place-making to give LPA a unique position among architectural firms in this region. This solid foundation of skill and thoughtfulness underlies every project LPA designs in the Sacramento area, across the nation and around the world. In a global economic environment of relentless change, this approach to design strengthens values in harmony with the natural environment. This sensitivity has and will continue to aid the Sacramento region face future growth in a responsible manner, creating an environment for people that is memorable and lasting.

The six-story headquarters building for Vision Service Plan is part of its corporate campus in Rancho Cordova.

The Natomas Marketplace, featuring shopping, dining and entertainment, was designed to reflect the rich agricultural history of the Sacramento Valley.

Marr Shaffer & Miyamoto, Inc.
Structural Engineers

Marr Shaffer & Miyamoto is actively engaged in preserving Sacramento's past as well as building its future. The firm has completed seismic retrofitting projects for the historical Sacramento Federal Building and 80 percent of Old Sacramento's historic buildings, including the Eagle Theater and National Hotel and more recently, the Woodland Hotel, a national historical monument.

West Coast headquarters of The Money Store

Some of the firm's latest work includes over 2.4 million square feet of commercial office development in 1998 and various buildings at California State University Sacramento, including the Student Union Center, the parking structure, Science Building II and, most recently, the six-story steel-framed Classroom II. The structural design for Classroom II incorporates "slotted beam" connections, a revolutionary connection design originating from studies of seismic events such as the Northridge earthquake. Perhaps its most distinctive building, the pyramid-shaped West Coast headquarters of The Money Store, is one of the most advanced structural designs in the United States, with seismic dampers incorporated throughout its steel frame for protection against potential earthquake damage. The firm continuously applies state-of-the-art methods (such as seismic viscous dampers and fiber reinforced plastic) where doing so will reduce clients costs.

U.S. Geological Survey Building

1304 O Street

Marr Shaffer & Miyamoto's collective experience includes commercial, industrial, schools, hospitals, government facilities, hotels, utility buildings and parking structures. While the firm is based in Sacramento, clients are located as far away as Alaska and Japan. This is due to the firm's internationally recognized expertise in the application of state-of-the-art seismic dampers, devices that act like a shock absorber while protecting buildings during an earthquake.

Marr Shaffer & Miyamoto began in 1946 as Arthur A. Sauer, Structural Engineer. Sauer opened the firm at a time when the region was rapidly growing. As communities in California grew, children needed additional classrooms. So for the next 40 years, Arthur A. Sauer specialized in school projects and hospitals, completing approximately 800 over his career.

Eventually, Arthur A. Sauer, Structural Engineer, became Marr Shaffer & Associates as partners Ken Marr and John Shaffer assumed leadership of the firm. Though now semiretired, Ken Marr and John Shaffer are still widely recognized throughout the industry as leaders in their profession. Their work is evidenced in literally thousands

of buildings throughout California. In 1997 the firm's name changed to Marr Shaffer & Miyamoto as longtime associate H. Kit Miyamoto became the president of the firm. Under his leadership the company has firmly established its expertise in the fields of earthquake engineering and seismic damping as well as overseeing the expansion of the firm's client base by 200 percent. The growth of the firm is evidenced by Mr. Miyamoto's decision to open a Santa Monica project office to better service clients in Southern California.

Considering the firm's 50-year history of expertise in structural design, Marr Shaffer & Miyamoto's consulting and design services continue to be an integral part of the structural framework of cities throughout California and beyond.

Cornelius and Company

Jack L. Cornelius Jr. deliberately located his accounting firm a stone's throw from the site of his family's mercantile origins in Old Sacramento. When he hung the new Cornelius and Company shingle at 2nd and R streets on October 1, 1997, it was a triumphant moment in his 30-year quest to become the undisputed captain of his own ship. Jack inherited his inde-

pendent spirit from his grandmother's grandfather, W.S. Cothrin, one of Sacramento's founding merchants.

W.S. Cothrin and Caroline Kip married in Avon, New York, and decided to start their new life as pioneers of the West. Family folklore tells of the honeymooner's overland journey to Sacramento from the East just as the gold rush began in 1849. The intrepid Yankee couple arrived when opportunities for traders were abundant, and W.S. wasted no time setting up shop to supply the hoards of immigrants pouring into the fledgling town. Demonstrating the signature resilience of Sacramento's earliest inhabitants, the Cothrins persevered as the family business went up in smoke or down the river over and over again.

W.S. experimented with many ventures, including successful land speculation, gold mining and livestock trading. Although W.S. was taken advantage of by some of his partners, he eventually found stability in the wood supply and general merchandise business on Front Street in Old Sacramento.

The Cornelius branch of the family became a multi-generational accounting dynasty. Following in his father's footsteps, Jack L. Cornelius Jr. earned his bachelor's degree at California State University, Sacramento in 1963 and accepted a staff accountant position with Porterfield and Company, CPAs. Jack served two years in the Navy Reserve's disbursing office, returned to Porterfield and Company in 1968 and completed graduate work in business administration.

Having accumulated 14 years of experience, Jack founded Cornelius and Company, Certified Public Accountants in 1977 as a partnership. A consensus of the partners to merge the firm with the Pfanner and Tate Accountancy Corporation was reached in 1983, but the new union strained relations between the principals. Several partners left in 1991 and the firm was renamed Cornelius and Company. However, all was not harmonious.

Much as his great-great-grandfather struggled with his various enterprises and business partners, Jack concluded that the only way to end the acrimony was to take sole command of his own future. On December 1, 1994, he formed Jack Cornelius and Company, CPAs with his daughter, Dawn, and three years later, he finally reacquired the exclusive legal rights to his own last name.

Cornelius and Company concentrates on business accountancy, with special emphasis on litigation support. Working closely with attorneys, the firm analyzes liability claims, does business valuation for marital dissolutions and consults regarding settlements and judgments. Jack has been a faculty expert for the Hastings College of Law and conducts seminars in continuing education for the The State Bar of California. Other areas of recognized expertise include tax planning and preparation, financial and estate planning, and management consulting for small- and medium-sized businesses.

Dawn M. Cornelius, a senior accountant for her father's practice, boasts some serious credentials. She received her bachelor's degree in economics from the University of California, San Diego. Her undergraduate career included studies at the University of Lancaster in England. She also earned a master's degree in business administration and one in professional accounting at the University of Washington, graduating with honors in 1994.

Jack L. Cornelius Jr.

Dawn M. Cornelius

Jack feels a deep kinship with the city of Sacramento, which continues to support his practice and his family's legacy. He returns that support through his service on the boards of numerous civic and charitable organizations. One of his favorite organizations is the Sacramento Pioneer Association, which is dedicated to preserving, documenting and communicating Sacramento's rich history.

When the time comes, Jack will pass the Cornelius and Company baton to his daughter, a sixth-generation valley resident. California's capital city owes its prosperity and vast influence to such venerable families — past, present and future.

The Spink Corporation

For more than 70 years The Spink Corporation has helped shape Sacramento. Now one of the largest firms of its kind in this area, offering sophisticated resources like bridge design and water resources modeling, and working with both public and private entities, it began as a one-man operation: civil engineer Joseph E. Spink opened his modest Spink Engineering Co. office in 1926.

The ambitious Spink cast a shrewd eye on the growing city to determine where Sacramento's challenges and his surveying abilities could meet. Realizing that flood control along the American River was a necessity for Sacramento's expansion, Spink campaigned to help establish the American River Flood Control District (ARFCD) and won the right for his company to act as the district engineer. He proceeded to have flooded areas aerially photographed and mapped so the ARFCD could establish flood control measures. The reclaimed land was then available for residential development.

Spink was something of an aesthete as well as a practical planner. He designed one of Sacramento's most endearingly beautiful and prestigious residential enclaves, St. Francis

Civil engineer and surveyor Joseph E. Spink (1889-1959), who founded The Spink Corporation in 1926, was instrumental in the early development of the Sacramento region.

The award-winning Guy West Bridge spans the American River at California State University, Sacramento and the upscale neighborhood of Campus Commons. The Spink Corporation not only designed the bridge, but planned and designed the residential development as well.

Oaks. Its eye-pleasing curving streets and deep housing lots — development features now taken for granted — were advanced concepts in the 1920s.

Throughout the 1930s Spink's company continued to help extend levees along the American River and to build McClellan Air Force Base and reactivate Mather Air Force Base as well. Answering another call to civic duty, Spink helped to establish Sacramento's electrical power provider, the Sacramento Municipal Utility District (SMUD). He was appointed its secretary and served in that capacity for many years.

After World War II, Spink was instrumental in opening unincorporated land to the east and north of Sacramento for badly needed housing development. His engineers and planners mapped and prepared thousands of lots for communities like Arden Park and River Park, as well as along the Highway 50 corridor to Rancho Cordova.

As his company grew, Spink added partners. By 1955 there were five — Enoch Stewart, Robert Hall, Melvin Stover, R. S. Stinchfield and Donal Dean — and they carried the company onward after Spink's death in 1959. The company incorporated in 1960, and in 1967 it acquired both R.W. Millard & Associates of Nevada and Western Aerial Photos Inc. to become The Spink Corporation.

Today, from its bright multistory, self-designed building in suburban Sacramento, The Spink Corporation continues to serve Sacramento's civil, electrical, mechanical, water resources and structural engineering, architecture, landscape architecture, planning, surveying and mapping needs.

To list them all would take an entire page, but some of the many distinctive Sacramento design and construction projects spearheaded by The Spink Corporation during the past 30 years are the Guy West Bridge over the American River, the Campus Commons and Gold River residential developments, Cal Expo, Point West housing/office complex and ARCO Arena. Regional projects have included the El Dorado Hills private community, the Sacramento-Yolo Port District facilities, the Broadstone Racquet Club and the Folsom Sports Complex.

In its capabilities, the corporation has "gone from slide rules to high technology," says 40-year Spink veteran and current Chairman of the Board Theodore J. D'Amico. But Joseph E. Spink's pioneering spirit endures, he notes: "Most firms don't survive the death of the founder. We've remained strong."

Quality of Life

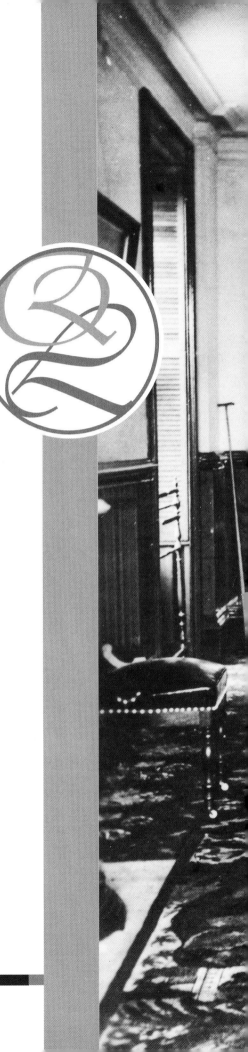

Medical, media, education and religious institutions, as well as recreation-oriented companies, contribute to the quality of life enjoyed by Sacramento residents and visitors to the area.

Sierra Health Foundation

Supporting Community Collaboration and the Improvement of Health Care in the Sacramento Region

Headquartered in Sacramento on the banks of the Sacramento River, Sierra Health Foundation is a private, independent foundation devoted to promoting the health and well-being of Northern Californians. The foundation seeks to impact the health of northern Californians through its grant programs: Health Grants, Community Partnerships for Healthy Children and the Conference Program. From Stanislaus County in the south stretching to the Oregon border and then east to the Nevada border, the foundation's region serves approximately 12 percent of the state's population, or 4 million people, and has distributed more than $40 million in health-related grants to nearly 1,200 nonprofit organizations since its creation in 1984.

In its lifetime, Sierra Health Foundation has addressed some of the most complicated and misunderstood issues of this health care era. From HIV/AIDS to managed care, the evolution of health care has invaded households across the nation,

Sierra Health Foundation Center is located on the Garden Highway in Sacramento.

but nowhere more dramatically than in the foundation's own backyard. For the last 14 years, foundation resources have been allocated to address a variety of the region's most critical health care issues while actively promoting preventive health care and problem-solving activities community by community. Grantmaking over the last 14 years has been focused in health grants, strategic initiatives, a convening/conference program and other educational activities.

Sierra Health Foundation's board of directors is chaired by J. Rodney (Rod) Eason, who is now retired after serving Mercy Healthcare as an administrator for 25 years. Since the inception of the endowment, the board has chosen community-identified concerns over popular issues to guide foundation grantmaking activities — issues that over time, have had a long-term impact on whole communities, families and the overall quality of health care service delivery in the

Letter From The President

Gold Rush Legacy, Metropolitan Destiny: An Illustrated History of Sacramento is an account of history spanning 150 grand years in the Sacramento region. In comparison, the history of Sierra Health Foundation is short. However, the perpetual nature of the foundation's endowment is such that it will provide continued support for Northern Californians well into the future. What follows is the story of Sierra Health Foundation and what it has done to provide for the health and well-being of Northern Californians. Sierra Health Foundation is proud of its accomplishments thus far, but it understands that the prosperous future of the region will also provide challenges to individual and community health. Sierra Health Foundation looks forward to creating partnerships to help address those challenges, providing all a chance for a healthy future.

region. In order to understand some of these issues, research projects were commissioned that have helped the board and foundation staff better understand the complex factors of health and health systems in the region. Publications from that research have served as educational tools for stakeholders in health care, including consumers.

Improved Access to Health Care Services

Sierra Health Foundation has made it a practice to increase and improve access to community health programs through strategic grantmaking initiatives. A study commissioned by the board in 1986 found that there were a marginal number of regionally organized services available to those affected by HIV/AIDS, and vulnerable populations of women in need of prenatal care. In the mid-1980s there was just one physician in the Sacramento area who would see a patient with HIV/AIDS, and community outreach services to pregnant women on Medi-Cal were nonexistent in some areas. After three years and a succession of grants, the foundation was able to forge partnerships with providers to create regional service sites for AIDS patients, some in rural areas where health and social resources were particularly scarce. For the first time in this region, persons affected by AIDS were able to access a comprehensive set of health and human services, including medical and mental health treatment.

This regional collaborative approach to grantmaking prompted a grant program targeted at improving access to prenatal care services for low-income women. As a result of this and similar coordinated efforts, premature births in the Sacramento area went down significantly and the number of nurse and family practitioners available to provide care increased dramatically during this period of time.

COMMUNITY LEADERSHIP

The foundation established its permanent Sacramento home by constructing its headquarters on the Garden Highway alongside the Sacramento River, affording a distant but clear view of the downtown skyline. Encouraged by the quotation attributed to Daniel Burnham, "Make no little plans; for they have no magic to stir men's blood," the Frank Lloyd Wright-inspired building, which is called Sierra Health Foundation Center, was designed and constructed. The center has become an institution of the community which accommodates foundation staff as well as the conference center.

Sierra Health Foundation's Conference Center opened its doors to the community in 1994. Believing that successful leadership in philanthropy comes through community collaboration, commitment, resolve and reciprocity, the foundation's conference program is designed to facilitate health policy and debate through community involvement and leadership. Nonprofit organizations whose missions and goals are compatible with the foundation's are invited to request meeting space.

The conference center is open seven days a week by reservation only. The goal of the conference program is to help health and human service organizations achieve their objectives by providing a neutral meeting facility where community members can gather to address regional health issues. Meeting space and additional convening benefits are given on an in-kind basis to a myriad of groups and affiliations who have come to know the work of the foundation solely through this thriving and much-needed community asset. More than 11,500 community members and leaders, representing 350 nonprofit organizations, utilized the conference center in 1998.

Sierra Health Foundation Board of Directors *top to bottom, from left to right:* Byron Demorest, M.D., Robert Petersen, Fr. Leo McAllister, James Schubert, M.D., George Deubel, Rod Eason, Manuel Esteban, Ph.D., Len McCandliss, Al Jonsen, Ph.D., Wendy Everett, Sc.D.

COMMUNITY MOBILIZATION AND CHILDREN'S HEALTH

The foundation believes that there is great deal more to an individual's health than germs and genetics. There are in fact, many social determinants of health — employment, housing, education and family environment, for example This means that through participation and involvement, communities can help improve the health of all, particularly children.

A desire to improve the health of children led the foundation to create an initiative called Community Partnerships for Healthy Children (CPHC). This 10-year, $20 million commitment was designed to assist communities in a widespread mobilization effort to specifically address the many factors affecting children's health and well-being. In order to maximize the impact of the work, the focus was narrowed to very young children, birth through eight years of age.

A Grant to the El Dorado County Public Health Department was used to purchase and renovate this vehicle for use as a mobile Health Clinic for rural, isolated children and adults.

Foundation staff were asked to identify community collaborative sites with leaders and community members who had "fire in the belly" for issues surrounding children's health — communities which were essentially interested in organizing a movement on behalf of children. Thirty-two communities were chosen for funding and were charged with forming collaboratives; identifying the resources available to them; and forming and implementing strategic action plans.

The CPHC initiative is now in its sixth year and 26 collaborative sites remain, five of them in the Sacramento area. The types of programs and services currently being administered in these communities address a variety of child and family-centered issues, including child abuse and neglect, parenting, affordable child care, safe neighborhoods, substance abuse in the home, isolation, and access to health care and dental services. Each collaborative is a unique success story, and the efforts of this initiative as a whole have gained national attention.

COMMUNITY ASSISTANCE

The Health Grants Program, which welcomes health-related grant proposals of all kinds, continues to be Sierra Health Foundation's touchstone with the communities of Northern California. In response to the need for greater dental health programs in the region, the board of directors recently approved the availability of $500,000 in grant monies to be earmarked for dental health. Many of the foundation's grants seem small in size but result in having a significant impact in their communities. Some examples of recent health grants are: the support for the purchase of a mobile clinic which provides traveling immunization and screening services to people who, for a variety of reasons, do not have access to transportation; implementation of a summer lunch program for children who do not have access to midday meals outside the school year; and the purchase of new mattresses and dental equipment for vulnerable populations in group shelters. Additionally, through the Health Grants Program, $1 million went to a foundation-sponsored research institute that has been built as part of a larger project on the University of California Davis Medical Center campus, establishing a laboratory dedicated to medical research.

Encouraging and strengthening partnerships has been and continues to be an important aspect of the foundation's grantmaking program; connecting with other regional groups and agencies with similar goals accomplishes far more than a single grant ever could. A terrific example of this type of community cooperative effort is the Boys and Girls Club of Sacramento. With land donated by the city, and private and corporate donations from several hundred different sources, this project will secure educational and recreational resources for inner-city youth for many years to come. Sierra Health Foundation is proud to have made a contribution to this important community project.

Most of the foundation's health grants have local significance, but two recent projects funded through the foundation's health grants program have received national attention: The Extreme Care, Humane Options (ECHO) project, a multi-agency effort that provides educational resources for the chronically ill in need of human care at the end of life; and the Health Rights Hotline, an ombuds project offering independent service for consumers who are experiencing difficulty with their health plan or providers in a managed care system. The Health Rights Hotline grant has particular significance because of the high penetration of HMO enrollees in the Sacramento market — among the highest in the country.

Many people do not know that the Sacramento region helped to pioneer the systems Americans have come to identify as managed care. In an effort to understand how exactly this happened, the foundation has published two books related to managed care: The Evolution of Managed Care and Health System Change in the Greater Sacramento Area. These publications were written to be readable, insightful and useful reference materials for anyone trying to understand the regional health care delivery system which exists in the Sacramento area today.

It is through these grantmaking programs, conference and educational activities, publications and partnering capabilities that the foundation provides support in its local community and funding region. So, at a time when a collection of Sacramento area communities are celebrating 150 years of history, Sierra Health Foundation is compelled daily to look around and consider all that

Sierra Health Foundation Center overlooks the Sacramento River and downtown cityscape in the distant skyline.

has developed here and all that has evolved. Once a small town, Sacramento is now a region of enormous size and potential, and the city is a major competitive force in the areas of health care delivery systems, technology and education. A diverse region, it has many riches, but also many needs. As is exhibited on the pages throughout this publication, the Sacramento area is blessed to have so many dedicated community partners identifying and filling those needs.

"THERE IS SOMETHING ABOUT THE INVITING OPENNESS OF SIERRA HEALTH FOUNDATION'S CONFERENCE CENTER THAT BRINGS PEOPLE TOGETHER. IN EACH OF THE (MANY) MEETINGS I'VE PARTICIPATED THERE, THE HEALTH CARE TOPICS UNDER DISCUSSION HAVE BEEN PRESSING AND IMPORTANT, AND MANY OF THE OTHER PARTICIPANTS DID NOT KNOW EACH OTHER. YET, EACH TIME, A MARVELOUS THING HAPPENED — A TREMENDOUS POSITIVE ENERGY AND INTERACTION BETWEEN PEOPLE OCCURRED. THE CENTER'S DESIGN AND LOCATION ON THE RIVER ACTUALLY SEEM TO WELCOME AND ENCOURAGE SOLUTION FINDING" CLARK E. KERR

Sierra Health Foundation was created when Foundation Health Plan converted from nonprofit to for-profit status in 1984. The proceeds from that transaction were $68 million, forming the endowment of Sierra Health Foundation. The endowment reached a value of $150 million in 1998.

A group of healthy children gathered to play at a Community Partnerships for Healthy Children (CPHC) planning event.

California State University, Sacramento

Through a strong tradition of combining quality academics, high-caliber instructors and affordable fees, Sacramento's "Capital University" is one of Northern California's most respected institutions. Encompassing some 300 acres, California State University, Sacramento (CSUS or Sac State for short) is justifiably proud of having celebrated its 50th anniversary in 1997/1998. Originally expected to serve 6,000 students, the school currently boasts an enrollment nearly quadruple that figure.

Legislation to approve a four-year college in Sacramento was signed on July 1, 1947, by then Governor Earl Warren. The college welcomed its first 235-student class on September 19 of that year with a budget of $88,854 and six faculty members. It was called Sacramento State College in those days and it shared quarters with the Sacramento City College campus. John J. Collins of Roseville was the university's first and only graduate on June 3, 1948. Collins helped celebrate Sac State's 50th anniversary by riding in the Founder's Day Parade in a carriage alongside Bernice West, widow of Dr. Guy A. West, Sacramento State's first president and namesake of the campus footbridge over the American River.

The university moved to its current location on the American River in 1953. It opened with seven buildings and 2,000 students. The college was renamed CSUS in 1972. Figures show that by 1998 the school's budget had blossomed to $240 million, and the facility had expanded to 2.6 million square feet. There were 24,000 students and 1,200 faculty members, with an average of one instructor per 23 students. Incidentally, CSUS has an above-average number of instructors with Ph.D.s. More than 3,000 trees have been planted, earning the university its reputation as one of the most scenic campuses in the CSU system.

The university has turned out a number of famous graduates, including Sacramento Mayor Joe Serna Jr., Sacramento Bee columnist Gloria Glyer, State Supreme Court Justice Janice Brown, County Supervisor Muriel Johnson, internationally renowned artist Wayne Thiebaud, Java City CEO Tom Weborg, AT&T's Director of Government Affairs Susan Cavzos, The California Lottery's Executive Director William Popejoy and five-time Emmy-winning journalist Giselle Fernandez. Television host Joan Lunden and Oscar-winner Tom Hanks are two other celebrities who attended CSUS.

The university's direct impact on the local economy has been colossal. With a 1998 payroll of $104 million and 5,200 employees, CSUS is one of the capital region's top 20 employers.

As the seventh largest of the 23-campus California State University system campuses, CSUS ranks second in dollars brought in for research, student services and other forms of sponsored projects.

The university prides itself on providing thousands of educated employees to regional businesses. Offering 60 undergraduate majors and 40 graduate fields, the campus awards more than 4,000 undergraduate and almost 1,000 master's degrees each year. One of every two of those graduates stays in the area. Some 300 company recruiters visit the campus each year.

CSUS graduates are in high demand, according to local technology giants such as Hewlett-Packard and Intel. To even be considered for admission, incoming hopefuls must place in the top one-third of their high school class. Those high standards pay off for hard-working students after graduation — Sac State consistently makes Hewlett-Packard's Top 10 list of schools for recruitment, along with big names like Stanford and Berkeley.

The university is recognized for its criminal justice program — the fourth largest in the country. Other popular undergraduate majors include liberal arts, psychology and

Graduates of the College of Engineering and Computer Science at California State University, Sacramento are highly sought after by the nation's premier engineering firms and computer manufacturers.
Photo by Sam Parsons, CSUS Media Services

California State University, Sacramento is located on the banks of the scenic American River. A unique pedestrian bridge, modeled on the world-famous Golden Gate Bridge, spans the river.
Photo by Sam Parsons, CSUS Media Services

communications. Approximately one-fifth of CSUS's undergraduate students enroll in the College of Business Administration, which features a burgeoning international program and active exchange programs in countries such as France, England and Korea.

One advantage of attending CSUS is the quality of available internships. Due to its proximity to the state government's center, CSUS is in a unique position to offer students valuable experience at the highest level. Best of all, a student need not be majoring in a government-related field in order to intern for the government. For example, nursing majors can intern for the State Nursing Board, or recreation and leisure studies majors might intern for the State Parks and Recreation District. Undergraduates from prestigious institutions such as Harvard vie for one of four capital fellowship programs at the CSUS Center for California Studies. These intense internships at the highest levels of California government have led some as far as Washington, D.C. for jobs.

CSUS offers other programs not usually found elsewhere — only a handful of campuses nationwide have construction management and government journalism studies programs.

Providing dynamic resources for the community, CSUS operates 30 research institutes and outreach programs that generate nearly $38 million in revenue. For example, Placer Hall is a unique joint venture between the university and the United States Geological Survey (USGS). The building houses the USGS water resources division and creates an opportunity for scientists, faculty and students to network and jointly research paleontology, mineralogy and hydrology.

As one of the few universities offering a master's degree in accounting with a tax concentration, CSUS offers a popular program, run by the College of Business Administration, that trains most of the state's tax preparers. The Tax Talk Partnership sponsors an educational seminar broadcast to 23 sites in California, Oregon and Nevada. The partnership consists of CSUS, the IRS and the Franchise Tax Board. The group is responsible for endowing the Center for Tax Education at CSUS to provide professional education to CPAs, lawyers, IRS agents, tax preparers and the general public.

The Insurance Education and Research Program is another stellar example of the university's outreach programs — its job is to coordinate insurance education programs with existing professional organizations. Its annual insurance career fair attracts more than 1,600 students and 175 local companies.

California State University, Sacramento celebrated its 50th anniversary during the 1997/98 academic year. More than 130,000 alumni now represent the university around the state, the nation and the world.
Photo by Sam Parsons, CSUS Media Services

The music department at California State University, Sacramento provides an outstanding series of concerts and recitals that draw not only students, faculty and staff, but many other residents of the capital region.
Photo by Sam Parsons, CSUS Media Services

Many credit a great deal of the university's recent success to President Donald R. Gerth. Gerth, among the most senior administrator in the 23-campus CSU system, has been a professor and administrators on three campuses since 1958. He has held the position of CSUS president since 1984. As president of the International Association of University Presidents, he has been instrumental in advancing the process of "education in a global marketplace." Although approximately 96 percent of CSUS students are Californians, there are some 600 international students representing 70 different countries. Worldwide, there are 96 CSUS-affiliated universities in 20 countries.

With its innovative programs, ideally located campus and reputation for providing quality education at a reasonable price, California State University, Sacramento is sure to be an academic force to contend with for decades to come.

Los Rios Community College District

On the surface, the Los Rios Community College District's main mission sounds simple — to continue to be the premier education and training resource for the greater Sacramento area.

Its complexities become evident upon examination of all that that mission entails. By the year 2007, the region's population is expected to swell to more than two million. The

number of graduating high school seniors in the area will increase by 46 percent, and the burgeoning health care and high-tech industries here continue to generate a critical need for highly skilled personnel. As more and more workers seek to upgrade their training or switch careers, parents and grandparents are joining young high school graduates in the pursuit of a quality post-secondary education.

The colleges of the Los Rios Community College District are up to the task and have been since Sacramento City College first opened its doors shortly after the dawn of the 20th century. The multi-campus public college district currently enrolls 59,000 students in credit courses and employs 3,800 staff members. This makes it the second-largest community college district in the state.

The district is composed of three — soon to be four — main campuses and eight outreach centers. Sacramento City

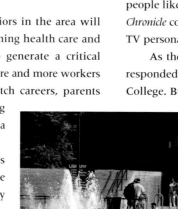

College, which opened in 1916, is the oldest of the three campuses. For nearly 40 years, it remained the only institution of higher learning in the capital city. Located along Freeport Boulevard, the college today lists among its many exemplary programs nursing, dental hygiene, physical and occupational therapy assisting, and aviation and railroad operations. Performing and visual arts programs, including commercial music and studio recording, are also SCC highlights.

With a student enrollment of 23,000, American River College is the largest of the three colleges in the district and one of the largest community colleges in the state. The college was established in 1955 to serve the rapidly developing areas around McClellan and Mather air force bases. At that time, Aerojet and McDonnell-Douglas had recently located in Sacramento, creating jobs for scientists, engineers and skilled electricians. The college, located on College Oak Drive, is known for academic excellence and is among the top community colleges in the state in transferring students to the University of California and California State University systems. ARC was one of the first community colleges in the nation to offer programs in gerontology and geographic information systems (GIS).

In 1965, American River and Sacramento City colleges joined under the Los Rios Community College District banner. Together they continued to meet Sacramento's educational and training needs and to graduate people who would go on to make a difference in the community and the world beyond — people like former Senator Albert Rodda, the late *San Francisco Chronicle* columnist Herb Caen, former Mayor Burnette Miller, TV personality Joan Lunden and movie star Tom Hanks.

As the area south of Sacramento developed, the district responded by creating a third college: Cosumnes River College. Built in 1970, CRC offers a full-transfer program, as well as many career programs including communications media, environmental technology, medical assisting, allied health, veterinary technology, culinary arts management and telecommunications. The main campus also operates the Folsom and El Dorado centers in Folsom and Placerville, enabling students along the Highway 50 corridor to avail themselves of a variety of educational opportunities.

A fourth college, Folsom Lake College, is being planned to replace the Folsom outreach center by 2003. Projections indicate Folsom's population will increase by 50 percent from 1995-2006, more than double the statewide

growth rate of 20 percent projected for the same period. Enrollment is expected to reach 11,000 by 2006. As the first accredited California community college of the new millennium, Folsom Lake College aims to set a new standard for community colleges nationwide that will significantly change the way education is delivered. Emphasis will be on access to technology and greater flexibility in classroom format.

Ever conscious of its role within the community, the Los Rios Community College District offers special economic development services in addition to its colleges and outreach centers, including a Center for International Trade Development, a Regional Health Occupations Center and a Workplace Learning Resource Center. The Training Source offers customized training and education for employers and their employees in the Sacramento area. Contract courses, scheduled throughout the year, vary from a single workshop to a series stretching over weeks or months. Since 1986, The Training Source has provided training to more than 30,000 workers in the capital city.

The Greater Sacramento Small Business Development Center caters to the unique needs of the small business community. It provides comprehensive assistance in the areas of general management, business planning, financial resources and marketing services to those who own or are thinking of starting a business.

In countless ways, the Los Rios Community College District has distinguished itself in excellence. Since 1985 the district has offered a transfer-guarantee program for applicants to the University of California at Davis, University of the Pacific and the California State University campuses in Sacramento, Chico and Fresno. This means that students who complete the prescribed general education program and receive grades of C or better are guaranteed admission as juniors to these institutions. Los Rios is second in the state in transfers, and studies show that students who take this route perform as well or better than students who entered those universities as freshmen — and save a lot of money in the process.

Another hallmark of the district is its tailored approach to community education: here there is no cookie-cutter program of study. When specific needs beckon, Los Rios responds by creating a curriculum specially suited to its students and the community. For example, when representatives of the high-tech industry came knocking on its door, the district initiated a program called TechForce 2000, which promises to graduate 1,000 students per year in the computer and electronic fields.

The word "community" in the Los Rios Community College District is truly an important word. The district is committed to improving the quality of life for all residents in the Sacramento area and takes seriously its integral role in perpetuating the region's prosperity. Its outstanding faculty and award-winning programs in virtually every department help make it an institution in which everyone takes pride.

Sutter Health

With You for Life...

Seventy-five years ago Sacramento was recovering from the devastation of an influenza epidemic. A group of physicians who had tended hundreds of patients met with other leading citizens and decided Sacramento needed a state-of-the-art hospital to better meet the needs of the community. Building upon the foundation of the city's first hospital at the site of Sutter's Fort, they began

what has become one of Northern California's leading centers of care — Sutter Medical Center, Sacramento.

From the founding of the first hospital, the sophistication of services provided by Sutter has grown with the needs of the community. In delivering more than 280,000 births over the years, Sutter has become the leading women's and children's center for excellence care in the Sacramento Valley.

Sutter opened the city's first cancer center in the 1940s, with the installation of the nation's second high-voltage radiation center in 1947. Over the years, the Sutter Cancer Center has been a national leader in clinical trials for treatment of prostate, ovarian and breast cancer. Sutter's pediatric hematology/ oncology program is one of the busiest in the world. The Sutter Cancer Center was the first facility west of the Mayo Clinic to use intraoperative therapy.

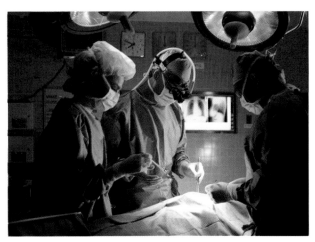

Over the years, Sutter Medical Center developed advanced medical procedures used throughout the world. Much of this research is conducted in conjunction with the Sutter Institute for Medical Research, the largest non-university research center in Northern California. Physicians around the world have used more than 40,000 Cutter-Smeloff heart valves developed by Sutter cardio-vascular surgeon Edward Smeloff, M.D. Sutter orthopedic surgeon William Bargar, M.D. helped develop a robotic surgical device used in complicated joint replacements called ROBODOC™.

In 1959, the first open-heart surgery in the Sacramento area was conducted at the Sutter Heart Institute. Sutter also has the area's only heart transplant center, recognized as having one of the highest survival rates in the nation. The Sutter Heart Institute also implemented the first pacemaker in a Sacramento patient. The institute has the third best medical outcomes in the United States.

The Sutter tradition of providing leading medical care continues today. Sutter Medical Center now has

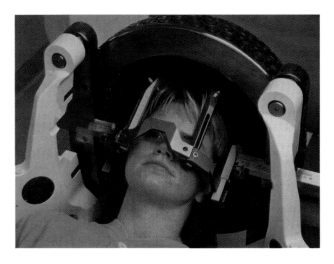

Sacramento Valley's first Gamma Knife equipment, which provides the most precise, fastest recovery rate surgeries for brain tumors and lesions. Patients have come not only from the Sacramento area, but from all over the world.

These advanced services provide the community with the best care available, and they also help establish Sacramento as one of the leading centers of medical excellence in the world. This reputation helps attract leading physicians, nurses, and other health professionals.

Since its beginning with that first community hospital, the facility has grown into a leading medical center. Some of the services Sutter Medical Center performs are listed below:

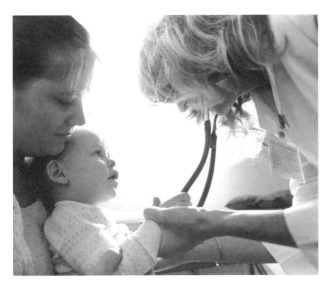

Sutter Women's and Children's Services

- Northern California's leader in obstetric care, with more than 6,000 babies delivered annually in the greater Sacramento area — a total of more than 280,000 babies
- Regional referral center for high-risk obstetric care and pediatrics
- Special care nursery, treating more than 1,400 critically ill infants a year
- Pediatric referral system that makes Sutter one of California's largest providers of pediatric general and intensive care services
- One of the world's largest treatment centers of pediatric hematology/oncology
- Pioneered ECMO (Extracoporeal Membrane Oxygenation) services for full-term babies with lung failure

Sutter Heart Institute

- More cardiac cases of all types referred to Sutter Memorial's Sutter Heart Institute than any other area facility
- Opened the first cardiac catheterization and performed the first open heart surgery in the Sacramento area
- Highest volume pediatric open heart surgery program in the area
- Only Sacramento Valley hospital performing heart transplantation — second highest survival rate in the nation; certified as a Medicare-approved heart transplant center from the Health Care Financing Administration
- Pioneers in advancing cardiac care including first pacemaker insertion and angioplasty in the Sacramento Valley

Sutter Orthopedic Institute

- A center of excellence for orthopedics, performing more joint replacement procedures than any other hospital in California
- Surgery using ROBODOC™, an active robotic surgical assistant, used in precision drilling during hip replacement procedure

- Consistently one of the nation's test sites for new orthopedic technologies, such as the Wiltse Lumbar Spine Internal Fixation System.

Sutter Cancer Center

- One of California's largest, most comprehensive oncology resource and treatment centers, serving over 2,000 new patients a year
- Advanced diagnostic and treatment services, including P.E.T. imaging, radiation therapy, chemotherapy and bone marrow transplantation
- Leading clinical research center, ranking sixth in the nation for the national Cancer Institute's Prostate Cancer Prevention Trial while providing access to over 50 other studies involving prevention, treatment and quality of life
- Patient survival rates for breast, colon and prostate cancer exceed national averages

Sutter Center for Psychiatry

- The area's most comprehensive mental health system
- Provides one of the leading Employee Assistance Programs in Sacramento
- The only children's acute mental health facility in Northern California
- Celebrating 40 hears as the Sacramento Valley's only not-for-profit mental health system

Thanks to community support over the years, Sutter Medical Center's services have flourished. This enables it to respond to the community's health needs with the best clinical service available. Together, the community and Sutter Medical Center have helped create a healthier Sacramento.

UC Davis Health System

The UC Davis Health System has the only academic medical center in inland Northern California, and it is one of the top institutions of its kind in the United States. One of five University of California teaching hospitals, it is the primary clinical education site for the UC Davis School of Medicine.

AS THE AREA'S ONLY PROVIDER OF MANY MEDICAL SERVICES, THE MEDICAL CENTER IS INTEGRAL TO THE HEALTH AND WELL-BEING OF NORTHERN CALIFORNIANS.

It is the leading tertiary-care referral center for 33 counties with more than eight million residents. It also has the region's only level I adult and pediatric trauma center, offering the highest level of emergency medical care available in Northern California.

The medical center is the top health-care provider for underserved and underfunded citizens. Although the medical center has just 18 percent of Sacramento's licensed hospital beds, it serves 30 percent of the area's Medi-Cal patients.

Located on 140 acres in central Sacramento, the medical center is three miles from the state capital and 20 miles from the main UC Davis campus. The university took ownership of the medical center in 1973 to support the clinical and research missions of its then new medical school.

The health system has a network of primary care offices in and around the Sacramento area consisting of 18 primary care offices in 11 locations, with 142 primary care providers. The network, which has a patient base in excess of 250,000, provides routine care and wider access to the

advanced, specialized expertise and technology at the medical center.

Some of those patients in outlying areas may consult with a UC Davis specialist without traveling to Sacramento, thanks to the UC Davis Telemedicine Program. The program uses high-speed digital lines to transmit medical information, including sound and pictures, and enables patients to remain in their primary care physician's office or local hospital while being examined by a specialist at the medical center.

THE AMERICAN NURSE CREDENTIALING CENTER HAS RECOGNIZED THE MEDICAL CENTER'S NURSING STAFF AS ONE OF THE BEST IN THE NATION, DESIGNATING THE HOSPITAL AS A MAGNET NURSING CENTER OF EXCELLENCE. IT IS ONE OF ONLY SIX HOSPITALS IN THE COUNTRY AND THE ONLY ONE IN CALIFORNIA TO HAVE RECEIVED SUCH A DESIGNATION.

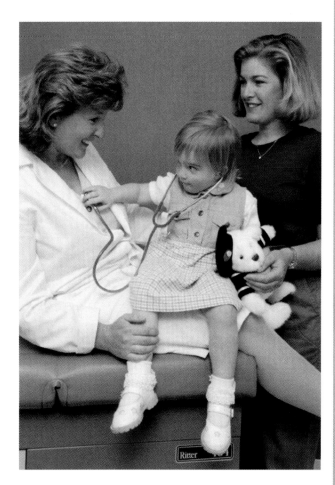

The health system has a number of clinical programs that integrate broad areas of expertise and employ a multi-disciplinary approach featuring state-of-the-art care and leading-edge research.

In the clinical neurosciences program, resources from neurology, psychiatry, neurosurgery and neuroradiology advance treatments for disorders like autism, strokes, headaches, epilepsy, head injuries and sleep disorders.

The clinical cancer program draws on 17 oncologic sub-specialties. New treatments are an integral part of the program's approach because conventional therapies are sometimes unsuccessful. These new therapies, linked to research projects, offer cancer patients sophisticated treatment options available at only a handful of institutions worldwide.

UC Davis children's services provide an array of services, including primary care, surgical and medical specialty care, and behavioral health care. Special services provided by UC Davis Children's Hospital include a level III neonatal service, pediatric trauma and pediatric critical care services, Child Protection Center, Child Life Program and the area's only pediatric emergency room.

The UC Davis Heart Center provides care for patients who experience heart attacks, coronary artery disease, heart valve problems and congenital heart disease. Doctors and patients have access to a full range of adult and pediatric services, including bypass, valve and congenital surgery, intervention procedures, risk reduction and rehabilitation programs, an arrhythmia/pacemaker clinic, heart failure clinic and the women's heart health network.

The Lawrence J. Ellison Musculoskeletal Research Center is developing into one of the world's preeminent clinical and research centers for a wide range of disorders involving muscles and bones, including sports injuries, arthritis and spinal problems. The center features experts from radiology, orthopaedics, physical medicine and rehabilitation, nuclear medicine and neurology.

The UC Davis Transplant Center performs single, solid-organ transplants of the kidney, kidney-pancreas, isolated pancreas, lung and liver. The center allows Sacramento residents in need of an organ transplant to avoid the long travel times and lengthy waiting lists associated with the procedure in the San Francisco Bay area.

The UC Davis School of Medicine plays a prominent role in training doctors for the region. It is the leader among the country's 125 medical schools in producing graduates who practice in California, and it consistently ranks among the top comprehensive public medical schools in primary care training. The school also ranks highly in the percentage of graduates who are underrepresented minorities. It has four student-run clinics that provide free medical care in underserved Asian, African-American and Latino neighborhoods. School of Medicine students, residents and fellows play a major role in educating the public about health, disease prevention and advances in medical treatment.

United Way

The concept of neighbor helping neighbor has always been the code of the West, and today that concept still thrives in the form of United Way California Capital Region. From its first attempts at fund raising, the local health and human services organization has evolved to become the lead catalyst for building the most caring community in the Golden State.

Each year, countless success stories arise from the 190-plus United Way California Capital Region agencies in Sacramento, Placer, El Dorado, Yolo and Amador counties. Families down on their luck are guided back into the workforce. Children who may not have a parent are connected with mentors. People with medical requirements beyond their financial means are provided what they need to survive. The list goes on and on.

Making it all possible are donors large and small who together have raised nearly $13 million a year in recent campaigns. In return, United Way promises to invest in programs and services that deliver measurable and specific results.

Programs such as the Job Training Program and Project Family are two examples of how United Way helps people find and and keep employment. Grant recipients in the job training and skills development category have prepared numerous individuals through job readiness training and have placed additional individuals in long-term competitive employment.

The third target area concentrates on making local neighborhoods healthy and safe. Thousands of individuals and families each year are provided with food, clothing and shelter. Adults and children who have been victimized by domestic violence receive counseling and other services through United Way-funded agencies.

The collaborative approach to fund raising took root in Denver, Colorado, in 1887 when four clergy members became concerned about the multiplicity of appeals in their community. They formed the Charity Organization of Denver to conduct a joint fund-raising campaign with hopes of preventing duplication of services and developing

Community Kickoff 1993

Through the United Way grant process, volunteers select programs with this aim in mind and meet regularly to determine community priorities.

Local United Way grant recipients are placed in one of three funding categories: children and youth; safe, healthy neighborhoods; or job training and skills development. More than 38,000 youngsters each year take advantage of programs funded through United Youth® — programs like Youth Substance Abuse and Violence Prevention, the Reading Tutoring Program and Project SUCCESS, a Greater Sacramento Urban League program that helps students obtain GEDs and create better futures for themselves.

cooperation among agencies that had been competing for community resources.

This process had its beginning in Sacramento in 1923, when 19 agencies banded together to reduce their appeals to a single campaign for all. The organization adopted the name Community Chest, and under the leadership of its first president, Harold McCurry, and its campaign chairman, Clyde Brand, the group raised $217,000 that year. Today, 12 of the 19 original members are still affiliated with United Way California Capital Region: American Red Cross, Boy Scouts of America, Camp Fire, Catholic Social Services, Grace Day Home, Jewish Federation, Sacramento Children's

Home, St. Patrick's Home, Stanford Lathrop Memorial Home, Salvation Army Citadel Corps, Traveler's Aid and the YWCA.

During World War II, fund-raising drives in Sacramento were split between two local agencies: the Community Chest and War Appeals. After the war, Community Chest's eponymous fund-raiser was dissolved, but the public remained dissatisfied with the continued myriad campaigns and overlapping drives.

A study committee was appointed in January 1950 to survey and assess the drives. After two years of study, it recommended the formation of a federated fund-raising organization. On August 14, 1952, the first Sacramento Area United Crusade was established.

William H. Johnson, then president of Anglo California Bank and an active member of several agencies, was named first president of the fledgling organization. Ed Combatalade agreed to serve as the first campaign chairman, and the first goal was set at $1,044,767 — an ambitious undertaking since in the previous year, separate campaigns had raised a total of only $858,070. The goal was exceeded by nearly $1,000 and the money was distributed to 37 local agencies.

Over the years, the Community Chest was phased out and United Crusade enjoyed steady growth, both in terms of member agencies and amounts raised. At the same time, similar fund-raising organizations across the country, all forerunners of United Way, were gathering strength. A major turning point occurred nationally when the Ford Motor Company began offering payroll deduction as a convenient way for its employees to contribute — and prompted United Way's historic shift from being an elitist organization to a populist one.

Today, the concept of "everybody giving a little" is so ingrained that folks may be surprised to learn about campaign tactics from earlier days. A campaign letter from a United Crusade executive to an owner of a small Sacramento confectionery, dated 1934, states that the executive was returning the confectioner's $10 check,

calling it a "ridiculous" amount. The executive then asked for a new donation of "at least $25."

By 1973, such tactics were unheard of. That year, the United Crusade accepted the name United Way Sacramento Area in response to a national effort to identify all community funds under one name while preserving their autonomy. Throughout the 1970s and 80s, the local United Way sought to strengthen its member agencies through programs that assisted in resource management skills. The gifts-in-kind program was also established during that time period.

Today, the United Way California Capital Region, renamed in 1998, continues to seek ways to improve the quality of life for all members of the Sacramento community and beyond, whether or not they are direct beneficiaries of its programs. For every person helped, the ripple effect makes a lasting and far-reaching impact on the integrity of the community as a whole. That is a goal well worth caring about.

Community Kickoff 1996 demonstrates United Way's partnerships with community employers.

University of California, Davis

In addition to its high-profile status and international reputation for excellence, the University of California, Davis, and the surrounding area offer a quality of life unmatched by any other town in Northern California. Known as an environmentally conscious city, Davis boasts more than 50 miles of bicycle paths and more bikes per capita than any other city in the nation. With students making up approximately half of the city's population of 53,000, Davis is one of the few remaining college towns in the state.

The northernmost and physically largest of the nine UC campuses (5,200 acres), UC Davis — originally founded as the University Farm — holds an impressive position for a non-

Ivy League institution. It was admitted in 1996 into the prestigious Association of American Universities, an exclusive "by invitation only" membership organization consisting of just 62 institutions of higher learning. *Money* magazine called it "one of the top 10 best buys" among West Coast colleges and universities. *US News & World Report* consistently ranks it among the top public universities nationally.

The UC Davis School of Veterinary Medicine is the only veterinary school in the state and is the top-ranked institution in the country in the field. The UC Davis Veterinary Medical Teaching Hospital offers care for small and large animals. Among its many clinical services are dentistry, zoological and nondomestic animal medicine and radiology.

The UC Davis Medical Center ranks among the United States' best hospitals, according to *US News & World Report*, in the areas of endocrinology, pulmonary disease, neurology, urology, orthopedics, cancer and otolaryngology.

UC Davis' public service and community outreach programs are a fundamental part of the campus's mission. In 1997 alone, nearly 4,500 UC Davis students, faculty and staff volunteered a staggering one million-plus hours of service to support community development, drug- and alcohol-abuse prevention, environmental causes, education and youth services. Students at the UC Davis law school help disadvantaged clients in such areas as immigration law, civil rights and domestic violence. A class of UC Davis students in human and community development spends spring break working in the Tenderloin, one of San Francisco's poor communities.

World-acclaimed musical performers come to UC Davis each year to share their talents with regional audiences and thousands of Sacramento-area public school students. A UC Davis K-12 partnership with Sacramento public schools, created in 1997, expands mentoring, tutoring and college preparatory programs. The partnership focuses on strengthening teacher training and curriculum, and it

Bright red London buses, ordinarily seen transporting students around the city of Davis, roll along the parade route on Picnic Day, UC Davis' open house, which is held each spring.

Shields Library, one of five libraries on campus that constitute the University Library, houses more than 1.2 million volumes in the subject areas of the humanities, arts, social sciences, biological sciences, agricultural sciences and mathematics.

also funds faculty research on issues surrounding the long-term improvement of K-12 public education. Students in 23 Sacramento-area high schools get a formaldehyde-free approach to biology with "Virtual Heart" computer software. Developed by the UC Davis School of Veterinary Medicine, this humane program allows students to examine a dog's heart without having to perform dissection.

Thanks to a University in the Library program offered in conjunction with the California State Library, residents of small towns in Northern California can select from an extensive list of UC Davis experts who are available to speak on a variety of topics, including local geology, children's literature, nutrition and urbanization of farmland.

And with the completion of the new Center for the Arts, slated to open in 2002, UC Davis will bring the arts to a new stage for the people of the capital region, adding yet another component to the campus's already rich and diverse offerings.

Chancellor Larry N. Vanderhoef eloquently summed up the university's dedication to the community in his annual report, writing, "It's our dedication to outreach that provides opportunities to bring this fine university to the attention of the nation and the world. ... We see education as Thomas Jefferson did, as the cohesive force of any democratic society, the force that provides common experiences and develops critical reasoning skills necessary to further the democratic

aims of our society. Essential to the achievement of these goals is a public education system that offers equal opportunity to all members of society."

It is this generous spirit and dedication to improving the quality of life for people everywhere that will undoubtedly continue to keep the University of California, Davis, one of the nation's most well-respected and highly ranked educational institutions.

Von Housen Motors
Sacramento Jaguar Saab

In 1954 19-year-old George Grinzewitsch, Sr. arrived in America fresh from Germany, with no inkling that he would someday own two of Sacramento's most successful automotive retail centers, Von Housen Motors and Sacramento Jaguar Saab.

After first arriving in New York, a city he didn't care for, he headed to Sacramento, where he had family. He went to school, at what was then called Sacramento City Junior College, during the day, and he pumped gas at night at what used to be Pete and Glen's Richfield station at the corner of 2nd Avenue and Riverside Boulevard.

expanded into sales and secured dealership rights to sell Peugeots, Range Rovers and a line of British cars known as Morgans, as well as the bizarre Amphicar, which was half-auto and half-boat. George Sr.'s longtime friend and partner Carl Meyer passed away in 1964.

1963 marked the beginning of a long-term relationship with Mercedes-Benz in the Sacramento community. At the time, Studebaker Company held the exclusive franchise to all Mercedes-Benz products sold in the United States. However, in 1964, Mercedes-Benz dissolved its relationship with Studebaker and formed its own distribution company,

Despite the fact that he spoke little English and knew little about cars, Grinzewitsch managed to talk his way into a job as a mechanic and later as a service manager for Oxford Motors, a downtown Sacramento auto dealership owned by race-car driver Sammy Weise. Shortly after he began with Weise, he met Delia Roth, whom he married in 1959. While working for Weise, Grinzewitsch developed an interest in road racing. Soon young Grinzewitsch was traveling the West Coast circuit, working as a mechanic and occasionally driving a race car. Later, he would travel the racing circuit as a top-ranked professional driver until the early 1960s, winning several North American driving titles, including the prestigious Pacific Coast Championship in 1962.

In late 1958, Grinzewitsch left Oxford Motors and opened his own auto parts and repair shop with partner Carl Meyer. They named the business Von Housen, which in German means "from the better house." In 1961, the Grinzewitsches had their only son, George Jr. They also

Mercedes-Benz of North America. Of the 800 dealers nationwide who had been selling German cars through Studebaker, only about 100 were retained as dealers by Mercedes-Benz of North America, Grinzewitsch being one of them. It was a rough beginning for Mercedes-Benz in Sacramento — Von Housen's sold only 60 to 70 cars per year.

Grinzewitsch Sr. ventured into many other facets of the automotive industry. In 1964, he opened and operated a BMW/Volvo dealership in Reno, Nevada, which he sold several years later. In 1974, he purchased Roddy Auto Parts, renamed it Von Housen Auto Parts and expanded the retail business into 22 stores before he sold them to Southern Auto in 1996. Grinzewitsch Sr. also partnered up with well-known Auto Dealer Chuck Swift from 1974 to 1980. They bought several Dodge and Chrysler dealerships in Sacramento, Reno and Davis. In 1978, the pair created Van Man, a van conversion assembly company that produced up to 200 units a month.

Quality of Life

In 1977, Grinzewitsch purchased British Motor Cars and later changed the name to Sacramento Jaguar. Once established, the Jaguar store moved to Von Housen's old location on Fulton Avenue between Arden and Alta Arden. Von Housen relocated to its present location at Howe Avenue in 1979.

The year 1984 brought big changes for Jaguar. The Jaguar Rover Triumph Company was dissolved, and only Jaguar would continue to be imported to the United States. Jaguar's success meant another move to a larger location and a subsequent move to the Von Housen Motors site in 1990. The service department moved into what was once the Von Housen body shop, and the sales department shared a showroom with Mercedes.

By 1974, George Grinzewitsch Jr. joined his father at Von Housen Motors, working part time after school as a porter in the detail department and as the warranty administrator. While attending college, he held positions in the parts department and as service department dispatcher. He sold cars at British Motors in 1980 and 1981. He then moved back to the service department where he worked as a service advisor. From 1984-1985 he became service manager at Von Housen. After his extensive training and experience, coupled with his 1985 graduation from the National Auto Dealers Academy, George Jr. became a partner in Sacramento Jaguar. By 1987, George Jr. was the general manager for both dealerships and also joined George Sr. as a partner in Von Housen Motors

Several years later, Jaguar began construction of its own sales facility. After the facility's completion in July of 1995, Jaguar moved into its own brand-new multimillion dollar showroom, and soon after it added a state-of-the-art parts and service facility. With the Jaguar service facility out of the Von Housen location, a top-of-the-line detail and used-car renovation department was established. While the parts and service facility was being built, Sacramento Jaguar acquired the only Saab franchise in the Sacramento area, changing its name to Sacramento Jaguar Saab and posting record sales.

Von Housen Motors was now exclusive for Mercedes-Benz again, and the company completed a multimillion dollar renovation in 1998, adding a new eight-car showroom, all new client areas and a high-tech, 45-bay service department. The previous year, the Grinzewitsches were awarded the light-truck franchise from Mercedes-Benz. Business for the light-truck and Mercedes-Benz cars has improved each year, with 1998 sales topping more than 1,000 new units and $68 million.

The Grinzewitsches were given the prestigious honor of piloting the first Mercedes-Benz Service Center in the United States, located in Rocklin, just 15 miles from Von Housen. The worldwide grand opening was held in June of 1998, and many of Mercedes-Benz's top dignitaries attended.

Sacramento Jaguar Saab stands proudly to display its fine automobiles in the brand-new showroom. In addition to the sales facility, a high-tech service facility was added to complete client expectations for top-of-the-line service.

Through the years both Grinzewitsch Sr. and Grinzewitsch Jr. have been active with numerous affiliations in the auto industry. In the early 80s, George Sr. was president of the Sacramento New Car Dealers Association and has been on and off of the Mercedes-Benz dealer board for the last 15 years. George Jr. recently completed a two-year presidential commitment with the Sacramento New Car Dealers Association, which during his tenure was renamed the Central Valley New Car Dealers Association. In addition to being on the board of directors of the California Motor Car Dealers, in 1999 George Jr. was elected to a two-year term on the Mercedes-Benz Retailer Board.

Very active in charitable activities, the Grinzewitsches support an annual fundraiser called "Unveiling the Best," a wine-tasting event held every year at Von Housen Motors since 1987 that attracts more than 1,000 participants. The event supports charities such as Meals á la Car and the Shriners Hospital. Also supported throughout the year are the River Oak Center for Children, March of Dimes, local schools and the Marble Valley Centers for the Arts.

The Von Housen Motors and Sacramento Jaguar Saab legacy is sure to live on in the Sacramento area for many years to come. In 1993, George Jr. married his wife Denise. Their children, George III and Catherine, may some day follow in their father's footsteps and continue their family's automotive tradition for a third generation.

The Mercedes-Benz Service Center located in Rocklin, just 15 miles from Von Housen Motors, is the first of its kind in the United States. The Grinzewitches were given the prestigious honor by Mercedes-Benz of piloting this new program.

Heald College

The information age was just a gleam in the eye of the future when Edward Payson Heald founded the first Heald College site in San Francisco in 1863. More than 135 years later, Heald College still maintains the school's original philosophy — preparing thousands of students every year to enter the workplace in the shortest practical time.

Two local Heald campuses, in Sacramento and Roseville, are part of the 13-campus network in Northern California, Oregon and Hawaii. Heald first opened a School of Business on the Sacramento campus in 1912, and a School of Technology was added in 1986. The Sacramento campus' School of Business added technology programs in 1999 in response to the growing demand for students trained in business and technology. A business and technology campus in Roseville was added to the Heald family in 1999.

Heald specializes in providing education that meets the demands of the marketplace, with a select group of programs in business and technology. Programs offered consist of

18-month associate in applied science degrees, 12-month diplomas and six-month certificates in networking technology. Most programs are offered through day or evening classes and involve hands-on training on computers or with electronics equipment.

Heald students receive personal attention in several program areas including accounting, computer business administration, business software applications, legal office administration, medical office administration, computer technology, electronics technology and networking technology in Microsoft® Windows NT™, Cisco Systems and Novell. The campuses provide lifetime job placement assistance to its degree and diploma graduates, reinforcing

Heald's mission to prepare and help students succeed in the workplace.

Heald College has a colorful history, which began when 20-year-old Edward Payson Heald rented two rooms on Post Street in San Francisco, organized the school and called it Heald's Business College. It was the first business school in the western United States.

Shortly after opening, the school moved to larger quarters on the same street and stayed at that location until the building burned in fires caused by the 1906 earthquake. Although the infamous disaster destroyed the initial building and nearly forced the school's closure, a group of quick-thinking students rescued the school's most valuable assets, its 26 typewriters, and buried them in Union Square to protect them from fire and looting.

By 1912, there were nine Heald Business College locations in California, and Heald added the engineering and automobile school in 1921. The schools were reorganized and consisted of four locations — San Francisco, Oakland, San Jose and Sacramento. The engineering school was the precursor to Heald Institute of Technology, a separate division of the college, which opened in 1970.

Over the decades, many other changes have taken place. In 1978, Heald Colleges became a nonprofit corporation, using its minimized taxation status to reinvest surplus dollars in equipment, facilities and personnel. In 1983, Heald's accreditation through the Western Association of Schools and Colleges (WASC) was affirmed. In 1995, Heald Colleges' Web site appeared for the first time on the Internet. In August 1998, Heald consolidated its San Francisco and Oakland campuses to create the new San Francisco Schools of Business and Technology.

Computers have become an important part of Heald's curriculum, as the college has more than 4,500 computers throughout the 13 campuses. At each Heald campus, students have individual access to the technology appropriate to the program they are studying, and learn by working with equipment that they will ultimately find in the workplace.

With the growing demand for technical employees, Heald Colleges has instituted a curriculum development process that will ensure its programs reflect market demands for employment in the information age. As part of Heald's overall expansion strategy, additional campuses will become combined business and technology schools, serving a larger number of students with a wider array of programs, student services and equipment to give each Heald graduate a head start on a successful future.

The Sacramento Ballet

Barbara and Deane Crockett founded The Sacramento Ballet as a regional ballet company in 1954. In 1986, it became a professional company. Under the seasoned artistic leadership of renowned choreographer/director Ron Cunningham and former Boston Ballet soloist Carinne Binda, the company is skyrocketing to national prominence. This married couple celebrated their 11th anniversary with The Sacramento Ballet during the 1998-99 season. Together, the pair has helped bring the ballet in Sacramento to a higher level of artistic excellence. Dancers who have trained in their apprentice program have gone on to dance with The Joffrey Ballet, The American Ballet Theatre, The San Francisco Ballet, The Houston Ballet, The Atlanta Ballet and The Richmond Ballet.

Cunningham, also formerly with The Boston Ballet, has created more than 60 ballets for the international stage. Receiving critical acclaim everywhere including London, Peking, Shanghai, Rome and Milan, his work is known and admired worldwide. He has worked with such notable artists as Rudolf Nuryev, Edward Villella and Agnes de Mille. His re-creation of *Cinderella* was the first American ballet to be seen in the People's Republic of China and was televised to over 30 million viewers. The December 1999 performance of *The Nutcracker* will mark the 32nd year it has been presented by The Sacramento Ballet and the 12th season celebrating Cunningham's re-staging of this beloved holiday classic. This annual Sacramento event features 420 children participating on stage for 19 performances.

Binda, having performed lead roles in more than 100 ballets, has also made a major mark in the world of dance. Audiences and critics have praised her work for her performances in more than a dozen international tours. She has thrilled audiences from Boston to China in her roles as the Sugar Plum Fairy in *The Nutcracker* and in the title role in *Cinderella*. She has acted as ballet mistress for Rudolf Nuryev's *Swan Lake* and *Don Quixote* and has coached Sacramento Ballet principal dancers into the final round of the International Competition in Paris.

All regular-season performances are held at the Sacramento Community Center Theater. The company performs for roughly 70,000 people each year. Revenue is derived largely through ticket sales, which cover only 65 percent of the ballet's yearly expenses. Therefore, The Sacramento Ballet seeks underwriting for its various performance expenses, community programs and collaborations. It employs 21 full-time professional dancers, plus apprentices.

Despite a relatively small budget — $1.4 million dollars — The Sacramento Ballet contributes generously through a number of community outreach programs. Dancepower is an in-school student program reaching 17,000 students in 65 schools. Concentrating its efforts on economically disadvantaged students, the program includes interactive dance presentations, the opportunity to attend ballet studio rehearsals, ticket vouchers for a ballet and selected scholarships to ballet summer classes. Free tickets and programming are provided to over 40 community groups including Operation Headstart, the Mustard Seed School, River Oaks Center for Children and the Salvation Army, to name just a few.

From: Graduation Ball
Pictured: Amy Seiwert *(in air)*, Rome Saladino and Kirsten Bloom *(rear)*

In addition, The Sacramento Ballet presents activities for children at community events such as Children's Festival and Kids Fest. At Saint Hope Academy, a team of dancers provides twice weekly summer dance classes for educationally at-risk students. The classes culminate in student-choreographed performances. The ballet works in collaboration with Axis, a company of physically challenged dancers, through choreography and performance. The ballet also works with the NorCal Center for Deafness to help improve communication and access for the hearing impaired. At Shriners Hospital, teams of dancers give demonstrations and talks on dance and ballet.

The Sacramento Ballet's general philosophy is rooted in the belief that a strong cultural life makes the city more attractive to businesses and individuals considering relocation. It is firmly committed to providing the best of both classical and contemporary ballet, increasing accessibility to the performing arts for the entire community, and ensuring that ballet and other arts institutions flourish in Sacramento.

Sacramento County Historical Society

From its small beginning over 40 years ago, the Sacramento County Historical Society has been an active, productive and prestigious organization. It is recognized as an outstanding local/regional history society whose reputation extends far beyond the nominal boundaries of its title. The founding meeting on May 28, 1953, was chaired by Dr. Joseph A. McGowan,

Joseph McGowan, principal founder and organizer of the Sacramento County Historical Society
Photo by Mary McGowan

Dr. Edward Howes is a charter member of the Sacramento County Historical Society still very actively involved after 46 years of membership. Now in retirement as a history professor, he remains highly engaged with the programs and activities of the society, recently serving as vice president and writing the "Gold Rush" chapter in this book.

of the Sacramento State College history faculty, and was held on the campus of that college (California State University, Sacramento, since the 1970s). From that first meeting of 2 persons, the society grew in its first year to 56 persons, of whom 47 were charter members, and ultimately to a membership of more than 400 in recent years. The society's roster of officers, directors and active members from all walks of life has read like a who's who list in Sacramento city and county, united in the cause of promoting and preserving our local history, which is in many ways a microcosm of our state and national history.

The format of regular monthly meetings from September through June included brief announcements, any business requiring members' action, followed by a featured speaker giving an oral presentation on some aspect of local/regional history, based on his or her orig-

inal research. The society also decided to publish a monthly newsletter, *Golden Nuggets*, with short announcements of future program speakers and special activities, plus brief tidbits of local history by society members. Further, a second publication, the quarterly *Golden Notes*, would include in each issue one or more longer articles of original research as well as edited documents from historical source materials submitted by members and other historians. The files of these publications, from their early modest beginnings, present an amazing array of significant and interesting pieces of local/regional history which cover a time span from the pioneer years before the Gold Rush Era to the recent decades of the 20th century. From the first issues these publications have found a place not only in our local and state public and private libraries and educational institutions, but in those of other states as well. In this way the society has made a contribution to the growing body of history in the western regions beyond California, as well as in its home base. A representation of the talented work by members of the society is found in the chapters of this new sesquicentennial history of the city and county of Sacramento.

Sacramento Light Opera Association

As the capital city's oldest professional performing arts organization and California's largest nonprofit musical theater, Sacramento Light Opera Association (SLOA) presents two seasons of musical theater: Music Circus and The Broadway Series. It also boasts a quickly growing outreach and education program. SLOA members gladly contribute support for projects such as the internship programs that provide professional training for aspiring students; "ArtsAlive!", which exposes under-served populations to live theater; dramatic-training programs for students and teachers; and the Martin Luther King Jr. Project, a showcase for theatrical works created and performed by African-Americans.

The original Music Circus was conceived in 1949. This unique venue showcased musical theater productions in an informal tent arena where everyone had a good seat. When Eleanor McClatchy, president of *The Sacramento Bee*, invited Broadway producers Russell Lewis and Howard Young to establish a Music Circus in Sacramento in 1951, the pair jumped at the chance. The Sacramento Music Circus was the first of the new "tune tents" west of the Mississippi and only the fourth in the entire country. It was a hit from the start, and became the popular thing to do on a summer evening.

Formally incorporated as the Sacramento Light Opera Association in 1953, Music Circus has become a training ground for Broadway-bound actors. Tony-nominated actors Joel Grey, Douglas Sills and Susan Egan starred at Music Circus before making their Broadway debuts.

Now under the leadership of producing director Leland Ball and managing director Richard Lewis, this first-class summer stock season that celebrated its 48th anniversary in 1998 has become the predominant landmark on Sacramento's cultural landscape. Each year nearly 100,000 patrons attend musical theater in the 2,500 seat arena-style tent, the last of its kind. The creative team, cast and crew are gathered from New York, Los Angeles and Sacramento to produce the seven-show season. Each year, more than 350 ushers and dozens of production workers volunteer their services for the honor of serving on these beloved productions.

Since 1989, Sacramento Light Opera Association has also presented The Broadway Series, an offering of the best of

Linda Thompson Williams sings out as Bloody Mary in the 1998 Music Circus production of Rogers and Hammerstein's *South Pacific*. *Photo by Steve Kolb*

Broadway-style theater on a traditional proscenium stage. Located across from the Capitol in the spacious Community Center Theater, The Broadway Series attracts more than 150,000 theater lovers a year to downtown Sacramento to see blockbusters such as *Les Misèrables, Cats, Miss Saigon* and *Phantom of the Opera*. Faye Dunaway, Robert Goulet, Tommy Tune, David Cassidy, Petula Clark, Savion Glover and Carol Channing are just a few of the stars who have graced The Broadway Series' stage.

In the summer of 1998, SLOA was awarded the prestigious Rosetta LeNoire Award by Actors' Equity Association, the professional actors' union, in recognition of the theater's "long-term leadership in non-traditional casting" — that is, casting women and ethnic minorities in parts that they previously could not access. It was the first West Coast theater, as well as the first musical theater, to receive this important national honor.

The Sacramento Light Opera Association is committed to presenting quality theatrical productions that enrich the cultural life of all citizens. The organization's goals include preserving and expanding American musical theater as an art form by educating new audiences and nurturing aspiring artists.

The one-of-a kind Music Circus Theater on a late summer evening
Photo by Diana Hudson

Sacramento Theatre Company

Since its inception in 1942, the Sacramento Theatre Company has committed itself to excellence. The group was formed when Sacramento citizens responded to the need to entertain the armed forces during World War II. After a successful tour of local military bases, the group, then known as the Sacramento Civic Repertory Theatre, was formally organized. One of the goals was to build a theater facility capable of accommodating the creative work that was being performed. On October 18, 1949, that dream came true with the opening of the Eaglet Theater, now known as The McClatchy Mainstage.

The new company experienced many theatrical challenges and successes. During the 1950s, West Coast premieres, plays straight from Broadway and theatre festival competitions were presented at the arena. During the 60s, the theatre responded to a changing world and reflected the turbulent times by thriving on works from master

Shakespeare's *Pericles* played on the STC McClatchy Mainstage November 3-December 6, 1998. Pictured are Bob Devin Jones as Pericles and Erinn Anova as Pericles' daughter, Marina.

playwrights such as Arthur Miller, Gore Vidal, Noel Coward, Tennessee Williams, Eugene O'Neill and Eugene Ionesco. Maxwell Anderson and Kurt Weill's daring musical condemning South African apartheid entitled *Lost in the Stars* spurred interest throughout the Sacramento community. By the early 70s, the Eaglet had spread its wings to include at least one musical each season. During the 1980s the organization had redefined its identity, renamed its famed arena and changed its name to the Sacramento Theatre Company, complete with paid positions in every artistic, technical and administrative capacity.

Today the nonprofit STC, as it is called, presents public performances of classical and modern plays in two theatres from September to June with eight performances a week and more than 300 performances per year. The two stages consist of the McClatchy Mainstage and STC's Stage Two. The McClatchy Mainstage, named for Eleanor McClatchy, whose inspiration and support made STC a reality, seats 300 patrons in a proscenium auditorium. There are three sections and each seat provides a clear view of the stage and excellent

acoustics. The Mainstage also includes a spacious, remodeled lobby offering a gift shop, concessions and a bar that which serves a variety of beers and wines. STC's Stage Two is a 90-seat, black-box theater in which theatergoers experience live theatre on the most intimate level possible. Providing only three rows of seats, the audience is thrust into the on-stage action. Stage Two also offers outdoor concessions and allows patrons to bring their refreshments inside the theater.

During the 90s STC embraced Sacramento's multiethnic population with a repertory of many colors. Stage Two has played host to new, cutting-edge works. Outreach and education programs have brought many Sacramentans closer to the power of the theatrical experience. While the sum total of all the sponsored programs are too numerous to mention in their entirety here, STC has been the recipient of numerous honors for its wide array of education and outreach programs. For example, Business Volunteers for the Arts, a Sacramento-based arts advocacy group, awarded STC its Business/Arts Partnership Award in back-to-back years for collaborative programs with The California Wellness Foundation and the Juvenile Justice System (for workshops held in youth detention centers), and City and County Waste Management & Recycling Divisions for recycling shows that tours area K-12 schools. These recycling productions focus on the process and value of recycling and reach more than 45,000 students per year.

PLAY, an acronym for Plays, Literature and You!, is a unique program that targets economically disadvantaged schools for comprehensive play study and attendance. STC regularly sponsors pay-what-you-can performances, a significantly discounted student matinee program and youth subscriptions. The Acting Out school tour reaches more than 20,000 students annually with professional actors' productions featuring multicultural themes. The Senior Circle program offers theatergoers 60 years and older with highly discounted ticket prices, a preshow lecture/discussion and a postshow question-and-answer forum with the cast. In addition, Senior Circle participants are seated in the front of the house to ensure the best possible conditions for hearing and seeing the show.

According to STC's mission statement, the company believes, "Our responsibility as a resident theatre means providing opportunities, both within and without our walls for all residents of the Sacramento region to learn about and experience professional theatre." By creating art of a national standard, developing new plays, reinventing the classics and promoting innovation in all areas of the theatre, Sacramento Theatre Company will help shape the American theatre of the future.

Technology

A large and diverse group of businesses combine to make Sacramento one of the country's leading centers of technology innovation, development, manufacturing and employment.

USCS International, Inc.

It used to be that all a business owner needed for customer management and billing was a good calculator and a pen. But in today's global marketplace — in which huge companies are handling millions of customer accounts, each with multiple detailed transactions — that just isn't possible. Sophisticated computer software and billing services are the solution, and USCS International, Inc. is the company that provides that solution.

As the Sacramento area's first high-tech company and its largest software developer, USCS International is the kind of homegrown-business-makes-good story about which chambers of commerce love to rave. More than 30 years ago, the parent company of CableData and Output Technology Solutions was launched locally as a one-man operation by company founder Bob Mathews, and it has since become a leading global provider of customer management software and statement processing for the communications, utilities and other service industries. Its clients include providers of cable television, wireless and wireline telephony, direct broadcast satellite, electricity, water, gas, waste management, utility and multiple services in more than 30 countries.

USCS International, Inc. Chairman and Chief Executive Officer Jim Castle accepts an award from San Francisco 49ers coach Steve Mariucci at Sacramento's 12th annual Best In Business awards ceremony in 1997.

Founded in Sacramento over 30 years ago, USCS International, Inc. is a worldwide leader in customer management software and statement processing services.

CableData

USCS International's subsidiary, CableData, is a leading provider of customer care and open billing solutions to the global communications and utilities industries. CableData's customers include some of the largest U.S. cable operators, representing a significant portion of the North American cable market. In addition to its headquarters in Rancho Cordova and its software development center in El Dorado Hills, CableData also has several other U.S. locations, as well as offices in England, Brazil and Australia.

Leveraging its market leadership in the traditional U.S. cable industry, CableData is poised to maximize the increasing opportunities in digital television, interactive services and direct broadcast satellite worldwide. A major vehicle that company leaders see for advancing its growth is CableData's Intelecable® product. With this revolutionary software, CableData was the first company to offer integrated cable and telephony open-billing solutions. The product is designed to tap into the convergence of cable and telephony services occurring in many parts of the world, offering a system that can manage multiple services on a fully integrated basis. Intelecable is installed in numerous countries, including Britain, Japan, Australia and the United States.

In 1998, Output's El Dorado Hills facility underwent a 118,000-square-foot expansion that is enabling it to double the facility's processing capacity. This expansion has helped create additional job opportunities at Output, which is already El Dorado County's largest private employer.

The company entered an exciting new era in statement processing in 1997 — electronic bill delivery and payment. With its electronic billing solution, Output can offer billers the ability to deliver statements for viewing and payment via their own Web sites, through electronic bill consolidators or through "invited-pull" technology. One of its first customers was none other than its sister company, CableData, which now offers electronic billing to its large customer base.

Output Technology Solutions

Output Technology Solutions, another USCS subsidiary, is a market leader in cable TV and telecommunications billing and is rapidly expanding its capabilities in order to serve other industries, such as financial services, waste management and express delivery services. Each month, Output prints and mails approximately 130 million pieces of mail, making it one of the largest first-class mailers in the nation.

Its teams of software engineers have designed sophisticated systems for electronically receiving billing data from its clients, processing the data and laser-printing it on statements. The company holds several patents for custom-designed software applications, and additional patents are pending. Output also produces the inserts and envelopes for the statements, which are then packaged and sorted for mail delivery to the airport, where they are directly mailed to local post offices. It is this supreme efficiency that distinguishes the company.

A Good Corporate Citizen

As a major high-tech company in the Sacramento area, USCS strives to address community needs in ways that reflect the company's values and overall goals. Its Mathews Educational Charitable Trust, for example, underwrites some of the most innovative local projects involving technology and education. A recent recipient was the Boys & Girls Clubs of Greater Sacramento, which received an $85,000 grant to fund a state-of-the-art computer learning center at its new facility in downtown Sacramento. The annual grant is funded entirely by USCS, its employees and vendors.

The company supports other local organizations including the American Heart Association, the Arthritis Foundation, Big Brothers/Big Sisters, Challenger Learning Center, El Dorado Women's Center, the Sacramento Public Library Foundation, St. Hope Academy and United Cerebral Palsy of Greater Sacramento, to name just a few.

USCS International has been named Best in Business by the *Sacramento Business Journal* and one of The 200 Best Small Companies in America by *Forbes* magazine. USCS was also lauded for its internal Web site, "The In-Site," by *CIO Web Business* magazine, which named the site one of the top 50 company intranets. USCS and its subsidiary, Output Technology Solutions, are past winners in the Vanguard Awards, which recognize companies in the capital region determined to be on the leading edge of their industries.

MATHEWS EDUCATIONAL CHARITABLE TRUST
2960 PROSPECT PARK DR
RANCHO CORDOVA, CA 95670

1012

August 7, 1998

PAY TO THE ORDER OF **Boys & Girls Clubs of Greater Sacramento** $ 85,000.00
Eighty-Five Thousand Dollars   DOLLARS

Bank of America

NON-NEGOTIABLE

Capital Records Management

Locally owned and serving Sacramento since 1923, Capital Records Management offers area businesses an alternative to expensive storage units. This client-oriented full-service company focuses on off-site storage and delivery of business records.

As every business owner knows, a good records-retention program is essential to maintaining history, developing strategic plans and protecting confidential information. The older the business, the longer its records have been stored, often at considerable cost. Efficient record-keeping can save money, reduce storage space, cut personnel time and improve access to important information. Perhaps most importantly, it can help ensure legal compliance and protect a company during litigation, government investigation or audit.

According to Capital Records Management CEO Tracy Calvillo, who runs the business with her husband Ralph, knowing how long to archive old records is another important ingredient in the records-keeping mix. The company's expertise allows it to effectively advise clients on such matters. For example, not everyone is aware that items such as employee medical records must be maintained for a period of 30 years. Depending on how big a company is or its employee turnover rate, the amount of accompanying paperwork can be quite large. And there's more — most experts agree businesses should maintain corporate records including articles of incorporation, licenses, permits, annual reports and stock records. Payroll and pension documents should also be kept permanently. Failure to keep certain personnel records can result in stiff civil penalties. Other important documents to keep include accounting and financial records, correspondence, environmental records, tax records and supporting documents, which again, should be kept indefinitely. All of these records add up to one colossal pile of paper.

On the other hand, since keeping records for too long can also sometimes become a liability for a company, Capital Records offers regularly scheduled shredding and recycled destruction services.

Capital's completely secure warehouse environment ensures safety.

Companies rely on firms such as Capital Records for a number of reasons. Throughout its long history, Capital Records has offered a secure, convenient and economical method for maintaining, retrieving and delivering important documents for its clients. Its spacious facility is fireproof and free of bugs and rodents. The firm provides pickup and delivery services as well as detailed inventory reports via its state-of-the-art computer system. Use of companies like Capital Records helps maximize costly — and often limited — office space and reduce labor costs by eliminating the need for employees to spend precious time searching through old archives. Records are confidential and kept under tight surveillance by 24-hour monitored security.

All of these services are surprisingly affordable. Capital Records Management estimates that using these services costs 40 percent less than the cost of renting a mini-storage unit.

Although Capital's inventory of client records is maintained using an intricate, state-of-the-art computer system, most of the actual records are kept on good old-fashioned hard copy, stored in boxes. One might expect the hard copies to be converted into some sort of electronic format, but the Calvillos carefully try to steer clients away from that, because paper isn't likely to become obsolete any time soon. Converting data every time the technology changes is not only time-consuming but, more importantly, expensive for the customer.

The firm's more than 200 clients include banks, accounting firms, bakeries and auto parts suppliers. In addition to storing records for the Sacramento County, the city of Sacramento and other municipalities, Capital also maintains some of the U.S. government's vital records, which is no small honor. The federal government's security, fireproofing and legal standards are extremely rigid.

Protecting several billion dollars of records in more than 200,000 boxes throughout its facilities, Capital Records boasts many long-term clients who appreciate its commitment to providing convenient, safe service at an affordable price.

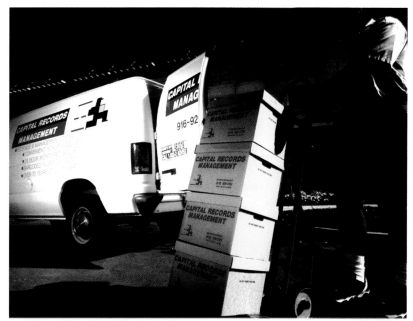

Capital Records Management's in-house delivery service provides convenience and value.

State-of-the-art systems for confidentiality and tracking service

Ferrari Color

Maggie Ferrari was exceptionally interested in manipulating photographic images in the darkroom, so in 1979 she went to work for Hacker Color, a Sacramento-based commercial photo lab. By 1990 she had worked her way up through the company from an entry-level position to vice president of the lab and outside sales. When the 90s ushered in digital imaging, making the traditional darkroom obsolete, her partner Floyd Hacker decided to retire and Ferrari bought the business. Ferrari purchased the company for $400,000 and three years later invested another $350,000 to transform the photo lab into a comprehensive digital-imaging facility. When computers entered the business, the darkroom door closed for the last time.

A composite photograph was created for Sacramento Magazine to depict the look and feel of Sacramento in a creative way. The region's bike trail, one of the best anywhere, took center stage.

In addition to providing photographic processing and printing, Ferrari Color specializes in producing large visual graphics, created either photographically or digitally, for use in advertising business products and services. Customers come to Ferrari Color looking for a visual image when words don't convey the message effectively. Some of the more popular uses of visuals for advertising include airport translight boxes, casino signage, vehicle wraps and point-of-purchase displays.

Through the use of digital imaging, a computer artist has incredible flexibility in preparing a customer's finished product. Photographs and illustrations may be altered on the screen using specialized graphics software, such as Adobe Illustrator, Photoshop and Quark Express, or a new image may be inserted, such as the addition of a building into an existing photograph of a city's landscape. The final product can be output in a variety of formats depending on the customer's end use — poster, banner, backlit sign and glossy point-of-purchase display are a few options.

Ferrari Color was a pioneer in the digital-imaging business. Ferrari Color's long-tenured staff remained throughout the industry transition, and everyone needed to invest time in relearning the trade. Customers received numerous newsletters and technical bulletins explaining how to prepare computer files for computer-generated end products. The impact on the business was immediate — using computers cut production time in half, allowing Ferrari Color to develop new business.

The company's next big step was to expand its commercial account base. In the early years, the lab had relied heavily on state projects and had limited exposure to the commercial marketplace. Developing retail display signage for Las Vegas casinos paved the way for developing commercial accounts. The company created advertising displays for Harvey's, MGM, Bally's and Harrah's. Ferrari Color then pursued business-to-business relationships for advertising graphics to companies such as Intel, Cable Data, Pacific Bell, Stanford Ranch in Roseville and a number of other real estate developers. As a result, sales volume between 1993 and 1995 doubled and the company expanded its market to include the area from San Francisco to Los Angeles and the Nevada casinos. Ferrari continued expanding north to Redding and south into the San Diego area, adding one satellite office in Reno, Nevada.

From 1995 to 1998, growth continued at a slower pace as other photo labs and related businesses converted facilities to accommodate digital-imaging services. Ferrari competed with companies never in the running before, such as print shops and reprographics houses.

By 1998 the staff was well-seasoned in digital-imaging techniques, and Ferrari hired an outside sales staff to generate additional revenue. Until that time, all of Ferrari Color's business came from referrals as a result of its outstanding reputation as an industry leader.

vinyl, graphics for window blinds and canvas applications. Using the electrostatic printing process with dye-sublimations inks, Ferrari anticipates that in the future almost any surface will be able to be printed on, including ceramic tile, wood and fabric.

Another product that is increasingly popular is a highly visible advertising method referred to as vehicle wraps. Businesses that want to attract attention while their vehicles are out on the road choose customized, eye-catching vehicle wraps. Using specially designed vinyl, vehicles of any size are literally encased in a graphic image to create a one-of-a-kind roving advertisement. KAT Country FM 103 radio of Stockton wrapped their traveling van with photos of celebrity DJs. The Peninsula Humane Society covered a motor home with images featuring people and their pets. Jelly Belly covered a tractor-trailer rig with its Jelly Belly Beans company logo and phone number.

Ferrari regularly shares the operational side of the business with her employees so everyone has the opportunity to be part of the solutions that lead to the company's success. Although she remains the sole owner, Ferrari treats her employees as business partners. In an industry driven by continuous innovation, which ultimately leads to substantial investment in equipment upgrades, it is important to Ferrari that everyone knows the expense line as well as the revenue.

As the owner of a business that considers Sacramento its home base, Ferrari looks for ways to position the company as a community resource. Ferrari is very involved in the Sacramento Area Commerce and Trade Organization (SACTO), which helps bring businesses into the region. Ferrari Color provides donations of cash and equipment as well as corporate sponsorships to local nonprofit organizations.

Given the rapid evolution of computer technology, Ferrari keeps a sharp eye on what is industry hype and what will move the company forward. "We don't want to become a company that is technology-driven, buying equipment just to impress our peers," says Ferrari. "If it improves the product, then it's time to make our move."

Advances in technology continue to expand the capabilities of Ferrari Color. The company creates signage with Kodak Duratrans Backlit Display material for displays at Arco Arena, Sacramento International Airport, bus shelters, casinos, mall kiosks and trade shows, and Duraflex opaque print material — which provides the glossy finishes used in posters, menus and point-of-purchase advertising.

By using a variety of digital printers, Ferrari Color renders realistic photo images with crisp, sharp type directly from the customer's digital files. The output images are applied to laminated paper for posters and banners, high-traffic vinyl floor coverings, magnetic

Vehicle wraps are extremely popular with food and beverage manufacturers, radio and TV stations, auto dealers and buses.

The sales office for Serrano in El Dorado Hills is one example of a retail business that uses photos and illustrations to attractively present a variety of products.

Sterling Software

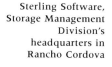

In this age of information, timely knowledge can be acquired instantly with the click of a button. But that data isn't just floating around aimlessly in cyberspace, ripe for the grabbing. It has to be stored safely and cost effectively and should also be readily accessible in order for businesses to compete in today's global economy.

For more than 20 years, the Storage Management Division of Sterling Software, Inc., headquartered in Rancho Cordova, has been an industry leader in storage management technology — a concept that has evolved from a necessary technical discipline into a business-critical operation. That is because users of vast amounts of data — insurance companies, airlines, government entities, financial institutions and manufacturers, to name a few — have storage-capacity needs that are growing beyond anyone's ability to predict. And data itself is more critical to the success of a business than ever before.

The Storage Management Division has product development laboratories in Rancho Cordova and San Bernardino, California; Stavanger, Norway; Boulder, Colorado; and Tefen, Israel. International sales offices are located in Australia, Austria, Belgium, Brazil, Denmark, France, Germany, Italy, Japan, the Netherlands, New Zealand, Norway, Portugal, Singapore, Spain, Sweden, Switzerland and the United Kingdom. The division uses distributors in other international markets.

The division's Dallas, Texas-based parent company, Sterling Software, Inc., is one of the largest independent software companies in the world, with 3,500 employees in 95 offices worldwide. The company has a unique business model consisting of four independent operating businesses, allowing it to expand rapidly and establish leading positions in each market — systems management, applications development, information management and federal systems. Its products and services are used by 95 percent of Fortune 1000 companies.

By responding effectively to the critical needs of its customers, Sacramento's Storage Management Division has distinguished itself as one of Sterling Software's shining stars. Organizations today are faced with the challenge of managing data storage in complex and dynamic distributed environments. Files are created on a wide variety of platforms with different file structures and naming conventions. The result is an enormously complex

Sterling Software, Storage Management Division's headquarters in Rancho Cordova

enterprise information system that requires highly flexible storage management.

Sterling Software delivers with its registered, trademarked SAMS family of products. The SAMS enterprise architecture is unique in that it provides data classification and the ability to differentiate between critical and noncritical data and manage data based on its importance to the organization. In addition, SAMS products feature interactive reporting, enabling users to view real-time information about the distributed environment and generate commands from a single screen.

SAMS architecture also provides automation that monitors and manages the storage environment 24 hours a day, seven days a week to ensure continuous data accessibility. SAMS' open architecture is designed to maximize investments in existing storage systems by providing interfaces to other storage products. Flexibility and scalability are also incorporated to give organizations the freedom to manage storage based on their unique needs.

One should expect no less from the division that pioneered the concept of MVS storage management — now known as OS/390 — and has always played a key role in advancing the technology of system-managed storage.

Even before Sterling Software, Inc. formed in 1981, the Sacramento office, then known as Software Module Marketing, was busy acting as a marketing arm for products developed by "techies." It was one of the first companies to be acquired by Sterling Software after the company went public on the American Stock Exchange in 1983. Since March 1990, Sterling Software has been traded on the New York Stock Exchange (SSW).

From the beginning, Sterling Software, Inc. has been a trailblazer in the relatively young industry of computer storage management. Before 1976, only nonintelligent, volume-only backup existed. Simple utilities were available, but they had limited function and had to be manually initiated. In 1976, Sterling delivered the first comprehensive storage reporting tool in the form of DMS/OS. A year later, the product was enhanced to incorporate archive and backup, becoming the first management tool. By 1979, DMS/OS became the first intelligent, incremental back-up industry-wide.

In the late 1980s, Sterling Software's Storage Management Division opened the floodgate for exciting new developments taking place within the industry upon the advent of IBM's DFSMS in 1988. That same year, the debut of SAMS: Automate marked the first online storage reporting tool. For the first time, with just the click of a button, information was available immediately.

SAMS: Vantage for MVS came on the scene in 1992 and with it the first graphic user interface (GUI) for MVS storage management. This technology melded the ease of use of a PC with the very complex task of mainframe storage management.

In 1996, Sterling Software delivered the first cross-platform, multiplatform storage resource management capabilities with the SAMS: Vantage, Network Edition, and the new and improved SAMS: Vantage for MVS delivered storage management capabilities for the new RAID devices. A year later, Sterling added MVS enterprise server and volume views to the SAMS: Vantage, Network Edition, making it the industry's first and only application independent cross-platform storage management tool to extend from Windows NT to OS/390.

Sterling Software will continue to bring new storage management products to the market and enhance existing products. It is the company's vision to combine the information from each Sterling platform-specific product into a centralized, multiplatform enterprise storage management automation and reporting system.

Crucial to the Storage Management Division's continuing success is the ability to keep a finger on the pulse of the customer while playing the role of the visionary. Rarely do these two very different talents reside in the same person or team of employees, but division headquarters in Sacramento — with employees from all over the globe — is blessed with the best of both worlds.

Sterling Software has become a leader in SAN technology as well, delivering the tools and the knowledge necessary to lead the industry in the exploitation of SAN technology as a strategic resource. SANs (Storage Area Networks) are the next wave of storage technology.

Sterling's SAN tools support E^3 (End-to-End Enterprise) storage management. That means managing data for multiple platforms. From desktop to data center. Across ATLs and RAID. For tape and disk. From the time data is created until it's obsolete.

The platform component of this definition is critical because SANs incorporate more than UNIX and NT data — just as the enterprise incorporates more than one or two platforms. In fact, it's estimated that 70 percent of all critical data still resides on mainframe systems. To ignore the mainframe environment, including OS/390 systems, as many storage-management software companies do, is to ignore a significant portion of the data upon which businesses rely. That's why Sterling Software emphasizes storage management and SAN management for the entire enterprise. That's E^3 storage management.

As information storage becomes ever more pertinent to the ebb and flow of business, Sterling Software, Inc. will be there, providing solutions that make sense in an increasingly complex world.

Synergex

What do contacting a congressman, visiting a bank, making hotel reservations and filling a prescription have in common? Chances are the answer is Synergex technology.

Synergex was one of the first high-tech companies to establish headquarters in the Sacramento area. Founded in 1976 as a single-product company, Synergex has become a dynamic industry leader and provider of computer technology throughout the world.

The privately held company creates and distributes its diverse Synergy product line of software applications, tools and solutions to enable companies that build mission-critical business applications to compete and succeed.

Fortune 500 leaders in virtually every major industry — banking, health care, manufacturing, distribution, communications, retail and government — count on Synergex to lead them through the fast-paced evolutionary stages of growth inherent in the software industry. Synergex-enabled software is used by more than 2.5 million end-users in more than 80 nations.

The name Synergex results from the blending of two words: synergy and apex. The company views its success as a full-circle process in which its customers' success must equal its own. Synergy is attained through dynamic, collaborative relationships between staff and customers. Only then will all reach the apex — the highest point to which they can aspire.

One of the ways Synergex achieves a competitive edge is by just such a collaborative approach. Every product it designs is based on customer feedback. The company hosts conferences around the world to give its customers opportunities to network with one another and with its own staff of professionals. In addition, an

independent Synergy Advisory Council, elected from within the company's global customer base, offers feedback and advice on all aspects of its business set. Synergex's highly trained support professionals are always available to help customers achieve success in critical situations.

Synergex also believes in taking good care of its employees. The company has been honored with Arthur Andersen's Best Business Practices Award for Sharing Knowledge in the Organization. Chosen from hundreds of

companies around the world, Synergex was recognized as a role model for corporate culture, with its internal Web site and such innovative meeting spaces as a "think room" featuring a 250-gallon aquarium, a "lodge," complete with a fireplace, and the high-tech Stanford room where business and corporate developers come for training. Other features include a homey kitchen/dining area where employees enjoy complimentary breakfasts and an outdoor amphitheater where Synergex staff meet to share information and concerns in a casual atmosphere of open communication.

Synergex's strategy for future growth includes accelerated production of new solutions and tools, acquisitions in adjacent markets and continued establishment of strategic partnerships with industry leaders like Microsoft, IBM, Merant and Compaq.

Synergex is proud to join other industry leaders in contributing to Sacramento's growth.

Kenneth J. Lidster, founder and chairman of the board, and Michele C. Wong, president and CEO, are committed to building success in Sacramento.
Photo by Lawrence S.K. Lau

Company employees contributed to the design of the Synergex headquarters building in Gold River.
Photo by Lawrence S.K. Lau

Daveyfire, Inc.

Daveyfire is genuinely unique in both the products it manufactures and its company history. Davey Bickford Smith & Co., its parent company, was founded in England

in 1831 to manufacture the first safety fuse. Although black powder had been used for hundreds of years, particularly in mining, no device had been invented to dependably ignite a charge while permitting the person who set it enough time to safely get out of the way. After a visit to a rope factory, William Bickford realized that if he could pour a vein of gunpowder into the core of a coated cord, he could create a reliable fuse for black powder. His invention, the Bickford safety fuse, transformed the use of powder from a life-threatening business into a process that could be precisely planned and controlled. Although Daveyfire did not come to Sacramento until 1988, the 19th-century gold and silver miners of California and Nevada must have made frequent and grateful use of the original safety fuse.

Through decades of change, Daveyfire, an ISO 9002 registered firm, continued to develop new products while maintaining stringent standards for safety and quality. The company now offers an extensive line of pyrotechnic initiation systems not only for traditional uses in mining, quarries, civil engineering and oil exploration, but also for fireworks, special effects, motion pictures, armaments, aerospace and automotive safety applications. As the company grew, Daveyfire's parent corporation sought new production sites for its expanding North American markets. Michel Herbinet, Jean Jacques Pinel and Alain Duchesne, the founders of the local operation, chose the Sacramento area as one of their new facilities because it offered an excellent pool of qualified contractors and skilled labor.

Daveyfire serves Sacramento by supplying funds, materials and expertise to local fire departments, the FBI

and police bomb squads, as well as the Bureau of Alcohol, Tobacco and Firearms. The company teams up with all of these organizations, helping with prevention, training and safety issues. As executive vice president in charge of the Sacramento area operations Alan Broca explains, "We maintain close ties with all the local law enforcement agencies. All of us work together to protect the public from misuse of explosives."

Daveyfire products are most visible during times of celebration. The company contributes to local celebrations, particularly on the Fourth of July. Those intricate showers of color in the night sky are created with firing sequences triggered by sequences of initiators. The Centennial of the Statue of Liberty was also highlighted by Daveyfire-initiated fireworks. Although the drama of these celebrations highlights the importance of Daveyfire products, they also serve the Sacramento community in less visible ways, and aspects of life that residents take for granted would be impossible without them.

top left:
Fabrication in the 1900s
right:
Initiation components

left and center:
Airbag initiator and
spectacular fireworks

Electric igniters used
for commercial and
military initiations

Barber, Edmund L. and George M. Baker. *Sacramento Illustrated*. Sacramento: Barber and Baker, 1855. Reprinted.: Sacramento Book Collectors Club, 1950.

Barth, Gunther. *Bitter Strength: A History of the Chinese in the United States, 1850-1870*. Cambridge: Harvard University Press, 1964.

Britton, Cooper Busch. *Alta California, 1840-1842: The Journal and Observations of William Dane Phelps, Master of the Ship "Alert."* Glendale, CA: The Arthur Clark Co., 1983.

California Historical Society. *California History*. Quarterly journal of articles on California history, including Sacramento, 1922-present. Issues and index available in libraries. Four double issues, 1997-2000, comprise the Society's California History Sesquicentennial Series, edited by Richard J. Orsi, published in book form for the Society by the University of California Press. The coeditors and volume titles are: Ramon A. Gutierrez, *Contested Eden: California before the Gold Rush* (1997); James J. Rawls, *A Golden State: Mining and Economic Development in Gold Rush California* (1998); Kevin Starr, *Rooted in Barbarous Soil: People, Culture and Community in Gold Rush California* (1999); and John F. Burns, *Taming the Elephant: Politics, Government and Law in Pioneer California* (2000).

Caughey, John W. *The California Gold Rush*. Berkeley: University of California Press, 1948. Paperback edition, 1975.

Chan, Sucheng. *This Bittersweet Soil: The Chinese in California Agriculture, 1860-1910*. Berkeley and Los Angeles: University of California Press, 1986.

Choy, Philip P., et. al., Eds. *Coming Man: 19th Century American Perceptions of the Chinese*. Seattle and London: University of Washington Press, 1994.

Conlin, Joseph R. *Bacon, Beans and Galantines*. Reno and Las Vegas: University of Nevada Press, 1986.

Connolly, Elaine and Dian Self. *Capital Women: An Interpretive History of Women in Sacramento, 1850-1920*. Sacramento: Capital Women's History Project, 1995.

Conrotto, Eugene L. *Miwok Means People*. Fresno, CA: Valley Publishers, 1973.

Cook, S. F. *Expeditions in the Interior of California, Central Valley, 1820-1840:* Berkeley and Los Angeles: University of California Press, 1962.

Cousineau, Ann and Terry Chekon. *Women in Sacramento: A Selected Bibliography*. Sacramento: Sacramento Public Library, 1975.

Cross, Ralph Herbert. *The Early Inns of California, 1844-1896*. San Francisco: Cross and Brandt, 1954.

Dana, Julian. *The Sacramento, River of Gold*. New York: Farrar and Rinehart, 1939.

Davies, J. Kenneth. *Mormon Gold: The Story of California's Mormon Argonauts*. Salt Lake City: Olympus Publishing Co., 1984.

Davis, Leonard M. *Citrus Heights: An Illustrated History, 1850-1997*. Citrus Heights, CA: Citrus Heights Historical Society, 1998.

Davis, Winfield J. *An Illustrated History of Sacramento County, California*. Chicago: Lewis Publishing Co., 1890.

Davis, Winfield J. *History and Progress of the Public School Department of the City of Sacramento 1849-1893*. Sacramento: D. Johnston and Co., 1895.

Didion, Joan. "Notes from a Native Daughter," in *Slouching Towards Bethlehem*. New York: Farrar, Straus and Giroux, 1968.

Dillinger, William C., Ed. *A History of the Lower American River*. Revised and updated edition. Sacramento: The American River Natural History Association, 1991. Original edition by Lucinda Woodward and Jesse M. Smith, Eds., 1977.

Dillon, Richard. *Captain John Sutter: Sacramento Valley's Sainted Sinner*. Reprint edition Santa Cruz, CA: Western Tanager Press, 1981. Originally published as *Fool's Gold: A Biography of John A. Sutter*. New York: Coward-McCann, Inc., 1967.

Driesbach, Janice T., et. al. *Art of the Gold Rush*. Copublished: Oakland Museum of California, Crocker Art Museum and University of California Press, 1998.

Galarza, Ernesto. *Barrio Boy*. South Bend: University of Notre Dame Press, 1971.

Gudde, Erwin G. *California Gold Camps*. Berkeley and Los Angeles: University of California Press, 1975.

Gudde, Erwin G. *California Place Names: The Origin and Etymology of Current Geographical Names*. 4th edition revised and enlarged by William Bright. Berkeley and Los Angeles: University of California Press, 1998.

Guinn, Prof. J. M. *History of the State of California and Biographical Record of the Sacramento Valley.* Chicago: Chapman Publishing Co., 1906.

Hafen, LeRoy R., Ed. *French Fur Traders and Voyageurs in the American West.* Spokane, WA: The Arthur H. Clark Co., 1995.

Heizer, Robert F. and Alan F. Almquist. *The Other Californians.* Berkeley and Los Angeles: University of California Press, 1971.

Holden, William M. *Sacramento: Excursions into its History and Natural World.* 3rd revised reprint edition Fair Oaks, CA: Two Rivers Publishing Co., 1998.

Holliday, J. S. *Rush for Riches: Gold Fever and the Making of California.* Berkeley: University of California Press, copublished with the Oakland Museum of California, 1999.

Holliday, J. S. *The World Rushed In.* New York: Simon and Schuster, 1981.

Hoobler, Dorothy and Thomas. *The Japanese American Family Album.* Introduction by George Takei. New York and Oxford: Oxford University Press, 1996.

Hoover, Mildred Brooke, et. al. *Historic Spots in California.* 3rd edition. Stanford: Stanford University Press, 1966.

Hurtado, Albert H. *Indian Survival on the California Frontier.* New Haven and London: Yale University Press, 1988.

Jackson, Donald Dale. *Gold Dust.* New York: Alfred A. Knopf, 1980.

Kelley, Robert. *Battling the Inland Sea: American Political Culture, Public Policy and the Sacramento Valley, 1850-1986.* Berkeley and Los Angeles: University of California Press, 1989.

Kelley, Robert. *Gold vs. Grain. The Hydraulic Mining Controversy in California's Sacramento Valley.* Glendale, CA: The Arthur H. Clark Co., 1959.

Lapp, Rudolph M. *Blacks in Gold Rush California.* New Haven: Yale University Press, 1977.

Larsen, Lawrence H. *The Urban West at the End of the Frontier.* Lawrence, KS: The Regent's Press of Kansas, 1978.

Levy, Jo Ann. *They Saw the Elephant: Women in the California Gold Rush.* Norman and London: University of Oklahoma Press, 1992.

Levy, Richard. "Eastern Miwok," in Robert F. Heizer, Ed. *California. Handbook of North American Indians, Vol. 8.* Washington: Smithsonian Institution, 1978.

Lord, Israel Shipman Pelton. *At the Extremity of Civilization: A Meticulously Descriptive Diary of an Illinois Physician's Journey in 1849 Along the Oregon Trail to the Goldmines and Cholera of California...,Thence in Two Years to Return by Boat Via Panama.* Necia Dixon Liles, Ed. Jefferson, NC: McFarland and Co., 1995.

Lord, Myrtle Shaw. *A Sacramento Saga: Fifty Years of Accomplishment - Chamber of Commerce Leadership.* Sacramento: Sacramento Chamber of Commerce, 1946.

Marryat, Frank. *Mountains and Molehills or Recollections of a Burnt Journal.* Reprint of 1855 edition published by Longman, Brown, Green and Longmans of London. Time-Life Books: Classics of the Old West Series, 1982.

McClatchy, Charles K. *Private Thinks by C. K.* Foreword by Senator Hiram W. Johnson. New York: The Scribner's Press, 1936.

McGowan, Joseph A. *History of the Sacramento Valley.* 3 Vols. New York: Lewis Historical Publishing Co., 1961.

McGowan, Joseph A. and Terry R. Willis. *Sacramento: Heart of the Golden State.* Woodland Hills, CA: Windsor Publishing Co., 1983.

Mellon, Steve. *Sacramento Then and Now.* Gibsonia, PA: Scripps Howard Co., 1994.

Morse, John Frederick, M.D. *The First History of Sacramento City.* The Sacramento Book Collectors Club, Publication No. 3. Sacramento: Book Collectors Club, 1945.

Neasham, V. Aubrey and James E. Henley. *The City of the Plain; Sacramento in the Nineteenth Century.* Janice A. Woodruff, Ed. Sacramento: The Sacramento Pioneer Foundation and the Sacramento Historic Landmarks Commission, 1969.

Nevins, Allan. *Fremont: Pathmarker of the West.* Reprint of 1955 edition. Lincoln and London: University of Nebraska Press, 1992.

Oliver, Raymond. *Rancho Del Paso: A History of the Land Surrounding McClellan Air Force Base.* McClellan AFB, CA: Sacramento Air Logistics Center, 1983.

Olmsted, R. R., ed. *Scenes of Wonder and Curiosity from Hutchings' California Magazine, 1856-1861.* Berkeley: Howell-North, 1962.

Owens, Kenneth N., Ed. *John Sutter and a Wider West.* Lincoln: University of Nebraska Press, 1994.

Oxford, June. *The Capital That Couldn't Stay Put: The Complete Book of California's Capitals.* San Jose: Smith McKay Printing Co., 1993.

Paul, Rodman. *California Gold: The Beginning of Mining in the Far West.* Lincoln: University of Nebraska Press, 1947.

Phillips, George Harwood. *Indians and Intruders in Central California, 1769-1849.* Norman and London: University of Oklahoma Press, 1993.

Rawls, James J. *Indians of California: The Changing Image.* Norman and London: University of Oklahoma Press, 1984.

Reed, G. Walter, Ed. *History of Sacramento County, California, with Biographical Sketches of the Leading Men and Women...from the Early Days to the Present.* Los Angeles: Historic Record Co., 1923.

Rohrbough, Malcolm J. *Days of Gold: The California Gold Rush and the American Nation.* Berkeley and Los Angeles: University of California Press, 1997.

Royce, Sarah. *A Frontier Lady: Recollections of the Gold Rush and Early California.* Lincoln: University of Nebraska Press,

1977. Reprint of Yale University Press, 1932.

Sacramento Bee. *Sacramento Guide Book*. Sacramento: The Sacramento Bee, 1939.

Sacramento County Historical Society. *Golden Notes.* Quarterly publication of articles on Sacramento history, 1954-present. All issues on file, some indexed, in the Sacramento Room, Sacramento Public Library.

Sanborn, Margaret. *The American: The River of El Dorado.* San Francisco: Holt, Rinehart and Winston, 1974.

Saxton, Alexander. *The Indispensable Enemy: Labor and the Anti-Chinese Movement in California.* Berkeley: University of California Press, 1971.

Severson, Thor. *Sacramento: An Illustrated History, 1839-1974, from Sutter's Fort to Capital City.* San Francisco: California Historical Society, 1973.

Smith, Jesse M., ed. *Sketches of Old Sacramento: A Tribute to Joseph A. McGowan.* Sacramento: Sacramento County Historical Society, 1976.

Stanley, Don and Frank McCulloch, eds. *The Sting of the Bee. 125 Years of Editorial Cartoons from The Sacramento Bee, 1857-1982.* Sacramento: The Sacramento Bee, 1982.

Sutter, John A., et. al. *New Helvetia Diary.* San Francisco: The Grabhorn Press in arrangement with The Society of California Pioneers, 1939.

Takaki, Ronald. *Strangers from a Different Shore.* New York: Penguin Books, 1989.

Thompson and West. *History of Sacramento County.* 1880. Reprint edition: Introduction by Allan R. Ottley. Berkeley: Howell-North, 1960.

Thompson, John and Edward A. Dutra. *The Tule Breakers: The Story of the California Dredge.* Stockton, CA: The Stockton Corral of Westerners International, 1983.

Willis, William L. *History of Sacramento County*. Los Angeles: Historic Record Co., 1913.

Wilson, Norman L. and Arlean H. Towne, "Nisenan" in Robert F. Heizer, ed. *California. Handbook of North American Indians, Vol. 8.* Washington: Smithsonian Institution, 1978.

Winter, Carl George and J. Martin Weber. *Heart of California: Sacramento County, Then and Now.* San Francisco: Fearson Publishers, 1959.

Wooldridge, Major J. W., ed. *History of the Sacramento Valley, California.* Chicago: Pioneer Publishing Co., 1931.

Zollinger, James Peter. *Sutter: The Man and His Empire.* New York: Oxford University Press, 1939.

SELECTIONS FOR CHILDREN

Altman, Linda Jacobs. *The California Gold Rush in American History.* Springfield, NJ: Enslow Publishing, Inc., 1997. (Grades 4-8).

American River Natural History Association. *Ooti, A Child of the Nisenan.* Sacramento: American River Natural History Association, n.d. (Grades 3-5).

Blumberg, Rhoda. *The Great American Gold Rush.* New York: Bradbury Press, 1989. (Grades 4-8).

Dunnahoo, Terry J. *Sacramento,* California. Parsippany, NJ: Dillon Press, 1996. (Grades 3-6).

Epstein, Sam and Beryl. *The Sacramento: Golden River of California.* Champaign, IL: Garrard Publishing Co., 1968. (Grades 4-8).

Honnold, Dierdre W. *Sacramento With Kids: A Family Guide to the Greater Sacramento Region.* Carmichael, CA: Wordwrights International, 1994. (Parents and all grades).

Hoobler, Dorothy and Thomas. *Treasure in the Stream.* Silverb. Publ., 1996. (Grades 4-6).

Krensky, Stephen. *Striking It Rich.* New York: Simon and Schuster Children's Publishing Division, 1996. (Grades 2-4).

Lewis, Oscar. *The Sacramento River.* New York: Holt, Rinehart, Winston, 1970. (Grades 4-8).

Trafzer, Clifford E. *California's Indians and the Gold Rush.* Newcastle, CA: Sierra Oaks Publishing Co., 1989. (Grades 4-8).